SERMONS

PREACHED ON

VARIOUS OCCASIONS

BY THE LATE

REV. JOHN KEBLE,

AUTHOR OF "THE CHRISTIAN YEAR."

SOLD BY

JAMES PARKER AND CO., OXFORD,

AND 377, STRAND, LONDON.

1880.

CONTENTS.

CONTENTS.

SERMON I.

MERCY FOR THE MERCIFUL.

S. MATT. v. 7.

" Blessed are the merciful, for they shall obtain mercy."

If we could remember clearly the time when first, as children, we became acquainted with these comfortable words of our Lord, which are commonly called the Beatitudes, I suppose we should all be conscious of something within us, which whispered, 'What noble, what beautiful sayings are these.' Our natural feelings bare Him witness, so far as they were not already corrupted by self-love, that He spake well when He said, "Blessed are the poor in spirit, Blessed are they that mourn, Blessed are the meek, Blessed are they that do hunger and thirst after righteousness." For all persons, hard as they might think it for themselves to be poor rather than rich, to mourn rather than rejoice, to endure ill rather than seek redress, to labour for righteousness rather than for the meat that perisheth—all persons, I say, whether they accept these sayings for themselves or no, do yet by a kind of instinct admire those who accept them, and secretly wish they had a heart to do the same.

B

At any rate, this is the case, with regard to that fifth Beatitude: "Blessed are the merciful, for they shall obtain mercy." The simplest and most un-educated acknowledges at once the fairness (so to call it) of this sentence: even as the fellow-servants in the parable of the Unmerciful servant, when they saw what he did, refusing to forgive when he had been so freely forgiven, "[a] were very sorry, and came and told their Lord all the things that were done." They were sorry: the Saints and Angels in heaven were very sorry, that anything so shocking should happen among the creatures of the good and merciful God; and they came in their natural indignation, and complained of it to their Lord. For a like reason, and much more, they rejoice when the merciful obtain mercy. And so, as I said, do simple persons among men. Our Lord appeals to the ordinary practice of such in that other sermon in S. Luke, which has so much common to it with this Sermon on the Mount. "[b] Judge not, and ye shall not be judged: condemn not and ye shall not be condemned: for-give, and ye shall be forgiven, give and it shall be given unto you: good measure, pressed down and shaken together and running over, shall men give into your bosom." And further on in this Sermon itself, with reference to one branch especially of the duty of charity He says, "[c] Judge not, and ye shall not be judged: for with what judgement ye judge ye shall be judged, and with what measure ye mete, it shall be measured to you again." These sayings are evidently parabolical; in a manner not unusual

[a] S. Matt. xviii. 28.   [b] S. Luke vi. 37.
[c] S. Matt. vii. 1.

with our Lord, representing God's doings with us
after the pattern of our doings with one another.
As if He should say, 'You know that it is the custom
of men to deal gently with those whom they perceive
to deal gently with others: and to be severe in
speaking of those men's conduct, who permit themselves easily to find fault with their neighbours.
Know now that in this they are but following the
lead of their Almighty Judge. For one law of His
judgement at the Last great Day will be, 'Did you use
to speak evil of your brother, and judge your brother ?
then you must expect to be spoken evil of, and
judged yourself: not by man only, but by Him who
can read all hearts. If you said, while living on
earth, " ᵈ Stand off, come not near, I am holier than
thou," He will say, " Depart from Me." If you
shrank back, and abode in the lowest room, esteem-
ing others better than yourself, He will say, " Come
up higher ᵉ." '

By such imagery our Lord gives us to understand
that His proceedings on coming to be our Judge
will be in harmony with those feelings which He has
implanted in His creatures: and it will be well for
us to remember this, in watching what goes on in
ordinary life. When we see any one indignant at
an act or word of unkindness, let us take it as a true
token from Him Who will come to be our Judge, how
He will treat the unpitying at the last day. Great
need, unspeakable need, shall we have of mercy in
that day ; of mercy in both its branches, giving and
forgiving. For how shall one stand before the throne
of the unerring Judge, laden with all the sins of his

ᵈ Isa. lxv. 5.　　ᵉ S. Luke xiv. 10.

earthly being, sins perhaps of a long life, "oft and
many times committed, long and many years continued;" sins of soul and sins of body: sins of
thought, word, and deed: sins secret and open, fleshly
and spiritual: sins grievous and deadly, some from
their foulness and horror taken singly, others as
forming part of a habit of wilful disobedience and
rebellion? Who can bear such a burden? Most
of us know something of the misery, when a person
has to stand before a parent, master, or any other
superior, or before one whom he has grievously
wronged, with all his faults naked and opened, his
duties all or almost all left undone: how ill he can
bear the face of his judge looking towards him: how
he is ready to sink into the earth. But all this is
nothing to the burden and shame of that day: any
more than the forgiveness of an offended father or
friend here is like our Lord's great final sentence of
pardon and acknowledgment.

So again in respect of that other great branch of
the virtue of mercy; the giving to those who are in
want: who can express, or worthily imagine, the utter
helplessness and craving need of a soul and body newly risen and standing on the edge of eternity? Not
but that in reality the creatures of the most High
God must always stand equally in need of Him; but
as long as we are here, the veil of the flesh stands
between us and Him, and we seem to want other
things, and not our God only: and it is an act of
great faith to discern through that veil, how that He
alone is sufficient for us. But in that day it will
be quite otherwise: the world and the flesh with all
their shadows, will pass entirely away, and the poor

helpless child of Adam will at last feel and understand that God is all in all to him : he will understand
it, whether he rejoices in it or no : he will acknowledge it in unspeakable thankfulness, or in unspeakable despair. He will understand and feel what hitherto he has acknowledged only in words, that he
must lean upon his Father in heaven from moment
to moment, both for being and for every good thing.
If he is ever to have joy, or peace, or delight, or
glory, it must come straight from Him, not through
any of the things which He has made. And all this
once for all, and for eternity : the river of mercy
will then be finally opened, or sealed up for ever and
ever.

The need then of those who shall be raised at the
Last day being so great and universal, in respect both
of giving and forgiving ; our Lord and Judge being
also our Saviour, will come prepared both with full
Absolution and with full and perfect Satisfaction
of all our wants. His Absolution indeed is not expressed in words, at least not in those endearing
parables, which most graciously set forth His final
mercy to sinners. In the parable of the prodigal
son [1] the forgiving father makes known his forgiveness by running out when his son was yet a great
way off, and falling on his neck and kissing him :
and when the son confesses, he stays not to absolve
him in words, but orders the servants to bring out
the best apparel, and the fatted calf. And in the
parable of the sheep and goats, the righteous seem to
know their pardon by being set on the right hand :
the words that are spoken are altogether words of

[1] S. Luke xv.

blessing. Surely we may understand hereby the exceeding eagerness of our heavenly Father to shew mercy to His penitents: even as we see love and mercy shewing itself continually by a mere kindly glance or gesture, before there is time or opportunity to speak a word: the watchful and anxious heart, knowing its own need, understands at once such signals, and is prepared with all humble delight and surprise to receive the benediction which comes after.

The final Absolution then (as we may believe) is expressed in signs only, to make the penitent understand at once that his Father's heart yearns towards him, and he is fully forgiven. But the Benediction is expressed in distinct and unreserved words: "[g] Bring forth the best robe, and put it upon him, and put a ring on his hand, and shoes on his feet: and bring hither the fatted calf, and kill it that we may eat, and be merry:" and again, "[h] Come, ye blessed of My Father, inherit the kingdom prepared for you from the foundation of the world." He puts no bounds to His words of invitation: that the lowly self-withdrawing penitent may not fear to come in and partake of His very best. Observe how charitable and hospitable persons press you to draw near and taste of what they have prepared, as though the favour were all done to themselves; as if they were partakers of the benefit and you the benefactor: observe them, and make sure that in them you see a faint image and token of your merciful Lord at His final wedding banquet, seeing of the travail of His Soul, and satisfied with it. "[i] If any man open the

[g] S. Luke xv. 7.   [h] S. Matt. xxv. 24.   [i] Rev. iii. 20.

door, I will enter in unto him, and I will sup with
him;" and not only he with Me. "[k] I will drink of
this fruit of the vine new with you in My Father's
kingdom." As if He should say, 'Come in and sit
down, that I may feast: drink, that I may drink also.'
What end or limit need there be to the hopes of a
true penitent, seeing that the Almighty and Infinite
One esteems it a part of His own unspeakable
blessedness to be ever pouring out on such an one
new blessings?

Blessed indeed are they, who as they go about
the world, so full of temptations to selfishness, carry
with them everywhere and in all company, the three
lessons which our Lord here teaches concerning that
Day as a day of mercy: how great will then be our
need of mercy, how rich His promises, more than to
supply all our need, and how impossible for any but
the merciful to have any share in those promises.
That we might never forget it, our Lord has put it
into His own prayer. He has commanded us never
to use any solemn form of devotion to Him, without
the words, "Forgive us our trespasses, as we forgive
them that trespass against us." He has warned us,
in the parable of the unmerciful servant, that refusing to forgive is such a thing, as will utterly blot
out and cancel for ever all the forgiveness before
sealed to us. And in regard to the other part of
mercy, bountifulness in giving; it is the one thing
mentioned when He declares whom He will set on
His right hand and whom on His left. Many no
doubt will wonder at that day to find themselves on
the wrong side of the throne, and to hear Him say,

[k] S. Matt. xxvi. 29.

"¹Depart from Me:" and when they come to know the reason, it will be simply this, that they were unmerciful. God set His poor and afflicted children in their way, that they might relieve and comfort them for His sake: and they passed rudely by on the other side. Try to imagine how it will be; think of the Judge speaking to you from heaven: think how all will depend on your present behaviour to your brethren: on this very hour perhaps, or this very minute. "ᵐ He shall have judgement without mercy, who hath shewed no mercy." Let us think of this, when we are inclined to complain and be cross on being called on to give of our substance: or again, when we are tempted to spend wantonly on ourselves what might be spent on Christ and His poor. I fear there are many of us who stand in need of one or other of these warnings. Sometimes, though we are in a manner willing to give, yet we are impatient when unexpectedly applied to: and harsh answers and angry looks betray it: yet all the while, for aught we know, it may be Christ Himself Who is applying to us: Christ in one of His really poor and afflicted. Sometimes we have a sort of reckless feeling, that we *will* have such and such a thing, cost what it will, instead of laying by for something better. These may seem little things, but there is great evil in them, if the feeling that lurks in them is indulged. The one is rudely driving away Christ, the other is setting up oneself in Christ's place. Both are marks of an unmerciful heart: we must watch and pray against them, else how shall we obtain mercy?

Again, in respect of the other branch of mercy,

¹ S. Matt. xxv. 41.   ᵐ S. James ii. 13.

'Forgiving.' We are all at times inclined to dwell on ill usage; and although it may be hoped, that, were it in our power, we should not really avenge ourselves, we scruple not to take vengeance as it were, in imagination and fancy: the wrong we have suffered recurs too often to our minds, and we permit ourselves to gaze on it with our inward eye: we speak of it to friends, and take pains, direct or indirect, to have it noticed; we are secretly pleased when others make mention of it, and make no effort to silence them as we ought to do. Thus it comes. to pass that a great part of the life, even of good people and of those who desire in earnest to be holy, is taken up with complaining and finding fault. Even if it go not so far, as to end in evil speaking and positive sin, it will be a sad blemish; and we shall be sure to hear of it again in that Day. As far as it goes, it will hinder our obtaining so much mercy, as otherwise, by the grace of God, we might obtain. We shall suffer loss, though we ourselves be saved through the merits of Jesus Christ.

Another test of our mercifulness will be this. It cannot be, but that in no long time after our leaving this, or any other of God's solemn assemblies, we shall see or hear, or in some way come to know of some ill or questionable behaviour, some part of our brother's conduct, which may seem to us more or less provoking and unpardonable. We shall be told of such things, and they will be to many a sore temptation. What shall we do, then? Shall we give way to the pleasure, such as it is, of judging harshly and hastily of them? Or shall we refrain our souls, and if we cannot praise, at least not be eager to

blame? Shall we in our hearts condemn them, or
shall we forbear? Shall we interpret their doings
severely, or with kindness and hope? Look to it:
surely it is a matter wherein to take counsel beforehand. What if we were even now, each of us seve-
rally, to resolve, here before Christ's Altar, to be
merciful, when we are next tempted to judge hardly?
You know not how trying the instance may be, nor
what difference it may make through all future time.
If the Evil one see that we are patient and forgiving,
not only in our doings and behaviour, but in our
very thoughts, the next time anything untoward
comes across us: who knows but it may discourage
him from ever vexing us more in that way? Who
knows but he may leave off tempting those by whom
he now tries to provoke us? and so there may be
peace and quietness in a whole family, neighbourhood, or kingdom, where otherwise all would be envy
and strife, confusion, and every evil work.

We all, I suppose, know more or less of the comfort of that verse in the Psalm, "[a] If Thou, Lord, wilt
be extreme to mark what is done amiss, O Lord, who
may abide it?" Many a sinking heart must have been
stayed by thus hearing out of God's own mouth,
that He is not extreme to mark what we have done
amiss. But what becomes of all that comfort, if we
ourselves are sharp and alert and well-pleased in
marking the transgressions of other men? how can
one who is unscrupulous in doing so have the heart
to say his prayers?

Another point in the merciful man's character, apt
to be forgotten more or less even by those who do

[a] Ps. cxxx. 3.

not mean to be unkind, is Consideration : putting
ourselves in other person's places, and thinking how
matters will strike them, and how they would like
you to behave to them. The merciful man is merciful even to his beast, much more to his brethren who
look up to him either as inferiors, or as being in
trouble and distress. He makes a rule of considering them, is troubled if he finds he has forgotten
them, puts himself out of his way to spare them, and
provide for them. Most of all is he anxious that no
offence should come by him : that he may not be
unmerciful to the souls of his brethren. True Christian mercy is altogether opposite to the false good-
nature of the world : for such goodnature cares not
how it ruins a man in the end, if only it may keep
things for the present smooth, easy and pleasant.
But Christian mercy, if it can but secure your soul
at last, minds not how it pains you for the time :
like Him, Whose whole life and being on earth was
mercy, yet none of His messengers ever spake so
openly as He did of "° the worm that dieth not, and
the fire which cannot be quenched." He came down
from heaven to save us : and part of His way of
salvation was, that He told us plainly of hell.

Blessed are they who labour and pray to be merciful, not after the false and spurious pattern of this
world, but after His pure and high example : remembering that they cannot be as if they had never
heard or read of Him : His Divine pattern must in
the end serve either to shame or to bless them.
There may be other features in the evangelical picture of our Lord, less in sight, and harder to copy :

° S. Mark ix. 44.

but this point of forgiving and doing good, is what all to a certain extent, can understand and admire. He " ᴾ went about doing good." Be not ye then content any more, to be merciful and helpful to your brethren, only now and then, as convenience and fancy suit : but pass the whole time of your sojourning here in mercy. If such a life be sweet and precious even here, what must the fruit and end of it be, when it comes to be made perfect in heaven ! when the work, the anxiety, the self-denial, will be all over, and only the love and joy and everlasting fragrance remain ?

ᴾ Acts x. 38.

SERMON II.

CHRISTIAN EDUCATION.

Gᴇɴ. iii. 23.

*" The Lord God sent him out from the garden of Eden,
to till the ground, out of which he was taken."*

Iᴛ is no new thing for Christian childhood to be
compared to the condition of our first parents in
paradise. When we stand by the Font, and gaze in
faith upon the countenance of the innocent infant
fresh from his second and better birth, surely we
behold no less than an outward and visible token of
the blessed Image of God in which Adam was first
created. First, the word of regeneration, or new-
creation, "I baptize thee into the Name of the Father
the Son and the Holy Ghost," answers wonderfully
to the first creating word, "Let Us make man in our
image, after our likeness." He was made in the
Image of the Trinity, and now the Trinity Itself is
mysteriously imparted to him, so that God dwelleth
in him and he in God. Next, the priest standing
there to bless him in Christ's stead, returns him
into his nurse's or godmother's arms, that is, into
the arms of the holy Church militant here on earth,

as the Creator, having made man, put him into the
garden which He had planted in Eden. We are
placed there with a word of blessing: "Of every
tree of the garden thou mayest freely eat," which being interpreted is 'All Christian privileges are now
freely made thine by covenant: seeing it hath pleased
God to regenerate thee by His Holy Spirit.' But
along with the blessing comes also a word of warning: "he must not be ashamed to confess the faith of
Christ crucified, and manfully to fight under His
banner against sin, the world, and the devil:" even
as Adam was warned, "Of the fruit of the tree which
is in the midst of the garden thou shalt not eat,
neither shalt thou touch it." And as that first warning concludes, " In the day that thou eatest thereof
thou shalt surely die," so we know that sin after
Baptism, wilful indulged sin, is especially mortal and
deadly: since until it is effectually repented of, it
destroys that heavenly life, which was given us in
that holy Sacrament.

All baptized infants then are in a manner put
into paradise, into God's garden on earth, to dress
it and to keep it: but it would seem as if the type
or comparison were with more especial exactness
suited to the condition of those young Christians,
who by God's good providence are being trained in
places of truly Christian nurture, under the more
especial care of the holy Church: such as we hope
and trust that College may ever prove, the birthday
of which, if I may so call it, we keep this day with
prayer and thanksgiving.

That which made and kept Paradise what it was:
the safeguard of all its other privileges, was, as we

know, its being God's own enclosure, separated and fenced off from all the rest of the earth's surface, from all ordinary and common ground: and what is it but Christian severity and strictness, our setting ourselves exact Gospel rules, which marks this our College, and other similar institutions, as a desirable place of shelter for the young children of the Church? The Church rules by which they are limited are to them as the wall of Paradise, shutting out as far as may be the noisome beasts, venemous reptiles, and even the infected airs of the world, and cherishing and protecting the growth of all good things: giving full advantage to the natural shelter, which even in the ruined world is left us for a while, of childish ignorance and simplicity, so that the instinctive trustfulness and innocency of babes may grow up into Christian faith and purity. O happy they, who learn in good time to prize the home of their Christian education as the very refuge provided for them against the dangers and temptations of their early years: who love their paradise for the tree of Life's sake, rather than for the tree of Knowledge, which is also set in the midst of that garden for their trial in various ways: who give no way to the impatient feelings and love of false liberty, which, as years go on, would make them wish themselves outside the protecting wall. Happy, thrice happy, those sons and daughters of the Church, who feel their school, their College, or their home, so much the more like paradise, because they live by rule and under restraint, and are not left to their own choice in many things in which frail nature might incline them to choose amiss.

Consider next their positive privileges, and see if they do not correspond in a marvellous way with the privileges of that holy and happy garden. What is that river, which went out of Eden to water the garden, and was parted into four heads, but the Spirit of Christ making Him known in the Church by the four blessed Gospels? which are come indeed into all the world, and bear every where their proper fruit, but are more distinctly made known and more continually thought of in these which may be called the schools of our prophets. They are themselves our chief learning, and by them is measured all that we learn besides. The early, literal, practical knowledge of our Lord's four Gospels is indeed a privilege worthy of Eden; and it is put within the reach of all who come to the Church for education. Those books of Christ's law depart not out of their mouth, they meditate on them day and night: whatever else is taught, these surely are taught with extreme diligence: taught when we sit at home, and when we walk in the way; when we lie down, and when we rise up: they are bound for a sign upon our hand, and are as frontlets between our eyes: and we write them upon the posts of our house and our gates: the very walls of our College bear witness to them, and to the other Scriptures, in the sight of all comers, by the inscriptions which they bear. Thus we have eminently the second mark of God's paradise, the fourfold river of the water of Life.

Moreover, we have here the tree of life: communion with Jesus Christ crucified as each one is able to bear it. We have Baptism and the remembrance of Baptism, Communion and preparation for Com-

munion. We have not been without visits from those
who are called God's Angels on earth: Christ has
given His blessing to this place by the hands of more
than one of the Bishops and pastors of His Church:
your own Bishop has been here, and laid his hands
specially on some of you in the holy Office of Confirmation: and you have been favoured with the
presence, by you I trust never to be forgotten, of
some of those who have gone forth like Abraham,
almost not knowing whither they went, to the lands
which God had assigned to their care as missionary
Bishops. These, I say, were visits of Angels, and
so far tokens of paradise. Endeavour to think of
them with humble delight as the Great Shepherd's
merciful encouragement to this portion of His little
flock. Be sure that these Bishops, these visible Angels coming here, were tokens of a more glorious
Presence, of the true invisible Angels, Angels of
your own, who abide here in perpetual guardianship:
for is not this a place for Christ's little ones? and
has not Christ expressly declared that His little ones
have Angels, high Angels, Angels which always behold the Face of His Father which is in heaven?
Nay, and here is yet another Presence, infinitely
more blessed and glorious: the tree of Life (as I said)
in the midst of the garden; the Lord God walking
in it daily, and causing His Voice to be heard. This
is the great privilege of all, God dwelling in us, and
silently discoursing with us: and the rules and ways
of this Christian school are intended to be such, I
think I may say are such, as to help you to realize
the blessing, and to keep you from forfeiting it.
Evil indeed is near, is at hand, it is separated by

c

but a hair's breadth from the cradles of Christian
infants, and from the tasks and plays of children of
elder years: it is near always, the very state of
fallen man may assure you of that: but it need not
hurt you, and if you are true to your rules and your
prayers, it cannot: and that shall be fulfilled morally
in you, which by a wonderful providence we sometimes see fulfilled outwardly in the case of young
infants left seemingly within reach of wild beasts or
venomous insects: God sends His Angels, and shuts
the lions' mouths: the sucking child plays beside the
hole of the asp, and the weaned child puts his hand
on the cockatrice' den.   They hurt not nor destroy
in all Christ's holy mountain, in the paradise of His
Church on earth, in the safe habitations of His little
ones, fenced and guarded by the loving wisdom of
His Church.

These, little children, and such as these, are your
special privileges as inmates of a Christian College:
God grant that you may be even now, one and all,
availing yourselves of them: but should it unhappily prove otherwise with respect to any one or more:
should the tempter have found and made his way
even within this guarded ground: should any one
be entangled in the snares of subtle wickedness,
fleshly or spiritual, such as envy, lying or impurity:
let him know for certain, and bless God for it, that
not only is there pardon and healing for him, as for
all other sinners, on his true repentance and amendment, but also that God graciously favours him, more
than many others, I might say more than the greater
part of his brethren that are in the world, in respect
of one of the chief helps to repentance.   Special

confession, opening your sin and your grief to God's messenger, ordained to counsel and absolve you, is far easier, generally speaking, to those who live under the shadow of a kindly sacred home, to whom the priest is as teacher and parent, than to such as have their lot in the ordinary highways of the world. This was not indeed one of the blessings of Paradise: for as sin was not there, so neither were the remedies of sin. They were not there because they were not required. But such as we now are, and with such a world as we have around us, surely we cannot be thankful enough for the opportunity and encouragement afforded in Christian homes, schools, and colleges, to the blessed ordinance of Confession, as recommended in the Prayer-book for the relief of burdened, and guidance of doubting consciences. We cannot say too earnestly to those who need it, ' Make haste and avail yourself of it: lose no time in bringing your sins by humble acknowledgement to the foot of the Cross, that being purged by Christ's Absolution, you may go forth from this your paradise, not indeed without the garb of penitents, yet wearing over it bright and clean armour, to fight the battles of the Lord in the ordinary world.'

For in this other respect also do our Christian homes and nurseries resemble that first Paradise, that the time soon comes for us to depart out of them, each in his turn for his appointed task upon earth: our first father and mother lost Eden for their sin, we lose our tranquil homes and the haunts of our youth by necessity of our condition, in the regular course of providence. Adam was driven out to till the ground from which he was taken: we go out

from our schools and colleges to do our life's work,
whatever it may be: as it is written, "Man goeth
forth to his work and to his labour until the evening." We may not stay in the quiet refreshing
shade: there is a great deal to do, and little time
to do it in: our place for a long time to come must
rather be the hot wearisome road, full of noise and
disturbance and anxiety. So we have found it, one
after another, all of us who are come to man's estate:
and so will all you who are younger find it ere long.
Do not grieve too much at this: it is the condition
of human life. In one way or another, the world is
full of little images of Paradise, and men are from
time to time made to feel as those did who were
exiled from Paradise. Those even who think little
of eternity are familiar with this thought as applied
to the passage from childhood to man's estate. They
know that after so many years a change will surely
come over them in body and soul and spirit, and
they shall never again feel so light-hearted, so buoy-
ant, so free from care as they have been. They will
have the earth to till, and not merely the garden to
dress. They know it must be so, and they make up
their minds to it. Some even desire and welcome
the change, by reason of certain hopes and fancies
which have got possession of them, and which, as
they think, will now be nearer fulfilment. Yet on
the whole it is a pensive and melancholy thought:
all of us, in after life, look back wistfully on our
young days, and muse on them somewhat in the
same way as Adam must have mused on the happy
garden which he had lost.

Moreover, all the way along, though no second

change occur so complete as the transition from youth to age, still God causes us occasionally to be put in mind of Paradise, and to feel as if we were in some degree parting with it. Hardworking persons have their seasons of retirement, their retreats, their holidays, their recesses, of longer or shorter duration: and when such seasons have been well and innocently spent, to be called out of their freshness and fragrance into the round of daily work, is so far like Adam being called away from the happy garden to till the ground. Nay, every week of our lives the same kind of feeling recurs: for is not Sunday, compared with other days, as paradise compared with other places? And the same may be said of Advent, Lent, Easter, and the other holy seasons: in proportion to their sacredness and the reverence with which they have been observed, is the change keenly felt when we pass out of them into ordinary days and weeks: we feel as if they had been all too short, we deeply regret our inadequate use of them, we long for them to come again, and when they do come, if by any means we are prevented from keeping them as we wish, are we not as those exiles from paradise, whensoever by any chance they were brought at all near it, and reminded of their sad exclusion by the sight of its outer fence, or of the ways leading towards it?

Yes, my brethren, we are all exiles from paradise, and the wise and merciful God will in all likelihood cause those among us who now least feel it—such as the young inmates of this College, to be made more and more seriously aware of their loss, as life goes on. But let us not complain nor be down-hearted.

The Lord God hath sent us, or will lead us out of Eden : but it will be well with us, if we are really busied in tilling the ground, our appointed task : well with us, if we so work, as to come back in His good time, I will not say to the same happy garden, but to that far happier one, of which even the first paradise was but a very faint shadow : much more our remembrances and fragments of it. Well for us, if we set-about our tasks, whatever they may be, in a patient and thankful spirit : owning our Father's great mercy in making man's very punishment, his penal task, a token and mystical pledge of his deliverance and a great help towards attaining it. For such surely is the effect of that part of our sentence, "ᵃ In the sweat of thy face thou shalt eat bread." Whether our calling be to hard bodily work or to mental anxiety, to want or to abound, to command or to obey, to act or to suffer, abroad or at home, in town or in country, to wait on souls or on bodies, still we have the comfort of knowing that every moment of pain and care and trouble if only we improve it in faith, is an earnest from God of His most merciful purpose, His purpose to relent at last, and bring us back to the paradise which we have forfeited : and moreover we may know by kindly experience, that these our cares, self-denials and toils are the very discipline to prepare and train us for that most happy change.

Thoughts such as these may naturally come with unusual force into our minds, when we turn from the confusions and troubles of this present evil time to such a safe dwelling and quiet resting-place as

ᵃ Gen. iii. 19.

our Lord's good providence has here provided for His little ones: when we compare this their paradise with the ground which they will soon have to till. Here, their days are so ordered and divided as to teach and help them to pray: the walls are covered with holy words and pictures, the Church and school bell speaks to them hour after hour, of some lesson of devotion and obedience: all or almost all whom they see are truly concerned for them, earnest to help them in the good and true way. O how far unlike is all this, my young brethren, to the outer world, the world which awaits you, the world which is to be the scene of your work! It is very near: a few minutes journey, and you are in the very midst of its wild confusions. There, for the most part instead of Church bells, and summons to holy duties, all the air rings continually with sounds of money-getting and hunting after pleasure: instead of kind religious sympathy, no man pretends even to care for his next neighbour: instead of the wholesome rules and parental restraints of a Christian college, all is left in a wild heathenish liberty. This is the sort of ground from which, by the good providence of God, you have been taken and transplanted into this His own sheltered garden: and in His time He will call you out into that same ground again: you will have to till the ground out of which you were taken: as school-masters, or as catechists, perhaps even as missionaries, in our heathenish great towns or in our more than half unchristian colonies, those of you who are found worthy will have to wait on the souls of your brethren; to do some good, as you may, in your generation, to Christ's

Holy Catholic Church. It will not be an easy service, as you have often been warned; nor, to the natural man, a pleasant one. As in the literal tilling of this outward visible ground, there will be very often bad weather, failing crops, mischievous trespassers. You will often have to rise up in the morning and to lie down at night with a heavy and foreboding heart, as if things in sight were all against you, your labours unrewarded by any fruit, the enemy winning souls out of your hand. It is well that you should have counted beforehand this part of the cost of Christ's service, as well as the more outward and obvious troubles of life, poverty, persecution, solitude, reproach, and the like. It is well that you should be in some measure aware how disappointing your best work is likely to prove in this world, not that you should faint and draw back from what God otherwise has given you a heart to do, but in order that you may lose no time now, in laying up a treasure of noble thoughts and good prayers, for yourselves and for one another. Practise yourselves now in thinking and praying, for then there will often be little time for either. When the conflict is really around you, a thousand pressing needs calling your attention this way and that at the same moment, and your soul all the while ready to faint within you at the thought how little you have done, how precious then will be to you any good habits which God's grace may have enabled you to learn here, of lifting up your whole hearts to Him, in short inward prayer: like a soldier who is used to his armour, and can take it up and buckle it on in a moment; while another, now perhaps

equally courageous and loyal, is embarrassed with
his, because he has not proved it in time past.

Practise yourself also in serious thought and meditation: I mean not now that blessed exercise of
meditation on divine truths, but rather I mean the
habit of carefully considering, every morning, the
duties and temptations of the day, resolving as in
God's Presence what we ought to do, and asking
His special grace to keep our good purposes. As a
holy writer of our own advises young people especially, 'Sum up at night, what thou hast done by
day, and in the morning what thou hast to do.'
Such a custom humbly and faithfully persisted in,
may help you more than you can tell in your future
trials and tribulations; more especially in one which
to many is the painfullest of all, I mean, the sore
trial of doubt and perplexity, when in after time you
shall have to make up your mind, for yourselves or
for others, in hard and entangled cases, such as the
pastoral care can never be without. I cannot tell
you earnestly enough how much it concerns you to
be trained against all this by the daily weighing and
measuring of your duties and performances, now in
your young days. Still less can I express to you
how deeply you will wish, when the hours of doubt
and anguish come on, that you had prepared for them
by keeping purity of heart. God grant that none of
you may ever know the miserable irresolution, the
wavering and cowardice of heart and judgement,
which are apt to hang around the best endeavours of
those who have given way to any grievous sin, when
in after time they would serve the Church, and do
good to the souls of their brethren. The grace in-

deed of true constant heroic penitence will sooner
or later cure this entirely, as it will the other sad
consequences of sin: and till it is cured, it must be
borne with resignation, as part of our just penance:
but may yours be the far greater blessing to hold
fast that which God has given you, and to let no man
take your crown: that when you go forth of this
your paradise, you may know right from wrong, both
for yourselves and for others, not by sad experience,
but by that instinctive wisdom, which the Holy
Spirit never denies to the prayers of humble innocents: and you may be spared the grief and pain of
continually fearing, lest those who look up to you be
the worse for your sad falls in former years.

But in order to this, you must watch, not only
against wilful and crying sins, but against the subtle
ways of sloth, vanity, self-will, greediness. You
must learn to govern your tongue, to keep your eyes
in order, to set about unpleasant, wearisome duties
at once, and to do them as well as you can. If you
desire to be good labourers in the field and vineyard
of Christ, this is the only training which can ever
make you so. Conform yourselves to it, humbly and
earnestly, as lesser children than you apply themselves to whatever they take an interest in: and then
when your time shall come to issue forth from this
your Paradise, the remembrance of it will abide with
you, fresh and fragrant, with no remorse to embitter
it, until your day's work is done, and you find that
by His unspeakable mercy, your way is won, not
back to this quiet home, but upward to the true
Eden; to the river of the water of life; to the tree
of life growing beside it; to the throne of God and

the Lamb : His Image perfectly restored in you, and your joy (if it so please Him) enhanced by the joy of having turned others, more or fewer to the same righteousness.

One word in conclusion to those who are less directly interested—

Who that knows at all what the world is, but must be deeply thankful that there are such places, where the little ones of Christ may be trained to pass through it unharmed? If such be our mind in earnest, let us remember that we too have our privileges, indirectly but not less really arising out of such institutions. Our privilege is, to keep them with our alms and our prayers, and so to repent and live, that by His great mercy through Christ, our alms and prayers may be acceptable. The offertory on this day, it is intended to apply to the enlargement of the college, so as to complete, if possible, the number of the scholars to thirty, and to provide more accommodation for the instructors. I do hope that this good work will be wholly or nearly accomplished this very day. It will be a good token, if so it please God, of His blessing on what is here doing.

SERMON III.

THE OFFERINGS OF LOVING HEARTS, MORE PRECIOUS, IF MADE IN DARK DAYS.

S. MATT. xxvi. 12.

" In that she hath poured this ointment on My Body, she did it for My Burying."

WHETHER or no the blessed Mary herself knew the meaning of what she was about, in that mysterious anointing, we are not told. It might be altogether an involuntary prophecy, an action over-ruled like the words of Caiaphas, to signify a great deal more than the doer was aware of. She might only think to express her overflowing love and gratitude to our Lord: He in His wisdom and mercy told His disciples that they would do well to take what she did as an expressive token of His approaching Passion. If after the tradition of many fathers we may suppose her the same person with S. Mary Magdalene, His words may perhaps admit of such a paraphrase as the following: 'She simply means to honour Me, but she is guided to employ that special sign of honour, which you all know to be most appropriate to the dead. "She hath done what she could." She cannot stay the counsels of Mine enemies, nor rescue

Me from their hands, but she is permitted to shew
forth her true and abiding love for Me in life and in
death. She will come, I know, after I am entombed,
to bring spices and ointments, and it will almost
break her heart to find that her Lord is taken away,
and that she is hindered from performing that sacred
office. But when she comes to know all the truth,
she will understand that I graciously accept this
honour which she pays to Me living as the full accomplishment of that which she will intend but will
be prevented from paying to Me after death. She
will know then that she did it for My Burial, that
she was chosen out of all the world to wait on Me
in that season, when men naturally select their
nearest and most trusted friends and servants to
wait on them. She will know it, and the whole
Church will know it: for "Verily I say unto you,
Wheresoever this Gospel shall be preached in the
whole world, there shall also this, that this woman
hath done, be told for a memorial of her." '

Thus understood, our Lord's words give the greatest possible encouragement to penitent sinners in
offering their best to Him: but taken in connexion
with His other sayings at the time, they seem also
to convey much instruction, and to warn us against
serious but not uncommon errors, as to the mind and
temper in which He will be approached.

For although this forgiven and favoured one
knew not distinctly what was going to happen, as it
is plain none of the Apostles knew, yet she might
have a dim foreboding as they most likely had.
There were many signs which caused all who loved
Him to feel that some great change was going to

take place: and although their very love, in its human frailty, hindered them from apprehending that which He told them so plainly, that to us as we read, it seems wonderful how they should have missed it, yet no doubt it caused them continually to be amazed and afraid, and to tremble as they followed Him.   Their hearts laboured with an uneasy sensation, like that of the mother of Jacob, 'If He should be taken away, what good shall my life do me!'   It was, I suppose, in part, to relieve such a feeling as this that she, whose delight had so long been to sit at His Feet, and hear His word, now ventured to draw near and anoint, not His Feet only, but also His Head and His whole Person: not caring for the waste of the ointment, if so be she might obtain acceptance for such an expression of her dutiful mind towards Him.   In this there was both a moral and a mystery.   The mystery our Lord Himself has partly explained to us, in telling us that it was over-ruled to be a type and token of His Death: and hath He not also not obscurely hinted the moral? "She hath wrought a good work upon Me, she hath done what she could, she is come aforehand to anoint My Body to the burying."   Some might have been slow to give, at least in that way, in proportion as their mind misgave them that their Lord was about to depart.   They might say, 'I would willingly spend it upon Him if it would do Him any good; or if the remembrance of it were likely to be useful in cheering Him, or encouraging others to honour Him through many years of a long life: but at such a crisis as this it is surely out of season: I will at least reserve it until we see whether these sad fore-

bodings which so many of us feel, are going to be
realized or no: if He put down His enemies, then
it will come in well, perhaps, to adorn His triumph:
but so to expend anything so valuable would at
present be idle and unmeaning, like providing rich
apparel for a person on his death-bed: better sell the
ointment at once and give it to the poor.' Thus they
might argue, coming round at last to the same point
with Judas Iscariot: and who shall deny that there
is some plausibility in their reasoning, if we judged
merely by human views of what is *useful?* But as
the loving heart contradicts it all at once, before it
has heard or read a word on the subject: so our
Lord in His condescension to loving hearts has not
permitted them to doubt, but has told them plainly
that He is on their side in this argument, and against
their reprovers. ' " She hath wrought a good work
upon Me: for in that she hath poured this ointment
upon My Body, she did it for My Burial." It is a
good work, though it be a costly, and as the world
would say, an useless mark of honour lavished upon
one who will not live long to enjoy it. It is better
than many things that look more useful, because it
shews more love.'

Thus we see that as the great reward given to
S. Mary Magdalene and the other holy women who
waited on Christ in His tomb is a Divine encouragement to those in all ages who wait lovingly on
the dead, so these words spoken before, as it seems
to the same saint, are His seal set upon those good
works, which affectionate spirits perform towards
the dying, while cold-hearted decency stands by
with somewhat of scorn in her air, thinking, 'all

this is superfluous: it comes too late : What real
good will it do?' There must be many here who will
recognize at once the kind of contrast which I mean:
for who that is at all used to sick-beds, has failed to
observe or feel this difference (among others) between
those who are nurses, for love's sake, and those who
are so for decency's sake—that the latter neglect
their patients in comparison as their cases become
more hopeless and intractable: the former are if possible more and more earnest and unwearied, as desiring to make the most of the short time which remains for so sacred and so dear an employment.   Go
into one cottage, and you shall find an aged man or
woman sorely oppressed in their last days with the
thought, that 'they are sadly in the way, and the
sooner they are gone the better:' go into another,
and all is placid joy and contentment, and if you
were to search out the reason, it would be, that in
the one attentions and kindnesses, especially if they
are at all expensive, are secretly or openly grudged,
—for 'what is the use,' people say to themselves,
(and sometimes they are not ashamed to speak it out)
'what is the use of laying out so much time trouble
and money, upon one who will so very soon cease to
be the better for it?' Whereas in the other and far
happier home the question is not 'What is the use of
it all?' but, 'What will most soothe and comfort
him, and least disturb him in preparing for his last
end ?'

I say, most who have eyes to see must have observed this kind of difference: and among our poor
especially something of the same kind is discernible,
in their willingness or unwillingness to give up near

kinsmen in old age to the care provided by the state,
be it scanty or abundant. Some too evidently would
think it too much to do anything themselves even
for their aged parents, and have no objection to pass
them entirely over to strangers: others would not do
so for the whole world, if they could help it. Why?
but because in some there is a deep living love for
their parents; in others love is worn out; or they
never felt it. They would be loth to neglect their
children, who are likely to live long, and some day
make them recompense. But the very old, the de-
crepit, the bed-ridden; the waiting on these appears
to them hardly worth while.

Now it is not hard to see, that against this whole
way of thinking and acting, which is nothing in fact
but a subtle selfishness, our Lord did in effect warn
us, when He intimated that the work of love which
the holy Magdalene had just been offering, was the
more acceptable from its coming so near His Death.
It is similar to that other intimation to which it is
immediately subjoined as a kind of corollary. "ᵃShe
hath wrought a good work upon *Me:* For ye have
the poor with you always, and whensoever ye will
ye may do them good, but *Me* ye have not always."
As those words mark a distinction between heathen
benevolence and Christian charity, the one seeking
merely to do good, the other to do it to Jesus Christ;
so do these which we have been considering, between
the heathen and the Christian notion of *what is good:*
the one tender and confiding, the other cold and cal-
culating: the one of faith, the other of sight. They
are deep lessons, and of manifold daily application:

ᵃ S. Mark xiv. 6.

D

let us now consider how they may help us in the
special work which has called us together this day.
The subject is the more appropriate, as it is taken
from the history of that Saint, after whom our new
Church is to be called: and surely it is well that
there should be in Christendom very many churches
named from her, whom our Lord has specially commended, with this her deed, to the remembrance of
all who listen to His Gospel at any time throughout
the whole world.   Neither is it a new thing to hear
S. Mary Magdalene's history appealed to in connection
with the work of Church building.   To the end of
time her breaking the box and pouring the ointment
shall stand as an example of eager love not nicely
measuring utilities, but lavishing all its best upon the
Adored One for very love's sake: Judas' complaint
shall no less exemplify the opposition of the world
to all generous piety : and our Lord's sayings shall
be rehearsed in all lands, to silence the one and encourage the other.   They are lessons for all times: but
it strikes me that there was something in our Lord's
tone which marks them out as peculiarly adapted to
times of trouble and anxiety in the Church.   Consider the thing in this way.   There is no doubt, that
the Son of God, Incarnate, and sojourning on earth,
to be the Head of His future Church, did by His Divine providence order things so that His doings and
sufferings, besides their own ineffable results, should
indicate and as it were typify the doings and sufferings of His Mystical Body, and as people behaved to
Him, so should the like sort of people in all times
behave to His Church.   Therefore whereas the holy
Magdalene made haste to pour the ointment on Him,

the rather because of the dim foreboding she had of
His being soon to depart from them; and He gave
her His praise and blessing: we are to understand
Him as vouchsafing His approbation to those labours
of love especially, whereby faithful men endeavour
to serve His Church in bad times, in cases when
mere worldly wisdom would say, 'You may as well
let it alone; you will do no good.' Such a work was
that of Josiah, in the latter times of the kingdom of
Israel. The whole nation was to the eye incurably
corrupt: the prophecies of coming destruction were
daily being repeated, and growing more aweful : yet
Josiah set himself, not only to put away the idols,
but to repair the house of the Lord. In the very
outset of that work the copy was found of the lost
prophecies of Moses, fearfully confirming the sentence
of condemnation : and when the matter was deferred
to a living prophetess, all the comfort she gave was,
that Josiah's own eyes should not behold the evil :
plainly enough implying that as soon as he was gone
it would break out. A dreary forethought! to toil
as though building for ever, with the certain knowledge that ere so many years were over, all would be
overthrown; the buildings burnt with fire, the treasures spoiled and profaned, the people carried away
captive. Yet he went on in faith, and his reward is
great: his fame is in the Church like that of the
blessed Magdalene; the whole house is filled with the
odour of the precious ointment. The remembrance
of Josiah is, as the Wise man saith, like the compo-
sition of the choicest perfume: " [b]sweet as honey in
all mouths, and as music at a banquet of wine." The

b Ecclus. xlix. 1.

temple indeed which he had repaired was quickly rased to the ground, and the vessels which he had purified were profaned again : but who shall dare affirm that his labour was thrown away; that what he spent would have told better had it been given to the poor ? Nay, herein, peculiarly he manifested his loyal devotion, that he did all ungrudgingly though he knew the visible result would last but a very short time. Doubtless he hath his part in the peculiar blessing of her who anointed the Lord's Body to the burying.

And what shall we say of the poor widow with her two mites, one of the few persons to whom we read that our Saviour gave them especial praise? Was not hers a good work when she willingly poured all she had, even all her living, into the treasury of God ? And what was the destination of the money put into that coffer? It was all to be spent in the repairs and ornaments of the temple: which temple, with all its goodly stones and gifts, was in less than forty years from that time to be so completely destroyed, that not one stone in it should be left upon another. Our Saviour prophesied of this ruin, immediately after He had seen and commended the poor woman's most bounteous offering: but He spake not a word as though that offering had been better and more usefully applied, had she known all, to some other purpose.

Wherefore, my brethren, if it appear to any of us, as surely to all it may more or less appear, as if the visible treasures of the Church were even now in danger of being rifled, her ornaments spoiled, her glorious sanctuaries profaned, not so much by open

violence, as by intrusive, heretical legislation, under
colour of seasonable reform : and if along with this
apprehension the thought came, 'Had we not better
forego this offering, and do something else with what
we have to spare? for what is the use of giving to
a Church only that it may be taken away by spoilers
and unbelievers;' I say, should a thought like this
come across a man's mind, let him remember king
Josiah, the widow with her two mites, and the blessed
Magdalene, how their several offerings were but the
dearer and more welcome to Him Whom they loved,
because to the eye they could bear but little fruit,
and were only to last a short time : let him remember our Lord's warning that He is not always with
us; and how that on that very account He encourages us to make haste and pour our ointment on
His Body, to honour Him as we may, or ever He is
buried as it were, out of our sight.   There are
countries, where His Mystical Body, once eminently
living and thriving, is now, alas! completely buried
as was His natural Body in the grave on Mount
Calvary.   There is North Africa, where the Church
has hardly looked up since the time of S. Augus-
tine : do you suppose that that blessed Saint and
his companions were the less earnest in serving
God, forming congregations and providing Sanctuaries for them because they saw the storm coming
on? or that they had less of God's blessing? We
should not surely measure the result of their labours
by what now appears in their own particular country : no more must we regret the counsels, the toils,
the prayers, the oblations, of this generation of believers, though it should happen for our sins, that

the spoiler may follow hard after them, and seem
for a time to desecrate all the hallowed ground
which they have provided. He against whom we
have to contend, we read, doth but quicken his
energies, because he knoweth that he hath but a
short time: He Whom we desire to serve, said even
of His own self, "I must work while it is day;" the
shorter the time, the nearer the Cross, the more
laborious did He shew Himself. Follow Christ's
example, you who profess to be His servants. Go on
with your Churches and your schools: I say, schools
as well as Churches, because I wish you to understand that the offertory of this day will be applied
not to the new Church but to the schools connected
with it: go on in faith and prayer, in penitence and
self-denial, and leave the result to Him. He can
stay the hand of the spoiler, or turn the heart of the
false prophet, so that neither earthly policy, nor
subtle heresy, may be permitted to mar your work.
Or if in His just judgement He deal with us sinners
more according to our deserts, if to human eyes our
efforts appear quite to fail: yet who can say how
much fruit may be borne in secret? Who can say
how many souls the work of this very morning may
help sooner or later to win to Christ? But suppose
it were only one soul, would not that be enough to
warrant all the labour, all the expense? Yes, my
brethren, could we but once perceive and know, and
keep the knowledge in our heart, what an infinite
loss or gain a soul is, that one thing would take us
all right in all that we try to do for our Lord and
His members. Knowing how precious a soul is, and
at how dear a price it hath been bought, we should

leave off murmuring as though money spent on poor men's souls had better be given to their bodies: and even in the worst of times, and at the greatest risk of intrusion and perversion, we should not, by God's help, cease from our works and our offerings.

Let this then be our special prayer to-day: that God would give us, now and always, a right sense of the value of souls. The most perfect has need of such a prayer, for it is an infinite thing which is asked for: a thing which in an especial way likens the servants of Christ to their Saviour. The least advanced need not fear to put it up, for it is the very beginning of religion. It is a good prayer for the occasion: for why are Churches founded but to save souls? And it is especially good for evil times, for it directly meets and overpowers the misgivings which might else bewilder and check us in such acts of faith.

Now, when this service is ended, and those who shall have waited on our Lord in Holy Communion are dismissed with His servant's blessing, our duty will be to proceed from this Church to the spot where the new Church is intended to be built, in order to lay the first stone with all due solemnity, as is usual in all Christian Churches. I am sure all those of you who mean to take part in that ceremony must feel what a shame and pity, what a sad falling off it would be, if by any irreverence on our way we should forfeit any part of the blessing which we trust will accompany us out of this Church. But if we are to be reverent we must be silent: there must be religious silence all the way till we come to the appointed place. And in this our silence what can we

do better than secretly offer our prayers to Almighty
God for ourselves and all who are dear to us; all
whom we most wish to remember in Holy Communion, and especially all who are concerned in this
day's work, that they and we may begin, continue, and
end what we do in a deep sense of the worth of
souls: our own souls, and the souls of our brethren:
that as we pass along the streets of Babylon, our
eyes may be turned away, never more to behold
vanity: and that if the times, as we apprehend, are
evil, we may nevertheless be found of the number
of those, whom the Holy and Prophetic Spirit meant
when He said, "[c]Blessed are the men whose strength
is in Thee, in whose heart are Thy ways: who going
through the vale of misery use it for a well, and the
pools are filled with water. They will go from
strength to strength and unto the God of gods ap-
peareth every one of them in Sion." But neither
shall we gather strength as we go, nor shall we find
God at last, if we be not careful to go *very reverently.*
So may we go out of Church today: so may we go
down to our graves: reverent, in thought of God
Who is with us, and of our own souls which are to
be with Him, or with His enemy for ever.

[c] Ps. lxxxiv. 5—7.

SERMON IV.

THE JOY AND BLESSING OF ALMSGIVING.

DEUT. xv. 11.

" The poor shall never cease out of the land : there-
fore I command thee, saying, Thou shalt open thine
hand wide unto thy brother, to thy poor, and thy
needy, in thy land."

THAT which was often practised by Him Who is the
Truth, in His teaching here on earth, namely to
speak the truth in such form of words, as that it
should sound like falsehood, and appear as if it con-
tradicted some other truth, no less plainly spoken,
either at the same or at some other time; whereby
the hearer was startled and awakened to unusual
attention, and persons who would otherwise have
only learned half the truth, were constrained in a
manner to learn the whole of it, viewing it on all
sides;—that seeming self-contradiction which our
Lord so frequently used in His teaching, when He was
among men after the flesh, we find Him in this part
of Deuteronomy practising long before His Incarnation, in teaching His people, by the mouth of His
servant Moses, certain rules of brotherly charity,
forbearance and almsgiving, whereby they were to
be marked from among all nations, as His own peo-

ple, and to secure to themselves a great and special
blessing.   For whereas in the fourth verse of the
fifteenth chapter, He puts the case of there being no
poor among them (or rather seems to promise that
there shall be none, if they carefully hearken to
God's voice, and keep His commandments,) in the
eleventh verse He distinctly says "The poor shall
never cease out of the land."   Thus the words of
holy Scripture *seem* to contradict one another; but
of course it is not so really, and in their true meaning.   The true meaning seems to be like this.   In
the fourth verse Moses is giving directions about
the release or remission from debts, which was to
take place among the Israelites every seventh year.
Every seventh year, the rich Israelite was to forgive
the poor one what he owed him, and could not re-
pay: but the prophet having given this rule, stops
as it were and corrects himself, as if he should say,
'Thou must forgive thy poor brother what he owes
thee: only that in fact thou wilt have no one that is
poor belonging unto thee; so blessed shalt thou be
in all things, if thou be really obedient to the Lord.'
So he speaks in the fourth verse, describing the
visible outward blessing which should wait upon
those few and rare cases, in which a person and his
family would wholly devote themselves to the Lord:
but in the eleventh verse he signifies how it would
be with the people of Israel generally.   *They* would
be far indeed from entitling themselves to the outward privilege of having no poor belonging unto
them: there would always be destitute Israelites
enough to exercise the charity of their brethren:
there would be need of that express and earnest

command, "Thou shalt open thine hand wide unto thy brother." In a word, there might be exceptional cases, where in reward of great dutifulness, a family or neighbourhood might have no poor immediately belonging to them, but even then they would have others within their reach, to whom they might and ought to shew bounty: for the general standing condition of the land would be, that the poor should never cease out of it.

So it was to be under the law: and so, and much more, might it be expected to be under the Gospel: by how much less is promised to Christ's faithful people now of the wealth of this world, than was promised to His former people Israel. Accordingly our Lord, having to declare His mind on a matter which greatly concerns us all, the true Christian way of spending money, laid it down as one thing continually to be remembered, that there would never be wanting, within our reach, fit and proper objects of charity. "ᵃ Ye have the poor with you always, and whensoever ye will ye may do them good." You see at once that it is the same promise almost word for word, as had been long before made by Moses.

I say the same *promise*, for this is the remarkable thing, the point to which I would now direct your especial attention, that both in the words of Moses, and much more in those of our Lord, the continuance of the poor among us is held out as a great *favour* and *blessing*, a token of God's love to those who desire to please Him. In both, the mention of it occurs in connexion with a great deliverance. In

ᵃ S. Mark xiv. 7.

Deuteronomy, and under the law, it was a main part of the solemn and joyful remembrance ordained to be kept every seventh year, of Israel's release from the bondage of Egypt, "that the poor should have their debts remitted unto them." The joy, the thanksgiving would be quite incomplete if there were no poor to be so relieved. Nor will you find any where throughout the whole Bible, a feast and a good day held unto the Lord, but what the poor and needy have their part in it. Portions are sent to those for whom nothing is prepared : commandment is given, and care taken that not only each Israelite himself, his son and his daughter, but the poor also, the stranger, the fatherless and the widow, that are within his gates, shall rejoice in his feast, and be the better for his good things. For the sake of His servants themselves, who were minded to be bountiful, the Lord took care that there should never be wanting a poor man to receive their bounty.

And so in regard of that other promise, yet more gracious and loving: "The poor ye have always with you, and whensoever ye will ye may do them good," it came to the disciples first as part of our Lord's dying words, one of the many legacies of mercy which He was about to purchase for us and seal to us by His death. The poor are always with us, and we are to note their presence as a remembrance of Him Who is no longer with us in sight, because He is gone up to complete our redemption and blessing. And to make the thought of the poor quite inseparable from the thought of Christ, you see that the solemn sacrificial remembrance of Him in Holy Communion is ever joined with the remem-

brance of the poor. The Jews in their state sacrifices might not appear before the Lord empty: every
one was to give according as he was able, according
to the blessing which the Lord his God had given
him: and the Holy Eucharist in the Church of God
is always accompanied with its Offertory. Christ and
His poor are set forth both in His promises and in
His Sacrament, as being, in a manner inseparable;
we cannot come to the one without waiting upon the
other: and therefore it is the greatest mercy in Him
Who so earnestly longs to bring us to Himself, that
He has promised never to leave us without His poor.
They are a kind of sacramental token of His special
Presence among us, and like all other sacramental
tokens, He proves and tries us by them in a way
peculiarly aweful: worthily received, they deepen
and exalt our mysterious union with Him; neglected, or used unworthily, they leave us farther from
Christ than we were.

There is no need of many words, to explain how
the presence of the poor is rendered thus instrumental to our highest spiritual good. We all perceive
that if there were no poor in the land; none that require aid in money or in money's worth; the readiest
opportunities would be wanting for the exercise of
some of the highest virtues; generosity, self-denial,
brotherly kindness, charity. Even a heathen might
understand so much as that: but they to whom the
Lord Jesus Christ hath revealed; nay more, hath
given and imparted—Himself—they have reasons infinitely higher and deeper for rejoicing in His implied promise, that the poor shall be alway with
them. For in that He hath made us His children

one of our high privileges is to try and be like Him, our blessed Father; and in this respect more especially He declares Himself to be our Pattern, that when He was rich, for our sakes He became poor, that we through His poverty might be rich. The way of the Cross, the way of self-denial, the way of stripping ourselves, the way of selling that we have and giving alms, and so laying up treasure in heaven; this is one principal way in which He hath left us an example that we should follow His steps: and our mutual wants and miseries are His merciful dispensation, for putting that way within reach of every one of us: so that though a man be never so poor, yet he may always find some one in some respect or other poorer and more destitute than himself, whose burden he may bear, and so fulfil the law, and follow the example of Christ.

But there is something more by far, and more marvellous than this, to make a Christian rejoice in having Christ's poor with him always. I need only just remind you of it; you all know the rule of the great and dreadful Judgement. You know that the day will very soon be here, when we shall each one of us see the Son of Man upon the throne of His glory, and hear His voice commanding us once for all to come to Him or depart from Him, and adding also the reason—that we had Him with us wanting our aid, and ministered, or refused to minister, to His wants. And then if not before, it will be made plain to us, that in dealing with Christ's poor, we were dealing with Himself: the hungry, the thirsty, the wanderers, the naked, the sick, the prisoners, the distressed of all sorts, were so many outward

signs, one might, as I said, almost call them sacramental tokens, of Jesus Christ present among us.
They were all in such true and real sort brethren
and members, of our Incarnate Lord, that what mercy
we shewed them for His sake, was truly and really
shewn to Him, and when we scornfully or lightly
denied any, we were scorning or trifling with Him,
O had we but faith as a grain of mustard seed, great
indeed is the blessing we should discern, whensoever
one really in want came near our doors, or was any
how brought to our notice by the good providence
of God. In such an one, how mean, how unworthy,
how unattractive soever, to us his outside appearance might be, we should behold our Lord, and hear
Him saying, as He once did to a certain rich man,
"Make haste and come down," 'come down from
thine high place of worldly ease and enjoyment,' "for
to-day I must abide in thine house:" and with all
haste we should come down and receive that afflicted
person, for Christ's sake Who is in him, very joyfully. See my brethren, what we should lose, if we
had not the poor with us always. We should lose
that special Presence of Christ, in them, whereby
He both miraculously enables us here to minister to
Him, and relieve Him, and also offers us a chance
of securing to ourselves His pardon and blessing in
our last and greatest need.

Observe, it is His pardon as well as His blessing:
for this is also one very gracious fruit of His coming
to us continually in the person of His poor and afflicted servants, that what we do for His sake by
way of relieving them shall be made to tell by His
mercy, towards relieving us from the sore burden of

our sins; as we plainly see in the case of the same
Zacchaeus : when he stood forth and said unto the
Lord, "[b]Behold, Lord, the half of my goods I give to
the poor," and when, accompanying this gift with
fourfold restitution to those whom he had wronged,
he made it plain that he was not bargaining to be
charitable at other men's expence, then, and not before, He Who will come to be our Judge, pronounced
beforehand the sentence of acquittal upon him : when
he so proved his faith by his works, then the Truth
itself declared, he also was "a son of Abraham."
Zacchaeus' gift to the poor availed in some way, we
cannot doubt it, towards obtaining pardon of his past
sinful life : he is a plain unquestionable instance of
that rule of Christian wisdom which was declared
of old, in anticipation of the Gospel, by a Jewish
prophet to a heathen king, "[c]Break off thy sins by
righteousness, and thine iniquities by shewing mercy
to the poor." By his example we may understand how
"alms deliver from death," and "[d]charity covereth
a multitude of sins." Not of course by atoning for
sin, in the strict sense of the word; nothing could do
that, save the Blood of Him Who is both God and
Man. But there are the prayers of the poor. Who
can doubt that they have power in aid of the prayers
of the penitent? And next and chiefly, as the holy
actions, properly called Sacramental, have by Christ's
ordinance an especial virtue in them to apply Him
with all His merits, His graces and blessings, to the
penitent soul, so the good works of Christian people,
wrought in them and through them by the Spirit of
Christ, and most especially works of charity, are de-

[b] S. Luke xix. 8.   [c] Dan. iv. 27.   [d] 1 S. Pet. iv. 2.

clared in these and other like Scriptures to have a mysterious power in them for the bringing Christ nearer, to the perfecting our pardon, and to the strengthening and refreshing of our souls.

And now, seeing that the presence of Christ's poor and needy among us is the very condition and instrument of so many and great spiritual advantages: without them we could have no practice of the best and highest qualities of our nature; no imitating of Jesus Christ: no personal waiting and attendance on Him, in the way that He most delights in; and that we should lose one chief portion of the very little we can do towards putting away our sins: surely we are bound with all thankful joy to acknowledge it as one of His tenderest mercies, that His afflicted ones are present with us and will continue to be so: that "the poor shall never cease out of the land:" that we "have the poor with us always, and whensoever we will we may do them good," and thereby much more do good to our own souls. All these are sentences which a loving and wise heart will teach a Christian to seal up among his treasures, among the most endearing and comfortable promises of the Gospel. Strange it were if such an one should ever begin to fret inwardly that such is the providential law of his being on earth, for this would be in effect repining at his Lord's giving him so much help towards working out his own salvation: like the Pharisees who complained of our Lord's receiving sinners, and did not perceive that if they could enforce their complaint they would but be shutting out themselves from mercy.

All this is so undeniable, so palpably evident to

E

such as at all believe the Gospel, that one is almost
ashamed to have taken up your time in rehearsing it:
and yet, my brethren (I would seriously ask), is there
not a cause?   I fear there may be not a few of us,
who have reason to be painfully conscious, that in the
state of society wherein our lot is cast, there are very
strong temptations to feel it hard that we should
have the poor with us always.   I do not now speak
of mere covetousness, simple dislike of parting with
money (and yet it is harder to rid one's self entirely
of that, than we commonly love to acknowledge to
ourselves), but those even who are cheerfully prepared to give to their power and beyond their power,
unless they are unusually free from selfish passions,
may often detect in themselves a secret impatience
at the multiplicity of objects, the endless stream of
demands on them.   They are inclined to limit themselves in the duty of giving, as S. Peter once in that
of forgiving.   'Lord how oft shall my brother ask
help of me, and I relieve him? until seven times?'
And the Giver of all good answers, "I say not unto
you, until seven times, but until seventy times seven." We know partly how it is with men, in this respect in the course of their private almsgiving.   They
cannot bear to see the same persons coming so often,
and fresh cases still occurring, as fast as the old pass
away.   Out of very sloth and childishness they will
send away one petitioner, or at least hearken to him
unwillingly and uncourteously, because they have
done so much for him before, and when the next
comes, he will be treated in like manner, because
they have done so much for others: a temper which
one of the old fathers ingeniously reproves, by ask-

ing, ' Why do you not make the same answer to your
own hungry appetite? Why do you not say to it, You
had your meal yesterday and the day before: are
you not ashamed to come again to-day? or, How can
you be so troublesome? such another has just had a
meal.' So it is with us often, I fear in our acts of
bounty: we are tired and vexed at having to repeat
them so often: which could not be, did we rightly
consider to Whom they are indeed done, and that
each one of them was intended to be to us a glean-
ing of so much more heavenly treasure. And then
there is our false refinement: the loathing and dis-
gust, physical and moral, which we cannot help feeling at many of the ways of those who most need our
charity: so that in the wealthier neighbourhoods especially they are driven as it were into corners, and
in our very Churches, if they find room at all, they
are so kept out of sight, that they can hardly help
feeling as if they had no business there. Could these
things be, if we and our fathers had received our
Lord's sayings in simplicity of faith? if we had regarded Him as uttering a promise not a threat when
He said, "The poor ye have always with you," "the
poor shall never cease?" or when He taught His
prophets to say, "ᵇ I will leave in the midst of you
an afflicted and poor people, which shall call on the
Name of the Lord?" Surely our acquiescing in such
customs, and in general our withdrawing ourselves
from contact with the poorest of our people, is alarm-
ingly near to what another prophet says of the mind
of some concerning our Lord Himself: "ᶜThere is no
form nor comeliness, and when we see Him, there is

ᵇ Zeph. iii. 12.   ᶜ Isa. liii. 2.

E 2

no beauty that we should desire Him : we hid as it
were our faces from Him, He was despised and we
esteemed Him not." What a depth of evil, what a
subtle poison must there be lurking and lying hid
in the seemingly light and thoughtless ways of the
world, to reconcile tender-hearted, generous persons,
to any thing so irreligious and undutiful as this!
And yet, would that we might reasonably hope that
it is not still the too prevailing tone of the higher
and more refined among us ! notwithstanding much
that of late years has been so nobly and religiously
done by earnest persons of very diverse schools of
opinion, towards restoring the poor of Christ to their
original and proper position in His kingdom. May
the blessings of the Almighty Saviour, great and
manifold, rest upon all such endeavours in every
quarter! and O that it would please Him to make
men's sympathies in the love and care of His poor,
His merciful instrument for bringing them back to
sympathy and union in the love and faith of His
Church !

With regard however to public charities in particular, whether their object be spiritual or temporal,
the immense quantity of the work to be done; its
growing, as it does, on our hands; brings with it a
peculiar temptation, somewhat akin to the despon-
dency which Moses felt, when he asked of God,
" [d] Wherefore have I not found favour in thy sight,
that Thou layest the burden of all this people upon
me ? Whence should I have flesh to give unto all
this people ?" As fast as new Churches, new schools,
new hospitals, new penitentiaries are built, others are

[d] Num. xi. 11.

required : the need seems to grow with the supply,
and the question, When will it end? is asked, by
some perhaps in grudging, by others in charitable
anxiety; by both sorts, we may fear, not unfrequently,
with somewhat of fretfulness and repining.   The
answer to the question of course is a very plain and
short one : the need of these charities will *never*
come to an end; not only will each generation of
the world still require the same kind of help; the
streets and lanes of every city, and the highways
and hedges of every neighbourhood, still abound
with such as are corporally or spiritually, poor,
maimed, halt, or blind, whom the Church and her
children will have to compel to come in; but the
nature itself of charitable work is such as to multiply its requirements; the more steps we take onward, the more widely does the field spread around
us : the higher we climb, the more plainly do we
perceive that there are further heights still to be
surmounted : more and more needy to be befriended,
better and better modes of befriending them.   But
what of that ?   There is nothing herein to disheart-
en us; have we not been told long ago that this is
one portion of the proper reward, the special encouragement of Christian bountifulness, to be allowed
fresh and fresh opportunities of waiting on Christ,
though it be in the person of but one of the least of
His poor on earth ?   Yes indeed: from our earliest
days upward we have been told of our great Master's
rule, To reward men's earnest obedience by helping
them to obey yet more earnestly, and to overcome
greater difficulties : as the Psalmist emphatically
says, " ᵉ I have thought upon Thy Name, O Lord, in

ᵉ Ps. cxix. 55.

the night-season, and have kept Thy law; this I
had because I kept Thy commandments." He was
very dutiful in the hours of daylight and work,
therefore God Who knoweth how to make His rewards suit our endeavours, helped him to be dutiful
also in the hours of sleep and darkness. Keeping of
the commandments is rewarded, in a manner, by
keeping of the commandments still better: the sincere endeavour to do good, by a higher skill and
perfection in that difficult art of doing it in the best
way. 'God,' says a wise and holy Bishop, 'as soon
as He perceives in you good desires of serving Him,
makes opportunities for the indulging of those desires,
that He may increase your blessing. He prepares for
you opportunities of trying your faith and brightening your crown by disappointing your first endeavours, or if they have succeeded, by shewing you
that there is still more to be done, without which
the first will be a failure. Thus He prunes and
purges the fruitful branch that it may bear more
fruit.' So it is in missionary work, whether abroad
or at home; the servants do what is first commanded, and still there is room; and their fee and
recompence is, to be sent out a second time, farther
into the highways and hedges, and labour on until
the house be filled: and it seems to them nothing
for the love they bear their Master: they are minded
as David, to account it a privilege when their task
becomes more costly and self-denying: we find
them, like the same good Bishop to whom I just
referred, increasing their alms as their means dimi-
nish. Perhaps this may be partly at least the account of the many cases, so startling at first sight,

in which it has pleased God by some stroke of
His providence suddenly to blight and bring to
nothing a whole harvest of religious and charitable hopes just as they seemed on the point of
ripening into good effects. How often have Cathe-
drals, and other religious foundations, been burned
down, or spoiled, or otherwise swept away, just as
the time semed to have come for them to answer
their founders' purpose! Or some patron, or chosen
instrument, has been providentially taken away without whom the work was sure to languish: or there
have been misunderstandings and false reports and
other like discouragements. And then, my brethren,
sore indeed was the trial, and great by His mercy will
be the reward and the glory, of those who in sweet
and courageous patience have gone on, renewing
their efforts as they might; and bye and bye when
their final crowns are awarded, they and we shall
understand more than we now do of the All-seeing
love which dealt with them so sharply for a time.

Far be it then from the promoters of good works
to faint and be weary in well doing, either for such
reasons as these, or on account of the more ordinary
misgiving, sure from time to time to make itself felt,
that 'do what you will the work is endless, and to
think of accomplishing it a mere dream: that any
such efforts as private individuals can make are but
as a drop in the ocean, or a single shower in a vast dry
wilderness: after all, it makes no visible impression:
as well give it up.' Nay, these are but the whisperings of the Evil one, but they will be effectually
silenced, if we settle it in our hearts beforehand, that
all this was to be expected for the greater blessing

of God's people; the work is endless, because the reward is intended to be so: when charity has done her best, her doings will yet be as nothing in comparison of what remains for her to do, God ordering it so, that she never may miss the privilege of having Christ's poor always with her.

And there is another trouble, of our time especially, which the same consideration may assuage. It is but too evident that the spirit of the age and country is setting itself strongly against permanent endowments, especially for any religious purpose. The moment they become important and influential, the state claims a right to control and direct them as to the majority may seem best. In proportion as this comes to be understood and acted on, persons wishing to do good will of course perceive that the day of endowments is over; that it is vain to think of imitating our noble-hearted ancestors, in their care for the generations to come: and who but will feel humiliation and sadness in the thought? But even this, rightly taken, will not be without its consolation and usefulness. It may be that in former times men have depended too much on the munificence of their ancestors: such and such good works, they may have imagined, are sufficiently done already, and age after age, in this way, may have underrated its own responsibilities in divers important matters. To be undeceived in this, is a wholesome, surely, though it be a very severe discipline, and the moral of it cannot be mistaken: 'Now, more than ever, let Christians be free and courageous in giving to their Saviour.' "'Take no thought for the morrow, for the

'S. Matt. vi. 34.

morrow shall take thought for the things of itself."
Think it not hard if your Lord come calling upon
you again and again, in behalf of the same good
work, not only for the first outlay, but also for the
perpetual maintenance of it. His mercies are new
every morning : why should His people decline
coming before Him every morning with a new thank-
offering ? Day by day we ask of Him and He gives
us our daily bread : what more abundant joy and
honour than to be permitted, day by day, to give
something to Him ? He hath fed us, and His whole
Church with food both spiritual and temporal, all
our lives long unto this day : why not lovingly
trust Him for the short time yet to come ?

SERMON V.

CHRIST'S GRACIOUS ACCEPTANCE OF DEVOTION TO HIM.

S. Mark xiv. 8.

" She hath done what she could."

This day's anniversary, my brethren, invites us to reflect with humble thankfulness, how all along, from the very beginning of the Gospel, our gracious Master has condescended to make use of 'women's work' in preparing men's hearts for His kingdom, and in promoting it when the time came. Before and beyond all, there is the momentous and mysterious decree, that we were to be saved by "the child-bearing;"—not without the instrumentality of a woman would the great Almighty God vouchsafe to be made Man. "*a God sent forth His Son, made of a woman," through His Mother alone partaking of the substance of our flesh: of a woman vouchsafing to be born, of a woman to be nursed, and in His man's nature cared for educated and ministered unto by a woman until He was full thirty years old. No other instance can come up to this; but it is observable how from time to time, doubtless not without a special providence, women were selected to be His agents on occasions for new steps to be taken, new

a Gal. iv. 4.

doors as it were to be opened in the progress and
diffusion of His marvellous mercy.   Thus when He
would shew Himself to the Samaritans, half heathen
as they were, and prepare them for the coming of
His Spirit, with His Evangelist to convert, and His
Apostles to confirm them, He drew by His secret
providence that woman whom we have all read of, to
Jacob's well, and caused her to inquire of Him the
best way and place of worship.   A woman was His
first messenger to that remarkable people.

To a woman, to her who had had an issue of blood
twelve years, was given, in reward of her faith and
humility, the privilege of being the first to have revealed to her the healing (might I not say the sacramental ?) virtue which abode in the very hem of
His garment, to meet the touch of faith.

Women, as far as we are told, were the first who
had the honour allowed them of ministering to Him
of their substance.

In His last journey from Galilee to Jerusalem, in
His lodging at Bethany, on His way to Calvary,
around His Cross both before and after His Death,
beside His grave both before and after His Resurrection, we all know what a part they took, and how
highly they were favoured.   The Saint of this day,
as has been often remarked, became an Evangelist,
commissioned to announce the Gospel of the Resurrection to the Apostles themselves.   She first found
grace to see our Risen Saviour, and with or without
her certain holy women, as appears by S. Matthew's
Gospel, were first privileged to touch Him.   None
of them indeed appear to have been present at His
Ascension : but not without the women and Mary the

Mother of Jesus, did the Apostles after that event
continue in the upper-room, in prayer and supplication: waiting, as the Holy Ghost said by the prophet, "[b] for His loving-kindness in the midst of His
temple." And to crown all, the narrative in the
Acts clearly implies, that the Holy Spirit actually
descending, found the women praying with the
Apostles with one accord in one place, and made
them partakers of Himself, sealing them with His
blessings, variously, according to the various work
which He had prepared for them. Thenceforward
the daughters as well as the sons began to prophesy,
the handmaidens as well as the servants had the
Spirit poured out upon them, and they prophesied
in that sense especially in which Miriam was a
prophetess, in festival ceremonies, in holy psalms
and hymns. Thenceforward again the Church had
her deaconesses, or whatever they might be called
whom S. Paul so often salutes as "women that
laboured with him in the Gospel" or "laboured
much in the Lord:" whether wives, as Priscilla,
whom God enabled so to help her husband in the
work of conversion, that all the Churches of the
Gentiles had to thank her; or widows, experienced
in bringing up children, in waiting on strangers, in
washing the saints' feet, in relieving the afflicted, in
diligently following every good work; or those
lastly, whom he congratulates as happiest of all;
who were willing to abide even as himself, caring
only for the things of the Lord, and enabled to attend on Him without distraction. Eminent of course
among them and over them all, Holy Scripture sets

[b] Ps. xlviii. 8.

forth to us, from the Annunciation even unto Pentecost as the chosen type of the Church and pattern
of all Christian women, virgins wives and widows
alike, our Lord's own highly favoured Mother; the
representative of the Christian as Eve was of the
natural woman.

But were we to select any one saying of our Lord,
which more than others might seem to embody the
whole duty of woman, and the secret of accomplishing it, so far as it is ever accomplished; it would not
perhaps be far wrong to lay one's finger on the simple utterance, "She hath done what she could," 'what
she had, she hath offered.' What form of words
could more exactly express the peculiar character
of womanhood; a deep sense of helplessness, but a
deeper of duty? That saying, with the occasion of
it, stands out as one of the most noticeable among
the few instances, each of them strongly and distinctly marked, in which our Lord vouchsafed to
utter words of personal praise to individuals in their
own hearing. I do not believe that these are more
than ten or twelve such instances[e] altogether in the
four Gospels, even if we include such sayings as
" Thy faith hath made thee whole."

Very interesting and instructive it would prove
to examine all these cases in detail : at present I will

[e] 1) Nathanael. S. John i. 47. 2) The centurion. S. Luke vii. 9.
S. Matt. viii. 10. 3) The woman of Canaan. S. Matt. xv. 28.
4) The woman with the issue of blood. S. Matt. ix. 22. S. Mark
v. 34. S. Luke viii. 48. 5) S. Peter. S. Matt. xvi. 17. 6) Mary
of Bethany. S. Luke x. 42. 7) The tenth leper. S. Luke xvii. 19.
8) Bartimæus. S. Mark x. 52. 9) Zacchæus. S. Luke xix. 9.
10) Mary of Bethany again. S. Matt. xxvi. 10. 11) S. Luke vii.
44—47. 12) The twelve. S. Luke xxii. 28—30.

only point out that five of the twelve relate to women, and two of the five to the same woman at different times: i. e. to Mary of Bethany, the sister of Lazarus. Of her, in her hearing, Christ had said some time before, "Mary hath chosen that good part, which shall not be taken away from her." Now He says, "She hath wrought a good work on Me:" "she hath done what she could." "Verily I say unto you, Wheresoever this Gospel shall be preached throughout the whole world, this also that she hath done shall be spoken of for a memorial of her." O blessed woman, to be so spoken of by Him, Who shall come to be her Judge, the Judge of us all! to be assured out of His own mouth that she was not deceiving herself, that the part which she was professing to have chosen was really the good part, that she had really chosen it, that it should never be taken away from her. Then as to the matter of the anointing: what would any one of us poor uncertain backsliders give, to be quite sure of having pleased our Lord but in one action of our lives; as sure as Mary of Bethany was of having pleased Him in pouring the ointment on His Head. In both instances, you will observe, Mary had been attacked and needed defence. Before it had been her own sister who found fault, now it was Judas Iscariot, backed up by some other of the disciples, but both times it was the same kind of censure, though passed on her by very different persons, with very different intentions. She would deeply feel both her sister's reproof and the scornful if not spiteful saying of Judas: the rather, as in both cases, opposite as the persons and their intentions were, there was plausibility enough in what they alleged to disturb a mind in the least degree scrupulous. What sort of a devotion is this, which leaves a sister to serve alone? which lays out on ointments and perfumes offered to Him Who needs them not, a sum of money which might go a good way in feeding the hungry or clothing the naked? Who can say that there is nothing in such a remonstrance? Or that it will not tell most upon the good and kind hearts, that care most for their kindred and for their poor neighbours? Doubtless, as the bystanders and some even of His disciples entered into the feeling which the traitor was first to express, and broke out in tones of deep displeasure, as though they were seriously shocked: so the beloved Mary herself could hardly help being in perplexity, as many on like occasions have been, before and since. But He that searcheth the hearts, and knoweth what is the mind of His good Spirit, the meaning and purpose which He puts into the hearts and doings of His holy ones; He interfered, as He never fails to do sooner or later, on behalf of His humble and meek ones, and spake out words of wisdom and power, which have settled the matter for ever to her and to the whole Church. Twice He spake: once to the traitor and once to those whom the traitor was misleading. To Judas apart, Do *thou* "let her alone. Against the day of My burying hath she kept this;" by His manner and look as well as His words speaking to what was in His betrayer's conscience: and startling him, it may be, with the thought, "surely this thing is known." To the rest, Do ye "let her alone: why trouble ye her? she hath wrought a good work on Me:" to all, "For ye have the poor with you always, and whenso-

ever ye will, ye may do them good : but Me ye have
not always." The drift of His words plainly being,
that both uses of our worldly substance are religious
and right : that each must be attended to in its season : that as the poor and their claims can never
cease out of the land ; they are always within reach,
and we are perpetually to be helping them ; so there
are special times and seasons, when such as love and
honour our gracious Lord feel especially called on to
lay out money in honour of Him, and as part of their
witness to Him before men. One of these occasions
would be, of course, His Funeral ; which our Saviour
proceeds to speak of as a thing so near at hand, that
to His all-seeing Eye this pouring out of the ointment was as a part of the ceremonial : and was so
taken by Him, though Mary herself knew it not, but
was simply offering her very best to show how dearly
she loved Him. We may remark by the way that
His approbation sanctions and hallows all the little
courtesies and self-denying services which Christians
practise one towards another in their daily common
life ; all the kind attentions, which the delicate loving heart suggests : while through a slight and almost imperceptible touch, in another narrative by
the same Evangelist, we are made to understand
with what a holy and charitable caution our Saviour
would have us guard our own and other persons'
demeanour on such occasions. The place which I
allude to is in S. John iv. The disciples, returning
from an errand to the place where they had left our
Saviour alone, " marvelled that he was talking *with
a woman.*" That is the only correct translation of
the words : do they not imply a general rule of re-

serve in our Master's conversation, which for our
sakes He vouchsafed to set Himself, and which all
who desire to walk warily and perfect themselves in
His Divine image would do well to bear in mind?

But to return to what took place at Bethany.
Doubtless He intended in so rebuking Judas to convey a spiritual rather than a social lesson. It is
commonly observed, and I see no reason to doubt it,
that He designed here to adopt as a law of His spiritual kingdom the sentiment which had been so long
before put into the heart of His favoured ones under
the dispensation of types and shadows. "*The house
which I build is great, for great is our Lord above
all gods." Do not ask only, 'What good will come
of these noble buildings, of these graceful sculptures,
of these enchanting sounds, forms and colours &c.?'
But where your God is to be honoured, strive without stint to honour Him with your best in every
kind, only taking care that it is your *own* best, that
you are not giving Him what is not yours to give.
I say, I cannot doubt that our Lord really meant
as much as this; He was not, as some have thought,
merely condescending to the innocent infirmities of
His people, when He thus accepted outward beauty
in holy things, but was promulgating a true part of
the more excellent way. But neither is this the
main point, to which His Scripture in that passage,
and His providence by this day's ceremonial draw
our attention. It is something broader and deeper
and higher. It is the great principle of Sacrifice:
especially of such sacrifice as His lowliest and weak-
est can offer, "She hath done what she could."

* 2 Chron. ii. 5.

F

What she had, she herself, this very person and no other, that she hath offered, hath given it all unto Me. What more can be said of the greatest saint, nay even of the highest Archangel? Yet what less can be said of the poorest and meanest worshipper, nay even of the most grievous sinner truly repenting to God by faith? It is the rule, the great charter of Divine equity: "[b] If there be first a willing mind, it is accepted according to that a man hath, and not according to that he hath not." Not, of course, all saints are alike holy, any more than all sinners are alike bad and miserable, but that He Who alone sees men as they are, vouchsafes in His mysterious mercy to accept them as they are, provided they truly submit and surrender their whole being into His hands.

"[c]She hath done what she could: she is come aforehand to anoint My Body to the burying. Verily I say unto you, wheresoever this Gospel shall be preached throughout the whole world, this also that she hath done shall be spoken of for a memorial of her." As if He said, 'She, i. e. this woman whom you blame, this Mary of Bethany whom you are trying to put out of countenance for what you call a wrong way of manifesting her love, I know that love, how deep it lies in her soul; I know her willing mind, what she would part with, what she would endure, if she could thereby save Me the the least of the pangs that are coming on Me. She knows not yet of those pangs, but I Who know them have put this instinct in her affectionate womanly heart, to pay Me this tribute while she has Me yet

[b] 2 Cor. viii. 12. [c] S. Luke xiv. 8, 9.

with her. I have, by My warnings to My disciples
or in other ways known to Myself, caused her to have
foreboding thoughts, how it may be with Me before
long: and having by her this costly thing, she humbly offers it for My acceptance in token that she
offers herself and her all, and would do so a thousand
times, if she could. And she shall not be disappointed of her hope: I accept her gift beforehand,
as I shall accept what she or others like her will offer
for My Burial: and My will is that her name and
this which she hath now done shall accompany Mine
own Name and the memory of My Passion in all
ages and nations to the end of the world.' Was
this decreed, think you, for a special honour only to
her, or was it not in part at least for our sakes? For
our sakes, no doubt, this is written, that all people,
nations, and languages, all sorts and degrees of the
sinful children of men might know how to draw near
to their Saviour, the Saviour of all alike, and be sure
of a loving welcome.

Is there any one for example whose heart is newly
broken with the consciousness, sudden or of gradual
growth, that his or her life, be it much or little as
men count life, has been hitherto worse than wasted;
that every hour of approach to death has been an
hour of departure from God: any who feels as though
nothing remained to be offered but the dregs of life,
years that can have no pleasure, a polluted body
perhaps and sin-sick soul, hopes blighted and chances
of doing good utterly gone and cast away: yet let
that afflicted one come and kneel at the Feet of Jesus
and offer him or herself with all that sin and sorrow,
to be punished if need be, but pardoned if it may be:

let him shew himself in earnest by doing what little he can in the way of confession and amendment: and so go on patiently waiting: sooner or later he shall hear in his secret heart, and hereafter it shall be said of him in the hearing of the whole world, 'This My servant hath done what he could; what he had, though it were but a wreck remaining of that which I had at first given him, he hath laid it all at My Feet; he hath kept nothing back: therefore I own him for Mine, Mine wholly and for ever.'

Suppose now a different case; a person brought up in the ordinary way, with a certain knowledge of God and of our Lord Jesus Christ, and leading a respectable life; outwardly screened from great temptations, and not tormented with strong impulses to evil; suppose, I say, such an one coming to see and feel after many years, how low his standard has been, how lukewarm his heart, how much evil he has done, how much more good left undone, because he was simply contented to be as other men: but now he wakes up like Jacob, with a feeling, 'The Lord has been here all this time, and I knew it not: how dreadful is my condition; I have been going on all these years in a common-place way, self-satisfied, self-approving, because my fellow-sinners seemed to approve, and through that whole time the Saviour's eye has been upon me; His heavenly messengers, I now perceive, have been coming and going between me and Him: and where am I still, and how am I the better? I cannot go on so. What must I do, that I may work the works of God?'

In many such cases, perhaps in the greater part, the answer of Divine grace to such a question will be the same as when it was once asked of our Saviour, " ᵈ This is the work of God, that ye believe on Him Whom He hath sent." Do not attempt great things, make no sudden outward changes, whatsoever you do now in the way of duty, go on doing it, but strive and pray, pray and strive, to do it all with a new spirit as to Him Who loved you and gave Himself for you.

But in every generation of Christians there will be some to whom the Divine voice will rather seem to say, 'If thy will, thy real longing is to be perfect, sell all that thou hast, and distribute unto the poor, and thou shalt have treasure in heaven: and come, follow Me.' Happy they who find grace in either of these two ways to understand and obey their Lord's call: of both it will be said, 'They have done what they could.' But Holy Scripture teaches beyond all question, that those who have the higher call are most highly favoured: and it is a special mercy to our time and country, that among Christian women especially that higher call comes to many more than it did in some former generations. The daughters of our people have been made aware by many remarkable turns of providence how great a power has been given them for good: great good to their sinful or suffering fellow-creatures, infinite good to their own souls; and what a pity and loss it has been, their using that power so little hitherto. It is well, that the idea of Counsels of Perfection has become a little more familiar to them, were it only to counteract in some measure the tendency of our age to grow more selfish as material comforts are brought more and

ᵈ S. John vi. 29.

more within reach. Indeed, my brethren, when we look round and see the condition of our poor, our forlorn, our sick, our children, our fallen ones, how can we choose but pray earnestly for more Maries, (if I may so speak,) in Bethany, that He may increase the number and holiness of such as are willing thus to sacrifice and surrender themselves to His immediate service. It is a great grace which they need, seriously to undertake, still more, soberly to carry out, such a plan of life. Mary did not mind breaking the box in order to pour it on our Saviour's head: and these our sisters must deal somewhat rudely with themselves, if they are to pour out all that they are and all that they have; some more some less, but each what herself can, on Christ's mystical Body; must deny themselves many things which they would naturally, and others, might innocently enjoy.

Will you not pray for them, and if you pray will you not give, lest your prayer prove a mockery? Will you not both pray and give to your power, that you too may have some small share in the comfortable words, "She hath done what she could?" There is great need in this case of both: for although the Penitentiary here has great tokens of God's continual favour to be thankful for, its funds, I am told, have lately fallen short. It was natural, the system extending as it does, that subscribers from a distance should transfer their gifts to their own respective neighbourhoods: but we must not allow the pattern-work to suffer through its very success in attracting so many imitators.

Finally, to speak one word more, if any person's

heart begin to fail him as to evils which may be feared for our Church, looking on present signs, and remembering the foreboding words, "* When the Son of Man cometh, shall He find faith on the earth," let such an one take comfort from our Saviour's word, "She is come aforehand to anoint My Body for the burying." So if the worst that any one fears should take place, we may remember that the mournful pleasure of waiting on our dying Lord was itself a great honour and blessing, and it led to the joyful, unalloyed transports of Easter. Do thou likewise, and thou shalt be likewise rewarded.

* S. Luke xviii. 8.

SERMON VI.

THE PRESENCE AND PLACE OF ANGELS IN CHRISTIAN WORSHIP.

Ps. cxxxviii. 1.

" Even before the gods will I sing praise unto Thee."

MY brethren, we are this day all of us here present before God, through a concurrence of three distinct providential calls. First and chiefly we are here duly to complete our celebration (God willing) of the holy festival of S. Michael and all Angels, a matter in which the whole Church visible and invisible is interested, by reason of the blessed Communion of Saints. Secondly, we are here to return solemn thanks for the great blessing of an abundant harvest, a matter in which this whole country is interested. And thirdly (since there can be no true religious thanksgiving without thank-offering) we are here to give the sacrifice of alms for the better preaching of the Gospel, and administration of the Sacraments to the poor in this particular Church and parish.

Consider now with me for a moment what is the special significance and instruction of Michaelmas-day, and you will understand what an appropriate season it is for such a thanksgiving and such a thank-offering. The collect, a very ancient one,

makes mention of two employments declared in Holy
Scripture to be those for which God has ordained
His blessed Angels. The first is, to do Him service
in heaven; the other, to succour and defend us on
earth. Sometimes we read of them as praising the
Lord; sometimes as fulfilling His commandments
and hearkening to the voice of His words. Now
they are His ministers, waiting on Him as a great
King; now His messengers doing His errands here
and there in all places of His dominion. The prophet saw them about the throne of the Most High
chanting one to another the heavenly strain, "Holy,
Holy, Holy, is the Lord of hosts." The patriarch
saw them ascending and descending the mysterious
ladder between earth and heaven, on the messages
of God to His people, and it may be, the prayers
and alms-deeds of the people to God. Once Daniel
saw them by thousands of thousands, surrounding
the throne of the Ancient of Days : once again he
beheld one of them and heard his tidings when he
was caused to fly swiftly with words of hope to the
afflicted Church. And so it is also in the New Testament. They are seen waiting on the Son of God,
hymning His birth, honouring Him after His victory when He had been tempted of Satan; rolling
away the stone from His grave, standing by Him
in shining garments as He went up into heaven :
and again they are seen waiting upon His saints,
opening the prison doors for the two Apostles, undoing S. Peter's chains and bringing him out of his
dungeon in the night, warning Cornelius to send
for him, encouraging S. Paul when in danger of
shipwreck : although indeed these two, waiting on

Christ, and waiting on His saints, are according to His great mercy and condescension, to be accounted but parts of one and the same employment; since what is done to His Church is done to Him, and the glory which His Father gave Him He hath given them, to be one with Him as He with the Father.

But further, the one book of the whole Scripture which oftenest mentions the blessed Angels, and gives us most information concerning them, is the Revelation of S. John : and there we find them from beginning to end, engaged in these two offices, praising God, and succouring His Church. And for this very reason perhaps, the Bishops are called Angels, in that Divine book, because they as chief priests have just the same offices to fulfil; they are the leaders of the choir of saints, honouring God in solemn assemblies; they again are His chief ministers in helping, guarding, feeding His flock, all their way through this miserable and naughty world. Thus, wherever we meet with Angels, we meet with this double office : honouring Christ personally, as admitted to be near Him, and honouring Him, as labouring for His mystical Body, the Church.

If therefore there is any one department of human life, any one employment of people here on earth, any one place which unites in itself both these—the solemn honouring of God, and the succour and defence of His saints, that place, and that employment would seem above all others to belong to the holy and blessed spirits, to the remembrance of whom this day is in a manner dedicated. Now such a place is the Church, and such an employment is the public worship of God. It unites in itself the two things, in

which as far as Scripture informs us the angelical
office chiefly consists; the giving most high praise
and honour to the Almighty Lord both of us and
them; and the helping us in the most effectual way
to put down our enemies the evil spirits and make
our part sure in Abraham's bosom and in the eternal
and perfect world afterwards; to both of which, we
know by our Lord's own words, it will be the angel's
office to carry such as have died in His fear and
favour. I say both the praise of God and the good
of Christ's little ones are in a remarkable way con-
joined in the solemn public service of the Church:
no wonder therefore, if the blessed angels are represented in the Holy Scriptures, and have always been
considered by the Church, as feeling a great interest
in that service; as being truly there present, though
out of sight; as concerning themselves really and
seriously in our behaviour; nay, as actually joining
with us in some parts of the service. Scripture does
so speak, for it directs certain points of dress and
behaviour in Church to be ordered so and so, ª *because
of the Angels;* that is, on account of the Angels who
are present, and who cannot endure any kind of dis-
order or irreverence in Divine Service. And the
Church so speaks: as those well know who are so
happy as to be well acquainted by their own devout
use of it, with the most solemn of all her services;
such persons will know what is meant, when I say
that the Church teaches us that we are a far larger
company than we see there assembled to give glory
to God: it is not only we who are in sight, but there
are Angels and Archangels and all the company of

ª 1 Cor. xi. 10.

heaven; all the spirits of the just made perfect, lauding and magnifying God's glorious Name with the same holy hymn, which they rest not day nor night, singing before God's throne in heaven.

For although the blessed Angels are present at, and concerned in all the Church services, yet there is one kind of service, as one may easily perceive, in which they may be supposed to join more expressly than in any of the rest. They cannot of course join in confession and acknowledgment of sin, because they never fell, they have no sins to acknowledge. They cannot join in prayers, except by way of intercession, for our wants and weaknesses are not theirs. The proclaiming of God's holy Word does indeed declare things which even they desire to look into, and some have not hesitated to say that even those blessed beings may possibly receive fresh knowledge, if such a word may be used, from the voice of God speaking through their fellow servants of mankind. "[b]To the intent that now unto the principalities and powers in heavenly *places* might be known by the Church the manifold wisdom of God." Yet neither in this can we imagine them coming to be instructed like ourselves. But it is in the heavenly office of praising God, it is in the singing and chanting of Psalms and hymns, it is in giving glory and offering sacrifices of thanksgiving, that the heavenly spirits may be understood to join, literally and really to join, and mingle voices, though not heard, with those of the frail and fallen children of mankind. This seems to set the office of singing or of chanting Psalms in Church, or of solemnly re-

[b] Eph. iii. 10.

peating them as we all do, in a different point of view from that in which it is commonly thought of. For consider: when we rise from our knees after the pastor's invitation, Praise ye the Lord, and our own answer, The Lord's Name be praised. And when the hymn of glory first sounds through the Church, to the Father, and the Son, and the Holy Ghost, as it was in the beginning, is now, and ever shall be: then the blessed spirits who are invisibly in our congregations take as it were their harps in their hands, and prepare themselves to join with us in those most high and holy praises of their God and ours, which His holy Spirit taught us by His prophet David. Surely this, if persons would allow their thoughts really to dwell on it with undoubting faith, would be found both a transporting and an aweful thought: transporting, inasmuch as really to be singing with Angels is so far making a beginning of the very happiness to which we look forward in heaven; aweful, somewhat in the same sense as it would be most aweful to have heaven's gate opened, and to be admitted then for one half hour with all our imperfections and unworthiness on our head.

Hear, accordingly, how the psalmist speaks of this part of Divine Service. "I will give thanks unto Thee, O God, with my whole heart, even before the gods will I sing praise unto Thee." Before the gods, that is, before the holy Angels who, as we have seen, are present in the whole of God's worship, but may well be supposed to take special interest in that part which consists of praise and thanksgiving. Even before these, says the Church by the psalmist, I will not be afraid nor ashamed to

give thanks unto Thee. So great is the Church's
love and trust, so deep her sense of God's inestimable
benefits, so entire her assurance of communion with
Him, Whose mystical Body she is, that she ventures
to lift up her voice even before those whose golden
harps and never-ending songs she never can hope to
equal : she encourages her children, unworthy as they
know themselves to be, to join their voices to the holy
and blessed spirits. Even before the gods, before and
along with those who compared with us sinners are
as gods, we are invited to sing praise unto Him.

Far, far indeed beyond what man could have imagined is the privilege indicated in the simple saying,
"Before the Angels will I sing praise unto Thee."
The words, when the Christian heart follows them
on to their full meaning as made known in Holy
Scripture, take you up into the highest Presence,
through that door which was opened in heaven to
shew the beloved disciple the throne of God, and
Him that sat thereon. They make you a witness
and partaker in spirit of the true Eucharistical Service : you see with the eye of faith, in the midst of
the throne, and of the Cherubim, and in the midst
of the elders, revealed as God and as Man, as it were
a Lamb that had been slain : the Cherubim and the
elders falling prostrate before Him each with his
harp, and with vials full of incense which are the
prayers of the holy people : you hear their new song,
" ᶜ Thou wast slain, and hast redeemed us to God by
Thy Blood ;" and then, not before, quite suddenly,
there is a voice of many Angels, round the throne,
the Cherubim and the elders : their myriads are

ᶜ Rev. v. 9, 12, 13.

counted by myriads, their thousands by thousands:
and this is what they sing, "Worthy is the Lamb
that was slain, to receive power, and riches, and wisdom, and strength, and honour, and glory, and blessing." The saints open the service, and the Angels
follow: the saints fallen and recovered, sound the
key-note, and the Angels who never fell take it up:
and so, in part, that would appear to be fulfilled, of
which I made mention just now: "Unto the principalities and powers in heavenly places might be
known by the Church the manifold wisdom of God."
The mystery of redemption is revealed unto them,
it would seem, after it had been revealed to the
saints; but so, that even they, the Angels, still know
it not in perfection, they still desire to look into it.
Thus, before the gods we sing praise unto Him; the
great hymn of praise and thanksgiving is offered by
the saints to their Redeemer in the presence of the
Angels encompassing them on every side. Before
the gods they sing praise unto Him, to Him Who
is in the act of presenting and offering Himself to
God for them, with all His Wounds, "as a Lamb that
had been slain." The pure beings learn as it were
a lesson in singing of sinful and forgiven man. And
not only they, but the lower creatures also, hitherto
groaning and travailing in pain together because of
the long abuse which they suffer at the hands of the
Evil one, they also break forth into singing, for they
too are to be redeemed out of the bondage of corruption into the glorious liberty of the children of
God. Accordingly we read that not saints only
and Angels, but every creature that is in heaven and
earth, and such as are in the sea, were all heard say-

ing, "Blessing and honour, and glory, and power,
be unto Him that sitteth upon the throne, and unto
the Lamb for ever and ever. Amen."

When we contemplate what is here revealed to
us, and recollect that to all this we are, one and all,
really introduced in the holy Sacrifice and Sacrament
of the Body and Blood of Christ, may we not, many
of us, say to ourselves, 'Alas, how lowly have we
hitherto rated our privileges! how seldom have we
drawn nigh! how slight and scanty our preparation!
how little have we cared for the unspeakable inward
blessing, or put ourselves out of the way to practise
more entirely the outward reverence and devotion
due to the unseen but most glorious Presence!' And
then, my brethren, will it not seem a meet offering,
and suited to this company of Angels, if with penitent yet thankful hearts, you bring what little you
can, towards the continuance and due solemnization
of the Communion, and other holy offices which our
Lord has hitherto granted you in this Church? Yes
indeed, whatever any of you may so save from the
world, and spare to Him, we may humbly hope will
be acceptable as a true Michaelmas oblation, and help
to the obtaining more of the grace of His Spirit,
more angelical aid to the accomplishment of other
and better works to come. And there is a strong
call upon you; for you may well understand that
the wider diffusion of the devout spirit which begun
the work here, thankful as we must be for it, tends
to draw off the supplies needed to maintain these
services. And let me say to those of you, my brethren, who form no part of the regular congregation
here, that where we find a Church and parish which

began early and has long continued the custom of
more frequent Communions than some of us remember, debarred by circumstances from splendour
of ritual, but only the more willing to persevere in
such a course as our Lord recommended when He
said, "She hath done what she could;" can we doubt
that such a congregation is especially dear to the
blessed Angels, and that to pray with it, and offer
for it, will be counted a special privilege by all who
have the mind of Christ?

And as your contributions will be for the promo-
tion of Angels' work (for surely the ministrations of
Christ's Church are not less than Angels' work on
earth) so the blessing, in acknowledgement of which
they are offered, this year's abundant harvest, may
with reason be accounted Angels' work also, in another kind. For Holy Scripture and especially the
book of Revelation gives us to understand that the
holy Angels are God's ministers, sometimes for
mercy, sometimes for judgement, not in spiritual
messages only, but in regard of this world's prosperity and adversity: and not to individuals only,
as our guardian Angels of whom our Lord speaks,
but to companies of men, realms and Churches and
races: nay we read of an Angel of the waters, and of
an Angel having power over the fire. As then
Daniel and the children of Israel had to thank God,
not simply for withdrawing the plague which was
wasting them, but for bidding the Angel sheathe his
sword: so we may reverently believe that famine and
plenty come in some sort by the like ministrations;
and every harvest, more especially such favourable
ones as these two last, is due, in part, to God's good

G

Angels waiting upon us, and providing us under Him, with bread to eat, and raiment to put on.

Thus I have tried to shew you how meet, right, and natural it is, that your Michaelmas-day should be a day of harvest-home thanksgiving, and a day of gifts and offerings for the maintenance of your parochial work; in Church, and out of Church: whether it be the devout waiting on our Lord Himself, or the charitable waiting on His poor and needy members.

And now that the good and gracious hours of this holy day are all but gone by, what remains but that we seriously remind ourselves how they ought to have been spent, and how we have been spending them?

Praises sung to God, and offerings made to Him in the presence of the Angels, and in communion with them, require in order to be acceptable, that the worshippers be angelically minded. Well for those who pray and labour to come here with such dispositions as may win the sympathy of those our unearthly friends. And well too in the second place, for those who having failed in doing so, look sorrowfully back upon their failings, and will even now, before they leave the Sanctuary, breathe an earnest prayer for pardon and amendment.

Would you know the mind of Angels when they adore? Remember the Seraphim in Isaiah's vision, shewn to him as a pattern of the never ceasing worship in heaven. "[d] Each one had six wings; with twain he covered his face; and with twain he covered his feet; and with twain he did fly." With the first

[d] Is. vi. 2.

pair he covered his face. Very serious and reverent must you be, when you are in choirs with the Angels; hiding your eyes, as afraid to look upon God. Very pure also, and very chaste and clean must you be, both in outward demeanour and much more in heart; for a token of which the prophet saw the Seraph with his second pair of wings covering his feet, like a priest, with his glorious long robe. And whereas it is written thirdly "with twain he did fly;" that is as much as to say, 'Obedient you must be, dutiful, resolved, courageous, the wings of your heart ever stretched out in act to fly swiftly whenever and wherever He may send you.'

Again, our heavenly fellow-worshippers are most zealous and unwearied in their services; "they rest not day and night." Will you strive to be like them, never satisfied with your own doings; never allowing yourself to think that you are or have been holy enough?

Zealous too are those blessed beings in that other and more ordinary kind of zeal: keen and eager in keeping God's watch; (you know the prophet calls them watchers;) full they are of charitable fear and indignation to see others lukewarm when Christ's trumpet sounds an alarm. The Angel of the Lord, we read, did once even curse bitterly a certain indifferent careless city for not coming to the help of the Lord against the mighty [c].

Lastly there is the blessed obedience and order, the thought of which comforted Hooker on his deathbed, the exact harmony and concord of the Angels, typified by voices blending together according to the

[c] Judges v. 23.

musician's high and perfect rule. Think much of this, dear brethren, always when you come together in the Church; as nearly as possible let there be no divisions among you; at any rate, let there be no schism, no wilful division; and where there are differences that cannot be helped, I would, if I may, beseech you all in the name of our Lord Jesus Christ and for the love of the Spirit, that you suffer them not to hinder you from joining heartily together in matters wherein you are agreed, especially where there is any work to be done for the protection of God's truth, and of the souls for whom Christ died.

Do your best to keep these rules, and I dare promise you that a day will come in which you will find that by God's mercy you have been praying and singing praises and offering spiritual sacrifices, not only before the Angels, but with them: and not only with them but with our Lord Jesus Himself, Who immediately after His first Eucharist permitted His disciples to sing a hymn with Him. And as they went out immediately into the Mount of Olives, so may these our services prepare us all, when our time shall come (if need be) to go out and suffer with Him.

SERMON VII.

CHARITY QUICKENED BY THE THOUGHT OF OUR LORD'S RETURN.

Acts i. 11.

" Why stand ye gazing up into heaven? This same Jesus, which is taken up from you into heaven, shall so come in like manner as ye have seen Him go into heaven."

WE heard, brethren, this solemn warning, this gracious promise, this earnest caution, in the second lesson for the day, and surely as we heard it, it must have struck some of us how fitly it comes in to introduce the Advent season. It was not so intended, but this year it so falls out : and it is one of the thousand instances in which by the providential arrangements of the Church the scattered lights of holy Scripture do, as it were, combine themselves in a wonderful order to the glory of God and the good of our souls. And we may notice another like coincidence in the service to-day : that the first Sunday in Advent should fall on S. Andrew's Day. It may remind us that as surely as we believe that He will come again to be our Judge, so surely do we believe also, will His saints in some mysterious way, come with Him.

But indeed if we be Christians in earnest, we cannot need these special tokens to make us begin Advent, aye and continue, and end it with the thought in our hearts of Jesus, returning, and the prayer in our hearts that we may be ready for Him. *How* to think, and what to pray for, He has sufficiently instructed us by this His farewell message, wherein He did especially exemplify the saying of His Apostle, "*His hour being come that He should depart out of this world unto the Father, having loved His own which were in the world, He loved them unto the end." In the very moment of departure, when the voice of blessing must cease to be heard, He did, as it were, speak to those two Angels apart and put a word in their mouths which they should at once repeat in His Name to His amazed Apostles. "Ye men of Galilee, why stand ye gazing up into heaven? this same Jesus, which is taken up from you into heaven, shall so come in like manner as ye have seen Him go into heaven." In this short sentence we have the sure word of prophecy, the great prediction to which the whole world is to be day and night looking onward, even as from all ages before it was to be watching always for the first Advent of Him Who is now departing. And it is, in fact, two prophecies in one: first, the same *Person* will come, secondly, He will come in like *manner*. 1. He shall come again, He, the same Jesus ; Him, and not another the Apostles' eyes are to behold. S. Andrew shall see Him as he saw Him when he followed

* S. John xiii. 1.

Him at the Baptist's teaching; and as he then asked, "[b] Where dwellest Thou"? and the Lord answered, " Come and see;" so shall he now be invited to come and see the place where our Lord dwelleth for ever. The places will be different, but the Voice, the Form will be the same. And so as to the other Apostles: He Who called them first to be His, from their fishing-nets, from the receipt of custom, from under the fig-tree, or wherever else they might be, He Who went in and out among them for more than two years, Whom they had seen agonized and betrayed, and bound and led away, crucified, dead and buried, Who did eat and drink with them after His Resurrection, He Whose true and undoubted Form had even now vanished from their eyes and touch, He, and not another shall again return and make Himself an object to their outward senses as before. So it was promised to the Apostles and so it is promised to all good Christians. The same Jesus Who took you in His arms in your childhood, Who called you by His Name, made His sign in your forehead, laid His hand upon you and blessed you in your Confirmation, Who has fed you all your life long with His own Body, and given you drink out of His own Heart; Who has been with you in your prosperity to chasten you, and in your dark hours to say "[c]Come unto Me, all ye that are heavy laden and I will give you rest;" the same Jesus Whom seeing not you have loved, shall shew Himself openly unto you. That is the Promise. The Ascension is the seal of it; the great Advent will be the accomplishment.

Now you see, my brethren, on what mysterious

[b] S. John i. 38. 39.   [c] S. Matt. xi. 28.

truth the glory and the blessing of this promise entirely turns. It turns upon *this* : that as our Lord and Saviour is Very God, of one Substance with the Father, Begotten of the Father before all worlds, so is He also, ever since His Incarnation, true Man; Very Man of the substance of His Mother, like all other children of Adam, of a reasonable soul and human flesh subsisting; so it was all through His Life and Death on earth, so it was when He ascended, so it is now that He is sitting at the Right Hand of God, so it will be in the Judgement and in the eternity that follows. The Manhood of our Lord Jesus Christ now on His wonderful Ascension has not vanished away, is not swallowed up in His Godhead, no, nor ever will be, but It continues taken for ever into God. He is God-Man, blessed for ever. Else where would be our faith and hope? for they altogether depend on His being one of us, as well as one with the Father: the one true Mediator between God and Man, being both God and Man.

Secondly: He Who will come is the same Jesus Who departed: and His message further assures us that He will come *in like manner* as He departs. He will come in the clouds of heaven, with power and great glory: His Sign, whatever that may mean (our fathers in the very early times supposed it to be the Cross), going before Him. He will appear from the cloud, even as He disappeared in the cloud. The Apostles had feared once before, when they saw Him with Moses and Elias entering into the cloud which overshadowed them on the mount of Transfiguration; they feared and fell on their faces, so that it needed for their Saviour to touch them and say,

"Arise and be not afraid:" but now they are enabled to look stedfastly toward heaven and even to rejoice in His departure. And those who are like them shall rejoice and lift up their heads when they see the skirts of His returning glory. God grant we may be of the number!

Then to enchance our joy and for a sure token that none shall ever take it from us, He will come as He went, with all His Wounds, with the print of the nails in His Hands and Feet, and the scar left by the spear in His Side. Holy Scripture takes particular notice of this. "[d]Every eye shall see Him, and they also which pierced Him:" Which of us has not pierced Him, pierced Him over and over again; pierced His loving Heart by unbelief and sin? But if you truly turned to Him, if you have so trusted in His Cross as to give Him your whole self, soul and body, thoughts, words and deeds (for this is the faith which justifies), then the sight of His Wounds which bought you salvation, will seal it to you for evermore.

Thirdly: As "two men stood by them in white apparel," two doubtless of His servants the Angels, so when He cometh in His glory, not only His saints will be there, as the twelve were there kneeling round, but all the holy Angels shall be with Him. Each of us, my brethren, will see his own Angel, to whom in this life God has given him in charge: and by that Angel, or some other, our Lord will send to each one of us a special message. May it please Him so to guide us here, that our Angels and we may then rejoice together!

[d] Rev. i. 7.

And besides all this, the true believers shall in that day know their Saviour by sound as well as by sight. They shall know His Voice, as Mary did by the sepulchre. For He will come as He went, with words of blessing. The manner of His going, Holy Scripture says, was this: "*He lifted up His Hands and blessed them. And it came to pass, while He blessed them, He was taken from them and carried up into heaven." Under the shadow of those out-stretched Hands, and by virtue of that blessing, we live and move and have our Christian being. The words of the blessing it is not yet given us to know. But He has Himself vouchsafed to tell us not only that when He comes again it will be with the voice of blessing, but even the very words, which, if we be worthy, we shall hear out of His Mouth. "'Come, ye blessed of My Father, inherit the kingdom pre-pared for you from the foundation of the world."

All this and much more, even a whole shower of blessings, is contained for the believing, loving heart, in that one gracious promise, "He will come in like manner as ye have seen Him go." Each Chris-tian person, I suppose, may reverently and humbly take it to himself in this way. He may say in his heart, 'Our Lord has dealt graciously with me in many many more ways than I know of; but from time to time He has permitted me to *see* and *feel* in some measure what great things He was doing for my soul. There have been providential joys and sorrows: Scripture words and words of the Church, have seemed as it were to find me out like sharp arrows of the Almighty. Prayers, and yet more

* S. Luke xxiv. 50.   † S. Matt. xxv. 34.

holy Sacraments, have seemed for a moment to lift
the veil, and His Eye has beamed out upon me.
Well, whatever He has done for me in this way, or
whatever more He may graciously vouchsafe to do,
especially whatever manifestation of Himself (if so
be) He may grant to me when my end draws nigh,
with that and more He will come again to me, to me
personally, when He comes to all the world.' He
will as much come to each one who is worthy, as if
He came to no other. Thou shalt know Him by
special tokens between thee and Him, as the beloved
disciple knew Him in the midst of His glory to be
the very same Son of Man Who in the days of His
flesh had loved him.

Those who are used to wait on the dying will understand what is here meant. If e.g. after a watchful and lowly life, a young person depart saying,
'I hope I am forgiven,' can you doubt that He
Who gave her that word will bring it back to her in
that day with an answer, not of peace only, but of
glory? If another, after pains like those of the
martyrs, which she had welcomed for His love's sake,
died exclaiming, 'Bless me, Lord, what is it that I
see? O the greatness of the glory, that is revealed
in me, that is before me!' to her also, doubtless, in
the day of Judgement shall be fully made known
that Countenance, of which in the hour of death she
could bear but a glimpse. Christ returning will perfect the joy of the departing saints and it shall abide
with them for ever.

In all these ways and by all these tokens, and
more far more than we can ask or think, will He
shew Himself the same Jesus, the same loving and

all-sufficient Saviour when He cometh again, as the disciples knew Him before He went into heaven, and as all His faithful people have proved Him to be ever since, interceding for them *in* heaven.

I will not now dwell on the other, the fearful side of this aweful mystery, how that the more gracious the promise to the Judge's friends, the more terrible the warning to His enemies. For them all the signs of love will be turned into tokens of anger. His saving Wounds which in life they scorned, will now bear witness against them that instead of coming to Him that they might have life, they have gone on crucifying Him afresh by their sins. The cloud from which He will appear will be to them as the pillar of the cloud appeared to the Egyptians, no refreshing shade, but mere darkness, hiding the light of God for ever. His saints and Angels will appear but to condemn them; the saints to shame them before heaven and earth, the Angels to "ᵉbind them hand and foot and cast them into outer darkness."

The, "Come ye blessed," will be changed into, "Depart from Me ye cursed." All this we know from the mouth of Him Who is Love and Truth: and because He is Truth, He cannot deceive us; because He is Love, He tells us, that we may be warned in time.

Now why did He speak so mnch of these things, the Blessing and the Curse, and put them so plainly before us all the time He was on earth, and by His Holy Scriptures ever since? Why did He command His Angels at the last moment to say to His people as His last word, that as surely as He was going, so

ᵉ S. Matt xxii. 13.

surely would they see Him return? He tells us why,
in the very words of the message. "Ye men of
Galilee, why stand ye gazing up into heaven?" If
we were never to see Him again, His friends might
look after Him with regret, His enemies with wonder
and perhaps with relief, and then both might turn
to something else. But now the word is *why* stand
ye gazing? He is not gone for ever: He will return
and you will have to meet Him: as He taught in
His own parable. He is that nobleman, that high-
born being, that Son of God and Son of David, Who
is now gone to receive His kingdom, leaving you
His servants in trust. And He will be here again
you know not how soon, to take account of each one's
task, to see what each has gained by trading. This
you will observe is the word to those who are gathered round Him in His holy mountain the Church,
professing to believe and care for Him. As for His
enemies who openly declare they will not have Him
to reign over them, for them He has a sharper and
keener word, "Bring them hither, and slay them
before Me [h]." But to us His special word is, "why
stand ye gazing?"

Let us take it, my brethren, this year as an Advent lesson or motto. Think for a moment, how
many ways there are in which, not meaning to be
absolutely irreligious, you may stand gazing after
Christ, instead of preparing yourselves to meet Him.
There is the *gaze* of what is called *mere historical
faith*; when a person reads or hears the Bible, or
the instructions of the Church, and knows and owns
it to be all good and true, and what it is every one's

[h] S. Luke xix. 27.

duty to attend to, but it makes no difference in his
doings. Sunday after Sunday, year after year, the
holy seasons and services come and go, and pass over
your head and leave you just where they found you.
The next week or the next year they come and find
you just where they left you, yet you would think
it very wrong to omit the accustomed attention to
them. What is this but gazing after Jesus when
you ought to be following Him ?

'Nay, but it is not so with me,' says another:
'I do more than look: I love; I feel in my heart
how beautiful these Scriptures are: it moves me
sometimes even to tears, when I read or hear of the
glorious things which Christ and His saints have
done and suffered; such a hymn, or such a sermon absolutely carries me away ; it is the joy of my heart.
Surely, with me, it cannot be so very much amiss.'
To one thus minded, the Angels seem to say 'Take
care: there is such a thing as dealing with God's
word as with a "lovely song of one that hath a pleasant voice, and can play well on an instrument: for
they hear His words, but they do them not[1]." '

Or a man may allow himself to think and speak
of heaven presumptuously, as if he were God's special favourite, and need not fear: or again in a slothful desponding way, like the unprofitable servant
who thought it was no use labouring, because he
had so little to work with, and that not his own.
These all in their several ways stand gazing, when
they ought to be about their Master's work. And
which of us, alas! is not inclined to err in one or
other of these ways?

[1] Ezekiel xxxiii. 32.

Brethren, do let me prevail with you, take this Advent warning, now in this year brought especially to your ears by the Ascension Gospel falling on Advent Sunday.

And as the twelve at the Angel's word turned away from Mount Olivet, overcoming their natural inclination to stand gazing after their Master, and to linger round the place of His last footsteps on earth: and as they applied themselves at once to holy meetings, with prayer and supplications, to make what preparation was needful for the coming of the Holy Spirit; and when He had come, to do and suffer all that He bade them; so may Almighty God grant us, if we have had any good thoughts to-day, not to let them die off unimproved. May He keep us from idly gazing after Him instead of, at once, setting about the next thing He would have us to do.

And this brings me to the special work for which our aid is now asked in His Name: the relief of hundreds of thousands of our brethren now suffering from the scourge of famine. Three hundred and thirty thousand is the last number I have seen stated, and it goes on increasing at the rate of thirteen thousand a week. Can we doubt, my brethren, that in this case, Christ has something for us to do? Surely not, any more than the good Samaritan doubted, when he saw the wounded man lying by the road side; any more than you doubt what that rich man should have done, who as he passed daily out of his doors, from his sumptuous fare and in his clothing of fine linen, saw, or should have seen Lazarus lying at his gate. We are not perhaps clothed as he was, nor do we fare as he did: but, my brethren, we are clothed and fed:

God Almighty for no special merit of ours, still gives
us bread to eat and raiment to put on: while there
our poor fellow countrymen have neither: they
would literally be starving, were it not for such help
as is now asked of you.   They are not indeed exactly
at our door, as Lazarus was at the rich man's: but
we can hardly go out of our doors without being met
by the report of them: it is almost as familiar to us
as if they were in our sight.   Can we find it in our
hearts to go on from day to day, enjoying the good
gifts of God, and not sparing some little, if possible,
week by week for them?   Ought we not almost to
be ashamed to ask a blessing on our own meals if we
do not in some small measure make our abundance
a supply for their want?   Can we help saying in our
hearts, 'Each of them is as a Lazarus to me, and if I
neglect to help him, our Lord has told me the end?'

Or we may go back to His Advent promise, Jesus
returning will be the same as Jesus departing, as in
other respects, so peculiarly in this; that He will
care for the poor and needy, just as He did when He
was suffering among them on earth.   When He shall
look down from His throne of Judgement, first to the
right hand and then to the left, and shall declare as
a Judge, not only His sentence but the grounds of it,
these, you know, will be His words, " [k] Inasmuch as
ye have done it, or did it not—unto one of the least
of these, My brethren, ye have done it, or did it
not, unto Me."   What tenderer, what more aweful
token could He give, how near His poor are to His
heart, how in all their affliction He is afflicted, in
all their persecution He is persecuted?

[k] S. Matt. xxv. 40.

He will speak the words, brethren, and we shall
be there to hear them.   Then, if not before, we shall
understand how they whom Christ shall finally bless
must have the mind of Christ, and that none have
His mind, but such as indeed care for His poor.   It
will be small comfort in that day to be able to say
in one's heart, 'True, I did suffer Christ's hungry
members to starve, but then it was other people's
business to feed them,' or, 'I had but a very little
to give, a few shillings, or a few pence, and what
was that among so many?' or, 'the distress was far
away, and I kept what I had until it should come to
my own door and touch those to whom I am more
nearly bound.'   What is the use of being members
all of one Body, and that the Body of Christ, if such
considerations are to interfere with our charity?   One
of the very last things that I have read of the endeavours that are being made to relieve this Lancashire
distress, is enough to put every such argument to
shame.   "A Lancashire lady writing from Switzer-
land, sends to the relief fund twenty-seven pounds
gathered from the neighbourhood.   She says, 'I put
a few lines in a local paper simply stating that I
would receive donations for the starving work-people.
I begged of nobody.   The whole of this twenty-seven
pounds has been given by Swiss and a considerable
share by peasants, servants, work-people and little
children.   It was indescribably touching when women so poor that I thought they came to ask charity
put their one franc or two francs into my hand, always with apologies: 'I am poor, I can only give
this little, but I cannot refrain; we must help our
neighbours.'   Many shed tears, while listening to de-

H

tails, which nearly all asked for. All the poor who
came were previously unknown to me and left no
name; there was no mixed motive: and surely these
mites are glorious treasures in God's sight."

Is not this the still small voice, which more than
any thing great and loud betokens the Presence of
God's good Spirit, the kind Father of the poor, in the
heart? Doubtless it is heard in heaven, and will be
heard of again when Christ shall come from heaven.
You too, my brethren, will respond to it; I am sure
you will: you will not if you can help it lose your
share in the blessing. The distress continues, there
is no doubt of that: and the early winter has been
trying the poor people sadly. On Friday and Satur-
day in last week a person in Manchester visited
thirteen families, all factory hands. ' I went into
the bedroom of each. It was grievous to see the thin
covering on the beds, and to notice that there was
not a blanket in any of the thirteen houses. One of
the men, a time keeper at a mill, has a wife and seven
children. The total receipts of the family last week
were twelve shillings and six pence, out of which
they have to pay three shillings for rent, leaving
nine shillings and six pence, for nine persons for a
week for food, coal, light &c. In one corner of their
bedroom were three fine boys, sleeping on the floor
with no covering but a patchwork print counterpane,
and their own scanty clothes. On the mattrass, in
another part of the room, was a little girl, covered
with her mother's shawl. There was no other
covering to this bed, and the poor fellow and his wife
and a baby three months old have only their own
clothes to protect them from the cold of the night.

In another room on the floor was the bed of the two daughters, fifteen and nineteen, both of whom are at our sewing school: the only covering on that bed was what appeared to have been once a table cloth. The house was remarkably clean and the father really a good honest man. They have sold and pawned every thing, rather than go to the parish.'

One part of the mind of Christ is to care for those who bear their cross so sweetly; and those again, alas! how many ten thousands! who are brought into grievous temptation: Satan taking advantage of their destitution. You will help them and pray for them for their souls' sake as well as for their bodies'.

If any have scruples about the right *way* of helping them, it might perhaps be well for him not to withhold that which he would give if he had no scruples, but to pour it in some other way into God's treasury, for Christ's sake: e. g. to give it for one or other of those loving plans which are being tried for the *spiritual* good of these poor people.

Christ Who loves them might feed them all in a moment. But for our sakes and their's also, for the sake of the souls as well as bodies of us all, He makes as though He had need of us. It is as if He came to us, saying, "Whence shall we buy bread that these may eat?" Do not turn away nor stand gazing. Bring your five loaves and two fishes, and see if He will not take them in His Hands and feed your brethren, and bless *you* with a very special Advent blessing.

SERMON VIII.

THE SPIRITUAL PROFIT OF BODILY HUNGER AND THIRST.

S. Matt. xxv. 34, 35.

" Then shall the King say unto them on His right hand, Come, ye blessed of My Father, inherit the kingdom prepared for you from the foundation of the world; for I was an hungered, and ye gave Me meat."

We all know what it is to be hungry and thirsty, and some perhaps know but too well the pain and care of sometimes not having enough for themselves or for those who depend on them. But have we ever considered in what a wonderful way God has caused this hunger and thirst of ours to help us in obtaining the salvation of our souls for ever? In themselves, these appetites of hunger and thirst would seem to pull us down to earth; they put us on a level with the lower creatures: for aught we know, they are just the same in us as they are in the beasts that perish. But our good God in His mercy and wisdom has instructed us how our being hungry and thirsty may be a great and real profit to us, in regard of that life which shall never pass away.

First, He took it on Himself, along with the other

frailties and infirmities of our nature. He knows
and feels for all that men need in that way, not only
because He created us, our bodies as well as our
souls, and made them to require that earthly nourishment, but also, even more wonderfully, because He
Himself became one of us, and for more than thirty
years hungered and thirsted, ate and drank, endured
pain and faintness from want, and received relief
from food, just as all the children of Adam do. And
He never forgets what He vouchsafed to bear. Even
on His judgement throne, when He shall come in
His glory to pass sentence on the quick and dead,
He will say, "I was an hungered." We are especially told in the Gospel, how on a certain day, the
multitude being very great, and having nothing to
eat, Jesus called His disciples unto Him, and said,
"*I have compassion on the multitude, because they
have now been with Me three days, and have nothing
to eat: and if I send them away fasting to their own
houses, they will faint by the way." Did our Saviour, think you, feel for those hungry persons only,
whom He had then in His sight? May we not be
quite sure, that He feels alike for all who suffer in
that way? Since He is perfect God, and all are
alike present to Him; He is also perfect Man, and
knows by His own experience what it is to be hungry and have nothing. In this way we may well
understand, though perhaps we never yet have been
used so to think of it, that every pang of hunger or
thirst which we feel is in reality a token of Christ's
love towards us: we know by our feeling it, that
He feels it in a manner with us, since in all such

* S Mark viii. 2.

points He was made like unto us. In all our affliction He is afflicted : of course *that* is not left out,
which is so great a part of the affliction of many :
we may truly say, In all our hunger He is an hungered, and in all our thirst He is athirst. We have
reason to remember it especially at this season of the
year. For now we are come to the time of Lent,
the forty days which the Church always keeps in
remembrance of what our Saviour did for our sake,
when He was openly setting about the work of our
salvation. He remained in a lonely place without
food forty days and forty nights : and when those
days were ended, " He was afterward an hungered."
For our sake He fasted : for us He bore all the pain
of it : and therefore in the Litany the Church teaches
us to put Him in mind of it, " By Thy Fasting and
Temptation, Good Lord, deliver us." As if we
should say, ' By the pains of hunger which Thou
didst take on Thyself, we beseech Thee, O Lord,
deliver us from all evil and mischief, which our own
hunger and thirst is apt to bring on us : from glut-
tony and drunkenness, from inordinate care about
our diet ; from selfish desire to please our appetite ;
from envy and grudging, from dishonesty and stealing ; from mistrusting Thee in want, and forgetting
Thee in fulness ; from the misery of famine, and
from the sight of those dear to us pining away in
destitution and faintness ; Good Lord, we beseech
Thee, deliver us and all Christians for ever.' What
blessings would our daily hunger and thirst prove
to us, did they but set us on thoughts and prayers
such as these ! How would they serve as gracious
means to lift us up towards heavenly desires, would

we but use ourselves, when we are hungry, to remember Christ fasting for us, and when we are
thirsty, to remember how He thirsted on the Cross.

In these ways hunger and thirst may remind us of
Jesus Christ, and bring us in spirit nearer to Him:
and there are yet other most effectual ways, in which
He graciously offers to turn those unpleasant feelings
to our good for all eternity. One of those ways is
fasting, another is alms given to the hungry. You
know what fasting is: it is living in some degree
lower than we commonly do: having fewer meals,
or taking less at a meal, or doing without something which we like; the better to please God,
and obtain His pardon and grace. I know indeed
that some good persons are very jealous of all mention of this duty: they have a kind of fear that it is
encouraging people to trust in something outward,
something of their own, instead of making Christ all
in all: but they need not fear this, any more than
in the case of any other duty. Our Lord speaks of
fasting, just as He does of almsgiving: and we can
no more please Him without the one than the other.
He says, Christians will of course fast; and we know
from other Scriptures, and from the example of holy
men of all times, and from the plain rules of the
Church in the Prayer-book, how greatly it is for our
good to do so. But now, it is quite plain, that if
there were no hunger and thirst, there could be no
fasting, no secret exercise of one's self in denying
those bodily appetites: and so Christ's servants
would lose that encouraging hope which He holds
out to them in the gracious words, "ᵇAppear thou not

ᵇ S. Matt. vi. 18.

unto men to fast, but unto thy Father which is in
secret; and thy Father which seeth in secret shall
reward thee openly."

But thirdly, I said that our gracious Saviour has
vouchsafed unto us yet a third way of turning men's
bodily hunger to our soul's good: it gives us opportunity to shew our love for Him, by relieving, as we
may, our brethren who are in hunger. That we
should do so, is so near His heart, that He will
make special mention of it in the last Judgement.
He will point as it were to those who have been poor
and needy in this world, assembled there before Him,
with all others, and will say to the happy souls on
His right hand, "Insomuch as ye gave food to these
My brethren in their hunger, ye gave it unto Me."
It is all one in His sight, whether a person living in
our Lord's own time upon earth helped Him gladly
and dutifully to food in His hunger, or whether,
living as we do long after, we do the same thing
gladly and dutifully for any of those whom He calls
His brethren. Absence in body, and distance in
time, are nothing to Him in such a case. A poor
famished person comes to your door; you give him
food for Christ's sake: Christ sets it down as so
much given to Himself. Think of it again and again,
say it to yourself over and over: 'It is not this poor
man whom I relieve or refuse, it is my Lord and
Saviour Himself. The poor man will thank me,
perhaps, and it will be a pleasure to hear his thanks:
but whether *he* be thankful or no, whether I hear
him or no, I shall have a good and sure hope of being
thanked at the Last day, thanked by our Lord Jesus
Christ Himself, Who cannot forget, Who will not

despise any the least act of loving-kindness shewn
to any child of Adam for His sake. I shall, if I do
not forfeit them, hear the blessed words, "Inasmuch
as ye did it to one of the least of these, ye did it
unto Me." ' Again, a thirsty person comes to your
door, you give him but a cup of cold water, it is all
perhaps which you have to give, but you give it
willingly for Jesus Christ's sake; he goes away refreshed, and you think no more of it; he too most
likely forgets it before long: but our Lord, as I said
before, cannot forget it: He has said, "such an one
shall in no wise lose his reward:" and depend upon
it, our Lord will keep His promise.

But although no work of mercy will lose its reward, yet it is quite certain that he who has least
to spare will have the greatest blessing in proportion
to his gift. Most of you have heard of the widow's
mite: and some may remember that remarkable
history of the widow who relieved the prophet Elijah
in his hunger, giving him part of her only handful
of meal[c]. It seemed hard to ask her, when she had
so little for herself; and more than that, when it
seemed as though every morsel she gave away was
so much taken from the portion of her starving child.
It seemed hard to ask her, but it was the greatest of
kindnesses. It seemed so much taken from her young
child's scanty portion, but it was the means of saving
his life twice over: first, while the famine was in
the land, that one barrel of meal, by a wonder of
God's mercy, wasted not until two or three years
had passed, and so the child's life was saved, who
would else perhaps have starved. Again, when the

[c] 1 Kings xvii. 12.

same little child fell sick and died, Elijah prayed for him, and God restored his life. Such was the bountiful, the overflowing return, which it pleased God to bestow on that very poor widow, because she parted with a handful of flour when she had for herself and her child but just enough for one day.

As there is thus a special blessing on those who give out of a very little, so also is there a special blessing on those who give to the very poor and miserable. The more wretched a person is, the greater his likeness to that Divine Person, Who says by the prophet, "d Behold and see if there be any sorrow like unto My sorrow." If there be any pain or misery more dreadful and distressing than usual, there is so much the greater joy and comfort in doing something to lessen the misery, because, whether we think of it or no, there is in it an unusual portion of the Cross of Christ. For instance, we all of us feel how great an honour and happiness it would have been, had we been permitted to wait upon one of the glorious martyrs, upon those whom Christ calls friends: to wait upon them in prison, in torture, or in death, and so a considerate Christian will always perceive that whatever brings him nearer to great affliction whether in himself or in another, does in reality bring him nearer to Christ.

My brethren, I would that we had as much faith in all this, as we may easily have understanding to see that it is true: I would that when we see or hear of deep sorrow, we were used presently to carry back our thoughts to the Cross, and forward to the Day of Judgement. I would that at this time, on

d Lam. i. 12.

this day, when God's providence is bringing before us what seems the greatest calamity which has befallen our country since the oldest of us can remember anything, I would we might have grace, to " ᵉhear the rod, and Him Who hath appointed it."

All of you know more or less of the sad occasion for which we now ask your alms. You know that in Ireland and in the Highlands of Scotland, the poorest parts of this kingdom, it has pleased God for two years following, but chiefly in the last year, to withhold His blessing from the fruits of the earth, so that hundreds of thousands, I may say millions, are really in a state of famine; they are really dying daily by hundreds. They are dying by famine, not here and there one, but in many instances whole families together: the cold winter has come upon them without food and clothing, and often there has been no friend, nor any means to provide even the common decencies of burial. Many of the saddest accounts in Holy Scripture of the Jews' sufferings when God visited them with famine seem to answer but too well to the present condition of our brethren in Ireland. "ᶠWhen I have broken the staff of your bread, ten women shall bake your bread in one oven, and they shall deliver your bread unto you by weight, and ye shall not be satisfied. Your land shall be desolate, and your cities waste . . . as long ˙as your land lieth desolate it shall rest," i. e. men will want the heart, or the power, to till it. "ᵍThou shalt carry much seed out into the field, and shalt gather little in . . . Thy life shall hang in doubt before thee, and thou shalt fear day and night, and

* Micah vi. 9.　ᶠ Lev. xxvi. 26.　ᵍ Deut. xxviii 28, 66.

thou shalt have none assurance of thy life." "ʰMine
eyes do fail with tears, my bowels are troubled, my
liver is poured upon the earth, for the destruction of
the daughter of my people ; because the children
and the sucklings swoon in the streets of the city.
They say to their mothers, Where is corn and wine ?
When they swooned as the wounded in the streets
of the city, when their soul was poured out into
their mothers' bosom." "ⁱThe tongue of the sucking
child cleaveth to the roof of his mouth for thirst :
the young children crave bread, and no man breaketh it unto them." These and other sad descriptions
are but too truly fulfilled even now at our very
gates : within a few score of miles from us, among
brethren speaking the same language. And we have
it in our power, more or less, to relieve them : or at
least to shew a good will towards doing so: and that
is a great deal. The country, as a country, is doing
all it can, trying to find both work and provisions :
and every one of us may at least add his mite, may
bring his cup of cold water. And what if our own
times are hard, prices high, and demands pressing ?
Faith, true courageous faith, sees in that an additional reason for taking pains to give all she can.
The greater their affliction, who ask, the more they
resemble our Lord Himself : the less our ability to
help them, the more abundant our blessing, if we
strive to do so. I have good hope that some of you,
nay, not a few, will consider these things, and lay
them to heart against next Sunday, when you will
be invited to make an offering towards the relief of
these our famishing brethren, if you have not done

ʰ Lam. ii. 11, 12.　　　　ⁱ Lam. iv. 4.

so before. What if you have families, persons depending on you here? depend upon it, what you offer in religious alms will obtain for them a greater blessing than all that you could save for them. If you have young children, you are the better able to understand what parents in Ireland feel, when their little ones cry for meat and drink, and they have none to give them. Let me then beseech you to prepare yourselves, one and all, those that have much to give much: those that have little to be diligent in giving of that little. Give largely, give willingly, and accompany your gifts with prayer. Bow yourself down on the knees of your heart, and there continue before God, in an aweful sense of His Presence: for in such visitations as famine He is surely present in a particular sense. Cast yourself before Him in all humility, as becomes one who knows that he is but sinful dust and ashes. Think again and again, think steadily, The Last Day is coming: Christ Himself hath told us that famines and pestilences are tokens of it: I will give what I can, I will repent while I may; I will not mind denying myself, if now at least, for the short time that remains, I may please God and lay up treasure in heaven.

SERMON IX.

————

THE CAUSE OF GOD'S VISITATIONS, AND HOW BY HIS MERCY THEY MAY BE REMOVED.

————

HOSEA ii. 8, 9.

" She did not know that I gave her corn and wine and oil : . . . . therefore will I return, and take away My corn in the time thereof."

WE are here this day, in obedience to our Bishop and our Queen, to humble ourselves before God on account of the grievous scarcity with which it has pleased Him to afflict our brethren in Ireland and elsewhere. And we have the comfort of thinking how all the country over our fellow Christians are even now employed as we are; from the highest to the lowest, from the Queen to the poorest cottager, we may think of many of all ranks as being at this hour present in God's House, to pray most earnestly to Him that it may please Him to forgive us our sins, and turn away the evil which threatens us.

We may have comfort and hope in doing so : first, because of His gracious promise, that " ᵃ Where two or three are gathered together in His Name, there is

ᵃ S. Matt. xviii. 20.

He in the midst of them," to hear and grant their prayers, if they be not unworthy. And in the next place, Holy Scripture encourages us by telling us of many times when God's people came in like manner before Him, and He on their sincere repentance was pleased to withdraw His heavy hand.

The Prophet tells us in the text, why famine was sent on the Jews. He is speaking of that whole people under the figure of a betrothed wife: in the same way as S. Paul tells us, the Church is the Bride or Spouse of Christ. So the Jewish people was in old time accounted the Spouse or Bride of the great King of heaven and earth: and their forgetting God, and worshipping idols, is compared to the sin and shame of an unfaithful unchaste wife; who preferring some other man, forsakes her husband's house, and forgets his loving-kindnesses. "She," i. e. the nation and people of Israel, "did not know that I gave her corn and wine and oil, and multiplied her silver and gold." Of all people, one would think that the Israelites would be least likely to forget that God is the Giver of plenty. Think what a number of remarkable histories there are, from beginning to end of the Bible, plainly teaching them Who it is that feeds us. By a famine they were brought down into Egypt; they were fed with manna in the wilderness; God's blessing was especially promised to their land of Canaan, if they were obedient, and His curse threatened, if they were rebellious. Yet we see that they did from time to time forget both the mercies and the words of warning. Seed-time and harvest went on as usual, and they sowed and reaped, and thought not of Him Who alone gave them strength to do the work, and the ground strength to bear the fruit. They thought not of Him, but very often instead of Him they chose them out other gods. They gave the glory of their good harvests to any one whom they most fancied *among* the idols of the heathen, who dwelt around them. What was the consequence? They very often had famine. We read of sore famines while the Judges ruled : of famine in the days of David : of a very sore famine, occasioned by long drought, in the time of Elijah the Prophet. In the next generation there was such a famine in Samaria, that women, driven beside themselves, were fain to kill and eat their young children. The like grievous miseries happened as we read in the book of Lamentations, when Jerusalem was distressed by the Babylonians, before that great captivity. Thus did the Almighty, from time to time, scourge His own ancient people by taking away their bread, when they forgot Him the Giver of it. And how did they recover His favour, and prevail on Him to take off the scourge? They humbled themselves before Him, one and all, in fasting and prayer, in outward and inward penitence ; and relief came. They put away the strange gods, from among them ; they turned from their evil way ; they put themselves to shame and pain ; they punished and vexed themselves, and God ceased to vex and punish them. So it was in the days of David: there was a famine three years, year after year, and on inquiry God told David of a particular sin which was to be punished : David punished that sin, and afterwards God was intreated for the land. Elijah slew the prophets of Baal, and destroyed his worship for a time out of Israel, and presently God sent rain upon the land. Jehoshaphat proclaimed a fast, and the enemies of Israel were overthrown. Daniel fasted, and God moved Cyrus's heart to let the people go from Babylon. And not to mention more instances; in the time of the prophet Joel there was a great threatening of famine, and Almighty God of His great mercy put it into the prophet's heart to tell the people what they should do for relief. It is the place which is appointed to be read for the Epistle today. "‘Turn ye even to Me, saith the Lord, with your whole heart, and with fasting and with weeping and with mourning, and rend your heart, and not your garments, and turn unto the Lord your God." And observe: the prophet bids them do this not only inwardly in their hearts, but in the way of solemn outward service also: "Blow the trumpet in Zion, sanctify a fast, call a solemn assembly; gather the people, sanctify the congregation, assemble the elders. . . . Let the priests, the ministers of the Lord, weep between the porch and the Altar: and let them say, Spare Thy people, O Lord." And he adds words of most merciful encouragement: "Then will the Lord be jealous for His land, and pity His people."

In these portions of Holy Scripture, we seem to find our own case provided for. We find both our sin, our punishment, and likewise, if so be, the means of our relief.

As to our sin: can we deny that we too, Christians as we are, have too often sadly forgotten Who gave us our corn and our other provision for the body? We have ploughed, sown, harrowed, reaped,

‣ Joel ii. 12, 13.

I

thrashed; we have taken our portion in the fruits
of the earth day after day and season after season;
God has most graciously fed us, and those who are
dear to us, all our lives long unto this day: and the
very abundance of the mercy has made us unthankful. Almighty God has been very bountiful to us,
as a country; for many many years, there has been
nothing like a famine in this island. And we have
grown so accustomed to the blessing of plenty, that
we have taken it as a matter of course. We have
reckoned upon a certain return of crops which we
put into the ground, and each one of us, generally
speaking, has reckoned upon such and such meals
in the day, almost as if it were a thing to which we
had a right, and as if it would be dealing hardly
with us, should God refuse it. And all the while
both the general harvest of the country, and each
person's own share in each meal that he has partaken
of, have been wholly and undoubtedly free gifts of
our good and forgiving God, free gifts bestowed on
people who were continually forgetting Him. We
have gone on lying down at ease in our beds, saying, "*To-morrow shall be as this day, and yet much
more abundant :" and have neither thanked Him earnestly for the bread of the day gone by, nor intreated
Him earnestly for the bread of the following day.

Sometimes, instead of trusting Him for it, we have
permitted our minds to be swallowed up by all manner of worldly cares. We have taken thought for
the morrow, quite overlooking His promise, "*Seek
ye first the kingdom of God, and His righteousness, and all these things shall be added unto you."

_c Isa. lvi. 12.   _d S. Matt. vi. 33.

What words could be more gracious? What could have been said, more entirely to put us at our ease? And yet we have been anxious and fretful and un-believing, and sometimes, perhaps, and in some dealings, hardly honest: at least I suppose it is not so very uncommon for decent persons to take liber-ties in buying and selling; to be too much on their own side; and scarcely to blame themselves for it: for how else, say they, should we get bread for our-selves and our families. Why, what is this, but forgetting that all the while it is God and none else Who gives us our corn and our wine? He has no need of our anxiety, nor yet can He be pleased when we are careless and unthankful. And there is ano-ther thing which may have gone some way towards forfeiting this favour. When we have had knowing and clever schemes for getting our maintenance, and they have answered well, presently we have begun to trust in those ways, and to rely on our own cleverness, instead of giving our Creator the glory. We have sometimes come too near that most pre-sumptuous saying, which God can so ill endure in His people, "*my power, and the might of mine hand hath gotten me this wealth." All sorts and degrees among us have been more or less guilty in that way; not only the rich man rejoicing in his large property and good management, but the la-bourer also, boasting of the skill and power of his hands. What more common than to hear from both sorts, expressions which shew that they have not really been remembering the Lord their God, and that it is He Who giveth them power to get wealth?

* Deut. viii. 17.

I 2

Here then, that is, in our worldly unbelieving ways in regard of God's merciful gifts, we may see quite sufficient cause for His sore judgement, Famine, to come upon us: though we were to say nothing of the innumerable sins over and above, which are swarming in all corners of our Christian land: the utter reckless irreligion of so many who might know better: their entire neglect of the Church, its holy days and services, their profane, contemptuous abuse of God's Name: their disobedience and irreverence to their elders and betters: their envy, and grudging and unpitying abuse of their brethren: their desperate uncleanness in thought, word and deed: their dishonesty and utter falseness, so that one scarce dares trust another: their lying and slandering, their selfish and discontented hearts. Surely the wonder is, not that the Almighty should at last have begun to break the staff of our bread, but that such a tribe of rebels should have gone on so many years with bread to eat and raiment to put on. Surely our own consciences will tell each one of us that he has himself long ago richly deserved to lose his allowance, and to be turned out of God's family.

And who can say how soon something of the sort may happen to us? God's tokens surely are near and very fearful: every day seems to bring more sorrowful accounts of our starving brethren in Ireland, dying now, we are told, by tens of thousands; and of the danger, lest from various causes, the very land should be left untilled this year. In France and other neighbouring countries the distress seems increasing: and what if our God, provoked at our still continued impenitence, should withdraw His blessing from this year's crops of corn, here in our own country? There is but the breadth of a hair, as one may speak, between us and another failing harvest: and in that case, I suppose, we should indeed know what famine is.

Our sin and God's judgement being both so open and notorious: a public sin, unthankful use of God's bounty; a public judgement, the withdrawing of the bounty: how can we earnestly enough acknowledge His goodness in so clearly pointing out the remedy also? The remedy, as we have seen already, is expressed in that invitation by the prophet Joel: "Turn ye even to Me with all your heart and with fasting, and with weeping, and with mourning. And rend your heart, and not your garments; and turn unto the Lord your God." Turn to God by true and inward repentance; and to help yourselves and one another in doing so, sanctify an outward Fast also. "Call a solemn assembly: gather the people, sanctify the congregation, assemble the elders, and those that suck the breasts: let the bridegroom go forth out of his chamber, and the bride out of her closet: let the priests, the ministers of the Lord, weep between the porch and the altar, and let them say, Spare Thy people, O Lord, and give not Thine heritage to reproach, that the heathen should rule over them." Do you not see how nearly these words represent the very service which we are trying to solemnize today? The people gathering here in greater number than usual, the priest saying the mournful Litany, and the people making the answers: from every Church in town and in country the sound going up at once of confession, supplication, and lowly submission to our God. Let this service prove but an earnest one: God grant it may be so: and surely the Scripture gives great reason to hope that it will prove an effectual one too. I say, a good hope, for it was not quite certain, even in the case of the Jews, who were more immediately under God's outward and visible government. The prophet says, "Who knoweth if He will return and repent, and leave a blessing behind Him?" as much as to say, ' There is good hope of it,' but we must not make too sure, at least not for this year: for we know not the depth of our own sin, how angry our God is with us, therefore neither can we know how long it may be necessary for us to endure the severity of His judgement, though we should be forgiven at last. But, as I said, there is good hope. Only let us all repent in earnest. Let every man, woman and child, consider for himself that his sins are a part of the heavy burthen of sin, which is now hanging so heavy on the land. Let him take off his own share, as he may at once, by true repentance and amendment: then the sin of the whole country will not cry quite so loud to heaven for punishment: he himself also will be in a condition to pray to God more acceptably, and so will all those who shall be the better for his help and good example.

Men appear sometimes to go on in their sin and irreligion, long after they are convinced of it, and more or less ashamed and sorry for it, for want of something to rouse them up, and brace their nerves, as it were, for one strong effort. At such times it is a great mercy of God, if He send upon us some sudden trial, or severe wound to our hearts, piercing through and through, and not suffering us to be at all easy in our sin. Now, if any among us have fallen into this listless way; and from my heart I fear that it is a fault which prevails very widely among us of this place; if, I say, any one among us is conscious to himself, that he wants awakening, let him not wait till the horrors of famine come close to his own door, till he hear his own children crying in vain to him for bread: but let him even now dutifully stir himself up, and take hold of the mercy offered him. Surely the call of the Almighty, though distant, is clear enough and startling enough: and indeed it is not so very distant: I know of a parish in England with a population of about three thousand, where sixteen hundred persons are being daily fed with charitable gifts at one door, and would not know where else to look for a meal. As yet, whatever some of us may suffer, we are not come to any thing like what we hear of: but why should we not permit ourselves to be warned by the certain report of such things? O my brethren, for our country's sake, for our poor helpless brethren's sake, for our own souls' sake, let us now turn unto the Lord our God: but take good care that you turn in earnest, that you turn with your whole heart: that you turn once for all, and never relapse again, or, if you do, that you recover and repent immediately. We stand as it were on a needle's point, were our eyes but opened to see it. True repentance, by God's mercy, may do every thing for us: but hypocritical repentance, or open stubbornness in sin, may plunge us without hope or stay in famine here and perdition hereafter.

SERMON X.

WARS TO BE EXPECTED, EVEN AMONG CHRISTIANS.

S. Matt. x. 34.

*" Think not that I am come to send peace on earth:
I came not to send peace, but a sword."*

It was but a few hours ago that we were keeping Easter, one of the great Feasts of peace. The Lord came among us from the grave, saying, "Peace be unto you:" even as the Angels when He was born came from heaven saying, "Peace on earth," It was a time of outward peace, when He so came down for us men and for our salvation; the very heathens of the Roman Empire noticed, how that at that particular time the Romans were at peace with all nations. It became Him, the great Peace-maker between sinful man and his forgiving God, to make known His power and Coming by the outward blessing of peace and quiet on earth. Melchizedek, the shadow and type of our Lord in that He was both Priest and King, was king of Salem, i. e. king of peace: for the word Salem signifies peace: Solomon, the type of our Lord as King and Head over His glorious Church, was also by God's special providence a peaceful king, and in his time God gave

Israel rest from their enemies on every side. Neither can you well open a page of the prophetic writings, but you will light upon a promise of peace. "[a] The Lord shall give His people the blessing of peace:" "Abundance of peace, so long as the moon endureth:" "[b] Nation shall not lift up sword against nation, neither shall they learn war any more." Such are the expectations raised by the Old Testament. The Gospel was to be the Gospel of peace, to guide our feet into the way of peace; and when it came, it professed to do so. Peace was the very legacy bequeathed by our Lord to His friends. "[c] Peace I leave with you, My peace I give unto you." And for the fulfilment of all these merciful and marvellous promises, we have been as I said praising Him for many days. Our Easter acknowledgements have been like those of holy Joshua. We have owned with all our hearts and with all our souls, that neither peace, nor any other good thing hath failed of all the good things which the Lord our God spake concerning us: all are come to pass, and not one thing hath failed thereof. During the whole of this Easter season, we have been thanking God for the blessing of peace, and now as soon as Easter is over, we are called upon by His mysterious providence to humble ourselves before Him as in a state of war: to beseech Him to save and deliver us from the hands of our enemies; not now our spiritual enemies, but men like ourselves, men and brethren, children of the same first father; and what is sadder yet—alas that we should say it—Christian men, renewed and regenerated as we are. We are praying

[a] Ps. xxix. 11.　　[b] Is. ii. 4.　　[c] S. John xiv. 17.

against them and they against us; and every day we
are expecting to hear about wounds and blood and
slaughter on this side and on that.

Some of us can remember another fearful war, a
very wasteful and murderous one, long continued,
and full of most intense anxiety: a war close at our
own doors, and in the course of which for months together, we knew not when we lay down to rest, but
we might wake in the morning to hear that the enemies were actually in our land. I dare say there are
some here to whom as well as to myself the very
sound of the prayer appointed to be said in the time
of war and tumults has brought back in a lively manner the remembrance of those anxious days; and
surely, my brethren, we ought to be very thankful
that we have to go so far back in order to remember
them: surely to those who know anything of history it must seem an exceeding mercy to have gone
on now nearly forty years years without occasion
to use that prayer, so that to the greater number
of us, the land hath been at rest as far back as they
can remember. Alas that we should have made no
better use of the good time! and now He Whom we
have too much forgotten is judging us, by bringing
upon us a war more distressing in one respect than
even that long French war was. For then we were
fighting against a power which had for some time
openly renounced the Gospel, but the Russian nation,
to which we are now opposed, was a Christian
people almost as soon as we were. And though we
have reason to believe that they are on the wrong
side in this dispute, we have no reason to believe,
that as a Christian nation, we are at all better in

God's sight, more dutiful, more obedient, truer believers, more like the first Christians, than they are.
God keep us from any such pharisaical thoughts !
We are warned against them in the Gospel you heard
just now; in which our Lord Himself tells us, that
we lose the fruit of our devotions if we come to
praising ourselves in our hearts, and fancying that
we are better than others. There is too much of this
disposition in us English people; it is greatly encouraged by a good deal of our ordinary reading;
and surely, if this is to be a day of humiliation, as
those who are set over us intend it to be, we ought to
humble ourselves in this respect also; to put down
any proud and boastful thoughts of our country, our
fleets and armies, our great generals and admirals,
our skill, wealth, courage, and the like. Indulging
such thoughts is trusting in an arm of flesh, and is
the very way to provoke the Giver of all victory to
withdraw His protection and help from us.

But I was speaking of the Russians, our opponents
in this war: how that they are Christians like ourselves, and that the war is on that account, a more
sad and fearful one to think of than the last great
war was. For what more melancholy than for members of Christ to be brought into such a condition,
that it is a kind of duty in them to hurt and damage
one another, even unto death ? And yet there is one
thing which makes it more melancholy still; and
that is, when the very quarrel itself arises or is
thought to arise on religious grounds; which this
one professes to do. For the Russians say, that what
they want is for the Christian people in the Holy
Land, and elsewhere, to serve Christ more securely,

and with more entire liberty, than they do now: if this were provided for, they say they would lay down their arms; and so, whether in pretence or in truth, the ways of honouring our Lord in the places which He has made most sacred on earth, in the cave of Bethlehem, or on the hill at Calvary, the ways, I say, of honouring Christ in those places are made among Christians a matter of such sharp contention that they cannot settle it without shedding each other's blood. And why is this? There may be mere worldly reasons, but no doubt the mischief is greatly increased by the sad religious divisions among Christ's people. The East has been separated from the West, Russia and Greece from the rest of Europe, now for many hundred years: there were faults on both sides, but whose ever fault it was, *there is* the separation: they have ceased to worship and pray together: outwardly, that which was one has become two or more. Our Saviour prayed that all Christians might be one, but this state of things would seem to make even His prayer void, so far as men can do it: and thus the war of fleets and armies, of outward wounds and slaughter, in which we are engaged, becomes even more terrible, in that it is very much caused by the inward strife and division in the Church.

Thus it would seem that in this present war (although I trust that on the whole our cause and our intention is good) yet two great Gospel blessings appear as if they were forfeited and taken from Christ's people; the very two blessings for which we pray so earnestly and continually in the most solemn of all services, the one, Unity, and the other con-

cord. Unity, outward and visible Unity, is gone,
since those two great bodies of Christians have found
that they could not worship together; and now concord and peace are gone also; they are not only separate in religion, but they are at war: God grant it
may be only for a short time! Now surely all this
would be most astonishing and bewildering; it would
seem as if God's word had even returned unto Him
void; only that He hath warned us of it all expressly beforehand; and *that* on many occasions, and in
many ways.

For, first, as to there being wars at all: after the
great Prince of Peace had come unto the world, after
He had taken to Him His great power in heaven and
in earth, it was natural to expect that such misery
would come to an end; that as the prophets had said,
"[d] they should not learn war any more." But our
Lord put an end once for all to such expectations,
when He told His disciples in the mount of Olives, as
one of the signs of His coming and of the end of the
world, that "[e] nation should rise against nation, and
kingdom against kingdom, that they should hear of
wars and rumours of wars:" and this after saying that
"many should come in His Name, saying, I am Christ:
and should deceive many:" as if the false religions,
that of the Turks especially, should be a great cause
of war even when His kingdom should be set up.
And one of the visions of S. John in the Revelation
relating to the times of the Gospel, is this: A person
"[f] riding on a red horse, to whom power was given to
take peace from the earth, and that they should kill
one another, and there was given unto him a great

[d] Is. ii. 4.   [e] S. Matt. xxiv. 6, 7.   [f] Rev. vi. 4.

sword." Whatever else this might mean, one part of
its meaning clearly was to keep people from reckon-
ing on outward peace among the nations of the world,
or quiet times, free from wars and tumults, after
Christ's kingdom should be set up.

But more than this: our Lord gave also plain
warning, that He and His religion would be the
very occasion of war. The text would certainly
seem to tell us: 'You having read and heard the old
prophecies, and knowing that I am come to be a
Peace-maker, may be supposing that now there will
be an end of war among the nations of the world, at
least among those who shall join themselves to Me,
and become Christians. This you can hardly help
supposing: but I tell you it is otherwise; inward
and eternal peace indeed I bring to all who do not
reject it; but as to the outward peace among nations,
which you are dreaming of, it not only will not follow, but will very often be even interrupted because
of the coming of My kingdom. "I came not to send
peace but a sword." I tell you, not peace, but rather
division.'

Yet further our Lord adds this very distressing
circumstance, that the war, the dispute, the factions,
the party feeling, about Christianity would often
times reach even into private houses, and divide (it
may be) quiet families, taking part with one or the
other: "ᵉ The father shall be divided against the son
and the son against the father, the mother against
the daughter, and the daughter against the mother;
the mother in law against the daughter in law,
and the daughter in law against her mother in law."

ᵉ S. Luke xii. 53.

No doubt, one part of Christ's meaning when He said this, was to point out the terrible trials young persons must be prepared to undergo: to part with father, or mother, or other nearest relation, rather than part with Christ. But the same words describe also the feeling of contention and controversy, which He knew would take occasion from the establishment of His kingdom, to set Christians one against another, even though they were spiritually one family: as children when they fall out with their fathers and mothers. We see this with our own eyes often; as often as serious differences arise in a family, on points of faith and worship. Thus in three distinct ways, our Lord, as the event proved, shewed that He had come not to send peace upon earth, but a sword.

Moreover, in our Lord's own history, and in the Acts of the Apostles, there were tokens not a few, that the subjects of His kingdom would be sometimes making a mistake, and thinking to uphold it by outward persecution and warfare. When Christ was about to be taken in the garden, S. Peter in his eagerness, having provided two swords, asked our Lord's leave to smite with one of them. The greater part of the people were at several times so inclined to support our Lord by violent doings, that the Pharisees and Chief Priests feared to make trial of their plots against Him in the day time. Any thoughtful believer having an eye to these things, would be more or less prepared bye and bye to see Christians going to war; doing at least as S. Peter was for the time forbidden to do, smiting with the sword by way of protection to themselves and to any one under their care. He would be prepared also for the case of Christians warring against the enemies of the Faith : as the Christian nations of Europe did several times, to free the Holy city from the dominion of the Turks; and in token thereof they went about wearing a cross on some part of their dress, to shew that they were Christ's soldiers. Nay and what is more and stranger still, the warnings of our Lord and the conduct of those around Him would make it seem before hand no incredible thing, that Christians from time to time should even go to war *with Christians* for Christ's and His truth's sake ; and kill one another, thinking to do God service. All these things were to be, have been, and are, and yet our Lord's promise of peace to His people is not broken : even as the other promise of unity in Church communion standeth fast, for all the schisms and separations in the world calling itself Christian. The inward and invisible, spiritual blessing is not gone from those who are worthy of it, though for our sins the outward and visible Church may seem in great measure to have forfeited the outward and visible blessing.

Believe this, my brethren, to your comfort: and believe also, and take special notice of it, that according to God's fatherly way of bringing good out of evil, His children may if they will make great spiritual good of this very sad calamity of war with our fellow Christians. S. Paul said it could not be but schisms and heresies would arise among Christians ; but, he added, This good will come of it, that they which are approved may be made manifest among you. In like manner may we say, There must be also wars among us, to bring out and exercise many parts of Christian goodness. To be at war at all is a grievous scourge, and when God 'scourgeth, what should His children do but humbly inquire what sins have brought His chastisement on them, and how they may repent? The sin of a nation is made up, I suppose, of the sins of each person in it. Each person of this very congregation has added more or less to the heap of transgressions, which, reaching as it were to heaven, has provoked Almighty God to visit us with one of His sore judgements, even war: and there are two others, famine and pestilence, nobody knows how near to us. As each one has contributed to the nation's sin, so let each one this very day begin to contribute to the nation's repentance. We know not how much harm our past ways may have done to our country: neither do we know how much good, even now, our earnest conversion and penitence may do to it.

And is there not enough in the circumstances of war itself to quicken the seriousness of all who are not quite hardened in heart? Think what war is: what an anxious time, how full of painful separations, of foreboding thoughts, of watching for bad news, of sudden losses and bereavements, of earthly hopes and dreams disappointed, earthly supports and comforts blighted and swept away in an instant. Who can think of it, and not wish that *his* treasure and the treasure of those who are dear to him were safely laid up in heaven, where no enemy can approach to spoil, to waste, or to destroy?

And then our Lord has expressly reckoned up wars and rumours of wars, distress of nations and perplexity, among the signs that shall go before the

K

end: each one as it shews itself is a token of the Day of Judgement: the confusion and ruin which wars bring upon the works both of God and man, are a shadow of the world burning up and passing away with a great noise: the sad and violent separations are a token of that last fearful parting, these to the right and those to the left. Will you not see the Lord's hand when it is so lifted up? Will you not accept His tokens, and prepare in earnest to meet Him?

And remember that when He shall come, one great question will be, 'Have you spared what you could for these, My brethren and yours, as I gave up all for you?' It will be a good beginning, a help to a better mind, if we try now to open our hearts and hands to the destitute families of those who are undergoing hardship and danger for our good and safety: if we overcome any little feeling of fretfulness or grudging, and cheerfully offer what we can for them. In this and other like ways, the fearful scourge may by His mercy be turned into a great blessing, a happy beginning of really good times.

SERMON XI.

THE MYSTERY OF ALMIGHTY GOD'S PROVIDENTIAL DEALINGS.

Ezek. xiv. 23.

" Ye shall know that I have not done without cause all that I have done."

Did you ever observe, my brethren, how often the question is asked in the book of Psalms, and in those prophets which are most like the Psalms, Why hath the Lord done thus and thus? what can be the reason, what can be the meaning of it? " [a] Why standest Thou so far off? and wherefore hidest Thou Thy face in the time of trouble?" " [b] Why withdrawest Thou Thy Hand? Why pluckest Thou not Thy right hand out of Thy bosom to consume the enemy?" In those sayings and in many more the Church wonders how the Almighty should seem to let things alone and not interfere: in others the wonder is that He should visit very severely, seeming as if He had forgotten His tender mercies. " [c] Lord, where are Thy old loving-kindnesses which Thou swarest unto David in Thy truth?" " [d] Why art Thou absent from us so long, and why is Thy wrath so hot against the sheep of Thy pasture?" " Why abhorrest Thou

[a] Ps. x. 1.   [b] Ib. lxxiv. 12.   [c] Ib. lxxxix. 48.   [d] Ib. lxxiv. 1.

K 2

my soul and forgettest my misery and trouble?"
And to mention no more, we hear the Almighty
Son Himself uttering for our sake that aweful and
mysterious cry, "*My God, My God, why hast Thou
forsaken Me.*"

We might think it no strange thing that ordinary
persons; the backsliders and wicked who have forgotten God, and the heathen who have never known
Him, should utter this kind of cry, and seem to
complain of His doings, not only as very sharp and
bitter, but also as very perplexing and unaccountable: *that* might well seem to us a matter of course,
for we know that when one is reproved or punished
for any fault, it is generally very difficult to make
him see the greatness of his own fault, and to understand and own that he deserves the punishment.
We should expect the common sort of people to cry
out in that way. But those who so cry out in
Scripture are not the common sort of persons: they
are such as David and the other prophets, Moses,
Job, Isaiah, Jeremiah; yea even Jesus Christ Himself in His Human and suffering Nature condescends
to speak as one wondering how the Father should
seem to forsake Him and be far from Him. The
holiest then and the best of men may naturally and
innocently wonder and long to understand how
things should be as they are: so very unlike what
God would have them; so much misery where the
Lord had given His blessing, so much error and
perversity, sin and wickedness, even among those
whom He hath loved and washed from their sins in
His own Blood.

* S. Matt. xxvii. 46.

In like manner it is but natural that even good
and dutiful Christians, and those who most unfeign-
edly desire to submit themselves to His holy will,
should nevertheless be sorely tried, filled with trouble, and perplexity, and confusion, at what happens
to themselves, their friends and acquaintance, in the
course of God's ordinary providence with each one.
Consider for a moment : is there any one of you, of
age to have had any experience of the world, who
cannot at once recollect some turn of God's providence, just contrary to what seemed best, according
to our natural will and the calculations of our human
reason ? Who is there of mature age who can look
back on his own past life without feeling that God's
dealings with himself or with some who were as
himself have been in some instances not only untoward but unaccountable ? He or his friends have
suffered losses and disappointments, the providential
use and reason of which, he feels quite unable to
fathom : although perhaps by the grace of God he is
enabled to receive them with all meekness and lowli-
ness, and to feel sure that they are meant for his
good, if he could but discern how. How often do
we read or hear of persons—how many have we
known ourselves—taken away in the prime of their
usefulness : just as they were beginning to bear
the fruit, for the sake of which, as to us erring
mortals it seemed, they had been raised up and sent
into the world ! How have we seen plans thwarted
and good beginnings swept away, when people as it
seemed to us, had set to work with the best intentions, and all seemed to promise a happy result !
How many times have we been made to feel the

mysterious and bitter disappointment, when the children of good parents, carefully educated, prayed for and watched over, turn out amiss, and go on in ways provoking to their God, and heart-breaking to their best friends! In such cases who can help calling upon God in his silent heart, and saying, 'Wherefore this sad disappointment? What can be the meaning, what the purpose and end of it?' And He, according to that which His merciful goodness knows to be best, sometimes enables us in part to understand why He deals so with us and our friends, sometimes goes on hiding the knowledge entirely; either way, if we will take it rightly, helping us to prepare for whatever in His providence He may see fit next to bring forth.

But the occasion of this day leads us rather to think of another class of mysterious disappointments, the sudden clouds, sometimes even whirlwinds, which sometimes by permission of the great King of heaven, sweep over whole kingdoms, or whole portions of God's Church, undoing in a moment the work of many generations, and scattering to the winds the best meant contrivances of man's wisdom and power for the peace and order of the world and the good of his fellow creatures. Such a storm is this which has arisen in India, and is still by the last accounts fearfully raging, and rather I fear seeming to spread than to abate. It has come at a time, when the true friends of that unhappy country were beginning, I believe, to be more hopeful than they had been concerning it. In respect of outward and bodily prosperity and comfort, great improvement was expected from the forming of railways, the es-

tablishment of telegraphs, the increasing number of
schools, and thriving prospects of trade: there
seemed to be no public enemy in the whole Empire,
and entire confidence must have been felt in the
native army, since as we heard the other day, the
great city of Delhi with all its warlike stores, was
left without misgiving in the care of Indian soldiers
only. So much for seeming outward prosperity:
and I believe that those also who had their hearts in
missionary work, were beginning to have more hope
and comfort as to the progress of the Gospel in
North India than they had had for a long time. In
the month of May last, a Bishop who had been
visiting the Churches there had the following account of one of them printed in England. 'I have
never seen a mission commenced with greater promise than the Delhi mission. I confirmed the first
twelve converts two or three of whom are men of
very high standing and attainments, and the most
hopeful converts I have ever known ... Your school
too, in the most famous city of Delhi, of more than
one hundred boys, is in a most efficient state, and
likely to be of the greatest service in the cause of
the mission. Your missionaries there command the
utmost respect, by their talent, discretion, and piety,
from all classes.' At the very time that this word
of high approbation was being published in England,
the revolt had begun, the principal clergymen and
others belonging to the mission had been cruelly
put to death, the rest were scattered away from the
place, and the work of conversion for the present
seems violently brought to an end. As for the
murders and worse than murders which those cruel

heathen soldiers have wrought in Delhi and elsc-
where, breaking the hearts and destroying the hopes
of so many, I will not dwell upon them here, farther
than to point out how strongly men are tempted
when they hear of such things, and much more
when such things happen to any one near and dear
to them, I say they are very strongly tempted to
many evil and ungodly thoughts. They are tempted
to an unbelieving despair, to give up all faith and
trust, as if there were no God to look after them:
to charge God foolishly, as if He were unjust and
partial: to be reckless, and quite to leave off caring
what happens to them, and how they behave: to
lose their charity, and hate their brethren, not only
those who have ill used them, but mankind generally, as if all the world were against them, and
they had better be against all the world.

'Why, O Lord, should these things be?   Here is
a sudden end of all the hopes of the great realm of
India, all its chance of becoming civilized, peaceful,
and Christian, cast away for ages and generations?
for ages and generations must surely pass away before the English can be one with the Sepoys after
what has now happened.   And wherefore'—so the
discontented aching heart will be apt to go on and
say, 'Wherefore O Lord dost Thou hide Thy Face,
and permit so many innocent babes and helpless
women to be so inhumanly butchered in the face of
day? so many made widows and orphans, so many
families ruined and their earthly hopes destroyed in
a moment? What, O Lord, can be the cause, and
what the end, of all these miseries?' So man might
ask, in his vexation and anguish : and what if it be

the answer of the Lord Almighty? 'Thou enquirest, Why is this? wherefore is that? I will tell thee, if thou wilt first tell *me* why God's famous and faithful servants have almost always had to endure disappointment and anguish more or less like unto this? why Moses was all the way compassed about with such a disobedient and gainsaying people, on whom all his labour seemed to be lost? why the worst plagues decreed for the ungodly; the sword, the whirlwind, the fire from heaven, the evil report of those who should have been his best friends, all seemed to gather themselves together against Job to overwhelm him? why the holy and loving prophet Jeremiah went on for years in danger of his life, warning God's people of their sins and of God's judgements, but in vain; so that his life was a burthen to him, and he wished again and again that he had never been born. When you have accounted for these things; and for the whole captivity of Babylon, so heartbreaking to the true believers of that time (for it seemed more than ever as if God's counsel had returned unto Him void, and as if His promise had come utterly to an end); when, I say, you feel that you can explain all those ancient dealings of God with man, then and not till then, you may begin to doubt whether God's ways are indeed just and right in regard of this Indian rebellion, or no.'

The history of the troubles of God's people of old is set before us so very minutely, in order that we in our troubles may quiet ourselves as they did, may receive the answer given to them as if it were given of God to us. What is that answer? In substance and meaning it was spoken by Moses at the Red sea. "[1]'Stand still and see the salvation of the Lord:'" and to S. Peter afterwards by the same Saviour: "[s]What I do thou knowest not now, but thou shalt know hereafter." Only be dutiful and patient, and you shall soon have this satisfaction of knowing that He has not done without cause whatever He has done to you, your friends, or your country.

And if the Almighty should now take off His hand, yet try to keep yourself always prepared for what His providence shall bring forth; and let it be a part of your daily devotions, that whatever temptation may be coming on, God would not suffer you to be tempted above that you are able to bear. The good Shepherd has infinite ways, ways of His own, of which we at the time know nothing, of preparing us His sheep for the storm or freezing blast, or whatever He knows to be coming to us. And in proportion to people's faith and devotion they are prepared. Though they know nothing beforehand of the particular calamity which is coming on, yet somehow no calamity can overtake them quite unawares. Be it what it may, they are ready for it, through Christ which strengtheneth them: as a soldier in complete armour is prepared against all the weapons of the enemy, from whatever quarter they may come. Such was the condition of the holy S. Paul: and of the saints of God generally. They put on Christ (so to speak) every morning, if not by Holy Communion, yet by earnest supplication and preparation of heart: and Christ stood by them and strengthened them all the day long. Consider, my brethren, had

---

[1] Exod. xiv. 13.   [s] S. John xiii. 7.

you been in the place of any of those our fellow
Christians, men or women, whose bitter sufferings
we think so much of to-day, consider, whether there
be not one thing which would have made all the
difference to you. What is that one thing? Whether, when you got up that morning, you were prepared for what was going to happen, or no. Some
of the sufferers we know were prepared: some we
may fear were not so. How were they prepared?
Not by knowing what would happen: of that all alike
were ignorant. But they were prepared, by committing themselves to God, through Jesus Christ, in their
morning devotions, whatever might happen. And
so, great and fearful as their sufferings were, they
are now no doubt blessing God for them: they
know and understand perfectly now that He did not
without a cause all that He did with them in giving
them up to their enemies. Those good clergymen
and other devout persons, for example, who both at
Delhi and at Cawnpore were murdered because they
were clergymen and Christians, can we at all doubt
that they are true martyrs, enrolled in that noble
army? And now they know by a blissful experience
what we cannot as yet know, how every pang which
they suffered was needful to complete the fulness of
glory prepared for them.

I say, they may most truly be called martyrs in
the strict and proper sense of the word: for according to all the reports we hear, this war in India is
truly a religious war, a war of persecution against
Christians as such, carried on by the heathen Indians
in some degree, but principally and properly by the
Mahometans. It is the Mahometan anti-Christ, so

to call it: that enemy of the Father and the Son, which has been for so many ages warring against the Lamb, in the East especially: that power it is which is now breaking out so violently, in great wrath, from a certain feeling perhaps that he hath but a short time. All therefore, men, women and children, whom these people murder because they are Christians, are indeed and in truth so many martyrs, so many witnesses, sealing the true Faith by their blood. If we will but believe it, dear brethren, what a comfort is here for us, and for all those who are now mourning their friends and relations, taken from them in a way so horrible to the eye of man, but in the Eye of God and His holy Saints and Angels so unspeakably blessed and glorious! What a privilege to have a sure hope that this our English Church has now so many more martyrs in Paradise, pleading for it and for us all, and crying out, "'How long, O Lord, holy and true, dost Thou not judge and avenge our cause?'"

And do you not desire, my brethren, every one of you, to be on the side of these holy ones against their cruel blaspheming murderers? Do you not feel as if you would rejoice to have a part in the war on Christ's side, and on the side of those so dear to Christ? Well, you cannot strike a blow for them with your hands. You may well wish to do so, for surely this war is on our side a holy war such as those which long ago Christians undertook against the like cruel unbelievers for the freedom of Jerusalem, and the holy places: and those who go out to it, or part with dear friends going out, in a right and

' Rev. vi. 10.

dutiful spirit, do in an especial sense take up the Cross, and may God bring home this thought to their hearts, to their great comfort, whatever happens. But there can be very few indeed among us so immediately interested in this war: and What can all the rest do? This day's service, my brethren, is appointed on purpose to teach you what you can do, and to exercise you in doing it. You can pray earnestly to God: and earnest prayer before now has turned the fate of battles and brought back victory when it seemed to be lost without hope. (Moses: Samuel). Who knows? this very day in India some decisive engagement may be going on, and one good Christian here, praying with all his heart, may for aught any one of us can tell, prevail on God for Christ's sake to give us victory in that battle. Especially if his prayer be joined, as the prayers of worthy communicants always are, to the solemn Offering which the great High Priest is evermore making in the heavenly sanctuary, the Offering of His own Body and Blood. I beg you, dear brethren, to think of this. Those of you who intend to communicate to day, I beg of you most earnestly to remember our brethren in India when you so join in our Lord's Sacrifice. That is one thing, the greatest of all, that you can do for them. Only observe; the efficacy of your prayer will depend on your coming with a true penitent heart. "*If I incline unto wickedness in my heart, the Lord will not hear me:" either for myself or for others.

And along with our offering of prayer, as always in Holy Communion, so now especially, our Lord calls on us for an offering of alms: free alms, loving alms,

* Ps. lxvi. 16.

liberal alms.   The need is great, far beyond any supplies that have yet been gathered; far beyond the necessities of the Crimean war.   For here are thousands of various ranks, many English, some natives: and surely the faithful natives should be especially considered who have lost their all in doing their duty. We cannot restore the husbands and parents that are lost; but we may do something by His mercy, towards binding up the broken hearts, by warding off from them the additional and very sore evil of want and destitution.   O let us not be found wanting either in our loving alms or in our penitential prayers. Think what you would wish, dear brethren, for yourselves and those dearest to you, were you among those sufferers : ask your own heart in earnest, and follow its counsel, for in this case it will surely be the counsel of our Lord Jesus Christ.   One thing more. Dismiss from your hearts, I beseech you, the bitter and unchristian feeling, of revenge : it will spoil all. But Christian courage and mercy by God's blessing, will more than recover all.   So we may hope even in this world to know the cause of all, when India reconquered by Christian courage, and won by Christian mercy, shall be the prize of the blood of our martyred brethren.

SERMON XII.

EASTER JOY, AND EASTER WORK.

1 Kings v. 4, 5.

" Now the Lord my God hath given me rest on every
side, so that there is neither adversary nor evil oc-
current; and behold I purpose to build an house
unto the Name of the Lord my God."

"Rest on every side!" What is this, brethren,
but Easter joy? "A house to be builded unto
the Lord our God!" What is this but Easter work?

The special joy of Easter is victory, not that rest
which consists in never having had any trials, any
temptations, any enemies at all; but the soldier's
rest after winning a battle: when besides feeling
himself free to repose and enjoy himself, he has the
proud thought of having been conqueror, overcoming
difficulties, sharing in the glory and noble deeds of
many whom he knows to be braver than himself, and,
if so be, of "pleasing him who hath chosen him to
be a soldier," of receiving praise and 'good marks'
from his commander, perhaps some great hero. This,
you know, is the soldier's joy: the joy of such as
David and his men, when the Philistines and other
enemies of God's people had been put down, and

the Lord had given Israel rest ; no adversary, no anxiety or fear as to what the heathen might do unto them.

When David's wars were over, this was his feeling and that of his people, and surely it was a kind of Easter feeling: it answers well to the mind of the true Israel rejoicing in the victory of the true David: the Christian people rejoicing in what Christ our Lord did as on Good Friday and Easter Day: by His Death giving a deadly wound to the great Goliah, our enemy the devil, and 'opening unto us the gate of Eternal Life.'

This is Easter joy, rejoicing in Christ's victory at Easter: feeling glad at heart that the Saviour Who loves us so dearly, and poured out His soul unto Death for us, hath now ended His sufferings, and lives and reigns for ever: glad at heart in the sure and certain hope, that if we go on earnestly serving Him for the short time that yet remains, we shall be partakers for ever of His joy and glory: and with us, all whom we love, except they wilfully cast away their hope. This is Easter joy, and it ought to lead us to Easter work ; as the joy and rest of David and of the people of Israel led them to a great work of thanksgiving. What was their work of thanksgiving ? It was building God's temple. David, now rejoicing in peace and glory, when he looked round on his own house, and saw how comfortable and beautiful it was, could not be easy in his mind to think that the Ark of God, the token of His Presence, had no better a home than a tent, where it was to dwell within curtains. And so he purposed in his heart to build a house to the Lord, exceeding mag-

nifical: as such a building ought to be. That was to
be his Easter *work*, his solemn thanksgiving, in return for the Lord's giving him rest. And accordingly, though by God's own message he was forbidden to attempt the actual building, yet for all the
remaining days of David's life he was greatly taken
up with gathering treasure and materials. And that,
under an especial blessing from God. For He vouchsafed to give David by His Spirit exact directions
how the temple should be built. As Moses when he
set about the tabernacle was warned to make all
things from the pattern shewed to him in the mount:
so the Lord caused David, by His hand upon him,
i. e. by His Holy Spirit, to understand in writing the
frame and pattern of the temple and all its furniture.
What a joy and consolation to good king David, to
be thus assured that the great Almighty Father was
well pleased with his way of giving Him thanks.
Make no question of it, He will be well pleased with
us Christians also, if in our Easter joy and thankfulness we apply ourselves to the same work.

For building—building the temple of God, is the
true Easter work, just as thanksgiving is the true
Easter joy. How was it with the holy Apostles after
that first and greatest Easter? We heard in the
second lesson for the evening of Easter Day. When
the Lord Jesus Christ by His Death had purchased
for them rest from their spiritual enemies, and by
His Resurrection and Ascension had led them the
way into that rest, and by the sending down His
Holy Spirit had given the signal for their work to
begin, and furnished them with counsel and strength
to do it: what did that work prove to be? It was

L

building, my brethren, building up not a temple of hewn stones and planks of cedar, but a temple of sanctified souls and bodies: living stones, one by one builded into the glorious and beautiful house which is the mystical Body of Christ, even His holy Catholic Church. This was the work which the Apostles set about, as soon as ever they were themselves filled with the Spirit, and to be made entirely partakers of onr Lord's victory. Like their forefathers the children of Israel newly delivered and come home from Babylon, because they were thankful, they arose and builded. How did they build? First they built up themselves, going on in all holy practices by which the Holy Ghost taught them that He would make perfect what He had begun in them. They continued stedfastly in their first doctrine, and in fellowship one with another, and in breaking of Bread, and in the prayers of the Church. By these the blessed Apostles and their companions builded *up* themselves day by day in their and our most holy Faith: and they kept on also building *in* others.

Take notice of this, brethren: it was not enough for those first and best Christians to be always building *up* themselves, trying to abound more and more; they could not be content without building in others also. Continually in the temple, and from house to house, both in public services and in private intercourse, they ceased not to teach and to preach Jesus Christ. They knew that for this very purpose they were called: not only that they might walk themselves in the light of the Lord, but that the same light shining before all their brethren might win them also to glorify the Father through Him. So earnestly and well did they begin building, that on that one day of the Church's Birthday, i.e. on the first Whitsunday, there were added unto them and unto Christ, by Holy Baptism, three thousand souls: three thousand living stones, builded into Christ's spiritual temple in the course of that one day.

What was Easter joy then, the same is Easter joy now: and what was the first Christians' Easter work then, the same (can you doubt it, my brethren), must also be your Easter work and mine, now and every year that we are spared to see another Easter. What though it be now eighteen hundred years since the good tidings went forth, 'Christ is risen, and His Spirit has come down—believe in Christ and you shall receive His Spirit:' yet our Lord's Blood has not waxed cold, nor is His Arm shortened that He cannot save. Our need is still what it was, born as we are each one of us in sin, and beset with endless temptations: and blessed be His Name, His Love is also unchanged. If therefore we rejoice in Jesus Risen, He expects us to shew our joy as the Holy Spirit taught those first Christians to shew it, by building up Christ in ourselves, and by building others into Christ.

And this year, brethren, we seem to be especially reminded of that which in all years alike is our Easter duty, in that God's providence has called on us at this particular time to join with our Queen and all our fellow-countrymen in thanking Him for mercifully delivering us from the miseries and dangers of that sad Indian Mutiny—the most heart-breaking in many respects of all the trials and troubles with which it has pleased Him to visit our land, as far back as the oldest of us can remember. And God forbid that the youngest of us, that any of our children's children should ever have to witness or hear of the like! But the more fearful it is to think of, the deeper surely should be our gratitude to God for having heard the prayers of His unworthy servants, and restored that unhappy land to something like peace and safety, after so many months of cruelty and horror.

And may we never forget that it is His doing, not man's. If governors and commanders were wise, it was He Who put the wisdom in their hearts: if soldiers were brave and faithful He helped them to be so: if weak women and children, if sick and dying persons, endured like martyrs the worst that man could do unto them; to His good Spirit be all the glory, Who endued them with martyrs' faith and patience. And who knows, brethren, how much of the present deliverance may be due to their earnest prayers, continually offered up in their affliction and agony? which prayers themselves were taught them by the same Holy Spirit.

This Indian deliverance, then, like all the great deliverances which our God at times bestows upon His people, may be looked on as a kind of faint image or shadow (as David's victories and the peace which followed were a type and shadow beforehand), of our Lord's all-redeeming Victory which He won for us by His Death and Resurrection; and of the peace assured thereby to all true members of Him. The mercy to our country calls for something like Easter joy: and by the same rule, He expects of our country, and of each one of us, something like Easter work. As David and Solomon felt in their hearts, that now the Lord had given them rest, they could not do less than build a house unto His Name: so it seems at this time impossible for a true Englishman to help feeling, that the English nation and all Englishmen, are bound to do their very best to build up God's spiritual house the Church, both here and in India, and wherever He gives them a chance. We have but too much reason to fear that one reason why God sent upon us all those sad calamities was the great irreligion of our countrymen in India, their too much indulgence of sinful lust, and the too great neglect of all care for the spreading of the Gospel, both there and among us at home. If, now that He has taken off His hand, we go on just as we did before:—" *after all that is come upon us for our evil deeds and our great trespass, seeing that Thou our God hast punished us less than our iniquities deserve, and hast given us such deliverance as this; should we again break Thy commandments, wouldest not Thou be angry with us till Thou hadst consumed us, so that there should be no remnant nor escaping ?" So the good and earnest Ezra that true patriot and reformer, mourned in his prayer over his countrymen, fearing that after all they would refuse to learn righteousness from the judgements and mercies of their God. I wish it may not be so with us Englishmen in our great and remarkable trials. I wish it could be said that our nation grows in faith and in religious reverence to God and His Church, at all after the same rate as He multiplies His mercies towards us.

* Ezra ix. 13, 14.

But what is the use of just *wishing?* let us up and be doing: let us all be earnest and busy, each one in his own place, in building up the Church of God, the proper employment of hearts thankful for Easter blessings. Our Queen and our Bishops have directed us this day to say in our prayers to Almighty God, "Grant, we beseech Thee, that every renewal of Thy lovingkindness towards our country may lead us to unfeigned thankfulness, and dispose us to walk more humbly and obediently before Thee," which is the same in meaning as the prayer which the Church puts into our mouths twice every day of the year, 'That we shew forth His praise, not only with our lips but in our lives.'

You say those words, at least you say 'Amen' to them, very often indeed. What if you were now to try and say it more in earnest than ever you did before? Does any one here doubt, that if he were to do so it would be a very blessed thing to him? Do you think, brethren, that David and Solomon, now in that other world, wish that they had laid out their money, their time, and skill, in the works and pleasures of this world, instead of planning and building that beautiful temple to the glory of God? Do you think—may God forbid that such a thought should find room in any of our minds—that the blessed Apostles and other members of that first Church in Jerusalem repent, where they now are, of having given themselves up altogether, body and soul and spirit, to waiting on their Lord? do you think they wish any of their goods back again, which they sold, all that they had, and gave the produce to the Church and the poor?

Well then, this is what you will do, if, as Englishmen you would follow David in his way of thanking God for victory and peace : and still more, if as Christians you would follow Christ's saints in their way of keeping Easter. You will put by foolish fancies and trifling objections, and difficulties which in fact are no difficulties at all, and you will set yourself to build up in earnest that holy Church and kingdom, which you know your great Father and Saviour has most at heart of all the things in this world, and which He would have you seek first and attend to before everything else.

Do not say, 'How can we build ? we who are neither rich, nor great nor learned : it is idle to talk to us of bearing a hand in so great a work.' There was once a person who might have said so, if ever any one might—a very poor desolate woman, who found herself at the place where offerings were being made for building up the house of the Lord, and she only had one farthing in the world : she might have well thought with herself—and I daresay she might have found many to encourage her in the thought, 'What is the use of my offering so small a sum ? it will go no way towards the work, but it would buy me a morsel of bread.' She might have thought this and who durst have blamed her ? But no, her heart was so full of love, so enlarged by the Spirit of God, that she offered her two mites, though it was her all, and went her way home, to serve God as she might, little imagining what the Son of God was saying of her, that she had in His sight put in more than all the rich men, because it was all that she had, all her living : and so her praise is in the Gospel, and shall be to the

end of the world. Only think what that poor widow
would have lost, had she thought like some of us, that
it was not worth while her giving at all when she had
so little to give, that she might as well keep it, so
far as it would go, to lay it all out upon herself. Is
not the same God, think you, beholding you, Who
was beholding her? Has He not the same power and
mind to bless you, and make what little you can
give to Him or do for Him go a very great way?

Observe, there are two ways in which you may
build for God, and you must practise both, or you
will not succed in either. You are to build *up* yourself in your most holy faith, to become a more and
more perfect member of Christ's Body; and if you
are in earnest in doing this, you will of course long
to build *in* others into the same Body. I say, you
must practise both these, or you will not please your
Saviour in either of them.

Of course, there is none of you but will at once
allow, that offering alms or any other outward work,
will never bring glory to your God, or save your
soul, except you be really endeavouring daily to draw
nearer to God in holy obedience: "[b] Though I bestow all my goods to feed the poor" or to benefit the
Church "and have not charity," true dutiful love of
God, "it will profit me nothing;" that you are quite
sure; you all know it very well. But there is another thing which you do not know: very few of you
seem to have more than a very dim notion of it:
namely that your love to God is unreal and cannot
be depended on, unless it urge you to win others to
love Him also: as it is written, "[c] Let us consider

[b] 1 Cor. xiii. 3. [c] Heb. x. 24.

one another to provoke unto love and to good works." I say, this is a necessary token of a heart truly converted and turned to God. "^d This commandment have we from Him, that he who loveth God love his brother also."

If you love your brother, can you possibly help desiring his eternal good? and if you truly desire it, will you not, when occasion serves, put yourself a little out of your way, make some little sacrifice, to promote it? Depend upon it, if you see people young or old, rich men or working men, turning away with scorn when they are asked to offer something for missionary work, those persons are not in the right way as to the salvation of their own souls. Think what you do, when Christ, (for in truth it is He,) when Christ comes knocking at your door, and vouchsafes to call upon you for aid in building up His spiritual temple, and you answer 'no,' or give no answer at all, but make as though you heard Him not. Even if there be no scornfulness, no wilful disrespect, yet such behaviour is a bad sign of your love to the souls for which Christ died, and to Christ Himself. For be sure you cannot really love one without loving the other.

Consider again what the Holy Ghost teaches, in the Old Testament and in the New, about persons caring or not caring for Jerusalem, how the Lord regards them as caring or not caring for Him. "^e Pray for the peace of Jerusalem, they shall prosper that love thee." And Isaiah says, "The nation" and those who "^f forget His holy mountain" are reproved as "forsaking the Lord." And He invites His people

^d 1 S. John iv. 21.   ^e Ps. cxxii. 6.   ^f Isa. lxv. 2.

to Him thus : "ᵍ Rejoice ye with Jerusalem and be glad with her, all ye that love her; rejoice for joy with her, all ye that mourn for her : that ye may seek and be satisfied with the breasts of her consolations; that ye may milk out and be delighted with the abundance of her glory." None, you see, are called to the glory and consolation, but those who really rejoice with Jerusalem and mourn for her.

And in much the same way He speaks of the Church in the New Testament. "ʰFeed the Church of God which He hath purchased with His own Blood." "ⁱHe loved the Church and gave Himself for it." And the dearest lovers of Christ were such as rejoiced in their sufferings "ᵏ for the Church." If then you care not for the Church, if you turn a deaf ear when there is reasonable and serious talk of spreading the Gospel, I am afraid it will appear bye and bye that you cared very little for Christ.

Well may an Englishman's heart ache when he thinks of such sayings, and compares them with the way in which the Church and the Prayer-book have been too commonly treated among us in late years.

The remedy for this evil state of things requires indeed much patience : but it is sure and cannot fail, for each one of us. It is simply this, Let every one mend one and all will be mended. Do you strive and pray, each one of you, to build up Christ in yourself, and in all whom He puts within your reach : give gladly some little as He shall enable you, when He asks your aid in His missionary work. And take courage : for He dearly loves

ᵍ Isa. lxvi. 2.   ʰ Acts xx. 28.
ⁱ Eph. v. 29.   ᵏ Col. i. 24.

when humble and holy persons come to Him, and try to bring others, such persons as S. Philip, one of this day's saints; Christ permitted him to find Nathaniel, and promised them the sight of "[1]heaven opened, and the Angels of God ascending and descending upon the Son of Man," and upon those whom He comes to save. This promise is for you, and that for ever: for the least and lowest of you, that will truly try to build up Christ in himself and in others. When will the world, the flesh or the devil, do half as much for you, serve them as devoutly as you may?

[1] S. John i. 51.

SERMON XIII.

EFFECTUAL CARE FOR OTHERS' SOULS,
ONE CHIEF MEANS OF HEALING FOR OUR OWN.

S. James v: 20.

" He which converteth the sinner from the error of his way shall save a soul from death, and shall hide a multitude of sins."

WITH these comfortable words the Apostle S. James finishes his Epistle: an Epistle so severe and alarming in many parts of it: so like the most strict and aweful warnings of Him Who shall come to be our Judge. The Holy Spirit however guided him to finish it with most gracious admonitions how to obtain forgiveness, and how to be in the way of receiving cure of the wounds which at any time sin may have made in our souls. This particular subject, the way in which Christian persons, sinning grievously, may be pardoned and healed, is not a matter on which the Scripture generally gives us any very full or direct instruction. The Old Testament indeed instructs us what method of recovery was ordained for God's ancient people, when they had grievously transgressed: and the New teaches how to enter into Christ's kingdom, so as to be forgiven sin in the first instance: but neither Old nor New says much expressly on the way in which those who belong to the kingdom may have their backslidings healed. Not without repentance and faith we may be sure; "*repentance towards God, and faith toward our Lord Jesus Christ." And this repentance is not a mere inward feeling, but is to be acted on in our whole life and in a great variety of ways; some of which, with promise of a special blessing on them, S. James in this place sets down. As for example, that we should improve our sickness, and of course any other affliction, to heavenly and divine purposes. "Is any sick among you? let him send for the elders of the Church, and let them pray over him, anointing him with oil in the Name of the Lord: and the prayer of faith shall save the sick, and the Lord shall raise him up; and if he have committed sins, they shall be forgiven him." Another remedy which he points out is, real confession of sins and mutual prayer. "Confess your faults one to another, and pray one for another, that ye may be healed." Last of all we are taught to hope that a wise and charitable care for others men's souls may go no small way in saving us from the ruin we have justly deserved. "If one of you do err from the truth and one convert him: let him know that he which converteth a sinner from the error of his way, shall save a soul from death, and shall hide a multitude of sins."

Effectual charity, then, to the souls of men; the real, practical, actual conversion of a sinner from

* Acts xx. 21.

the error of his ways, is one of the methods appointed in the Gospel for healing the wounds made by sin in Christian souls. It has some kind of virtue in covering, i.e. in hiding and veiling over, the backslidings even of Christian people; heavy as those backslidings are, and severe as are the warnings of Holy Scripture on their consequences. Yet the conversion of souls has in it some kind of power to obtain of God that infinite mercy, that He will pass over those sins, and account them as if they had never been. " ᵈHe will cast them," as the prophet says, "behind His back:" He will remember them, as the Prayer book says, no more.

And this, not because of any power or virtue or holiness which our labours and fruits in that kind have in themselves, but because they are a principal way ordained by Him for our laying hold of the Cross, and applying the Blood of Christ, the sovereign remedy, to the disorders of our own souls. It will avail for our pardon, in the same kind of sense as confession of our sins will, if hearty and sincere: or the prayers of the Church and of good Christians in our behalf: or as fasting and weeping and mourning, with which we are invited to turn to the Lord our God: or as alms, and shewing mercy to the poor, by which a great king of old was instructed to break off his iniquities: or as charity in general, which as S. Peter teaches, in the same words as S. James, will surely cover our multitude of sins. The holy writers in all such places as these mean no doubt to teach Christian people, that all these are so many parts of the remedy which God has provided for the sin and backslidings even of Chris-

ᵈ Isa. xxxviii. 17.

tians: they are means, the sincere use of which
will help greatly, each in its way, towards our obtaining the benefit of Christ's Cross: and yet all the
while whatever pardon and salvation it may please
the All-Merciful to bestow upon us comes from that
Cross, and from it alone. There is the Fountain
opened for sin and for uncleanness: the good works
and penitential rules of Christians are healing, because they help us in some mysterious way to lay
hold of that Cross: to sprinkle ourselves with that
Fountain: in that way they cover sins, and break
off iniquities, and obtain pardon: therefore the Apostles and Prophets and the Church of God in recommending them as remedies to the sinner do by no
means make void faith and the Cross, but rather
bring them home to the consciences and daily lives
of every one of us.

Let us not then doubt, but earnestly believe, that
the conversion and amendment of other men's sin
and unbelief, practised as a part of repentance, will
truly help towards obtaining forgiveness: will hide
even in God's sight, a multitude of sins: provided, of
course, that those sins be truly repented of and
forsaken: for otherwise the doing good to others in
order to obtain leave to sin ourselves, would be the
worst kind of pharisaical hypocrisy.

But the Apostle recommends the conversion of
sinners not only to those who have unhappily fallen
into sin themselves, as one way of obtaining grace
and pardon through the Blood of Jesus Christ,
but also to those who have kept their baptismal
vows, as a wonderful increase of their blessing. For
his word is, "He that converteth a sinner from the

error of his way shall save a soul from death." What a promise is that ! he shall save a soul from death ! a soul, an immortal, never-ending soul; made at first in the Image of God, and of so great value in His sight, that Jesus Christ came down from heaven to live for its sake as Man on earth, and die as a sinner on the Cross: and in which, moreover, if it be a baptized, a Christian soul, the Spirit of God dwells as in a holy temple, vexed by its rebellions, grieving for its sins: even so precious a being as this God Almighty permits us to save from death, when by our means He converts it from sin to holiness. Christ indeed is the Fountain of that as of all other salvation: yet still man, as the instrument in the hand of His Spirit, may be spoken of as saving in some manner.

And what is it that we save the soul from ? if God is so gracious as to prosper our labours to convert, i.e. to bring it to true repentance ? We save a soul from death. And the death of the soul is everlasting : and more fearful than tongue can tell or heart imagine. To be saved from it is to be saved for ever ; saved, as the Prophet says, with everlasting salvation. It is a great thing to save bodily life, but what greater honour can we imagine bestowed even by God Almighty Himself on the very Angels that behold His Countenance, than for them to be in a manner instrumental in His Son's work, and destroying the works of the devil, and saving a soul ? Yet even this, you see, He offers to every Christian ; to the penitent, as a help to making his repentance perfect; to such as have kept their vows, for the making their rewards brighter and more glorious.

One thing however, is very much to be observed: that the Apostle seems to make this our reward depend on the *success* of our endeavour. He does not say, if a man be very charitable, very earnest to save the souls of his brethren, God will put it to his account, reckon it a part of his repentance, make it a help to hide his sins; but he says "if one err from the truth, and one convert him:" if you really prosper in the good work you attempt, it will hide a multitude of sins. He does not say that the mere attempt, if made with a good and earnest mind, will do a man no good: far from it: we have reason to think that in this as in other parts of evangelical righteousness, if there be first a willing mind, it is accepted according to that a man hath, and not according to that he hath not. We are encouraged to hope that as a cup of cold water given to one of Christ's little ones in the name of a disciple shall in no wise lose its reward, so neither will any one sincere prayer or word spoken in good meaning. Yet still it remains true, that the particular promise in the text is made, not to him who merely endeavours to do good, but to him who succeeds in it. As far as these words of S. James go, we are not told that merely wishing and praying and striving to convert a sinner will hide a multitude of sins, but that really converting him will do so. Whatever other meaning or purpose of Divine goodness and wisdom we may see in this, one thing at least is very plain: that it tends greatly to hinder slothfulness, and to make men do their very best in Christ's service: just as people promise rewards to their children and servants, not for attempting but for really accom-

M

plishing this or that difficulty. The consequence is, that people who are so quickened do their very utmost, and try always to have all their senses about them, lest by any means they should miss their reward. Whereas if they were merely told to do well, or do their best, there would be far more room for the natural slothfulness and unsteadiness of man to come in. They would be more likely to reckon on the good-nature of him who employs them, and on the chance of his accepting the will for the deed.

Again, by this way of speaking, the Holy Spirit discourages, not only slothfulness, but also an imperfect irregular way of trying to do good to other men's souls. Many, even bad men, make occasional efforts to do so: much more those who mean on the whole well. They have now and then, perhaps at certain regular intervals, a strong feeling and wish to bring such and such a man, whom Providence puts in their way, to a better mind: they exert themselves perhaps for a time, are elated if they seem to succeed, dejected if they fail; but whether elated or dejected, their feelings and efforts do not last very long: they are like the morning frost or the early dew which vanishes away; and their charity, we may fear, will come to but little, either in saving other men's souls, or in hiding their own sins. Whereas, if they stedfastly set before them from the first not only the relief of their own feelings by trying to do some good, but the actual doing of the good, and converting the soul: this would be far more likely by God's blessing to make us both diligent, and circumspect in what we did.

And it has this further advantage and that an unspeakable one; that it leaves us all our life, more or less in uncertainty, how far we have done according to the Apostle's advice, and have really hidden a multitude of sins by converting one more of our brethren. This must be more or less uncertain, because it cannot be surely known, until the last great Day, whether any of those for whom we have laboured were truly converted or no, so as to have their souls saved from death. They may seem to repent for a time but we know not what they are in heart, and we know not how soon they may fall away. Therefore our success in this kind of charity must be always more or less uncertain. And this is really a great advantage to us as penitents; just as it is a great snare, when people allow themselves to think that they have done and are doing great things in the way of converting their brethren. They are tempted in a blind sort of way to think that they have done enough, and need not much doubt about *their* sins being forgiven. They speak more rashly and positively than they ought of such and such plans and ways being blessed: whereas we have small right to make sure of the blessing of God on anything which He has not Himself ordained in His Church. However, it is certain that for the most part He does leave men in doubt how far their charitable labours have really done good to the souls of their brethren. This tends to keep them humble and earnest, and watchful to lose no opportunity: and in another way it tends to keep them hopeful. For the quietest person can never know how far his mere good example may have gone without any knowledge of his towards converting some one or

other who may have observed it and been the better
for it in silence.

But what if the person to be converted be at a
distance, so that neither you know of him nor he of
you: is it possible, then, for you to convert him
from his error? It is possible, by God's infinite
mercy: He in His providence has provided this way
for it, that you may offer some of your substance, be
it little or great, for spreading the Gospel of repentance. And He will measure your offering not
by the quantity of it in money but by the sacrifice
and self-denial you make in order to bring it. Now
as of old when sitting by the alms box in the Temple; He will count the widow's mite, to spare which
she pinches herself with hunger for the day. He will
count it more than all the gifts of the rich men,
which they give only out of their abundance. This
very day it is in your power, by His especial grace,
to obtain for yourself a portion in her blessing. If
you give to-day to your power and beyond your
power, out of a sincere desire to please God, you
will stand a good chance of helping to turn not
one but many sinners from the error of their ways.
Many persons here will most likely know that the
alms which will this day be collected by her Majesty's and the Bishop's command, will go towards
strengthening the hands of the Church for propaga-
ting the Gospel in foreign parts. Many in this place
subscribe something half-yearly to this good and great
end. I trust it is a real charity, and this year we
have an additional reason for humbly depending on
His blessing: viz. that a great step is being taken
in furtherance of the Gospel, by our Bishops and

pastors, sending out not only missionary priests and deacons, but missionary Bishops, to the distant dominions of her Majesty : for the fuller establishment of the Gospel where it has taken root, and for the spreading it far and wide into other countries. Now this is a proceeding on which we have special reason to hope for His blessing, provided we really set about it with a dutiful mind, and therefore we have special reason to give to-day what we can ; that so far as any, by God's grace, have kept their Baptismal innocency unstained by any but sins of infirmity, they may obtain a brighter crown, the crown due to those who save a soul from death : and that the other and unhappily larger portion of us who have fallen into wilful or habitual sin, may do something towards covering and hiding it : may lay if it be but ever so little firmer hold of the Cross, which alone can save us.

SERMON XIV.

PERSEVERANCE IN INTERCESSION AMID SMALL BEGINNINGS.

1 KINGS xviii. [42] 43, 44.

" Elijah went up to the top of Carmel: and he cast himself down upon the earth, and put his face between his knees, and said to his servant, Go up now, look towards the sea; and he went up, and looked, and said there is nothing. And he said go again seven times. And it came to pass at the end of the seventh time, that he said, Behold, there ariseth up a little cloud out of the sea, like a man's hand."

You will hear in the first lesson this afternoon somewhat of the meaning of this unusual behaviour of the prophet. The children of Israel and their king Ahab had grievously sinned in following after other gods; and God by way of punishment had visited the land with a drought. "*It rained not on the earth by the space of three years and six months." Elijah prayed that it might be so, and so it was. But why should the prophet make such an unkind prayer? For unkind, no doubt, it would seem to most of us. Because God put it in his heart to do so. God filled

* S. James v. 17.

his heart with love towards them, and in his love he prayed God to visit them, and bring them by His chastisement to a better mind. Well: the prophet prayed, and the Lord heard his prayer: the drought came, and after the drought the famine: and still the people repented not. At the end of three years and a half, it pleased the Lord to make another trial of them. Elijah the prophet met Ahab the king, and dared him in God's name to seek a sign, which of the two was the true God; the Lord, or the idol Baal. Elijah did, as we should say, dare and challenge Ahab to make this trial. There is a high mountain called Carmel, which overlooks the sea to the westward of Judea, and lies in a situation convenient enough for assembling a great multitude of the people. To this mountain Elijah challenged the false priests and false prophets to come: eight hundred of them, and he was to meet them alone. They were to offer their sacrifices to Baal, and Elijah was to offer his to the Lord, and the God that should send fire on the sacrifice offered to him, he was to be accounted God. Of course it would have been very wrong in Elijah or any one else, to make his faith and duty depend on such a thing as this, had he done it out of his own head: but no doubt the whole thing was of the Lord, to bring about His counsels concerning the good and the bad Israelites. He put it into the prophet's heart: for He knew what He would do. The sacrifice then was offered on each side: the prophets of Baal in their wild way, crying out, and cutting and maiming themselves: Elijah in the Lord's own quiet and humble way, beseeching God to turn their hearts; and the consequence was, that whereas the one party had been crying all day unto Baal, and there was no voice, nor any that answered : no sooner had Elijah ended his prayer, than " the fire of the Lord fell, and consumed the burnt sacrifice, and the wood and the stones, and the dust, and licked up the water that was in the trench." This, for the time, thoroughly convinced the people. They not only acknowledged the Lord to be the God, but they took the idolatrous prophets and priests and put them all to death at the word of Elijah. Their heart was truly turned back for the time : it was true repentance, if it had but lasted : yet (and this is very remarkable) it did not immediately obtain the blessing they sought for : i.e. rain upon their thirsty land. Before that was to come down, Elijah was to intercede yet a little while. And how did he intercede ? In the remarkable way told us in the chapter. He went up alone to the top of the mountain, from which he could see the sea. (For the servants of God in all ages have sought out lonely places for their most earnest communings with Him : and places where His mighty works, such as the sea, are in sight.) Elijah, being then here at his prayers, casts himself into the very lowliest posture of prayer : he falls on the earth and puts his face between his knees : so he prays earnestly for rain, and he sends his servant to look out towards the sea, if there were any sign of the rain's coming. The servant reports that he sees nothing, no token of a change of weather : but the prophet bids him go again seven times : he all the while continuing to pray in that same most lowly and irksome posture. At last, returning for the

seventh time, the servant says, seemingly in a tone
of disappointment, "Behold, there ariseth a little
cloud out of the sea, like a man's hand." And this
cloud presently spreads and blackens, until it covers
the whole sky: there is not only a sound of abundance of rain, but the whole heaven is black with
clouds and wind, and there is a great rain. Thus
upon the repentance of Israel, such as it was, and
the slaughter of the false prophets, and upon the
prayer of Elijah, the heavens gave rain, and the
earth brought forth her fruits. Thus we see how
true that is which the Apostle S. James remarks
upon this history, "[b] the effectual fervent prayer of"
but one "righteous man availeth much." *That* is
very plain: we understand it at once: would we were
but careful and persevering to *do* accordingly! But
what is this about the going seven times before any
change was seen: and the other circumstance of the
little cloud, no bigger than a man's hand? What
are these things intended to teach us? Surely this:
that when God has a great work in hand, when He
is setting forward His holy and eternal kingdom,
and calls upon us, as He always does, to pray for it,
He means that we should not be content with one,
two, or three prayers: we must lead a whole life of
prayer: for that is the meaning (as I have told you)
of the number seven: it means the whole, the sum
of a thing: those that pray, must pray seven times,
like Elijah did: i.e. they must go on saying to God
without ceasing, 'Thy kingdom come:' and those that
look out and watch and work, they must go again
seven times: i.e. they must try again and again: they

[b] S. James v. 16.

must give the Lord no rest, until His promise be
fulfilled : they must still work and pray, and pray
and work.   And again, when something at last does
seem to come of our efforts, we are not to be disappointed or confounded, if it appear for a while to
be very little : somewhat hardly worth thinking of.
Observe the disappointed tone of Elijah's servant,
when he returned from his first look out over the
sea.   No doubt, after the wonderful miracle which
he had seen, the fire of the Lord falling, and the sacrifice consumed in a moment, and after the people
had given such a token of penitence as to seize and
slay the false prophets who were known to be favoured by the king and queen, the prophet's servant
expected to see the weather change all in a moment:
and we can well imagine his look and the tone of his
voice, when he first had to say, ' There is nothing.'
Like too many of us, my brethren, when we have
been praying for some mercy of God a little more
earnestly than usual, and are looking out for an
answer; when friends are ill and we long to have
them better : when children go astray; too often
by our own fault; and we wish and pray for their
repentance : day after day and week after week,
sometimes year after year, we have to say to ourselves "there is nothing," no visible fruit of our
prayers.   And again, when it pleases God to hear
us, and the blessing we ask is really about to be
granted, especially if it be a spiritual blessing, how
very small, commonly, and slight, are its first beginnings : an hour or two's sleep perhaps in a bad
and painful illness : or a reproof well taken and attended to by one who had seemed quite a reprobate:

these and such as these are commonly the beginnings
of entire recovery and complete reformation: we
perhaps, when we mark them, in our impatience think
little of them: we are tempted to say, "There is
just a little cloud, as big as a man's hand," or as
was said on another occasion, "[c] There is a lad here
which hath five barley loaves and two small fishes;
but what are they among so many?" But we are
soon ashamed of our childish complainings, when
we see the cloud overspreading the whole heaven,
and refreshing the whole earth with a timely rain;
when the loaves and fishes are multiplied to be the
food of thousands and their families.

And so it is in spiritual things. Elijah prayed
without ceasing to God for that three years and a
half, and his prayer is at last answered: and although
the whole people too soon fall into the same idolatry
or worse, yet he is told of "seven thousand in Israel,"
"a little cloud as big as a man's hand" in compari-
sion of the whole people, "who have not bowed the
knee to Baal:" and they are a type and an earnest of
the Christian remnant, the innumerable multitude
who in the Gospel times will worship the Lamb in
Spirit and in truth. So it has always been: so it
was in the beginning of the Gospel, when after the
labours and prayers of the Son of God during the
three years and a half of His marvellous ministry,
"[d] the number of the names together was about one
hundred and twenty." And so it is still, my brethren,
those who pray that God's kingdom may come, must
be content to wait long for an answer to their
prayer, and to see but small beginnings when an

[c] S. John vi. 9.   [d] Acts i. 15.

answer *is* graciously given. We heard and saw
something of this, as you remember, last Monday. I
look upon it as a great favour, a great privilege
granted us by the good Providence of God, that we
in this little country village have had at one time
two Bishops, two fathers under Christ of the Christian family, two successors of the Apostles, from
the other side of the world, telling us things, which
we could hardly so well have known any other
way, of the Holy Catholic Church, as they have to
wait on it. The same Church it is no doubt with
our own: there can be but one Catholic Church: as it
is written, "*My dove, my undefiled is one:*" but far
harder and ruder is the Church work in those countries; far more of outward self-denial and suffering
is needed, both for ministers and for people, than in
our quiet country parishes. And still they teach us
the same lesson, that Christian missionaries—those
who hope for that greatest mercy of God, to be permitted to turn many to righteousness, must go on
in patience and prayer: for years, perhaps for generations, hardly seeing any reward of their labours, yet
with every encouragement to hope for a great reward
at last. They taught us that the Church in their
country had been for many ages, praying as Elijah
prayed, looking out seven, yea seventy times, and
yet it might be almost said " There is nothing." Still
they persevered, and now they see in some places,
the little cloud no bigger than a man's hand, in
others the heaven almost generally beginning to be
overspread with tokens of "abundance of rain." As
to one of those Bishops, the Bishop of New York,

* Song of Sol. vi. 9.

the very existence of a Bishop at all in that land is
indeed a great instance of God's mercy to persevering prayer, and to the faith which watches and is
thankful for small beginnings. For New York, as
many of you know, is one of those portions of
America which in old time belonged to Great Britain :
but unhappily, in sending out colonists to them,
little or no care was had to send clergymen, and no
Bishops at all were sent. For full two hundred years,
since the time of Queen Elizabeth, when the first
settlers went from England to North America, from
1585 to 1785, there was no Bishop of the English
Church. The children there could not be confirmed ;
very few clergymen could be ordained ; the Church
could not be as our Lord commanded it to be ; and
no wonder it went on badly, indeed it would have
been quite extinct (as far as we see) but for the missionaries sent out by the Society for the Propagation
of the Gospel. That Society began in London one
hundred and fifty years ago, by a few people meeting
in a Bishop's study, and that very year they sent out
to America, how many do you think ?—*two* missionaries. That was the cloud no bigger than a man's
hand, which was to spread afterwards so widely, for
now in that land there are thirty three Bishops and
more than one thousand six hundred clergy ; besides
seven Bishops and four hundred Clergy in the
provinces which still belong to England. Bishops,
however, there were none, as I said, until after the
first two hundred years ; all that time Churchmen did
as they might, by communion with the Bishops in
England whom they never saw. But at the end of
the two hundred years, in a remarkable way, by the

good providence of God, Bishops were raised up
among them : in answer, we may humbly say, to the
prayers of the few earnest persons who had been all
the while taking the matter to heart; even as the
rain came by the prayers of Elijah. And I would wish
you all to observe this, that from the moment of
Bishops beginning among them, the word of God
grew and multiplied and the numbers of the disciples
increased greatly. It was the little cloud beginning
to swell and gather visibly, and giving good hopes of
its overshadowing the whole firmament. You heard
what the Bishop of New York told us, that he con-
firms as many persons turned from other ways of worship, as he does of those who have been brought up
in the Church ; and this is but one among hundreds
of instances of the blessing of Christ on those to whom
He said, "' As My Father hath sent Me, even so send
I you."

But it is very much to be noticed, that as in the
great work itself, so in each part of it, there is need of
long patience and of hopefulness under small beginnings : it is always prayer seven times repeated, and
the little cloud at last. The Bishop of New York
might have told us, how that in the western parts of
his country there is a zealous brotherhood of priests
of the English Church who in fact have no home;
their mission is to those persons who, being engaged
in clearing out the wild woods of that country, have
not as yet any Churches or ministers among them :
whenever they know of any such, they make their
way, sometimes in waggons, sometimes on foot, often
wading through rivers and swamps, and never resting

' S. John xx. 21.

in anything better than a log hut; when they come
to the place which is being cleared, the first thing
they do is to choose out a convenient tree, on which
they hang a very small Church bell which they carry
about with them; they sound this as for prayers, and
call the people together: they say the service of the
Church in the open air, and then speak to the settlers,
often no doubt very wild irreligious people, of the
duty of serving God, of having a regular Church and
minister, and they commonly succeed after no long
time in persuading them to form themselves into a
parish, and apply to the Bishop for a minister: which
done, the brother-missionaries take leave of them to
set about the same work somewhere else. Now what
are the cares and labours of these men, on coming to
each new station, but Elijah as it were over again
praying and watching in Mount Carmel? and what
is their success, when the settlers agree to form a
parish, but 'a little cloud no bigger than a man's
hand,' an earnest of great things to come?

By such labours and self-denials as these is the
Gospel being preached and the Church established in
such dioceses as that of Fredericton. The Bishop told
us of a clergyman with a parish ninety miles long
with five Churches in it. He told you of the English
who go to live there, how they miss their Churches
and their services, how their hearts were touched at
the sound of some Church bells, which he had provided, when they heard them for the first time: how
far they will come to a Church service, even in the
worst of weather: what notice they took of his instructions, so that when he visited them the second time,
he was quite struck with their improved behaviour in

Divine service and use of their Prayer-books, how
though they are by comparison a poor people, they
have already come to raise one thousand pounds a
year for Church purposes; and he also told us, what
may well come home to ourselves, of his preaching
in London and mentioning how ill-furnished his
Churches were with vessels for the Holy Communion,
whereupon a poor widow whose name he never heard,
sent him a silver cup, the only such thing she had,
for an offering to supply that want: which cup the
Bishop had made into a paten or plate, and by it the
Bread of Life is even now ministered, and will, we
trust, long be so, to a simple New Brunswick congregation. Other like things he told us, not read by him
in books, but known to himself, and he said that whatever offerings we of this parish might make him, he
would lay them out in completing his new Cathedral,
which he hopes will be consecrated on S. Peter's day
next year, and which will be, I understand, the most
beautiful Church in North America. I advise and
beseech you then, dear brethren, to contribute your
best with a glad mind towards this holy purpose: I
advise you to think this in yourselves: that God,
Who knows the hearts of men, if He see in you a
good mind to deny yourself that you may give something to-day like that of Elijah's poor widow, whom
I mentioned, may in His mercy make much of that
small beginning, that little cloud of grace with which
He has overshadowed your heart. Only do you make
much of it by prayer and dutiful obedience. Then
shall His hand be upon us indeed, unworthy as we
are; our Church and we shall grow in grace, and not
cease, even through the years of eternity.

SERMON XV.

OUR LORD'S MERCY IN GRANTING TOKENS, AND THE RIGHT USE TO BE MADE OF THEM.

S. THOMAS' DAY.

S. JOHN xx. 27.

*" Reach hither thy finger and behold My Hands, and
reach hither thy hand and thrust it into My Side,
and be not faithless, but believing."*

IT may be that this feast of S. Thomas was appointed
in the order of Divine providence to come so immediately before Christmas Day, as a lesson to us concerning that faith, to the exercise whereof Christmas
especially invites us, i. e. faith in our Lord's Incarnation. For to this assuredly our thoughts are led,
when we read or hear of the timid but loving Apostle, convinced at last of the reality of his Master's
risen Body, and crying out " My Lord and my God:"
convinced by the sight and touch, that this is indeed
his very own Master, present again in the Body,
convinced also of His Godhead by finding that He
knew his most secret thoughts, the inward wishes
and dreams of his heart: convinced above all by the
loving sympathy which the tender and forgiving

N

Jesus then shewed towards him : which was indeed
but an instance of that eternal love which brought
Him from heaven to be partaker of our frail condemned nature, because His Incarnation is the only
remedy for which He has all along taught that nature to yearn.

This is the point in to-day's Gospel, to which, at
this present time, I desire especially to draw your
attention : namely, the admirable condescension of
our blessed Saviour in giving His disciple the very
sign he had asked for.   Very natural, to our apprehension, were the misgivings of S. Thomas.   It was
not that he doubted his Lord's truth and goodness,
or ceased to love Him : how could he do so, he who
but a few weeks before had earnestly urged his fel-
low-disciples, "Let us also go that we may die with
Him?" but when he heard that they had seen the
Lord, his feeling most likely was, that he dared not
believe it, it was too good to be true.   And so he
was led to do the very same thing which his unbelieving countrymen did : to seek a sign, though in a
very different spirit from theirs.   *They* required a
sign from heaven : the Son of Man coming in the
clouds, according to their notion of the prophecy of
Daniel, to receive all earthly power, dominion, and
glory, their hope being that themselves should be
partakers of the same.   S. Thomas' anxiety was concerning our Saviour's Presence : he wanted to be
quite sure that the Blessed Jesus had not departed
from him : it was the impatience of love, waiting to
be indulged with the promised sight of the beloved :
we dare not blame it as undutiful ; yet we shall do
well to be warned by it, against a kind of undutiful-

ness which is apt to mingle itself with our longings for spiritual comfort. In all ages the religious heart and mind, longing of course for unseen blessings, is full of the prayer of the Psalmist, "Shew some token upon me for good:" and He Who alone can be touched with a full feeling of all our infirmities, has dealt with this longing in His wisdom and mercy variously according to the various cases of His servants. Many are left, in mercy or in judgement, to the general signs and tokens, which He has given in His Word and works to all who will attend to them. There has no sign been given unto them but the sign of the prophet Jonas, the Resurrection of Christ, and the wonders which ensued, written in the Bible, and remembered in the Church for our learning. In other instances, perhaps the greater number, He grants not the very sign which was desired, but some other equally true token of Himself, which He knows to be better for us. But from time to time we may also not doubtfully mark a condescension like that which He used towards S. Thomas. The exact sign is vouchsafed which the loving but imperfect believer had set his heart upon.

Would it be too bold, my brethren, if one were humbly to suggest, that the special occasion of our meeting this day affords something like an instance of a sign or token, we trust for good, granted by Almighty God to the prayers of His people in this land, and in the Church of this land; to some, perhaps, the very sign which they had been earnestly praying for, to others, a different blessing, but fully amounting to that for which they had prayed? I need not explain to you the special occasion of our

N 2

meeting. You know that we are now in this Church to join with the solemn service of the day, the sacrifice of our alms, as an expression of thankfulness to Almighty God for the blessings which He has granted to the Society for the Propagation of the Gospel, and also to pray earnestly for His further blessings upon it. I need not point out to you what a signal token of His blessing we have even before our eyes, in the presence of the Chief Bishop of the Churches of the southern Ocean. Why is he here? He is here, my brethren, because of the unusually rapid growth of the Churches committed to his charge. It is eighteen years since he was last in England. At that time in his colony there were but twelve clergyman and eight Churches. Now, by the good providence of God he has under him five or six Bishops, each of them, I believe, with a far greater number of clergy and people committed to his care than his diocese contained at that time: and the daily increase, and demand for more spiritual aid, is most remarkable. To provide for the needs of this great tree, so quickly sprung out of a small grain of mustard seed, the Bishop of Sydney has found it necessary to make a second voyage to England: and therefore I say, that his mere presence among us, were we to enquire no further, is a token shewn upon us for good, a sign from heaven, as we may humbly hope, in answer to the many prayers of the Church of England. Thank God, it is not a solitary sign; it is one among very many things, which encourage thoughtful persons to hope that English missions among the heathen, as well as among heathenized Christians in our colo-

nies, are at present in a way to prosper far more
happily than they ever have done: that by our
Bishops and priests the sound of His Gospel is indeed on the point of going out with our trade and
our money into all lands, and the words of His holy
Creed unto the ends of the world. We may hope
this, I say, far more confidently now than we could
eighteen years ago. We may hope it more and more
confidently every year.

Now this prosperity of English missions is, if not
the very sign, at least the *very sort of sign* which devout Churchmen were longing and praying for; it is
as the print of the nails, the scar in the Lord's Side,
which S. Thomas was permitted to feel. We have
been in great distress for a long time, great and very
trying distress, and the prayer of many has been,
' Only shew us that Thou art with us, shew the Light
of Thy Countenance and we shall be whole.' In His
infinite condescension He has given us this sign, not
alone, but chief perhaps among several, "* the Isles "
by the ministry of the English, are beginning in good
earnest " to see Him and fear, the ends of the earth to
be afraid, draw near and come." Now, my brethren
what pity were it that such gracious answering of
our unworthy prayers should fail of working its due
effect upon us. What may that due effect be ? What
is it which He expects of us ? Our Lord has told us
in two words, the remarkable words which He used
to S. Thomas, in the moment of granting him the
special sign which *he* had craved for. " Be not faithless but believing."

Perhaps some of us before now may have wonder-

* Isa. xli. 5.

ed why such a caution should have been addressed
to the Apostle at that particular moment.   It might
seem as if he could not choose but believe, when his
hands were upon the very marks of our Lord's
Wounds.   Why then press on him so earnestly, just
then, the duty of believing? First, perhaps, because
the spirit of unbelief is so very restless and subtle,
and if not kept down by the energy of a dutiful heart,
will be sure to go on disturbing us, inventing new
scruples as fast as the old ones are answered.   Thus
S. Thomas, had he been minded to listen to such
thoughts, might have said to himself, as certain here-
tics did in after times, "How can I be sure that the
sense of touch is not even now deceiving me, as I
imagined that the sense of sight was deceiving the
other apostles?" 'Nay,' says our Saviour, "be not
faithless, but believing," 'you may, if you will, go
on doubting My Presence, after all the tokens I have
given you of it, after the very touch which you desired: but it will not be for want of proof, but for
want of a good and steady will to believe.   For such
as are quite wanting in that, no evidence will be
sufficient.'

But perhaps the words may go deeper and spread
more widely than this.   For our Lord's way of dealing with S. Thomas may seem on reflection like
many other of His dispensations towards each one of
us and towards the whole Church.   In many ways
His overflowing mercy is wont to condescend to our
weak faith.   He grants the blessing, He shews forth
the sign, on which we in our imperfect knowledge
have set our hearts: but religious and thoughtful
spirits always understand it to be granted with a cau-

tion like that to S. Thomas, "Be not faithless, but believing." A sick person, we will suppose, has longed with unusual earnestness to recover; or a dear friend, the hope of a family, the pattern perhaps of a neighbourhood, has been ill, and prayer has been made without ceasing of the Church unto God for him; there has been more than ordinary importunity: some, it may be, have even forgotten themselves, and demanded the favour as a sign. Bye and bye it is granted; hope and health are restored; the thing which we greatly feared is withdrawn from us; and is it not so, that in the very act of bestowing such mercy God speaks to the loving grateful heart in a way which it cannot mistake? as if He should say, 'I grant your wish, and now you see My love for you, now you understand how I am touched with a feeling of all your infirmities, and also how entirely you are in My hands, unable by yourself to do the least thing towards securing what you most fondly desire. Will you not learn then to trust yourselves entirely with Me?' Will you not in all your future wishes and prayers try earnestly to submit yourself beforehand to whatever your gracious God shall appoint, not at all to demand the blessing as a sign, but having earnestly asked for it, to leave the event as cheerfully as you can, in the hands of your loving Father?

All persons allow this, if they cannot feel it, in respect of those wishes and prayers which concern the goods of this life: but it is not always observed, even by devout and earnest worshippers, that the same holds good in respect of spiritual comforts; observe, I say spiritual *comforts*, as distinguished from those graces which make us inwardly more like Christ; as for example, in the matter of prayer, there is no danger in being quite unreserved, quite as earnest as ever you can, in wishing and longing to be *sincere* in your prayers (to ask in faith, nothing wavering); but there is a certain risk in setting one's heart on *feeling* that one is sincere. Joy and comfort in spiritual exercises is one thing; perseverance and dutifulness is another thing: it is safe, right and necessary to pray absolutely for the one, but for the other, as for all *comforts* on this side the grave, we should pray, not as for a sign on which we are to depend, but as for an overflowing mercy, which we would not ourselves wish granted, except so far as He may know it to be best for our final and eternal abiding with Him. I should suppose that a deeply reverential mind, whenever it is indulged with high degrees of consolation in prayer and Holy Communion, fears and trembles exceedingly, lest it should be exalted above measure, and tries to be more and more on its guard against requiring such consolations, or asking them as a sign, or repining if they be not vouchsafed.

Again, who can doubt that it is a very great spiritual help to have the company and sympathy of others like-minded, keeping "the unity of the Spirit in the bond of peace," reciting the same creeds and the same prayers with one heart in one meaning; standing fast in one spirit, with one mind striving together for the truth of the Gospel?" and well may we long and pray that so it may be in our families, our parishes, our Churches; but we have no warrant so to pray for it, as if its not being outwardly and visibly granted, would be a token of God's rejecting our prayers, whether as a Church or as individuals. Outward and visible unity, concord and sympathy is to be prayed for as a blessing, not to be depended on as a sign, nor to be so accounted of, as though the absence of it implied the loss of our God and His Truth.

By these instances it would appear, that even in respect of spiritual blessings, when God grants a sign, it is often, if not always, accompanied with a certain temptation to unbelief, viz: that if afterwards we make similar prayers and no favourable answer come, we are apt to lose patience, to question His Goodness, perhaps, to doubt whether we are not altogether in the wrong Church and the wrong Faith. And it is a token of a wise and dutiful heart to bear this danger in mind, and not to set itself too strongly and too absolutely upon any special answer to prayer, but to leave it entirely in His Hands, only refusing to let Him go, until He have blessed us in this world with knowledge of His Truth, and in the world to come with life everlasting.

My brethren, it may be that some of us of this generation, to whom in great and undeserved mercy it is granted to see the growing diffusion of the Church, and to rejoice in it, may be conscious (such is human infirmity) of weak misgivings in time past, or what is worse, of lazy acquiescence in the too common neglect of missionary work: as though the supernatural power of God's Church were somehow worn out or withdrawn in these latter days. Because little appeared to be done, because the converting energies of the Church were so very imperfectly put forth, the very thought of what is implied in the

Holy Catholic Church, the Communion of Saints, was allowed in a great measure to pass away. The providential mercies which we now acknowledge may be intended among other things to rebuke this error, and warn us and our children against it. As the Almighty, by means of missionaries in our Communion, opens the door of faith to one Gentile tribe after another, we are naturally led to reflect, how great a mistake it was in some good men of past generations to think scornfully of their mother Church for the seeming unfaithfulness of her members and ministers. We may be sure henceforth that the Church is real, whether it seem to prosper and be effective; or no. As the coming of the Holy Comforter must have made all those ashamed in Jerusalem, who might be inclined to scorn the way of Christ, because after more than three years' teaching the number of the names was but about one hundred and twenty, and because as yet hardly any of the rulers nor of the Pharisees believed on Him : as the conversion of the Gentiles was the comfort of those who were disturbed at the Jew's unbelief : (according to the prophetic saying, "[b]Though Israel be not gathered yet shall I be glorious in the eyes of the Lord, and my God shall be my strength :") so the visible blessing of God on any portion of His Church at one time, may and ought to silence the sceptical, doubtful and sometimes scornful thoughts which might arise on contemplating its deficiencies at another time.

My brethren, it is a gracious as well as a very aweful voice which has been sounding in our ears to-day, 'Behold the signs of My loving Presence and

[b] Isa. xlix. 5.

be not faithless but believing. I have shewn Myself to you in such wise that you may be assured of My having been with you in times past when I did not so shew Myself, and of My purpose to be with you in times future, though I should again cease to shew Myself in that particular way.'

We have heard the voice; let us accept the lesson. While we thankfully and joyfully receive these signs of God's mercy, so far beyond our deserts, let us beware of so depending on them, as to lose patience, to relax our endeavours, to prove disloyal or unfaithful, if the signs should be withdrawn. In our dealings each one with his God, let us beware how we set up spiritual comfort, sensible refreshment, noticeable answers to prayer, and the like, as true and sufficient tokens how we stand. "The peace of God," we read, "passeth all understanding." Many have it, who think they have it not: very many, alas! have it not, who feel sure that they have it. Looking to parochial and pastoral work, though we cannot pray and long too fervently for an earnest clergy and an obedient people, yet let us make up our minds that the Church is true and real just the same, whether her children do their duty or no: just as a man's parents are his parents whatever faults there may be on either side, and his account must be given accordingly. Neither ought our love of missionary work, or our faith in it, to be measured by its visible results. Faithfulness, be sure, is a better sign than seeming effectiveness. Personal piety is then most thoroughly tested, when the soul perseveres in spite of dryness and discomfort: as it is written: "ᶜ I will

ᶜ Isa. viii. 17.

wait on the Lord who hideth His Face." A few earnest communicants in a destitute and neglected district are a sign from Heaven not so striking but perhaps even more unequivocal, than a much larger member where it has become the custom to communicate. A few zealous believers in the last ages, believers, I mean, in the whole Creed, "one" here and there "of a city, and two of a family," may for aught we know avail more as witnesses of the truth, our God and Lord Jesus Christ and His elect Angels being judges, than a whole generation in a more orthodox time. The alms now to be offered will tell, not according to their absolute amount, but according to the means of the giver, if only he give all that he can.

We have need to watch and pray always, as for ourselves, so for the Church, on the one hand that we be not spoiled by apparent outward success; on the other, that we pervert not Christ's call to soberness and patience into a cloke for heartless, unthankful indolence. As for "our own salvation," so for the Church's increase, it will be well when we have learned, to "[d] work always" with "fear and trembling," aware that in both "it is God that worketh in us both to will and to do of His good pleasure."

[d] Phil. ii. 12.

SERMON XVI.

THE PATTERN OF OUR LORD'S BOUNTIFULNESS AND HOW WE MAY COPY IT.

S. Mark viii. 2.

" I have compassion on the multitude, because they have been with Me now three days, and have nothing to eat."

THE great and wonderful miracle, which you have heard of in this day's Gospel, the feeding four thousand persons with seven loaves and a few small fishes, was itself but one among many like unto it, the crowning act of three days of mercies and wonders. For we read in S. Matthew, that our Lord had at that time retired, as His custom was, with His disciples into a mountain apart, and there came to Him great multitudes, having with them lame men, blind, deaf, maimed and many others, and they cast them at Jesus' feet, and He healed them, so that the "ᵃ multitudes wondered, when they saw the dumb to speak, the maimed to be whole, the lame to walk, and the blind to see, and they glorified the God of Israel." In such works, accompanied no doubt by many a spiritual miracle, many a word of grace and

ᵃ S. Matt. xv. 32.

healing to men's souls, our Lord had spent three whole days: and on the third day when it was time for them to depart, He had compassion on their weak and tired bodies, and multiplied the small store which the disciples offered to Him for that purpose, into an ample meal for each one of them: so manifesting forth His glory, and rewarding them for their dutiful faith in so long waiting upon Him.

Here then is another instance of what the Church so earnestly teaches us in all the services of this week, that our Almighty Lord and fatherly Benefactor, the Author and Giver of all good things, having once grafted in our hearts the love of His name, expects us to grow, and go on and improve. He offers to *increase* in us true religion, to *nourish* us in all goodness. We cannot, if we would, 'continue in one stay,' becoming neither better nor worse. How is it when a young child, having no noticeable defect or illness, yet ceases altogether from *growing?* Is the mother or the nurse satisfied with it? do they judge well of its chance of living and thriving? No, it is a great care to them, and in like manner it is a great grief to our spiritual friends and fathers, to the Church of God, and to God our Saviour Himself, when we Christians make no spiritual progress, when we are contented to go on just as we are, and think it well enough if we do not feel that we are drifting away farther from our God. Such a state of mind is just as foolish and as hurtful as if a sailor should rejoice in a dead calm, and say it was enough for him not to be turned back on his voyage.

Well then, my brethren, the miracle in this Gospel is one of many lessons in to-day's services which

would warn us not to be content with this way of
thinking, but still to be endeavouring to go on unto
perfection; to yield our members more and more
thoroughly as servants to righteousness unto holiness,
and withdraw them more and more carefully from
the service of sin and uncleanness. I say, this Gospel
is a call to *progress*, and *improvement:* it bids us
never tire in our works of charity, but as fast as one
kind purpose or action is accomplished, set about
another : let charity, gentleness, love, be as it were
the breath you draw every moment : think it not
hard to be told this, for what is it but telling you
to dwell in love, and he that dwelleth in love dwelleth in God and God in him ? it is no hardship then,
but the very secret of all earthly as well as heavenly
joy and consolation, when we tell a person not to be
weary in well doing; not to faint, nor think he has
done enough, because he has gone on for so long.
This indeed is too natural to our corrupt and fallen
hearts, in which, so long as they are unrenewed by
grace, self rules instead of love. When any one of
us has waited on another, or denied himself for the
other's sake, for a short time, or in a few instances,
he is too apt to say : ' Now I have done enough, I will
hold my hand, why should I help him any more;' and
if he be pressed to give more largely or to continue
his services longer, he says, ' This is endless, I really
cannot go on : to be sure the person is in want and
in other respects it would be reasonable and right
for me to help him ; but I cannot, because I have
done so much for him before.' This, I say, is natural to our selfishness, but it is not at all what Christ
expects of us, nor what we have promised to Christ.

He tires not of doing us good, day after day, and year after year. He encourages, teaches, commands us to come to Him, asking fresh help, every moment of our lives. He says " Pray without ceasing,' and, ' When ye pray say, Give us this day our daily Bread:" He does not say to us, as we are sometimes tempted to say to one another, 'Why do you come to me to-day ? did I not supply your needs yesterday ?' If then we will be like Him in mercifulness, as He expressly commands us to be, we must learn to rejoice instead of grudging, when we are called on to give more and more. True love, heavenly love, if it in earnest had taken possession of our hearts, would open our eyes to see our Lord Himself in every person coming to be helped, for His sake, and that as often as ever he came, we should no more tire of giving and doing good, than a mother would tire of waiting on her infant. As long as we could honestly afford it, every fresh application would be received by us with more and more cheerfulness, and we should always be glad to increase instead of lessening our gifts. So did our Lord, the day of that miraculous feast; because He loved His people and willed them to love one another; it was not enough for Him to teach them heavenly truths, to heal their diseases, to relieve their sad infirmities, but He also takes notice of their present hunger, and works a miracle, to relieve it: and He so works the miracle as to teach us the way of charity and encourage us to walk in it, He might have supplied the people's hunger at once, by a mere act of His Power, without employing His Apostles at all; but you see He distributes the bread through their hands, that they even more than

the receivers might have a blessing. Again, He requires of them to deny themselves in order to relieving the multitude. For finding that they had among
them but seven loaves, He receives at their hands
all those seven, and gives it away to the hungry
crowd around Him. And to reward them for their
charitable willingness so to part with their scanty
supplies, He multiplies the food so, that what remained to them at last was more than what they had
at the beginning; it was seven baskets full of bread,
instead of seven single loaves. As much as to say,
'Trust Him, and He will provide. Give *to* your
power, yea, and *beyond* your power, and He will
multiply your seed sown, and increase the fruits of
your righteousness.' For, as good Bishop Wilson
said, God will be no man's debtor. "He that hath
pity on the poor lendeth unto the Lord, and look,
what he layeth out, it shall be paid him again,"
with large increase.

And mark it well, my brethren, here is this miracle providentially read to us all, the very week in
which *we* have been invited to do what little we
can for a fainting multitude. Two of our Lord's
special messengers, two of those whom He calls Angels, in the book of Revelations, have this week
come among us upon one of their Lord's errands.
They have told us of thousands and tens of thousands coming to Christ, or only waiting to be called
to Him. Over and over again, as we heard from
the Bishop of Capetown, you meet in that colony
with villages or small towns, earnestly desiring to
have Churches, schools, and ministers, and quite
ready to give bountifully towards them, but unable

o

to find enough money to provide for them among themselves. For this, the Bishop in many instances has pledged himself, depending on us here in England. And for this especially he is full of anxiety just at present. He is very anxious to find a certain number who will promise him so much for five years and enable him to fulfil his engagements. And to promote this wish of the good Bishop, we hope, over and above the offerings of the day, to obtain within this parish some of these five-year subscriptions. Whoever is able and willing to give such help, we invite him in God's name, without loss of time, to put his name down in a list which we are preparing to send round, and opposite to his name the sum, be it ever so small, which he hopes to be able to offer every Easter for five years to come, towards the support of the poor and infant Church in South Africa.

We cannot well help seeing that this case answers very nearly to that of the multitudes whom our Lord so compassionately fed. Those congregations longing so earnestly for priests, and Churches, and schools, but not having wherewithal to provide them, yet continuing steadfast in faith and prayer, and welcoming Christ's Sacraments so joyfully, whenever they were brought within their reach, do we not as it were behold in them the multitude waiting upon Christ for three whole days, and having nothing to eat? Do we not hear His express will and word that He will not have them sent away fasting, He will have them provided with the Bread of life, lest they faint by the way, lest their faith and hope begin to fail them, and they yield to the many sad temptations which are all around them, enticing them away from our Lord and His Church : for divers of them come from far, some from the very depths of the most impure and cruel heathenism ; many from among sects which though they call themselves Christian, have wandered more or less from the truth as it is in Jesus. They say, ' We have stuck fast to our Church, we have been with you, our fellow Christians, now as it were three days, some considerable time of man's life, we have not swerved, though often, it may be, we have gone on months and years without any chance of Church ministrations, now do have compassion on us and send us a priest to look after our souls.' This is the poor settlers' call to the Bishop, but when the Bishop repeats it to us, what is it, my brethren, but God's call to each one of us ? Our Saviour, the great everlasting Bishop of their souls as well as of yours, He has compassion on these starving multitudes, and would fain have them kept safe with Him; He says in a manner to every one of us, as concerning these our brethren, 'They need not depart, give ye them to eat.' What if we have but our own small portion in a sum which altogether is not large, our one loaf, and less, out of seven ? He will not despise it, He will take it of us, if we really offer it with all our heart; He will bless it, and make it enough both for us and them. The seven loaves of the poor of this Christian land, if they come with all the desire of their mind and willingly present it at Christ's bidding, He knows how to multiply it, and make it sufficient for the seven hundred thousand heathen in that distant diocese. I say for the heathen : since what we may now offer, though in the first place, it will be applied to the support of the poorer Christian congregations, for which the Bishop has made himself answerable, will at once act upon the poor heathens around, since it will set the Bishop, and others his fellow labourers, at liberty to look after them. But whether heathen or Christian, I want you every one to feel and understand how much, how very much, Almighty God may in His mercy make of the meanest and humblest of our gifts. I saw this morning some of the little ones offering their pence and halfpence, like the poor widow: and I thought to myself, 'Who knows but one of those pence may pay for some little book or tract, which may touch the heart of some poor ignorant heathen, or heathenish Christian; and so that trifling sum may be God's instrument for the saving of that man's soul: and not of *his* soul only, but of theirs also who may be dependent on him, and whom he may bring with him, or after him, to Christ.'

And there is yet one thing more to be thought of, and it is a very great thing indeed. Those seven loaves, the store of our Lord's disciples, have a deep spiritual meaning: they represent to us the seven gifts and graces of the Holy Spirit, given to the Church and to each true believer, as it were Bread, along with our Lord's Body in the Sacrament of Holy Communion. Seven, as I have often told you, is in Holy Scripture, the number which means perfection, and the seven loaves are therefore the type of perfection in all spiritual nourishment. And in like manner, the few small fishes which were also blessed and distributed to the people, may be taken to mean the saints and holy persons whom God raises up from time to time in His Church, few and small in comparison of what they ought to be, yet greatly blessed by our Lord. Now both the Christian graces of the whole body, and the special good examples of the few remarkable Saints, are by His mercy made to help in converting the heathen, in refreshing those who come from far to wait upon Christ. If "* one member be honoured," saith the Apostle, "all the members rejoice with it." If any one Christian here strives in earnest to be as good as he can be, and so obtains honour from God, then God hears his prayers which he makes for his brethren who are ever so far off, and so, as well as in other mysterious ways, the holiness and repentance of any one portion of the Church is of the greatest service to the whole, and to every other portion.

To this feast then we are invited, as the Apostles were to that in the Gospel for to-day. Their blessing was greater than that of the multitude, inasmuch as "it is more blessed to give than to receive." Believe this, my brethren, for it is Christ Himself Who saith it. Believe that whatever you have offered to-day, or may hereafter offer for the same holy purpose, with a true penitent heart, will be to you as those seven loaves to the dutiful disciples of Christ. When it seems to be all given away, there will be the precious fragments remaining, good thoughts, holy and loving desires, wise and effectual purposes of well-doing, which the Holy Spirit will enable you to gather up, over and above the outward gifts, which the good God, somehow or other, will still furnish you with, to bestow on those who need them here-

* 1 Cor. xii. 26.

after. Gather up these remains, I beseech you, as our Saviour Himself directs. Do not forget any good and loving thoughts with which our Lord may have blessed you in this our missionary week, but store them up, with your five years' subscriptions, for another such feast of charity and self-denial : and so on through all your life, until He come, Who shall say to you, 'Ye did it all to Me.'

SERMON XVII.

THE MISSION OF CHRIST AND OF HIS SERVANTS.

Isa. xlviii. 16.

"From the time that it was, there was I: and now the Lord God and His Spirit have sent Me."

In one little short verse, He sheweth you the mystery of the Trinity. So speaks an old father of the Church, interpreting this portion of the prophecy of Isaiah. He teaches us to believe that when it is said, "The Lord God and His Spirit have sent Me," the three Persons mentioned are indeed the Three Divine Persons, the Father, the Son and the Holy Ghost, Whom Holy Scripture reveals to us subsisting eternally in the One All-perfect Being. That three Persons are mentioned, you perceive at once on reading or hearing the verse; "The Lord God and His Spirit have sent Me." Here is a Person sent, speaking of Himself; One Who says, 'Such and such Others have sent *Me*:' and He speaks distinctly of Two Who have sent Him; "The Lord God and His Spirit." The Father and the Spirit are two of the Persons spoken of. Who is the other, sent by Them both? It is One Who says of Himself, "From the time that it was, there was I." 'From the time that any thing at

all was, I was and am always: without Me was not
any thing made that was made ;' Who can it be, to
speak thus, other than He Who told the Jews, "Before
Abraham was, I am," i.e. our Lord Jesus Christ Himself: the same Who in Proverbs, under the title of
Wisdom, declareth how He "ᵃ was set up from everlasting, from the beginning, or ever the earth was,"
"ᵇ Before the mountains were settled," saith our Lord,
"before the hills was I brought forth."   "ᶜ When He
gave the sea a decree, that the waters should not
pass His commandment, when He appointed the foundations of the earth; then I was by Him, as one
brought up with Him: and I was daily His delight, rejoicing always before Him ?"   You understand at once as we read, that the only Person
Who could say this, the only Person Who could
say that He is from the beginning, or ever the
world was, and that now the Lord God and His Spirit
have sent Him, is the Second Person of the Holy
Trinity, God the Son, the Lord Jesus Christ our Saviour: and so the Three Divine Persons are all
mentioned in this short end of a verse, the Lord God
and His Spirit have sent Me.

But here it might naturally come into a Christian's
mind, How can it be said that the Son of God is
Himself sent by the Spirit of God ? since He tells us
expressly that He will send the Spirit from the Father:
"When the Comforter is come, Whom I will send
unto you from the Father :" and again, "If I depart
I will send Him unto you." How should this be,
that the Son of God should both send the Spirit of
God and be sent by Him ?   That the same Person

ᵃ Prov. viii. 23.   ᵇ Ib. 25.   ᶜ Ib. 29, 30.

should say in one place, I will send you the Spirit
of Truth, and in another place, the Lord God and
His Spirit have sent Me? Why thus it is, brethren:
I suppose that in so speaking our Lord willeth to
put us in mind of that other deep mystery, of His
Incarnation: that He is Man as well as God, true
Man with soul and body, as we are, and with a special work to do on earth as each one of us has; and
in this sense He was sent by the Spirit, His own and
His Father's everlasting Spirit: conceived by the
Holy Ghost in the womb of the ever blessed Virgin,
and of the Holy Ghost anointed at His Baptism by
S. John in Jordan, that being one of our fallen race,
He might suffer and do all that was to be suffered
and done in order to our pardon and salvation: and
all as our Apostle: sent by the Father and the Spirit
at His Baptism, when, as the second lesson told us
just now, the Voice which had been saying to Him
from before all worlds, "ᵈThou art My Son, this day
have I begotten Thee:" said unto Him in the hearing
of men and Angels, "ᵉThis is My beloved Son, in
Whom I am well pleased:" and immediately the
Spirit drave Him into the wilderness for the trial
which was to go before His ministry, and the Scripture was fulfilled which saith, "the Lord God and
His Spirit have sent Me."

And whereas just before this saying, He had declared by His prophet, "From the time that it was,
there was I;" we are to understand that although of
course His Human Nature had a beginning; it began
at the moment of His Incarnation, yet in His Divine
purpose and decree it was everlasting. For ever

ᵈ Ps. ii. 7.　　ᵉ S. Matt. iii. 17.

and ever, before the world was, before there existed
any thing besides the Almighty Himself, it was in
the Counsels of the Most Holy Trinity to restore
fallen and lost man by the Incarnation and Sacrifice
of God the Son; by Him to save and glorify all good
Christians.   Therefore in counsel and purpose the
Incarnation also was from the beginning, from the
time that the earth was, from the time that sin was.
The remedy was to reach as far back as the disease,
and accordingly our Lord, you know, is called in
the Book of Revelations, "'the Lamb slain from the
foundation of the world." This which was always in
God's purpose, came really to pass when the Son of
God was conceived in the Virgin's womb by the
power of the Holy Ghost.   Then, the Father sent
the Son to be the Saviour of the world.   And afterwards the Son was outwardly and visibly sent by
the Father and the Holy Ghost also: not glorifying
Himself to be made an High Priest, but waiting till
the Lord God and His Spirit commissioned Him
openly in the sight and hearing of men.

Now all the great and mysterious doings of the
Most High God with His Son our Saviour are made
to answer in a wonderful way to His dealings with
the Church, which is the Body of Christ, and with
every individual member of it.   The calling, the obedience, the sufferings, the glory of Christ are by His
unspeakable condescension made a true pattern and
ensample of the calling, the obedience, the sufferings,
the glory prepared for every Christian man, woman,
and child.   When therefore we read or hear of the
Lord God and His Spirit sending Christ on the er-

' Rev. xii. 8.

rand prepared for Him since the foundation of the
world, it is His will that we should think also each
one of his own self, and the work to which he in
particular is called.   For every one, depend on it,
has his own work, and that work appointed for him
before ever he was born.   We can easily understand
that it is so in all the greater doings of our heavenly
Father's providence and grace.   For instance : when
it was His will to call the Gentiles to the knowledge
of His grace and faith in Him, we know there was
a chosen vessel, a special instrument, whom He
raised up for that purpose; that vessel, that instrument, was the blessed Apostle S. Paul.   He by the
Holy Ghost, writes thus concerning himself: "[s] It
pleased God who separated me from my mother's
womb, and called me by His grace, to reveal His
Son in me, that I might preach Him among the
heathen."   Here we have, at an infinite distance it
is true, but yet in reality and in very deed, a copy
of what was done in the sending of our gracious Saviour Himself.   We have the beginning of S. Paul's
mission in our Saviour's wise and loving choice of
him, before ever the Apostle himself was born : God
separated him from his mother's womb, for that very
work and no other.   He called him by His grace ;
called him from being a persecutor to be first a Christian then an Apostle, made him know and understand
that He had a special work for him to do, provided
him with all the endowments necessary to prepare
him for it; and at last actually sent him upon it;
He revealed His Son in him, that he might preach
Him among the heathen.   So that S. Paul too might

[s] Gal. i. 15, 16.

say, though in a sense as far below our Saviour's, as earth is lower than heaven, "From the time that it was, there was I," in God's counsels, "and now the Lord God and His Spirit have sent me."

And not S. Paul only, but every saint in his turn, all the chosen vessels whom the Great All-wise House-holder hath from time to time created and formed for Himself—the same words in their measure might be applied to every one of them. Each one had his own work in the Church, and was raised up in his season for it. So it was with the Apostle whose memory by God's providence comes this year to be celebrated on Trinity Sunday, S. Paul's friend and comrade the holy S. Barnabas. He was called into the Church just when the Lord had need of him, to set an ex-ample of bountiful religious almsgiving, and of mak-ing peace among those who ought to be friends and were not. So it has been all along, thanks be to God for it, all through the one thousand eight hun-dred years during which the Church has lasted. The Lord God and His Spirit have never wanted instruments, special members of the Lord's mystical Body, to send out for any special work which it was His merciful purpose to have done. His hand hath not waxed short in that way, no not in our time, un-worthy as we surely are. Even now, we may hum-bly hope, it is His will to have His Son preached among the heathen far and wide, farther and more widely than for many, many generations past: and, it is not presumptuous to say it—He hath permitted us to see with our eyes, so plainly that it would be unthankful to doubt it, what manner of men He is

raising up for the work. Surely, brethren, if you
will put your minds to it for a moment, those of you,
I trust and hope not a few, who have from half year
to half year attended our village meetings in behalf
of missionary work, surely you will go along with
me, when I say it is a very remarkable thing, yes, a
very solemn and serious thing indeed, that in such a
little place we should within these three years have
seen (to mention no more) three Bishops of Christ's
Church, from three dioceses most distant from us
and from one another, the Bishop of Fredericton, the
Bishop of Capetown, and now lastly the Bishop of
New Zealand, each one so evidently raised up for the
very work in which he is engaged; each one entering
into that work with all his heart and soul, each one
earnestly calling upon us to help them, as best we
may, by our alms and our prayers. What, think you,
were Jacob's thoughts, when as he went on his way,
the Angels of God met him? "This is God's host," he
said, and he did what he could to keep up the remembrance of it: it made him more serious than
usual, more afraid lest he should be wanting to such
exceeding mercy as his God was shewing him.
Ought not you and I, at this very time, to have somewhat of the like thoughts? God has been shewing us
something of His great work, how it is being carried
on by those whom He calls the Angels of His Church
on earth. O let it not all pass away as in a dream:
let us not be in a hurry to drive it out of our minds
and memories with ordinary news, with common
work and diversion: and yet it will quickly be so
driven out, its fragrance will vanish away in a very

few moments, if we take no special care to keep it up. How may we keep it up? One thing of course we must do—we must listen to the call made upon us, and offer something, according to our means, towards the good works we have heard of. All that we can spare, and much more will be wanted, you may be quite sure, for the great mission which the Bishop last told us of, the mission to the heathen islands which lie north of New Zealand. Twenty millions of our fellow men, twenty millions of souls for whom Christ died, but not one of whom, as far as we know, ever heard of His Name. There they are, within our reach, shewing many signs of a favourable disposition towards us, and there, very soon, if it please God to spare and help him, will be the man to carry the message of God among them: but he must have help here, his own diocese cannot possibly furnish him with means for so vast a work. Shall we not offer to God through him what little help we can? and be very thankful to Him for the opportunity?

Depend upon it, my dear brethren, there is far more in occasions like this, than you might discern at first thought. They are as Angels coming near you; if they do not make you serious, what ever will? They are as if the great Shepherd knocked at your door and asked you for a cup of cold water to refresh him in looking for those many millions of his lost sheep: if you churlishly turn away, who will pity you in your time of need?

Consider, moreover, that not only Bishops and Apostles have, as Christ had, their appointed work and errand, for the doing which earnestly they must answer to the Great Master. All, every one of us, every man woman and child, has his task in life, known to God, determined beforehand, set him in due time, and of course to be compared bye and bye with his performances. The Lord God and His Spirit have sent us, as they sent Isaiah to prophecy, as they sent Jesus Christ to be our Apostle and High Priest. Only we are sent on different errands; some few to be guides, master-workmen, instructors : the more part to be hearers and learners and inferior helps. But what of that? if we in our lower calling will not attend to our necessary duties, will not hear, will not learn, will not do what little we can, we are as guilty, and lose ourselves as entirely, each one in this his lower place, as prophet or Apostle who should neglect his calling. We are not only wanting in the special work, which we slight, but we also lose our Lord's Blessing on the general work and end of our whole being. We cannot in such case truly say what our Blessed Master said on coming into the world, "Lo, I come to do Thy will O God." Let us offer then now the most that we can spare : and not only now, but always, be it our care to do the very duty of the moment, knowing that God Who has brought us to that moment has prepared *it* for *us*, and destined *us* beforehand to *come to it*. Perhaps the duty is in some respects unpleasant. Perhaps we feel not so willing and cheerful about it as we could wish; and this makes us backward, fearing lest such service should prove quite unacceptable with God. If such is your apprehension, know for a certainty that the way to obtain God's blessing, and to change your evil mind, is to be as earnest as you can on great days like Trinity Sunday: as charitable and self-denying as you can, when the true missionaries are to be helped. Practise this, and He is sure to be with you. Having given you first a willing mind, He will give you before long a willing and cheerful heart; your duty will turn by degrees into delight: i.e. you will have more and more of heaven on earth for His sake, Who came to lift you from earth to heaven.

SERMON XVIII.

MISSIONARY WORK THE DUTY OF ALL.

Rev. xxii. 17.

" He that heareth, let him say, Come."

THAT is, he to whom God has given the blessed privilege of hearing and receiving the Gospel, let him not selfishly keep all the blessing to himself, but let him, as he best may, make it known to others, and invite them to seek a share in it also. If you have the mind of Christ at all, you will of course wish and pray for the conversion and salvation of all men: for you know that He would have all to be saved, else why did He die for all? And if you wish and pray in earnest that they may be converted, you will do what little you can towards their conversion. Is not this plain common sense? does not every one perceive it of himself, if he give the matter the least serious thought?

But over and above your feeling and mine, *He* has spoken to us on this subject, Whose words none of us may dare for a moment to gainsay. Not to mention other Scriptures, observe Who it is, that speaks so earnestly in the text, "He that heareth, let him say,

P

Come." It is our Lord Jesus Christ Himself. He
is finishing the last of His Scripture lessons to His
Church sealing up as it were the vision and prophecy :
leaving a few last words, parting commands to His
beloved disciple, and to all who desire to love Him
and be loved by Him : and then He withdraws behind
the veil to speak no more personally, face to face,
with any one of us, until the day come for all to behold Him, some looking up, some seeking in vain to
hide themselves. He is declaring *His* last will : who
would but listen? And what are His parting words?
A short summary of the Gospel which He had preached, and commanded us to preach from the beginning. 'The time is fulfilled and the kingdom of God
is at hand,' that was the opening of His first address :
" ª Behold I come quickly," so He begins His last.
Then He speaks of the Judgement, " ᵇ My reward is
with Me, to give every man as his work shall be : "
of His own Divine Nature, " ᶜ I am Alpha and Omega,
the Beginning and the End, the First and the Last :"
He to Whom the Angels belong : " ᶜ the Root and the
Offspring of David :" " God and Man :" " the bright
and morning Star," Jesus risen, light dawning after
death. He speaks also of the Spirit, the Holy Ghost,
and of the Bride, the holy Catholic Church, and He
joins all with Himself to utter one good and gracious
word, come. "The Spirit and the bride say Come,
and let him that heareth say Come ; and let him that
is athirst come." Observe the word Come is in the
singular number. He is vouchsafing to take each one
of us as it were apart, and talk to each one, as a man
talketh with his friend, and to each one He says, Come:

ª Rev. xxii. 7.   ᵇ Ib. 12.   ᶜ Ib. 13, 16.

the same that had been His word from the beginning.
To all who are conscious of sin and misery, " ^d Come
unto Me, all ye that travail and are heavy laden:" to
such as are just beginning to take an interest in Him,
"^eCome see where I dwell:" to the Apostles "^fCome
ye after Me and I will make you to become fishers of
men:" calling them to their work; and then to their
refreshment, " Come ye apart into a desert place, and
rest awhile." To the multitudes eagerly but thought-
lessly running after Him "Come take up the cross
and follow Me:" to the specially invited first, and
then to all in the highways, "^gCome to the marriage:"
to Zaccheus in the tree, "^hMake haste and come
down:" to Lazarus in the grave, "ⁱCome forth:" to
S. John the divine and to certain martyrs, "^kCome
up hither:" lastly to those on the Right Hand, "^lCome
ye blessed of My Father."

Such is our loving Lord's constant word of invitation. Knowing that we can never be happy, truly
happy, without Him, He is for ever bidding us come
unto Him. And the Spirit and the bride His invisible and visible witnesses; or as we may call them,
His inward and outward voices, they both are continually repeating the same. For what was it but
saying "Come," when the Holy Ghost by the mouth
of S. Peter said to the congregation on the Day of
Pentecost, " Repent and be baptized every one of you
in the Name of Jesus Christ, for the remission of sins."
And again when the same Spirit in sight of the same
S. Peter descending on Cornelius and his friends,

^d S. Matt. xi. 28. ^e S. John i. 39. ^f S. Matt. iv. 19.
^g Ib. xxii. 4. ^h S. Luke xix. 5. ⁱ S. John xi. 43.
^k Rev. xi. 12. ^l S. Matt. xxv. 43.

gave the signal for the Apostle to say, " Can any man forbid water, that these should not be baptized ?" Once again the Holy Ghost spoke out expressly at Antioch in answer to the earnest offerings (Liturgies) and fastings of devout and holy men, prophets and teachers, there gathered, and told them to separate " ᵐ Barnabas and Saul for the work whereunto they were called." And the Bride, the Church of Christ in like manner. All through the Acts and Epistles, we see that it was at least half of the Church's work to spread the Gospel among those who as yet knew not Christ. The gatherings which we read of in the Acts, at Jerusalem to appoint deacons, at Antioch to make arrangements for S. Barnabas' and S. Paul's going out on the work of conversion in Cyprus and Asia Minor; and again when S. Paul went out with Silas, which journey ended in his founding Churches in Europe, these all were in reality missionary meetings, assemblies holden by Christians from time to time, to consider how they might best carry on the great and good work of turning the heathen to Christ. It was the Spirit and the Bride saying " Come," to one portion after another, of those who had been hitherto afar off, but were now to be made nigh by the Blood of Christ.

This went on to the time when the history of Christ's Church as far as we learn it from the New Testament comes to an end, i. e. as far as our Lord's final appearance to S. John at the end of the Revelations. And He, our dear Lord Himself, by these His parting words which I have been speaking of, plainly shews His will that so it should go on con-

---

ᵐ Acts xiii. 2.

tinually, in this His chosen family and Church on earth. Until He come again to us, we are invited, and are commanded to invite one another, to come to Him. The Spirit of Christ, the Holy Ghost, the Comforter, abides with us for this very purpose to recall our Lord's blessed words, " ª Come unto Me, all ye that labour and are heavy laden, and I will give you rest." " º Come eat of My Bread and drink of the wine which I have mingled." He will not let you forget the words, and if you will suffer Him, He will keep up within you a good heart and a brave spirit, not only to remember them yourself, but to put others in mind of them also. He, the Holy Comforter, will cherish in you the sense of our Lord's miraculous sweetness, the joy and consolation of being called by His Name : and how can it be but that He should also cause you to feel in some measure our Lord's own longing that all the ends of the earth, should look unto Him and be saved ? Thus the Spirit that is within us, greater than he that is in the world, saith " Come " : and the Bride, the holy Church, the whole mystical Body of Christ, the company of Christian people around us, from it also we hear the same voice ; to every soul within her pale, and to every one of every people, nation and language without, the Church by her very presence says, " Come :" 'all these privileges are for you : my gates are open continually, they are never shut day nor night, they are open to all, all without exception, not one is forgotten, despised or shut out.'

The Spirit of Christ then, and His spouse the Church, are for ever doing missionary work, for ever

ª S. Matt. xi. 28.　　　　º Prov. ix. 5.

saying, silently or aloud, 'O come, come, come to your Saviour.' But what of each one of us, private individuals? What of the farmer, the labourer, the tradesman, the servant, the men of business, the youths, the mothers and daughters of a Christian land? Of course it is their duty, like the rest, to come to Christ themselves. He died for them as for all, and there is salvation in no other: they must come themselves: but are they too bound, as the clergy and the learned are, to call others to come? Yes, for the Saviour of us all distinctly orders, "*Let him that heareth say Come*:" let him take up the good word, the word which is given him as a soldier, a watchful servant of his Lord: let him take up the word and pass it on to others: "He that heareth :" *that* is Christ's saying: not here one and there another, but *every* one without exception who is called on to have faith himself, is then and there called to do what he can according to his means and station, for bringing others to the Faith also. As sure as the Great Father gives you the witness in yourself, that you are by Baptism one of the family, you are bound in your degree to be a witness to others also. The missionary spirit has been from the beginning, a mark of God's people, a note of the true Church: just as the children of the Wicked one have been known by their not caring for the souls of their fellow creatures; like him who being asked "Where is Abel thy brother," could find it in his heart to say "P I know not: am I my brother's keeper?" Alas! my brethren, many and many a one, who little thinks of imitating Cain, proves himself, before God and

P Gen. iv. 9.

His Angels, in this a follower of that wretched man, that although he would shrink from being wilfully the murderer of his brother's soul, yet he is not ashamed to take up, in a way, that saying of the first murderer, and to answer the voice of conscience, i. e. the Voice of God, calling him to account, much as Cain did. How many a parent, when asked in God's Name, 'How comes that child of yours to be so unruly, so lewd, so profane,' instead of taking up the matter in earnest, will coolly reply, 'He must answer for himself, it is no use for me to speak to him!' And if it is so as between parents and children, you may judge how utterly indifferent men will be towards those who are only their neighbours, only their brethren for whom Christ died; how utterly strange and unaccountable it must appear to such persons, when you call on them to pray, to work, to make sacrifices for the everlasting good of the poor neglected millions a few miles off in their own land, much more for the untaught heathen on the other side of the world.

And yet this must be done, if we are to be acknowledged by our Judge and Saviour as members of Him in the day of account. The soul of every baptized person is as a lamp touched with His Holy Spirit, a torch lighted and shining, not to be put under a bushel, or under a bed, hidden away where no one will be the better for it, but on a candlestick, where burning steadily it may give light to all in the house: all persons within reach of it may see how to do their own work, and others may come and light their own lamps at it, and so that may come true in a novel and blessed meaning, "how great a

matter a little fire kindleth !" Thus while times and
seasons pass away, the light of the Gospel goeth
not out, this generation has received the holy fire
from the generation which went before, and will
hand it on (D.V.) to that which shall come after.
And again as in times so in countries: England,
fourteen centuries ago and more, caught fire from the
altars of Rome and the East, and now by God's
mercy Africa and the South, Australasia and the Isles
of the East, are lighting their fires from England.
True, we have had cold and dead times, when little
or nothing was done in that way.   But it has pleased
the gracious Lord to have pity on our unworthiness,
and to give us hope that this our rich and brave
England will do more and more of her duty in that
respect.   All honour to the good men who in the
midst of those unbelieving years, a century and a
half ago, set themselves to stir up the dying embers
by founding this our Gospel Propagation Society, and
to those who from time to time have ever since been
watching and fanning the flame.   All love and
thanks and praise to the Good, Holy, Converting
Spirit, so graciously blessing the work, that whereas
at the time I am speaking of, the beginning of the
century, there was not a single Bishop in our colonies, now there are at least forty five, labouring
either in the Queen's dominions or among the heathen and others with whom we have been brought
into connection through the colonies: forty five new
Bishopricks, my brethren, Churches in the same sense
that Ephesus and Crete were Churches, under their
respective Bishops as Ephesus and Crete were under
Timothy and Titus.   Drawbacks there are, of course:

there must be.   Is it not written "*⁋All that will live
godly in Christ Jesus must suffer persecution," or
troubles as bad as persecution? If it were not so,
where would be our cross? and where and what
should we be without our cross? E.g. we are not to
be disheartened, when as of late we hear in one diocese of the chief missionary station, being for the
present abandoned partly for health, partly through
the enmity of the natives and others, not enduring the
Gospel which expressly forbids man-stealing, i. e.
enslaving human beings for sale.   This has happened
in one diocese of Africa: and in another, what is far
sadder, it has been necessary to deprive a Bishop of
his place by reason of false doctrine and unbelief, he
refusing to be corrected.   Therefore, as you know,
we in our parish have of late said the Litany and
offered the Holy Communion for the Churches of
South Africa by name: and we have mentioned also
those of another province, New Zealand, because of
the dreadful war which is raging there between our
colonists and the natives: yes even the native Christians.   These things are worse than persecution,
because in these the mischief comes in a great degree
from within the Church, from the sins of baptized
men: nevertheless even of these we may hope that
by God's mercy they may tend rather to the furtherance of the Gospel.   Doubtless it will be so, if the
true believers meet their trials, in wisdom faith patience and charity, and when I have named the two
chief Bishops among them, the very names will be to
you a token, that please God we may look on
courageously and hopefully to the end.   They are

⁋ 2 Tim. iii. 12.

Bishop Selwyn of New Zealand and Bishop Gray of
Capetown. Some of you, my brethren, have seen
and heard them in this place, and have read of them
in the reports, and know in some sort what manner
of men they are. The last accounts left Bishop
Selwyn tending night and day the wounded and dying of the British army, and in no small danger from
the lurking parties of the natives as he went from
station to station: and Bishop Gray setting out on
a wearisome ride of five hundred miles, to visit the
scattered congregations, comfort them and confirm
them in the faith, after they had been disturbed by a
certain unbelieving teacher: and all this besides
that which cometh upon them daily, the ordinary
care of all the parishes under them. I could tell
you of others: of a Bishop who has left one of the
most delightful of English homes to spend the best
part of his life in an unknown and dangerous ocean
in searching out one wild island after another, putting
as David did his life in his hand, venturing himself
alone among hundreds of savages, if haply he may
find some young men willing to go away with him
and be taught, and parents willing to spare them:
the rest of his time, he spends chiefly in educating
them and doing a father's duty. Or I might tell
you of a clergyman dwelling with a wife in feeble
health in the midst of hundreds of rude half clothed
Africans in a hut with almost as few comforts as
theirs, waiting on them in every way, as their
schoolmaster, physician, helper and adviser in all
kinds of outdoor and indoor work: and all for
Christ's sake, watching all opportunities, and leav-
no way untried to win here and there a soul to Him.

Which of you all but would heartily rejoice to have
given to such as these, but a cup of cold water in
time of need for Christ's sake?   Which of you again
but is able, if he would but believe it, to give much
more? Only let us have true faith in Him Who has
pledged Himself to make even scanty alms and feeble
prayers, if they are the best we can give, real helps
in His great and saving work: fellow labourers (so
says the Apostle) with God.

"He that heareth, let him say, Come." Would it
not have been a blessed thing, think you, to have
been one of those to whom it was said on Easter
morning, " Go tell His disciples that He is risen from
the dead," who went about Jerusalem accordingly,
and were rewarded by meeting our dear Lord in
His own Person: to be saluted by Him in the gracious tones of His own Divine Voice; to fall down
and hold Him by the Feet and worship Him?
Well, the same errand, the same Presence, the same
blessing is offered to each one of you, only by faith,
not by sight.   In your parish and neighbourhood,
wherever it be; in your own house and home; in your
work and trade: in your daily discourse with those
around you: in your house-hold service (if such be
your providential calling): you have many ways of
bearing witness to His Resurrection; of saying to
those whom you meet, ' Come, by faith see the place
where the Lord lay.' You may say, Come, not so
much with your lips as with your lives: you may
by His grace live so, as that the very sight of you,
of your pure, modest, humble, dutiful, cheerful, kind,
self-denying ways, may be an invitation to come to
your Saviour. Men, taking knowledge of you that you

have been with Jesus, may be moved to say, Would
it not be well for me to go and be with Him also?
Deeds tell more than words. Actual coming is more
persuasive than merely saying, Come. E.g. every
one of you every Sunday, has a missionary work to
do. Our Lord expects us all to come if we can to
the place where He has promised to be, to greet
Him on His Resurrection Day, to humble ourselves
before Him in earnest and holy joy. As often as
you do so, you surely are so far obeying that farewell word of His, "He that heareth, let him say, come."
But if a man being in sufficient health, merely says
to his child and servant, It is time for you to go to
Church, and stays away himself because he likes
something else better than his Saviour's Presence—
you know whether or no that man is a likely one
to make people about him better Christians.

By good example, then, and by encouragement
given to good, our Lord, you see, would have us,
one and all, to be constantly doing missionary work,
i.e. winning souls to Him, and if any one be really
such at home, he cannot of course hear of what is
going on abroad without longing to have at least
some small share in it: and if you really long for
what God invites you to, be sure He will help you
to find the way to it. He will put it into your
heart, e.g. to set by a little of what you might spend
in ordinary ways, in dress, diversion, or innocent
fancies. Be it ever so little, if it be offered with a
willing heart, and a loving prayer, you know not
how much good it may do; the more if it be brought
regularly from time to time: for this shows a *constant* love, and not a mere passing flash of interest

in the work. The widow's mite, repeated a few times, may pay for some good reading, or for some kindness done to a sick heathen, which may in the end save a soul alive.

But observe one thing: you are not to look too anxiously for tidings of any actual good being done by what you give. It is enough that you have placed it in your Lord's treasury, as the poor widow did her farthing: and *you* know what *she* did not: that He is looking on all the time. We are not even told that she heard His words of praise: but so much greater, be sure, was the transport, when she came to know of them in that other world. Try to be like her: give with simplicity; with a simple heart, just to please Christ, leaving Him to do what He will with it. This is a sure way to a blessing.

If the promises seem, as well they may, too high and miraculous to be realized in such small things, in alms by a child offering the value of a plaything, a servant putting by a portion of his wages, a young person refraining from an amusement; or again, in conversation, by a word spoken in due season, or if it were but a grave look or tone, to reprove the dissolute; then remember Who it is that vouchsafes to be on the same mission with you: not only the Bride, the Church, but the Spirit also, the Almighty Teacher and Guide. His glorious Voice will sound in unison with your unsteady and feeble voice, crying to the unbeliever, the backslider, the imperfect, Come, and who knows what power may be thereby given even to yours for the saving a soul alive. For the Spirit of God is all-powerful, and is Himself that Living water of which He invites us to come and drink: making us hear that good word of our Lord. "Let him that is athirst come: and whosoever will let him take of the water of life freely." The only condition required of us is that we be really, truly athirst.

But no time should be lost. The world is waxing old: the time is short: and your lives and the lives of those whom you might help are fast passing away. As yet, however, the promise stands. Ask *now*, and ye shall have: come *now*, while you are called, and invite others to come. There is really no limit to the number of those whom by the grace of God you may win, or to the blessing of each one who may be won by you.

SERMON XIX.

THE LIBERALITY OF THE ISRAELITES A PATTERN TO CHRISTIANS.

EXOD. xxxv. 29.

" The children of Israel brought a willing offering unto the Lord, every man and woman whose heart made them willing to bring, for all manner of work, which the Lord had commanded to be made by the hand of Moses."

THERE are, I believe, in the Old Testament two instances only especially mentioned of a general collection being made among God's people, and both those collections were, as we may say, for the purpose of Church building. The first was made by Moses, under especial directions from God Himself. The second by David, who also, we are told, was guided in that work by the Holy Spirit of God. Of the one you read in the end of the Book of Exodus, of the other in the end of the first book of Chronicles. It may be well to give a short account of each.

As to the first, it was a material part of God's great work that He did with the children of Israel, when He gave them the Law on Mount Sinai. The great blessing which He assured them of, by that

Law and covenant, was His own especial Presence
among them: and for an outward sign and pledge
of that Presence, He willed to have a tabernacle
among them: a tent of His own, to stand openly
apart from the other tents, but in sight of them:
where His Glory might appear, and they might come
regularly to offer Him solemn worship. The tabernacle was to be among the other tents, while they
were living in tents, on their march through the
wilderness, as the Church is among other houses and
buildings, in any town or village of ours: and because it was God's own tent, it was to be more
beautiful and glorious by a great deal, than any
of the rest. The making, the ordering, and fitting
up of it, was a very solemn thing indeed: for it was
all to be according to the pattern which God shewed
to Moses in the Mount. For Moses, you know, was
in the Mount forty days and forty nights; hidden
from men's sight in the thick darkness where God
Himself was: and all that time he received instructions how God's will should be done with His people,
and this of the making and furnishing the tabernacle
was a very particular part of those instructions.
We in our short sighted way might be apt to imagine
such things of small consequence: we might have
thought, that to the great God of heaven and earth,
gold and iron, precious stones and clay, one pattern
of work and another, were all alike: but you see
that in this case it was not so. The materials and
workmanship of the tabernacle were of so much im-
portance in His sight, that He revealed them all
distinctly beforehand to His Prophet. Not a pin
nor beam was set up in the holy place, not a stitch

of work, if I may so speak reverently, was done there, but He had expressly ordered and arranged it before. It was said to Moses over and over again, "[a]According to all that I shew thee, after the pattern of the tabernacle, and the pattern of the instruments thereof, even so shall ye make it." "[b] Look that thou make them after their pattern which was shewed thee in the mount." "[c] Thou shalt rear up the tabernacle according to the fashion thereof which was shewed thee in the mount." "[d] As it was shewed thee in the mount, so shall they make it." So far, assuredly, we learn hereby, that such things pertaining to the outward service of God, may be of far more consequence that we in our rough way might suppose.

But there is another part of this history, very much indeed to be thought of by all who desire to be good Christians. This work of God's tabernacle, so great and holy and perfect, nay, and it may be called Divine, planned as it was by the Almighty God Himself, this work was to depend for its accomplishment on the free-will offerings of the men, women and children of Israel. If it had pleased God, of course He could at once have created all the gold and silver, the blue, purple and scarlet and fine linen, the spices, the costly wood and the precious stones: He might have created and furnished it, all at once, for the purpose: He might have caused everything to come to hand, ready made, according to the heavenly pattern: He needed neither human skill and labour to bring the works into their proper shape, nor the bounty and free-will offerings of the congregation to furnish the materials of them.

[a] Exod. xxv. 9.   [b] Ib. 40.   [c] Ib. xxvi. 30.   [d] Ib. xxxvii. 8.

Q

God had no occasion, as far as we see, for such human means, yet it pleased Him to make use of them. As He called by name Bezaleel and Aholiab, and other skilful and wisehearted men, to make the holy things according to the pattern, so He called upon the whole congregation to offer materials for the work according to their ability. He vouchsafed, as we should say, to make a *collection* from among them. This was part of His original purpose, declared unto Moses in the mount. He had said, "*Speak unto the children of Israel; that they bring Me an offering: of every man that giveth it willingly with all his heart ye shall take My offering." And accordingly Moses, in reporting His words to the people, said, "'This is the thing which the Lord commanded, saying, Take ye from among you an offering unto the Lord: whosoever is of a willing heart, let him bring it, an offering of the Lord, gold, silver, brass; blue, and purple, and scarlet, oil, spices, precious stones," and whatever else was wanted, either for the furnishing of God's tabernacle, or for the carrying on the service afterwards. This was the message from God: how did they answer it? "*All the congregation of Israel departed from the presence of Moses. And they came, every one whose heart stirred him up, and every one whom his spirit made willing, and they brought the Lord's offering to the work of the tabernacle of the congregation, and for all His service, and for the holy garments. And they came, both men and women, as many as were willing-hearted, and brought bracelets, and earrings, and rings, and tablets, all jewels of gold;" and so of

* Exod. xxv. 2.   ' Ib. xxxv. 4—6.   * Ib. 20—22.

the other materials which were wanted: "the children of Israel brought a willing offering unto the Lord, every man and woman whose heart made them willing to bring, for all manner of work, which the Lord had commanded to be made by the hand of Moses." And such a good heart had they for the service, that we read, how after the work had begun " [b] The people yet brought unto Moses free offerings every morning: and the workmen spake unto Moses, saying, The people bring much more than enough for the service of the work, which the Lord commanded to make. And Moses gave commandment, and they caused it to be proclaimed throughout the camp, saying, let neither man nor woman make any more work for the offering of the sanctuary. So the people were restrained from bringing. For the stuff they had was sufficient for all the work to make it, and too much." Thus the whole of that sacred and glorious work was completed by the free-will offerings of the people. If they had been backward, it would have been at a stay: God's gracious purpose of dwelling visibly among them would have been made void, and what would have become of them?

We seem then to learn by this history of the foundation of the tabernacle, that the perfection of God's outward service is of great consequence in His sight, and that He in His wisdom and love calls upon men freely to provide for it, with promise of a great blessing, i.e. His especial Presence, if they cheerfully obey the call in the best way they can, but with great fear of losing that Presence, if they draw back and refuse to offer.

[b] Exod. xxxvi. 3—7.

Q 2

Now let us go on to the other chief collection, which, as I said, we read of in the Old Testament. It was known to be God's will and purpose that after His people became settled in Canaan, He should no longer dwell among them in a moveable tent, but in a fixed and solid temple: a settled place to abide in for ever, somewhere in the midst of their tribes. And after many years it pleased Him to raise up David, the man after His own heart: and one token of David's great and exceeding love of God was, that he earnestly sought and prayed to be the builder of that temple. God in His wisdom told David, that he might not himself build His temple, but that his son Solomon should do it: He also revealed to him the place where it should be builded: which David no sooner knew, than he began to make preparation for it: wrought stones, iron, brass, and cedar for the building, and for the expense and ornament of it so much gold and silver, that he said, there was no numbering of it: and yet in addition to all this, when the people came to know of it, and David had said to them, Who is willing to consecrate his service this day unto the Lord? they offered willingly, and much more than doubled what David had offered before: and observe how happy it made them all: "[i]The people rejoiced, because with perfect heart they offered willingly to the Lord: and David the king also rejoiced with great joy. Wherefore David blessed the Lord before all the congregation:" and part of his blessing was as follows: "[k]Who am I, and what is my people, that we should be able to offer so willingly after this sort? for all things

---

[i] 1 Chron. xxix. 9, 10.   [k] Ib. 14, 17, 18.

come of Thee, and of Thine own have we given Thee."
"O Lord our God, all this store that we have prepared
to build Thee an house for Thine Holy Name cometh
of Thine hand, and is all Thine own. I have willingly offered all these things: and now have I seen
with joy Thy people, which are present here, to
offer willingly unto Thee. O Lord God of Abraham,
Isaac, and of Israel, our fathers, keep this for ever
in the imagination of the thoughts of the heart of Thy
people, and prepare their heart unto Thee."

You see, my brethren, that the two greatest works
which we read of as done in the Old Testament for
God's honour, the building of the tabernacle first
and afterwards of the temple, did both require the
free-will offerings of men: and that those, being
offered abundantly and cheerfully, brought down an
especial blessing, a kind of heavenly joy, upon the
work. That blessing, and that joy, were confirmed
out of the mouth of God Himself, and sealed for
ever unto the poorest of His people, offering ever so
little with a willing mind: when our Lord, sitting
over against the treasury, saw the poor widow
casting in her two mites, and pronounced His well
known blessing upon her. For the treasury was
the box into which people cast their offerings for
the repairing and adorning of the temple: and that
poor widow's two mites were offered for the very
same purpose as David's and Solomon's thousands
of talents. And so it has been, all along, in the
Church and kingdom of our Lord. The great work
of that Church and kingdom, God's glory in the
saving of our souls, cannot ordinarily be carried on,
without Churches to worship in: and the faithful

have all along delighted to offer freely to the building and adorning of those churches. They have felt
as David did, ashamed to dwell in ceiled houses
while the ark of God was within curtains : ashamed
to have things elegant and comfortable at home, while
the place where Christ had promised to be was left
as if it were little thought of. They have felt as
Moses did, anxious that all God's outward service
should be according to the pattern shewed in the
mount: i. e. that it should, in a kind of type and
figure, represent the heavenly truths of which it
teaches. Our fathers in the faith, the first Christians, were earnestly desirous that there should be
Churches everywhere, and that every Church should
be so ordered, that a Christian could not well look
at it, or go into it, without seeing something to put
him in mind of the Presence of God, the judgement
to come, the sufferings of Christ, the glories and terrors of eternity. Surely, my brethren, we do well,
to try to have the same mind as they had. We
are not surely so heavenly minded, so carried away
by the thoughts of another world, that we can afford
to do without those outward helps which all generations of God's servants have found necessary. We
surely are called upon, according to our means, to
offer unto Almighty God both for the building of
new Churches, where such are wanted, and for the
adorning and beautifying of old Churches, to make
God's service solemn and devotional, as it was always intended to be. Surely it is for the good of all
our souls, first that we should have a Church to worship in, next that when we come into that Church,
everything that we see and hear should draw our

thoughts away from the ordinary world, and lift them up to that world, where all is beautiful and glorious.

If then Almighty God approved and blessed the willing heart of those Jews, who offered abundantly to the tabernacle and to the temple, we may have good hope that He will approve and bless all, who in our days come cheerfully with a tribute of a free-will offering to assist in the building and adorning of Churches. If our Lord looked graciously on the poor widow's two mites, as she cast them into the treasury for the repair of the temple, doubt not but that He looks graciously also upon the small coins and lowly offerings of the poor, upon the halfpence and pence and farthings, which He sees cast into His treasury here, for the very same kind of purpose.

The more we think over the matter, with any degree of faith, the more reason shall we see to be earnest and cheerful in offering what we can spare. It is our Bishop who asks us for it, our chief pastor on earth: he finds a great want of new Churches in many parts of his diocese, and for the souls' sake committed to his charge he beseeches us for aid in bringing them to Christ's holy house, and in using them to be very devout when they are there. How are they ever to know and love their Saviour, if they are left to wander without common prayers and Sacraments, without the Church's instruction and guidance, without the special Presence of Christ, such as is promised to them in His solemn assemblies? Charity to our brethren's souls, no less than zeal for God's honour, would stir us up to this good work.

Then consider, if the Israelites in the wilderness,

having been delivered out of Egypt, were so full of
love and thankfulness; what ought to be our feeling,
if we really believe what we say in the catechism,
that we being born in sin, were in our childhood
made members of Christ, children of God, and inheritors of the kingdom of heaven? Which is the
greater, to be freed from Egypt and Pharoah, or to
be redeemed from the world, the flesh and the devil?
Which journey has the more blessed hope, the way
to Canaan or the way to heaven? Which marks us
more entirely for God's own; to have His law written
outwardly in our sight on two tables of stone, or to
have it written inwardly in our hearts by the Holy
Spirit of God and of Christ? Now the Jews' thankfulness for those lesser favours made them, we see,
most willing and joyful in offering for the service of
the sanctuary. They went on till no more was
wanted: the collection was stayed by Moses himself, because more than enough was brought. When
shall we see and feel the like willing spirit among
ourselves, who have so much more to be thankful
for? I will tell you: we shall see it in that day,
when the hearts of Christians in general are truly
and deeply touched with a sense of the great things
that have been done for them. When we come to
have right and true thoughts of the souls of men
and the Cross of Christ, then we shall not grudge
any thing that is ours to offer for the salvation of
souls and the honour of Him Who died on the Cross.

In the meantime it is written down in Scripture,
that "God loveth a cheerful giver," and I do hope,
my Christian friends and brethren, that what you
offer now, or on any like occasion, will be offered

not out of mere custom, nor grudgingly, but with a free and open heart: so that even at the moment of giving, you may experience what our Saviour taught, That "[1] it is more blessed to give than to receive." If grudging thoughts arise, as they are sure to do in many, stir up your faith to put them down: think you behold our Lord Jesus watching, as when He sat over against the treasury: be courageous in giving, like that poor widow: remember how often, perhaps, in times past, you have been bold to spend your money in things which you are now ashamed of: it will be a good sign of true repentance, if you overcome your misgivings now, and give freely and boldly for the love of God, though it seem to you at the time as if you could scarcely afford it. David, when he saw such a mind in his people, prayed earnestly that God would keep it in them: for he knew how great a blessing it would bring them from God. His words were, "Now have I seen with joy Thy people, which are present here, to offer willingly unto Thee. O Lord God of Abraham, Isaac, and of Israel, our fathers, keep this for ever in the imagination of the thoughts of the heart of Thy people, and prepare their heart unto Thee." And indeed, what better prayer could a shepherd and Bishop of souls offer for the flock put under his charge, than that they might all have their hearts so set upon pleasing God, as to part willingly with their earthly goods for His sake?

Cast your thoughts onward, my brethren: represent to your minds the last great day; when those who for Christ's sake have "[m] cast their bread upon

[1] Acts xx. 35.   [m] Eccles. xi. 1.

the waters" will "find it" again for ever and ever.
Consider what joy it will be when brethren who are
now at a distance, and cannot in this world know so
much as the names of those who do them good by
giving towards the supply of their spiritual needs,
when they shall meet and own their benefactors before the throne of their God and Saviour! What
joy to hear it said, 'You helped to build or adorn a
Church, and that Church with its solemn worship
was the salvation of my soul.'

Consider again, even in this world, what untold
benefit you may receive by the prayers of those to
whom you give your charitable help. When a
Church is consecrated, there is always a prayer for
those whose pious offerings have provided it—who
would not wish for a part in that prayer? Who
knows how far it may go towards obtaining for him
the grace of true repentance, which is sure to be
followed by pardon for Christ's sake?

May Almighty God make us willing, to our power
and beyond our power, in this and in every good
work.

SERMON XX.

THE UNSPEAKABLE GIFT[*].

---

2 Cor. ix. 15.

"Thanks be unto God for His unspeakable Gift."

THE gift, the free gift, the gift of God, are all of
them expressions occurring in the New Testament
with a higher and more mysterious meaning, than
we are generally apt to take notice of. We are
accustomed, as we read, to think only of this or that
mercy, which in the particular part of the Scriptures
happens to come into our mind: especially, I suppose, when "the free gift" is mentioned, we are apt
to think most of this one great thing, namely, the
pardon and forgiveness of our sins, by the death and
passion of our Lord and Saviour. And truly that
is an unspeakable gift, and by it alone are we made
capable of any other mercy or gift at all: yet it
seems very plain, that pardon and forgiveness by
the Blood of our crucified Lord is not the very
gift, of which so much is said in S. Paul's epistles
and elsewhere. That gift rather means, the Holy
Spirit of the Father and the Son, poured into the
hearts of Christian men to make them partakers of
Christ. It is the Lord God, the Blessed Comforter,

[*] Preached at a collection for Church-building.

dwelling in our hearts to unite us to the Father and the Son: according to His own promise: "[b]If a man love Me, he will keep My words, and My Father will love him, and We will come unto him, and make Our abode with him."

To make this plain to you, I will bring forward all the places, where the gift of God is mentioned, and you will see how well they suit with this meaning, some of them not at all admitting of any other.

The first, and the key to all the rest, is our Lord's saying to the woman of Samaria: "[c] If thou knewest the gift of God, and Who it is that saith unto thee, Give Me to drink, thou wouldest have asked of Him, and He would have given thee living water." The gift of God then is the same as the living water which our Lord here and elsewhere speaks of: and this, we know by S. John's own words, "[d] He spake of the Spirit, which they that believe on Him should receive." The Spirit of God, received in Holy Baptism, is the living water which purifies the whole man: and "[e] as every good gift, and every perfect gift cometh down from the Father of lights," so this in a more especial way, in a way which no words can express, is, as our Lord Himself teaches, "The gift of God."

So it is called repeatedly in the Acts of the Apostles. S. Peter on the day of Pentecost, inviting his hearers into the Church, says, "[f] Repent and be baptized every one of you, and ye shall receive the gift of the Holy Ghost." Afterwards, when he had preached to Cornelius, they who came with him were

[b] S. John xiv. 23.   [c] Ib. iv. 10.   [d] Ib. vii. 39.

[e] S. James i. 17.   [f] Acts ii. 38.

astonished, "ᵍ because that on the Gentiles also was poured out the gift of the Holy Ghost." And giving an account of it afterwards to the Christians of Jerusalem, he uses the word "gift" in the same sense: "ʰ God gave those Gentiles the like gift as He did unto us."

So to Simon the sorcerer, who wanted to buy for money such spiritual powers as the Apostles had, a curse was spoken by the same S. Peter, because he thought "ⁱ the gift of God might be purchased for money." Here again the Holy Spirit is described as being the gift of God. S. Paul too, many times speaks the word in the same sense. As to the Ephesians: "ᵏ Unto every one of us is given grace according to the measure of the gift of Christ: wherefore He saith, when He ascended up on high, He led captivity captive, and gave gifts unto men." This gift of Christ, bestowed after the Ascension, in sundry ways to sundry persons, what is it but the Holy and promised Comforter? No doubt then, the same Divine Person is intended, where the same Apostle speaks a little before of his having been made a minister of the Gospel, "ˡ according to the gift of the grace of God given unto him."

It is the same again, where to the Romans he speaks of "ᵐ the grace of God, and the gift by grace:" first, that is, of His free pardon and favour obtained for us by the Blood of Christ, and then of the actual gift of His Spirit, whereby that favour is sealed and brought home to every one; and where just after he mentions certain persons, as receiving "ⁿ abundance

ᵍ Acts x. 45.   ʰ Ib. xi. 17.   ⁱ Ib. viii. 20.   ʲ
ᵏ Eph. iv.   ˡ Ib. iii. 7.   ᵐ Rom. v. 15.   ⁿ Ib. 17.

of grace and of the gift of righteousness;" the gift of righteousness plainly is, true holiness poured into the hearts of men by the Holy Spirit.

Lastly, in the Epistle to the Hebrews, setting forth the great danger of wilful sin after Baptism, his word is, "° It is impossible for those who were once enlightened, and have tasted of the heavenly gift, and were made partakers of the Holy Ghost, if they shall fall away, to renew them again unto repentance :" thus again intimating, that to taste the heavenly gift is to be made partaker of the Holy Ghost.

These which I have now gone through, are all the places in the New Testament, in which the gift of God, or the heavenly gift, is spoken of, besides that one in the text: "Thanks be unto God for His unspeakable gift." It seems almost certain, therefore, that here also the sanctifying Spirit is meant: the Lord and Giver of life, the gift which includes in itself all other gifts. Well, indeed, is it called unspeakable: for what tongue of man or angel can can speak worthily of so great a thing as this ? God the Holy Ghost, the Good Spirit, in whose unity the Son liveth and reigneth with the Father :—that He should come and make His tabernacle in the souls and bodies of the children of Adam, of man His enemy: that He should vouchsafe to abide there for years, striving against sin and corruption, and changing the heart more and more into the holiness of our Lord and Saviour Himself! Such a thing could never be thought or imagined, much less can it be uttered by the tongue of man : but the more

° Heb. vi. 4.

unspeakable it is, the more it should fill our hearts; and the text seems to teach us that we do well to remember it, and mix it up with all our thanksgivings to the Most High, for any of the lesser mercies, which make part of it or flow from it; just as we make mention of our Lord Jesus Christ, His merits and sufferings, in all our petitions to God.

For how is it that the Unspeakable Gift comes to be mentioned in this part of S. Paul's letter? He had just been speaking of a collection which he had sent to have made in several Churches at a distance, for the benefit of the poorer Christians at Jerusalem. He had been rejoicing in the bountiful and loving temper which the Christians had shown, among whom that collection was made. And he says concerning that kind of charity, that is, alms offered in the Church for Christ's sake, that it carries with it a great blessing, over and above the immediate benefit of the persons for whom it is raised. "[p] The administration of this service," he says, "not only supplieth the necessities of the saints, but is abundant also by many thanksgivings unto God." It lifts up the hearts of those who receive it, with all thankfulness to Christ our Saviour, for many great and signal blessings at once.

"[q] They glorify God," he says, "for your professed subjection to the Gospel of Christ:" that is, 'the Christians of the mother Church of Jerusalem, where the Gospel was first preached, rejoice in the alms which you send to them, not only for the relief they themselves get by it, but also because of the proof it gives them of the wide growth of the

[p] 2 Cor. ix. 12. [q] Ib. 13.

Gospel; that you Gentiles, so far away, should nevertheless be Christians, feeling yourselves brethren with them, and ready to give abundantly for their wants, as members of the same body. And as they thank God for making you Christians, so they pray earnestly in your behalf; they have a longing desire to know you and do you good, which can only be satisfied in this world by earnestly praying for you.'

It is a beautiful and glorious picture, which the holy Apostle here sets before us, of one part of the Communion of saints. Christians as far removed from one another as Jerusalem was from Corinth, not speaking the same language, not knowing one another's names, not in the least likely to meet ever at all in this world, yet with all their hearts trying to do one another good, and obtain a blessing each for his distant brethren by his prayers. No wonder that the thought coming strongly before him, of members of Christ so distant in the flesh, yet so closely bound together in the spirit, their prayers wafted up by their several Angels, and meeting and mingling together, like clouds of incense before the mercy-seat in heaven : no wonder that the sound of their many voices, all praising God and blessing one another, full of all love and thankfulness : no wonder, I say, that the thought and hearing of these things filled the affectionate Apostle with that eager joy, that he could not, if one may say so, contain himself, but cried out with all his heart, "Thanks be unto God for His unspeakable gift."

Because this holy agreement and fellow-feeling, of so many Christians in so many different quarters,

was a kind of token, to the very eye, of their all
being inhabited by the same Holy Spirit, all made
living stones in the same true Temple of the Lord,
all made partakers of the same great unspeakable
gift. It was like the rushing wind, filling all the
house; or like the fiery tongues, settling on every
one: it brought home to the believing soul, with
irresistible force, the gracious presence of the Comforter.

Now the same holy and adoring joy which then
filled the heart of S. Paul, is even now offered, by
the grace and providence of Almighty God, to the
members of His holy universal Church, as often as
they are invited to give alms in the old way, offering them in the Church, for some good and charitable purpose, far away perhaps from themselves.
For though so many years have passed, we trust that
we are still, by God's especial grace, in the same
body, the same household of God, as S. Paul and his
Corinthians were; and if we are of the same body,
then we are sure the same Spirit is among us; nay
(most aweful is the thought), He is within us, to move
men's hearts one towards another; to cause us to be
of one mind in an house; to make us take interest in
the wants of our brethren at a distance, not simply
out of human pity, but because, they are brethren,
" faithful and beloved, partakers of the benefit."

We are not in general used, I should fear, to
think of Church collections of alms in this sort of
way. Too many account it just a convenient method
of gathering what little can be spared, and go away
and think no more of it.

But as nothing which is done in God's house

R

ought to be thought so lightly of, so we have seen that a charitable gathering there is such a thing, as, in the first and best days, filled the heart of the zealous Apostle, and caused it to overflow with joy.

We are bidden to be followers of him, as he also was of Christ. Let us try to have such thoughts of a Church gathering as he had: faint and low they must be in comparison with his, yet they may be the same kind of thoughts. We may use ourselves to consider these occasions, as each being one among the ten thousand ways, in which our Lord and His Spirit shew themselves in His Church.

All Church gatherings may be thus considered: but in this which we have to-day recommended to us, there is something over and above this.

For, in the first place, it is recommended to us by our Bishop: and the approbation of their Bishop is always a special comfort to good Christians, and his presence and direction is a token of Christ's.

Next, the particular purpose of to-day's gathering, is to raise a sum for building and enlarging Churches within this bishoprick to which we belong. Now, a Church, a building set apart and hallowed by the Bishop's prayers and blessings, for solemn prayers, and teaching, and administration of the Sacraments, is one of the plainest outward signs of the presence of the Holy Spirit among us: being the very place where our Lord has promised to be, since there, whoever are gathered together, are surely gathered in His Name.

When we ask an offering, therefore, for the building of Churches, we do in a more particular manner remind one another of the holy unspeakable Gift.

Our very asking means no less than this: 'You have been so many years members of the Body of Christ, endued with His Spirit; you have come here from time to time, trusting to His promise, have heard His holy Word, have received His blessed Sacraments; and now some of your brethren at a distance, who for one cause or another have less share in these outward and visible means of grace, seek to you for aid to be brought nearer their Saviour.'

Perhaps they are inhabitants of some crowded town, where even if they desired to worship God in His Church, they would find it almost impossible to gain admittance, so few and so small are the holy buildings in comparison of the number of people.

Perhaps (and this is the commoner case, in our part of England particularly) they might indeed find room if they came to Church; but the Church is so far from them, that it would be a great charity to help them to one at their own doors.

Perhaps their Church is old and decayed, or so unworthily and meanly fitted up, as to be quite unworthy of the house of the Most High; so that to let it stay as it is, would be bringing on us the rebuke of the Lord by His Prophet: "ᵃIs it time for you, O ye, to dwell in your ceiled houses, and this house to lie waste?"

Surely in each of these cases there is a call on us to feel for our brethren, who are less favourably circumstanced than ourselves. We know, or ought to know, the blessing of having the Church close to us, of being able, without much trouble, to find a place in it when we go there; therefore we ought

ᵃ Hag. i. 4.

R 2

to make a point of sparing something for our less fortunate brethren, who have less of these helps to draw near God, these tokens of the unspeakable Gift. It is but doing as we would be done by.

A good and fair beginning has been made in the work; such as, by God's blessing may help to save many souls; and one way of obtaining that blessing on what has been already done will be, not to grow weary in well-doing, but still to go on offering of what we can spare.

A great deal remains to be done. For taking the whole number of persons in the Diocese, and comparing it with the whole number of places in the several Churches, it appears that there is not room for one-fourth of the people. And another thing to be considered is, that in many crowded places nothing like this quantity of room can be found. In one town, where there are forty-five thousand, and more, there are places for only seven thousand four hundred. Who can doubt that it will be a real charity to help in providing for such cases as that? or a real act of devotion, to give something, as David did, out of regard to God's honour and glory, for making God's service more magnifical, and worthier of a Being so great and glorious?

And may I not be allowed to say, that those especially seem called on to contribute to this fund, who have had the benefit of Churches long ago builded for them, without being called on to contribute any thing themselves.

And this indeed is the case generally with regard to the inhabitants of any country which God's providence long ago made Christian. As the children

there born are made members of Christ before they
can know or choose any thing, so when they grow
up, they find a holy place made ready for their worship, as part of a regular sacred inheritance, without
any cost or labour of their own. Thus, if they be
at all thoughtful persons, the Almighty brings home
to them the fact of their election; their very outward eyes, among the first things they see, are made
aware of this great and distinguishing mercy, that
they are chosen in Christ out of the world, to be
made partakers of His holiness and salvation, while
so many others are left in darkness and the shadow
of death. It is supposed that not above one in four of
those who now live on the earth are called to be
outwardly and nominally Christians. All that we
see are so, and therefore too many of us have thought-
lessly esteemed it a matter of course, and forgotten
to be duly thankful for it. Let us not be always so
childish. Let us realize to ourselves, and never forget, that our being Christians at all is an instance of
mysterious favour towards us, denied to the far greater
part of our fellow creatures, and vouchsafed to us, our
friends, kindred, and countrymen, of God's free and
sovereign grace, surely without any desert of our
own. The more we meditate on this plain truth, and
bring it home to ourselves, the greater surely will
be our fear, lest we fall short in our acknowledgments
of His merciful election. The less we ourselves had
to do with the first foundation of these our Churches,
or with our own admission to them, the more earnestly, as it seems to me, would a right-minded person, a man having true faith, lay hold of all opportunities to praise and thank God for the gift of His

Spirit in His Church, not by words only, but by some free and cheerful offering.

Only let us take care that what we give, be given reverently; not merely given, but offered, with true and real thought of the aweful Presence we are in; and that it be not offered, as I fear sometimes happens, with a heathenish mind, as though alms had some power to make up for sins in some other kind, and prove in themselves satisfactory to Almighty God. Again, that it be offered thankfully, not grudgingly; devoutly, not lightly and at random: and that whilst we are sparing an alms to Churches elsewhere, we lose not the blessing which those alms might have hoped for, by neglecting our own Church, or coming to it profanely.

SERMON XXI.

***

THE HOUSE OF PRAYER.

***

1 Kings viii. 38, 39.

" What prayer or supplication soever be made by any man, or by all Thy people Israel, which shall know every man the plague of his own heart, and spread forth his hands towards this house: then hear Thou in heaven Thy dwelling place, and forgive, and do to every man according to his ways."

THE temple at Jerusalem, concerning which Solomon made this petition to the Lord, was especially intended, we know, to be a house of prayer. The name was expressly given it by the prophet Isaiah. Speaking of the Gentiles, who should one day come in, and join themselves to the Lord and to His people, Isaiah says, in God's Name, "*Even them will I bring to My holy mountain, and make them joyful in My house of prayer." And we know that in all times, whilst that temple lasted, good men, who could conveniently do so, went up to it for their solemn prayers. Hezekiah, when he had a letter that distressed him, went into the temple and spread it be-

* Isa. lvi. 7.

fore the Lord. And the New Testament plainly tells us, first as in our Lord's parable of the pharisee and of the publican, that different sorts of men " went up into the temple to pray :" afterwards that S. Peter and S. John went up there together in one of the Jewish hours of prayer, viz: three in the afternoon. This was the first and most obvious use of Solomon's temple; it was a place for men's coming regularly to worship God. This also all men understand to be a great and special use of such buildings as that in which now, by God's good providence, we are again assembled to hold our feast of dedication. They are houses of prayer, places where people may say their prayers at certain ordained times. All allow that it is the duty of Christians not to forsake the assembling of themselves together for such sacred offices. All thoughtful persons are aware, that if this be wilfully neglected, out of idleness, or pride, or ill custom, nothing can well go right with a man. The despiser of the Church prayers has forfeited God's favour : nothing can go right with him till he has truly repented of that sin. On the other hand, a very great blessing, no less than our Lord's own gracious Presence, is promised to those who wait for Him in His Church with a dutiful and willing mind. He who truly loves Christ, desires of course to be with Christ: and he is with Christ, by virtue of Christ's promise, as often as he comes here to any of the Church's solemn services. For at such times, there are two or three gathered together in Christ's Name, and by His own Word we know, He is of course in the midst of them. For this reason, to every one who has the love of his Saviour in his heart, Church dedications are days of great joy and thanksgiving. Both for ourselves and for brethren and companions we are bound to acknowledge with all our hearts the great goodness of our Redeemer, in thus providing for us that we may draw near Him continually.

This use of a Church is plain and well known to all: but there is another use of it, not so much thought of, yet very true, surely, and real, and very distinctly set forth in holy Scripture. I mean the use which the Church may be of to those even of the place who are hindered from being present at it. Men may remember, when they are elsewhere, what they see and hear in this place: and the remembrance may do them, by God's mercy, much good. I do not now mean so much the instructions which they hear, but the words and order, and tones of the prayers and psalms and hymns and creeds, the parts and ornaments of the building, the Font and the Altar, the decent ceremonies, the white apparel, betokening the inward purity which the Lord expects in those who come to serve Him: all these and the like things put together make up something which cannot be soon forgotten, something which takes hold of men's minds, and which they can cherish there, and turn to, if they will, when they are at a distance from it: just as all people who are not utterly hardened remember their own native homes, the ways and doings, the sights and sounds, the persons and things, to which they were there accustomed: and this remembrance helps greatly to comfort them when they are at a distance, to make them inwardly ashamed of wrong and undutiful ways, and to cheer and encourage them in what they know their parents would approve. The Church is the natural home of Christ's children, and they remember it when they are at a distance from it, and the remembrance does them good somewhat in the same kind of way as we all remember the places on earth most dear to us.

This use of such holy places as that wherein we are now assembled is evidently distinct from the first and principal use of them, though entirely depending on it: still it is a real and a great use, and may afford us on the present occasion matter of profitable thought, and of great thankfulness.

I said, that Holy Scripture sets forth this use of a Church, viz. that those even who cannot come near to worship in it, may have great good by thinking of it at a distance. It could hardly be otherwise when once God had promised to record His Name in any particular town. When He had chosen any one place out of the tribes of Israel to set His Name there, those who had once worshipped in that place would not easily be able to forget it. Wherever else they were saying their prayers the beauty of Jerusalem would have possession of their minds. If they kept the Passover at home, the holy place itself being too far from them, still while they were eating the lamb their thoughts would be with their brethren, more fortunate than themselves, who were even then keeping the same feast in the very place where it ought to be kept.

This would be the natural feeling of devout and dutiful Jews, though nothing were said about it in the Scriptures. But when we come to the psalms

we find that a great deal is said. The psalms were
written, most of them, before the temple was built,
when God's holy place was but a moveable tent:
but even then the souls of devout worshippers were
full of what was to be seen there: their notions of
holy prayer were such as these following: "As for
me, I will come into Thine house, even upon the
multitude of Thy mercy, and in Thy fear will I worship toward Thy holy temple." What the psalmist
most desires is to worship *in* God's house, but if that
cannot be had, he will at least worship *towards* it.
In that way he does what little he can towards accomplishing the desire of his soul, when it is athirst
for God; when he is pouring out his heart by himself, sadly recollecting how he had been used to
conduct the multitude into God's house in the voice
of praise and thanksgiving among such as keep
holiday. He represents to himself the power and
glory of the Lord such as he had been used to see
it in the Sanctuary. In his worst affliction it
gives him hope and comfort, not only to cry unto
God, but also to lift up his hands towards the mercy
seat of His holy oracle. Again, when David is
planning the great work which Solomon finished, a
settled temple for the Lord, this is the way in which
he describes the purposes of it: "[b] We will go into
His tabernacle, and fall low on our knees before His
footstool." We will go into His tabernacle: that is
the first and most evident use of a Church; it is a
place to worship *in:* Then, "we will fall low on our
knees before His footstool;" it is a place to worship
towards. And lastly, when the psalmist is rejoicing

[b] Ps. cxxii. 7.

to have the Angels present in his devotions, he gives
us to understand that such glorious Presence is not
limited to the house of God itself, but vouchsafes itself, wherever people pray in remembrance of that
house.   "Before the gods," i. e. with the Angels all
around me, "will I sing praise unto Thee : I will worship toward Thy holy temple, and praise Thy Name."
Thus earnestly did the holy prophets remember
God's chosen place in their devotions, even when it
was only a tent, and not yet a settled habitation.

And when through Solomon it became settled, and
was builded up as a regular temple, and the day of
consecration was come, this was matter of special
supplication : that God would not only hear the
prayers that were offered up by His people coming
before Him in that place, but would also look graciously upon those prayers which in any other place
should be directed towards Jerusalem.   Solomon in
his long prayer of dedication makes this petition over
and over : " ° Hearken unto the supplication of Thy
servant and Thy people Israel, when they shall pray
towards this place. . . . When heaven is shut up, and
there is no rain, because they have sinned against
Thee ; if they pray toward this place, and confess
Thy Name, and turn from their sin : then hear Thou
in heaven, and forgive."   Again, as in the words of
the text : " If there be in the land famine, if there be
pestilence, blasting, mildew, locust, or if there be
caterpillar ; if their enemy besiege them in the
land of their cities : whatsoever plague, whatsoever
sickness there be : what prayer or supplication soever be made by any man, or by all Thy people Is-

° 1 Kings viii. 30, 35, 36.

rael, which shall know every man the plague of his
own heart, and spread forth his hands towards this
house: then hear Thou in heaven Thy dwelling
place, and forgive, and do to every man according
to his ways." And then he goes on to implore the
like blessing on any foreigner who should pray that
way: on the armies of Israel, turning that way to
say their prayers before a battle: and lastly and
most remarkably on the whole congregation, if at
any time they should be carried away captive for
their sins, and should bethink themselves in the
land of their captivity, and return unto their God,
confessing their sins, and praying towards the land
which God gave to their fathers, the city which He
had chosen, and the temple now builded in God's
honour.

So ran king Solomon's dedication prayer: and it
was not offered up in vain. Many a time, in after
days, we find God's servants in various afflictions,
far away from the temple, yet making it present to
them in thought when they were praying, claiming
and receiving the benefit of Solomon's prayer. Thus
Jonah in the whale's belly, when things seemed at
the worst with him: "I said, I am cast out of Thy
sight; yet will I look again toward Thy holy temple." And so praying, he soon found that he prayed
not in vain. Even while he was calling, God answered; and before he had done speaking God heard.
"When my soul fainted in me," (so says Jonah a
verse or two after,) "I remembered the Lord, and
my prayer came in unto Thee, even unto Thine holy
temple."

Daniel's case is well known: how even in his

busiest time, being as he was the prime minister of
the greatest kingdom then in the world, he yet
found leisure to say his prayers on his knees three
times every day, and that with his window open in
his chamber *toward Jerusalem :* how also he chose
rather to be cast into the den of lions, than even to
seem to leave off this his daily worship, and remembrance of God's fallen house, though but for one day;
and how God sealed His gracious approbation of
these doings of His servant Daniel by sending an
Angel to shut the lions' mouths, so that they could
do him no harm.

Now the very same use which Jonah, Daniel, and
David made of the holy service in the tabernacle or
temple, at times when they could not themselves be
present at it : that very same use we also may make
if we will of the yet holier services, for such we
trust they are, which are celebrated in all our
Churches, some oftener, some seldomer, even when
we are forced to be away from them. We may take
occasion sometimes to pause in our hurried round
of pleasure or business, and imagine ourselves for a
moment with our brethren in Church : we may solemnly say to ourselves some part or other of their
devotions, the Lord's prayer, suppose, or the belief;
uniting ourselves, as we say it alone, in heart and
intention, to them, who say or sing it in company.
The more silently and secretly we do this, the better:
God will surely hear it in heaven : it will be no
secret to our Blessed Saviour. Some Christians before now have made it a rule to offer some such service as this whenever they hear the Church bell go :
they pray in their hearts, wishing that their prayer

may go up together with those prayers, which they know will presently be offered in the solemn assembly. Truly the sound only of a Church bell is an exceeding blessing to a neighbourhood, were it only for the help it gives to thanksgiving, and to thinking of God as always present. Many are the sick beds which have been smoothed, many the aged men and women whose forlorn and helpless state has been effectually comforted, by regularly noticing the bells inviting men to prayer, and endeavouring, though absent in body, to be present in spirit at those prayers. May we not hope, that many a sin too has been prevented, many an evil thought of lust, sloth, pride, or discontent, been stayed and put down at its beginning, by the remembrance of holy services, which persons longed to attend, but were unable? Thus the blessings of a Church in any place go far beyond the inclosure of the Church itself, they are like the fragrance of that precious ointment which S. Mary Magdalene poured on our Blessed Saviour: they cannot be hid: the whole neighbourhood is filled with their odour. And thus we are encouraged to go on offering the Church's daily sacrifice of prayer in her appointed place, (provided we can do it without neglecting other duties) though scarce two or three appear in Church to meet us there. We know not how many are there unseen, not only good Angels and saints, assisting at the solemn services of their brethren on earth, but also among living persons we know not how many may be present in spirit, wishing themselves there, on a sick bed perhaps, or in some far country, repenting that in their days of health they had not made more use of the

Church : or travelling along the road, they may be moved to join us with their good wishes, even if they be altogether unknown.

One thing however is quite plain : that both this use of the Church, and its first and more evident use also, as a place of actual assemblage, will in a great measure be made void, if persons are not careful to train both themselves and those with whom Christ has entrusted them, in true and devout notions of such holy places. For instance ; you see at once that they who wilfully neglect attendance here, or come irregularly, just as the fancy takes them, cannot have so much *remembrance* of the services to do them good at a distance. Again, what a difference between *his* thoughts, who has been used to regard this as just a convenient place for common prayer and hearing sermons, and *his* who has entered it with Jacob's saying in his mind, "d How dreadful is this place ! this is none other than the house of God, and this is the gate of heaven." This is the token and pledge to our very eyes of the holy Church throughout all the world : when we enter in we are at once in the company of the saints and Angels, the martyrs and Innocents, the holy and penitent men and women of all times : and being with them we are with Christ. For as the building is the visible presence of the Church, so is the Church the visible Presence of Christ : Christ diffused through all His members, all Christians, here and elsewhere, living and dead. This is why we desire and pray dearly to love and faithfully to honour our Churches, whether in sight or out of sight : because Christ has pro-

d Gen. xxviii. 17.

mised to be there and they are, we trust, sure tokens of His Presence. This is why we think it well, as did our fathers in the time of Moses, David and the prophets, to turn, in heart towards our Churches, even when we are praying elsewhere. Use your Church in this way, as a true pledge of the Presence of our Saviour, and you know not how much good it may do you, more than you now imagine. Where-ever you are, think sometimes of the Font in which you were baptized; it will help you towards perse-vering in your baptismal vows, or recovering your-self if you have grievously broken them. Think sometimes of the Altar at which you are used to kneel at Holy Communion; it will greatly lift up your heart to your crucified Lord: it will help you in your anxious intercession for all your brethren. Walk by faith, not by sight. Remember the holy things which God allows you to behold, even when they are out of sight; take them as sure signs of His peculiar Presence in your hearts : so shall they be means, through His blessing, of preparing you by degrees for the far holier and more glorious things which as yet no man hath seen nor can see.

SERMON XXII.

CHRIST PRESENT IN HIS CHURCH.

Ezek. xlviii. 35.

" The Name of the city from that day shall be, The Lord is there."

Now that we have been permitted, by God's good Providence, to bring our Church work so nearly to a completion, and our Consecration Day is actually fixed: what are the thoughts which best become us as Christian men, desiring to make the most of all His good gifts and undeserved mercies? For certainly *some* religious thought we must have: no dutiful affectionate heart will let such an event pass lightly away, like something in a dream, unnoticed and unimproved. If a man were but changing his own abode, it would be a serious matter and might well remind him of the last great change: how much more, when in common with all his neighbours he is called on to meet his God, coming as we hope mysteriously but really to dwell among us again in the same place where we have been used to meet Him.

And the first thought is one of thankfulness, earnest thankfulness to Him Whose Name is Merciful, that He has brought us so nearly to the end of our work without any calamity or accident: there have been no severe falls, no hurt of life or limb, to cause a sad and bitter recollection when we think of the undertaking in after years. Hitherto the Lord (blessed be His Name) hath helped us. Neither is it a small thing that He has watched us with His protecting providence, and given His holy Angels charge over us, so that while the very air all around has been full, as it were, of great calamities, we have been left free to serve Him and do the work of His house in peace. Would we had done it more worthily! For the months that have passed since we began to open our new foundations have been no ordinary months. On all sides around us the wrath has been going out from the Lord. We began almost in famine: we have gone on in wars and rumours of wars: we end in alarm of something like pestilence. But none of it has come nigh us: as He has kept all our bones and suffered none of them to be broken; so has He preserved us from the beggary and decay, which have fallen now for some time on so many around us. He has given us bread to eat and raiment to put on: our labours have not been interrupted by the interference of unkind enemies, as the Jews were interrupted in building the second Temple, neither have we been brought to a stand, as so often happens, for want of means; but we have been helped steadily on, and trust to be helped even unto the end. O, surely we cannot think enough of it: we cannot do less than give ourselves up entirely to Him Who has so far accepted us and our weak doings.

Surely also we must feel that the great duty of
the time is to address ourselves in earnest to the
making of such preparation as our Lord and His
holy Angels will expect of us, that we may come
into His house, when it shall be opened again, with
reverent and dutiful hearts. It would be a great
pity, when we have done what little we can towards
the outward beauty and solemnity of the holy place
and its Services, that after all it should be made un-
pleasing in God's sight, as the temple of Jerusalem
was in old time, by our coming thither unclean and
unprepared. And though it would be a far less evil,
yet it would be an evil greatly to be regretted, if
any of us, for want of being put in mind, should
enter the gates of God's restored sanctuary, with
thoughts not indeed wrong in themselves, yet not
so very deep and serious as the occasion clearly requires. For instance, I can imagine a person thinking most of the comfort it will be to come back to
the old Church and Church-yard, and worship God
nearly in the old place, and with more convenience
and comfort than now: and not lifting his thoughts
any higher. Or again, I can imagine some of us
carried away by the fair beauty and proportion of the
work or some part of it, or by something else which
may take their fancy there: and *resting* in that: not
endeavouring to use such things as steps whereby to
climb higher, but contenting themselves with the
present satisfaction of seeing and hearing. Or we
may let ourselves be carried away by mere excitement
and curiosity, as people are apt to be about all new
things. There is no doubt that in these or in some
other ways the Evil one will be busy among us just

now, to hinder our making that use of God's goodness which He, we may be sure, intends. He intends that His house, and whatever is done regarding it, should always put us in mind of His near and immediate Presence. See how He taught His prophet Ezekiel to finish the long account of the vision which he saw of the temple at the end of his prophecy. "The name of the city from that day shall be, The Lord is there." As much as to say that when the people should have returned to Jerusalem, as we read in the book of Ezra, God would also return to His temple, and would go on to be present there. It was to be always His house, the place of His abode, the place where people must go in order to meet Him. As such, it was a type and figure of the holy Church throughout all the world, the Body of Christ, wherein He dwells by His Spirit. It was also a type of heaven, that blessed place, whereof the peculiar blessing is, that there, "*the tabernacle of God is with men, and He dwelleth with them, and they are His people: and God Himself is among them and is their God." But if the temple at Jerusalem was thus a figure and a pledge of Heaven, and of the Church Universal in her glory, to all who look after it: so also, doubt it not, is each particular Church: and when for any cause a new Church is set up in a place, or an old one thoroughly repaired, the day of the Bishop's coming to bless and hallow it is a day on which we may well say of that place, "The name of it from this day shall be, The Lord shall be there." From this day forth all Christian people shall know for certain, that in coming near to it they are coming

* Rev. xix. 3.

near Christ, and in entering into it they are entering into Christ's shadow. Christ will be henceforth in that place, in a way and manner in which He is not in ordinary places. That is the great thing, 'Christ will be there:' and we, in order to go there worthily, must of course go, as if to meet Christ.

Consider then, my brethren : how would it be with us, if we knew for certain that on the day appointed our Lord would come visibly down (as He did sometimes by His Angels in the Old Testament) and would take possession of this our restored building, and there would remain, Sundays and week-days, to receive us and our children coming to worship Him, and to bless us with His good gifts? As we should wish to behave then, so let us behave now, and we cannot be wrong. What if you knew beforehand, that on the Church door being opened, as soon as you entered in, you would see our Lord Jesus Christ both God and Man, with His glorified Body, sitting on a glorious high Throne over the Altar? Would you not wish to come with a heart full of deep reverential devotion, giving up your whole self to Him, and not to your knowledge, keeping back anything at all? If He called to you from that Throne, to come near and confess your sins, would you not presently fall on your knees, and not merely own yourself one among other miserable sinners, but tell Him your own sins in special, trying and praying to be truly contrite for them? If He told you, 'Now I am going to pronounce the absolution, Now I am going to say, " [b] Thy sins be forgiven thee," ' would you not listen with all your heart for the blessed words, and

[b] S. Matt. ix. 2.

drink them in as the sure words of comfort, and pray
and vow that never whilst you live might you do anything to forfeit them ? If you heard Him say, ' Now
you may pray to Me, now I am ready to attend to your
wants, and here is My own prayer which you may
use ; I shall know your meaning :' would you not fall
down and say the Lord's prayer with all the devotion you could use both of soul and body ? If He
gave the signal for you to praise Him, and if the great
prophet David at His command sounded out the first
note of praise : could you help doing your best to join
in that psalm with the best of your heart and voice ?
If He began to teach, which of us would not hold his
breath to hear ? If He spread out His Divine Hands
to give us His solemn blessing, would you not think
very much of it, and try to receive it as meekly and
thankfully as you could, and altogether to behave
so that you might be sure of carrying it home with
you ? Above all, if He began to say, "°Come eat of
My Bread, and drink of the Wine which I have
mingled :" "ᵈMy Flesh is meat indeed, and My Blood
is drink indeed :" you would not surely in wilfulness
refuse to come unto Him, that you might have life :
neither would you have the heart to draw near in
your uncleanness, affronting Him to His face.

This, I trust, would be your mind, if you were to
see our Lord in His glorious Body, waiting to receive
you on your entrance into the Church. Only have
so much faith as to believe that He is there, although
you see Him not with your eyes, that He is there
for all these gracious purposes ; and you will see at
once what your mind and your behaviour should be

° Prov. ix. 5.   ᵈ S. John vi. 55.

now. You will not see Him, but He will see you.
He will hide Himself on purpose, that He may try
our faith. And the great trial of our faith will be
this: that as we try to make ourselves outwardly
clean and decent when we are to come to Church,
in respect to His aweful Presence; and as even for
the same reason we desire to make His holy place
and the holy things in it venerable and beautiful even
in their outward appearance; so we should above all
be careful to cleanse and prepare our souls, or ever we
go in there. We should get ready to meet Christ in
His Church, as we would get ready to meet Him in
heaven. If we have not hitherto considered it, now
at least let us consider how sad and shocking it must
be, to appear continually before our God and Judge
and seem to confess our sins, while in reality we are
flattering ourselves that we have little or no real sin
to confess: let us reflect what the Angels must
think of us, if while we pretend to join in psalms we
are not even trying to fix our thoughts upon God:
and how we can expect our prayers to do us any good,
if we make no real effort to turn from the sins which
we pray against, and obtain the virtue and grace
which we ask. If such unhappily has been the custom of any one of us hitherto, now let him make a
strong effort: now let him rouse himself once for all,
and break the chain of his evil and dangerous habit.
Let him by God's blessing make a good and firm re-
solution, that the new Church shall never see him
behaving as ill as the old Church did. If he went
in and out there without reverence, let him now
make a rule to himself, never to enter in here without recollecting, "*How dreadful is this place: this is

* Gen. xxviii. 17.

none other than the house of God, and this is the gate
of heaven." If he permitted himself there to talk
and gaze around him, now let him set a watch upon
his mouth and keep the door of his lips: let him
make a covenant with his eyes that they rest not on
anything which may lead his heart astray from God.
If he have disregarded the rules of the Church, sitting when he ought to have knelt, and remaining
silent when he ought to have joined in the responses,
now let him use his Prayer-book in good earnest,
and not bring it here as if merely to show how little
he cares for it. If he has come and gone, week after
week, and is conscious that God's All-seeing Eye
has discerned in him little or no improvement: his
evil habits yet unsubdued, his temper undisciplined,
his words uttered at random, his prayers too often
unsaid, or hurried over: let him now make up his
mind, by the grace of God, to use the new Church
as a real help in reforming himself: let him go there,
not only when he is in the humour, but regularly,
and always let him examine himself how he has behaved, and what good thing he has gained. For
coming before God must needs be a serious thing:
if a man is not the better for it, there is too much
reason to fear he may be the worse.

And not only in respect of our behaviour in
Church itself, and of the use we make of the services
and sermons there, but in respect of our whole
Christian behaviour and being, towards God, our
neighbour and ourselves, it will be well if we make
such a moment as this a kind of turning point.
Every great change, no doubt, is so intended by our
heavenly Teacher. Whether it be for comfort or

discomfort, for joy or sorrow, the changes and turns of a man's life all come upon him with a kind of awakening power: they rouse him up, as it were, to consider, What next?   So it is when people alter their abode, or their state of life, or their profession. All such things are so many providential calls on us, to reflect on our past conduct and future hopes: how we stand before God, whether our faces are towards heaven or hell: and many a man by God's blessing has been led at such times to begin a happy change of life.   Now what more suitable moment for such reformation, than when we are invited to take part in the services of a new Church, for the first time? All of us, my brethren, I am quite sure, know of something in ourselves which ought to be mended; something seriously amiss in our heart and behaviour. There is not one but has somewhat about him, somewhat in his life and conduct which he would be very sorry to bear with him to his grave.   He lives in hope of improving it some day: only as yet he has been irresolute and imperfect.   Now then what I say is, let *this* be the time of improvement.   Wait no longer: wait not till to-morrow, for to-morrow may never come: but wisely and resolutely from this day foward, set yourself to fight against that evil, whatever it be.   Do not say, What is there so much in a new Church, why should I care for that so much more than for the old one?   Rather make use of any good thought which the merciful grace and providence of Almighty God may dart, as it were, into your mind, on such an occasion as this.   Should there be anything in the new building which on your first entering may seem grave and aweful, and remind

you of God's Presence: keep fast hold of that
thought, take it away with you out of Church, pray
to our Lord to make it habitual to you.   Or if there
be anything in the psalms which delights you, in
the voices of many joining with one accord, and it at
all comes into your mind to think, 'So and much
more it is in heaven; all there is perfect harmony:
what if my worldly untuneable heart should exclude
me for ever from that most blessed company?"—encourage that fear, for it is a godly and wholesome
fear: and try by all means, night and day, to bring
your ways and thoughts into agreement with the
ways and thoughts of the saints.   Speak, act, live,
in such a way, as may not jar, nor be unseemly,
compared with the heavenly music and beauty of
God's house.

In any case, as I said before, try to make this
change of God's house, a happy change for your own
souls.   Turn to Him in earnest, you who have not yet
done so.   You who have made a good beginning, but
are yet far from steady consistent walking; clear
off now, by little and little, the remnant of your bad
habits.   Look about you: see what is to be done:
plan how to do it: begin in earnest: go on manfully :~lose no time.   Confess, make amends, forgive;
judge and deny yourselves, according to the Scriptures: be more ashamed of sinning and less ashamed
to confess your sins: never grow tired of the work
of repentance.   Since you are called to be where
God is, strive to be holy as He is holy: to perfect
holiness in the fear of Him.   To this end, use yourself to discern Him in all things: not in beautiful
Churches only, but in all His works, and in all the

ways of His providence. O, if each one of us would thus set himself in earnest to obey this call of our God, it would prove to us a blessed and joyful time indeed.

I beseech you all, pray in your hearts for such help of God's Holy Spirit, that our new Church may never be profaned by rude irreverent wilful behaviour, as the old one too often was: that no hypocrite may come near it, except to repent and amend; and that every visit we pay to it may prove to each one of us a step in the way to heaven.

SERMON XXIII.

THE HOLY EUCHARIST THE CROWN AND CENTRE OF CHRISTIAN WORSHIP.

Rev. xxii. 14.

" Blessed are they that do His commandments, that they may have right to the tree of life, and may enter in through the gates into the city."

Here the Holy Spirit sets before us a picture. We may conceive in our minds a number of travellers, approaching to the gates of the holy city, new Jerusalem, and waiting till the gates be quite opened, and they may see whether they shall be allowed to enter in. We seem to behold the city, all bright and glorious, all gold and precious stone, only far brighter and more precious than anything we see on earth. The gates are so far open that those who are near enough may look in and see growing in the streets the tree of life, the immortal, never failing tree, growing by the side of the water of life : ever fresh with leaves, ever loaded with fruit : the leaves of the tree being for the healing of the nations, and the fruit such, that if a man put forth his hand and take thereof in due season, he shall live for ever. And no man may enter in, nor taste of this tree, but they who in earnest keep the commandments of God.

In all this, you presently see, the holy writer
would have us bear in mind the account of our first
father Adam, and of the Paradise from which he was
driven. We seem to behold him waiting as it were
outside the gates through which he had passed in
the day of his sin, anxiously looking and longing
for the time, when for His sake Who is the true
Seed of the woman, he and those who had fallen
through him may be admitted again to his first
blessed privileges: when the Angel who keeps guard
at the gate will let him enter in once more, and not
lift up the flaming sword to repel him: when being
let in, he may go straight to the tree of life, and put
forth his hand, and take of that tree, and eat and
live for ever.

This condition which was in a manner Adam's
condition just after the fall, is also in a very true
sense a type of that in which we are all now living.
For we are yet without the gates of heaven: the
best account that can be given of the most perfect
on earth, is that he is waiting beside those gates.
Bye and bye, when our Lord shall come, the gates
will be thrown wide open, and then it will be seen
whether we shall be admitted or no. If we are admitted, we know not yet what we shall be; but thus
much we know, that we shall have access to the tree
of life, i. e. to the Cross of Christ, and to Him that
hung thereon, and became the fruit of that tree for
our sake. We now see Him "through a glass
darkly; then" we shall behold Him openly, "face
to face:" now we feed on Him sacramentally, then
we shall partake of Him by some far higher communion, beyond what can be now imagined. And all

will depend on our keeping and doing His commandments.

This is our condition in respect of heaven: it is also too like the condition of most of us in respect of the highest Church privileges. For the Church of God is our glorious city, our heavenly Jerusalem, our paradise, our heaven on earth. In one sense we are not waiting without the gates of it, since we were all admitted there by holy Baptism. But in another sense, too many of us are still without: in that they go not in to partake of the tree of life, the Body of Christ offered to them in Holy Communion. All would be set right, if they would in earnest apply themselves to the keeping of the commandments. Blessed are they that do so: for here is God's own Word, saying, that they and they only "have right to the tree of life, and may enter in through the" inner "gates into" the most glorious part of "the city."

Now as the vision of S. John in the book of Revelation represented all this to his inward eye, so the very frame and arrangement of a Christian Church represents it to our outward eyes, if we will but attentively consider it. For the Church, the holy building where the Lord has come and vouchsafes to dwell, is as it were a paradise, a heaven upon earth. And the sacrament of the Holy Communion is the tree of life in the midst of that garden: seeing that in it we partake of Christ Who is our life. The gates whereby sinners are admitted to this and all other divine privileges are first holy Baptism, and afterwards, our Lord's Absolution: Baptism making them in the first place members of Him, and our

Saviour's Absolution afterwards restoring that com‑
munion and fellowship when it had been interrupted
by sin.   Whereas therefore, on going into a Church
we see presently that one portion of it is in a manner
parted off from the rest, the portion, namely, which
we call the Chancel, as if there were something espe‑
cially sacred about it: this signifies that the Holy
Communion is the highest act of Christian religion
on earth, and the Presence of our Lord therein
nearer and more gracious than His Presence in any
other way.   Again, whereas holy Baptism is as it
were the wicket of entrance, the straight gate and
the narrow way for admitting people into God's
house: we ordinarily see the font or place of Bap‑
tism very near us at the first coming under the sha‑
dow of a Church.   And again, the place where the
priest stands, to give us our Lord's Absolution, after
we have confessed our sins, is commonly by the en‑
trance of the chancel: to signify that in no other
way, but only upon the Voice of our Redeemer and
Judge, saying to us, "[b] Thy sins be forgiven thee,"
can we be warranted in drawing near to partake of
His aweful Sacrifice.   We make ourselves clean,
and put on decent apparel, to signify the marriage
garment of Christian righteousness, and without
which whosoever cometh in is sure to be "[c] cast into
outer darkness, where is weeping and gnashing of
teeth."   We men uncover our heads, to testify our
deep reverence for our heavenly Lord and King, into
Whose especial Presence we are coming.   But the
women keep their heads covered, in token of de‑
cency, modesty, and submission.   All, when they

[b] S. Matt. ix. 2.   [c] Ib. viii. 8.

pray are turned towards the Chancel, for the same
reason that they finish their prayers with saying
"Through Jesus Christ our Lord;" namely that
they may remind themselves continually that their
prayers are nothing without faith in His aweful and
merciful Sacrifice. All stand up when they say the
Creed, signifying that they hope to stand stedfast in
that faith, and continue Christ's true soldiers: and
all at the same time look towards the Altar, because
the very chiefest point of that faith is to believe on
Christ crucified, and He has ordained the Sacrament
of the Lord's Supper to be a continual remembrance
of that Sacrifice. One might keep on a long while,
explaining in like manner other parts and other circumstances of Divine service: and one should find
concerning one and all of them, that they agree in
pointing out to us the Holy Communion as the very
greatest and holiest of all things that are done in
the Church. The very outward look and sound of
things, all that we see and hear around us, seems to
say that without attendance on the holy Altar all is
incomplete, and that if we do but rightly attend
there, all else is sure to go right. The tree of life,
planted within the city, is that one blessing which
comprehends all others, and for the sake of which
chiefly we are invited to enter in at all. Blessed
are they that have a right to it: they, and they
only, may enter in through the gates of that eternal
city, of which these our visible Churches are no more
than signs and tokens. Blessed are they that come
worthily to the holy Altar: they, and they only,
have the full promise of eternal life. Any person
who should have entered into that first paradise,

T

which the Lord planted for Adam in Eden, would no doubt first be caught by the tree of life in the midst of the garden. We may suppose by what is written in Genesis, that all eyes would be drawn towards that one tree: all the rest, how fair and noble soever, would seem to be gathered around it, and to wait upon it. Not otherwise, on entering into a Church, is the eye and heart of a believer drawn towards that one place, where He Who is the Fruit of the true Tree of Life gives us His Flesh to be our Meat indeed, and His Blood to be our Drink indeed. The whole Church looks as it were towards the Chancel and the Altar table: not for any holiness that naturally is in that place more than the rest, but for His sake, Who vouchsafes to be there with us continually, offering the remembrance of His most precious Death, and feeding us with what He offers.

My brethren; attend to this, I beseech you. The whole Church, looks to the Altar: and shall not we, the worshippers, do the same? Observe what the Holy Ghost tells us of the rules and orders of the Christian paradise. "Blessed are they that do His commandments; *they* have a right to the Tree of life; *they* may enter in through the gates." Does it not plainly appear, that entering into the city through the gates is only in order to the tree of life? that it is vain and dangerous for any man to depend upon his Baptism, his faith, his good character, or any thing else, as a mark of his being within the city, while he wilfully neglects this Sacrament? Surely there can be no doubt of it. Partaking of Christ must be all in all to a Christian. And how can you partake of Him, if you slight and pass over that way of doing so, which He specially ordained?

It is very true that not all persons, calling themselves Christians, have right to this tree of Life. Too many, alas! are leading such lives, that even if they were heathen and unbaptized we could not ask them so much as to receive Baptism, without first making a great change in their goings on. They are not fit as yet to enter through the gates: neither then, being in the city, are they fit to eat of the tree of Life. It would be mere profaneness: it would do them more harm than good. I speak not to such: but to all others, whether innocents or penitents, I say, 'Come near, eat and live, your Saviour invites you to eat bread with Him:' "ᵈ O taste and see how gracious the Lord is:" "ᵉ Come eat of His Bread, and drink of the Wine which He hath mingled:" "ᶠ Come, buy wine and milk without money and without price." Some of us, I fear, are apt to regard these many gracious invitations of our Lord, as if they related to something over and above the common way of salvation: to a sort of spiritual enjoyment, not at all to the very substance and necessary being of a Christian's life. Some of us are used to look on this Sacrament as a kind of thing which does many a great deal of good, but which they themselves may very well do without. I would they would consider it seriously over again. Christ says, You *may* come: none of you can deny *that:* but you think He does not say, you *must* come. But surely, where there is true love and dutifulness, there is no difference between *may* and *must*. If a father say to his son,

ᵈ Ps. xxxiv. 8. ᵉ Prov. ix. 5. ᶠ Isa. lv. 1.

T 2

'Now you may come near, my child, and receive my blessing,' and the child were to disregard it, saying in his heart, 'He does not say, You *must* come:' could you look upon such an one as on a good and obedient child ? Nay, good Christians, you may be quite sure, that if Christ says, You *may* come, then you *must* and *ought* to come; for love and gratitude's sake, and for your soul's good, you *ought* to come; though it be a great undertaking, though there be more or less of doubt and danger and jeopardy in it.

For love's sake you ought to come, and for fear's sake also : for how can you live without it ? As you cannot live the life of this world without constant supplies of meat and drink : so neither can you live the spiritual and heavenly life without constant supplies of the Body and Blood of Christ. You have heard His words over and over, many of your children know them by heart: I will now say them to you once again: "s Except ye eat the Flesh of the Son of Man, and drink His Blood, ye have no life in you." Are you not afraid when you hear this, as many as have hitherto neglected Holy Communion ? Is it not alarming, when you consider, how fast the time is passing, and as yet you have only had good imaginations and half purposes to come: as yet the Holy meal is untasted of by you: as yet you will not come to Christ, that you may have life.

I have no doubt there are many, among those who are not yet communicants, who really intend and wish to become so ere long. They hear these warnings from time to time, they see their neighbours draw near, while they turn their backs, they feel,

s S. John vi. 53.

they cannot but feel, that the days, months, years, are passing faster and faster away, and they have not yet come to Christ, that they might have life. Their parents brought them when they were children, but they have never yet come of their own accord. I make no question but there are many who feel this, and really intend to begin or to renew the good custom, if left off, some time or other. I say to them all, Why not begin now? Why not take occasion, from the solemn opening of this new Church of ours, to set in order the things that are wanting, and thoroughly prepare to meet your God? It is something out of the common: depend upon it, our merciful God intends it in His Fatherly providence as one call more upon you to consider your ways. The Bishop's coming, were that all, is a great thing: for the Bishop stands, as you know, in the place of our Lord and Saviour: his coming is a true token of our Lord's coming: his presence in Holy Communion, a token of our Lord's most sure and certain Presence with us. Again, when you enter our new Church, you will see I hope with your eyes, many things, which will draw your hearts towards Holy Communion. All, you will perceive, points eastward, because there God's Altar is set. The Chancel is fitted up more carefully and beautifully than the other parts of the Church, because there especially Christ comes to give us Himself. These very words on which I have been speaking to you are engraven on the step which leads from the body of the Church to the Chancel: I mean the words, "Blessed are they that do His commandments, that they may have right to the tree of life, and may enter in through the gates into the city." These things, and whatever else we may see and hear, which may put us in mind of the greatness of Christ's last Sacrament, I would we might all take them as so many calls from Him Who we trust will be there; calls uttered to every one of us: to those who are yet in their sins, saying, 'Behold here what I suffered for you, see here the remembrance of My Cross: can you have the heart to go on, rejecting Me and ruining yourselves for ever?' To those again, who are trying in earnest to repent, Christ will speak from our Chancel and say, "[i] Blessed are they that mourn, for they shall be comforted:" to those who have kept their hearts pure, or are trying in earnest to purify them, He will say, "[k] Blessed are the pure in heart for they shall see God:" and to all, both bad and good, who seek to Him earnestly desiring to be made better than they are, He will say, "[l] Blessed are they that do hunger and thirst after righteousness: for they shall be filled."

One call especially Christ utters to us all *to-day*, which I am sure we must all feel in our hearts to be a very grave and serious call indeed: I mean the notice which you just now heard, that in the new Church it is hoped by God's blessing to celebrate the Holy Communion every week. I have thought it right to give this notice: but I could wish to do it in much fear and trembling: for it is a very great undertaking, surely: and requires on the part of those who make use of it, more earnest care of their souls than ever. To those who truly endeavour to prepare themselves it will, I trust, be a real step towards

[i] S. Matt. v. 4.   [k] Ib. 8.   [l] Ib. 6.

heaven : but we must all beware of growing weary in well doing : we must all watch and pray more earnestly than ever against that most frightful danger, which frequent Communion of course brings with it, of feeding ourselves without fear.

And let us all pray for one another, that our weak endeavours to serve and honour our Lord most especially in His Holy Communion may be accepted in Him Who is All and in all ; our many and most grievous sins pardoned, and our few remaining days so ordered, that our very prayers and Churches and Sacraments may not hereafter rise in judgement against us, and condemn us.

SERMON XXIV.

THE PRESENCE OF THE EVIL ONE AT HOLY TIMES AND IN HOLY PLACES.

Job i. 6.

*" There was a day when the sons of God came to pre-
sent themselves before the Lord, and Satan came
also among them."*

A VERY startling and fearful thought, surely: that
the Evil one should be present among the good
Angels, that in the glorious assembly itself, which
is round the throne of God in heaven, *he* should be
any how permitted to appear, who for his pride and
rebellion was long ago cast down from heaven. *How*
it should be so, we cannot at all imagine, but that so
it is we may not doubt, for Holy Scripture plainly
declares it. That Satan does somehow present himself before God among the good Angels, appears not
only from this place, but from a well known passage
in the book of Kings also; where the prophet sees
" ᵃ the Lord sitting on His throne, and all the host of
heaven standing by Him on His right hand and on
His left:" and a spirit comes forth, and offers, and
is permitted to deceive Ahab by putting a lie in the

ᵃ 1 Kings xxii. 12.

mouth of the prophets whose advice he took. It is
a strange and fearful thought, when we read of the
author of all evil coming as it were so very close to
the great and holy God, the only Author and Giver
of all good: but it is no wonder, to us who know
that he once went still further, he even tempted the
Son of God to sin. Three times he came near and
tried to make the most holy Jesus break the laws
of His Father. If he was permitted to do that, we
need not be too much surprised at his finding a place,
as in this history, among the blessed Angels, though
he never could be as one of them, and getting leave
to tempt and try holy Job, as he did unholy Ahab.
We cannot understand how it should be so: we
cannot understand how a good God should bear
with evil at all: but we know it is so: and Scripture tells us so much of it, in order to put us continually on our guard. Further: it should seem that
one purpose at least of the devil, in entering into
the solemn assembly of Angels, was to bring an evil
report upon God's faithful servant Job: enviously
making the least of Job's goodness, and ascribing it
in good measure to a mere selfish desire of being
prosperous in this world. This is especially his part,
in that he *is* the *devil:* the false accuser; for that
is what the word devil, properly means. As he
was a murderer, so was he also from the beginning
a false accuser. The book of Revelations calls him,
" [b] the accuser of our brethren, which accuseth them
before our God day and night." This is just what
we find him doing to Job. As our Lord is always
pleading for us, so Satan, it would appear, is always

[b] Rev. xii. 10.

pleading against us: bringing our iniquities before
God, and our secret sins in the light of His countenance.   As it is in the prophet Zechariah: there is a
vision of the high priest, Joshua, standing before the
Angel of the Lord, and Satan standing at his right
hand to resist him.   That as the good and friendly
Angels bring our prayers and our good works for a
memorial before God; as one in the book of Revelations offers incense with the prayers of all saints
on the golden altar which is before the throne: so
Satan on the other hand should be allowed to practise his spite against us even in the court of heaven,
and as good men in the Church have always believed,
in the hour of death and in the day of Judgement,
those are two moments in which the assaults of our
ghostly enemy are to be more than usually apprehended : and therefore against those two most criti-
cal and dangerous moments, we must lay up in store
all the helps we can obtain, we must provide ourselves with abundance of spiritual armour, proved
and well tempered, for our last and most fearful
combat.   Think of the matter so, and you will
perceive that the day mentioned in the text, wherein
the sons of God came to present themselves before
the Lord, may have been a type of the Day of
Judgement: and as Job, by truthfulness and patience, was prepared for the one, so may we, by
God's mercy, be prepared in like manner for the
other.

But the special point to be learned by Job's history, to which I would call your attention to-day, is
this : that in all our solemn meetings for prayer and
praise, and even for the receiving the most holy Sa-

craments of Christ, we have reason to apprehend
that the Evil one, the enemy of praise, the abuser
of Sacraments, and he who turns prayer into sin, is
at hand. In this lower world there is no place free
from him: like the air, whereof he is called the
prince, he finds admission everywhere, winds himself into every place, is present unseen to breathe a
curse and a blight upon our blessings, if we guard
them not by humility and devout care.

It is sad to think that on bright and happy days
like this, when we meet to give God thanks for His
mercy in providing us a Church, there should be
need to make mention of Satan as being among us.
And yet, my brethren, if it is the truth (and none
can gainsay it, it is too plainly written and declared in the book of God), it must be necessary for
us to think of. If the danger is close at hand, we
must be on our guard. And therefore I know you
will bear with me, if even on this feast and good
day I direct your thoughts to this aweful and sorrowful subject, Satan present in our Churches—in
this Church—doing his best to corrupt and spoil our
privileges. A serious heart, believing this to be
true, can hardly help learning from it such lessons
as these following.

First, that if even he, the Evil one, the enemy of
God and man, is here, it can be no great matter for
any one of us to praise himself for, that he is here:
we know that ignorant persons sometimes do so;
they value themselves upon their careful Church-
going, and seem to rely upon that as a sufficient token
that all is right, and they are in a safe way. I say,
to such as these it ought to be a sufficient reproof,

that if coming to Church were all, Satan himself
would be in no such bad way, since Holy Scripture
tells us of his coming among the sons of God to present himself before the Lord.

Further, Scripture teaches that Satan's employment
concerning us, both here and in other places, is partly
to note our faults, and accuse us for them before our
God, partly to tempt us, and lead us away from goodness. Do you not see then how circumspect you
ought to be, the moment you enter within these holy
walls? You know the good Angels are looking down
on you, you see on each side figures to remind you of
their presence, it is well that you should remember
the presence of the wicked angel also. Remember,
he is watching you; take care to give him no advantage. Let him not have to write down against you
now, to plead against you by and by, On such a day
that man profaned God's holy service by unclean,
envious, unholy looks and ways, he brought his common every-day thoughts and behaviour into the
temple, he would not listen, nor learn, nor take warnings. Remember, yet more seriously, that he is very
likely tempting you: at least you know he is always
seeking opportunity to do so. Alas, we have, most
of us, too much reason to know this. We know it
by what we see, and have seen; and still more sadly,
we know it by what we feel, and have felt. Our
inward consciousness helps us but too certainly to
understand what we see in others' outward behaviour.
We see men or women coming rudely or irreve-
rently into a Church: we see them sit down at once
in their places, without any acknowledgement of
God's Presence, such as all good Christians are used

to make in the most reverent posture they can : we
see their roving looks, their unsteady behaviour:
too plainly we see how little they are minding the
holy work for which they profess to have come. We
see these things, whereby the great God and our
Saviour is every day affronted to His face, and we
are not at all surprised at it: we understand it, most
of us, too well, by our own distressing experience,
by the evil inclinations and fancies which keep on in-
terrupting our prayers : by our wandering thoughts,
sometimes merely idle and foolish, sometimes positively bad and corrupt: all this we know, more or
less, of ourselves, conscience reproaches us with it:
and we are not therefore much astonished at the outward ill-behaviour of others. But what is it which
interrupts us, even when we wish to attend, and say
our prayers in a Christian manner ? We have great
reason to believe that it is in part the work of the Evil
spirit. Why did that Pharisee in our Saviour's parable spend all the time of his devotions in proudly
comparing himself with others, and making out that
he was better than they ? There seems to have been
in that man a great deal of good: he was what would
commonly be called a decent religious person: he
fasted, and paid tithes very exactly : he was not an
extortioner, nor dishonest, nor an adulterer: but he
listened to the evil whispers of the devil, who came
with him into the temple, and persuaded him that
he was not as other men are, but far better, and so
he lost all the fruit of his goodness and his very
prayer was turned into sin. It may be, some of us
may have been tempted before now to the error of
that Pharisee. In Church, in prayer, on our knees,

yea even before God's Altar, yea even in the very
act of receiving our Lord in His Sacrament, we may
have given way, for a time, to that sad way of praising and thinking well of ourselves : and we have at
least lost, or greatly damaged, the fruit of that prayer,
or that Communion. And often again, as that Pharisee did, so we have allowed unkind notions, unchari-
table suspicions of other men, perhaps far better than
ourselves, to mingle with our meditations at such
holy times.   Sometimes again the disturbing thought
has been different; it was not pride in ourselves,
it was not uncharitableness towards our neighbour,
but it was doubt and mistrust towards God which
came over our fancies, even in the midst of our most
solemn services to God.   There have been passing
thoughts, too distressing to mention exactly, as if
there were no God, no God at least that cared for
us : as if our prayers and Sacraments were nothing.
Why was all this ? it was not always, nor altogether,
with our own full consent.   The proud, the unchari-
table, the unbelieving fancy semed to come of itself.
We did not drive it away as we should have done :
but neither did we seek it in the first instance.   How
came it ? Whence did it arise ? Surely through envy
of the devil came this mischief upon us in the Church.
The whole disturbance was his doing: we indeed
might be greatly blameable for too easily admitting
the bad thought, and not turning it out immediately :
but still he it was who introduced it.

Thus you see what reason a Christian may have,
even from his own sad personal experience, for
dreading the interference of Satan in his devotions,
whether at home or in Church.   The most miserable

thing, is when he disturbs us with evil thoughts
in Holy Communion, as the most shocking case we
read, of his entering into a man, was what we are
told of Judas. After the sop which our Lord Himself had given, Satan entered into him. A dreadful
case indeed! well may it warn us, not to trust in
our Church privileges, our solemn services, and our
many Sacraments, how nearly soever they bring us
to our Lord. Well may the case of Judas warn us,
not to depend on privileges alone, since the very
near Presence of Christ could not keep Satan away
from Judas: in that presence, almost in the very
act of Communion, Satan, we read, entered into
him. But why? because Judas himself loved to
have it so. His heart was so set upon the wages
and mammon of unrighteousness, that he would not
partake of Christ, when Christ gave Himself to him.
Else, if he had indeed relented, if he had at all answered that loving care which our Saviour shewed
towards him in giving him the sop, who knows but
he might have repented as S. Peter did, even at that
eleventh hour, when his sin was so nearly completed?
And who knows what miracles of grace the good and
loving Saviour may work in us by His Spirit, if we
will but resolutely set ourselves against the evil sug-
gestions of the enemy, if we will but try in spite of
him, to attend to our prayers, to put down proud,
censorious, doubting thoughts. And we may do so
if we will: for greater is He that is in us than he
that is in the world: greater, far greater, is Jesus
Christ, Who abides in this place, giving Himself to
us both at the Font and at the Altar, than that Evil
one who only comes in at the door and goes out again

with us and other imperfect and erring worshippers.
Christ, and His good Angels and saints gathered
together round His Altar table, will be far too powerful for Satan, then seeking to enter into us, except
we give him such advantage as Judas did. Yea, by
His great mercy the very crafts and assaults of the
devil, which were meant to work our ruin, shall add
to the brightness and glory of our eternal crown. It
will be with us as it was with holy Job. The prayers and Communions, the Sundays and holidays, the
Churches and Bibles which he has vainly tried to
turn into sin, will be witnesses for us at the last Day,
that we by God's help would not suffer them so to
be perverted: Satan, confounded, will retire, and
not come near us again for ever. O that it may be
so with each one of us! then will this Church be a
blessing to us indeed, and we shall keep our Feast
of Thanksgiving for it through all eternity.

SERMON XXV.

CONSTANT FAITHFUL CHURCH-GOING, A CHOOSING
OF MARY'S PART.

S. Luke x. 42.

"*Mary hath chosen that good part, which shall not be
taken away from her.*"

This day in its yearly return may well draw our
attention to many blessings, for which we ought to
be very thankful to the good providence of our God :
many things in which He hath shewn Himself *peculiarly* merciful to us, choosing us out of mankind,
for no desert or goodness of ours, that we might be
partakers of those blessings.

First and chiefly, the day of the Dedication of this
outward and visible Church; the building made of
ordinary stones, in which we are assembled; may
and ought to stir up our thankfulness, for our being
made members of the Holy Church Universal: living
stones in the "[a]building not made with hands, which
rests upon the foundation of the Apostles and prophets, Jesus Christ Himself being the Head Corner
Stone." *That* is the great privilege, upon which all
the rest depend, viz : our having been made, and con-

[a] Eph. ii. 20.

U

tinuing to be, members of Christ. Who are we, and
what have we done, that while the greater part of
our fellow creatures who have been from time to time
born into the world, should have passed through
it without having a chance to know and to love
Jesus Christ, to live by Him, and to be one with
Him, we should have been admitted into those blessed privileges before we could know or understand
anything, and not have had them taken from us, long
before now, for our manifold sins? Who are we,
and what is our father's house, that we should be a
portion of the elect people of God? We are sinners,
conceived and born in sin: our father's house, the
family of our father Adam, hath been from the beginning a lost and sinful generation: and yet here
we are, brought near, brought close to Him: brought
to Him in Baptism, and permitted still to abide with
Him. This, I say, is the first and principal blessing,
which ought on such a day as this to make all Christian hearts overflow with thankfulness. We may
say each one to himself, As surely as ever I come
under this holy roof, I know that I am a Christian;
not a Jew, Turk, infidel, or heretic; chosen in
Christ to be saved by Him, if I do not cast myself
away. That is the first and great thing, the fountain from which all other Church blessings flow.

If you ask, what those other blessings are, there
is no counting them for they are innumerable; there
is no measuring them for they reach on to eternity:
they are deep, and rich, and many, as the drops of
Christ's Blood, by which they are purchased, or the
promises of God's holy Word, by which they are
sealed. When we think of them we may well cry

out with the Psalmist, "ᵇ How dear are Thy counsels unto me O God: O how great is the sum of
them! If I tell them they are more in number than
the sand!" and they are various, suited to the needs
of all people, from the most desperate sinner to the
purest and holiest of believers. Let us only take
one of them, one which the providence of God invites us to think of, in that it is contained in the
second lesson this morning. Let us, my brethren,
on this our Church Feast-day, take especial notice of
the promise of our Lord to the devout Mary of Bethany, "The good part which she hath chosen shall
not be taken away from her." Let us see whether
that gracious promise is not particularly suitable to
all, who try to come constantly, quietly and lovingly,
to worship Him here or in any such holy place.

Mary of Bethany, the sister of Lazarus, is the
pattern, as it were, and representative of all such,
as her sister Martha is of those who are more outwardly busy: who, having a great deal to do in the
world, so give themselves up to it as to be content
without doing their best for the serving of God in a
devotional way. Martha, to be sure, was a good
and holy person: she loved our Saviour with a deep
and reverential love: at this very time that the text
relates to, the "much serving" about which she was
"cumbered" was contriving and managing and providing things for the more respectful entertainment
of our Lord. The mistake was, that in eagerness
to have all those outward things right, she thought
too little of the great privilege itself, of so having
our Lord in her house, that she might sit at His Feet

ᵇ Psal. cxxxix. 17.

and hear His word: as if persons engaged in building
a Church, or in taking care of it after it was builded,
should have their minds swallowed up with making
every thing as beautiful and solemn as they could,
and so be distracted and think little of the meaning
of holy services, and the aweful Presence of Him
Whom they are serving.   On the other hand, when
we read of the devout Mary, how she withdrew herself from the hurry and distraction of getting things
ready in the house, and made the most of every moment she could get for sitting at our Lord's Feet and
hearing His word, may it not remind each one of
us of some few at least whom we know or have known,
spending the whole of their spare time, as far as in
duty and charity they might, in waiting on Jesus
Christ: never willingly missing any of His solemn
services: coming here as often as they could, because
this is the place where He hath promised to be, the
house where His honour dwelleth: arranging and
contriving their employments so as to give them the
best possible chance of always being among the two
or three, gathered together in His Name, to whom
the gracious assurance is given, "cThere am I in the
midst of them."   Yes, you will find, if you consider,
that Mary sitting at Jesus' Feet is indeed a likeness
and image of such regular Church-goers, such devout
readers of the Bible, such punctual observers of the
appointed hours of prayer, such watchful improvers
and gatherers up of all fragments of time and thought
that may be redeemed and laid out on Christ's service, as I am now speaking of: and you will hardly
help perceiving, that as Martha complained of Mary,

c S. Matt. xviii. 20.

so the busy and well-meaning but perhaps less devout among Christians are apt to blame those who keep such rules as these : each one is apt to blame his neighbour who is a little stricter than himself, and say, 'Why does he not rather come and help me?' as if being so fervent and constant in prayer made a person slothful in business. They ask, sometimes with a sort of scorn, What is the use of so many services, such incessant Church going, so many hours spent in public worship? and at home they feel a sort of grudging at the sight of persons trying to make the most of *all* opportunities for sitting at Jesus' Feet. And they are not always so much to be censured for this, so very profane, as they may appear at first sight: for unhappily there is a good deal of self-deceit and foolishness mixed up with too many of our devotions, and sensible, busy, hard-working people, when they once see such a thing, naturally take a prejudice against any thing unusual in the way of devotion and think it more or less Pharisaical. This is a trouble and a hindrance : it must be borne patiently and sweetly, and it will pass away in time, if men take care to be as exact in all their earthly and temporal duties as they are in the house and services of God : meanwhile here is this word of comfort for them, such comfort as the world can neither give nor take away, They have chosen the good part, the one thing needful, and it shall not be taken from them. And as often as they come here, or do but think of the place when they are elsewhere, the very sight, the very thought of the building, the very continuance of it with its solemn services among us, is a pledge to all such earnest,

of the good part which they have chosen. "Mary," He saith, "hath chosen that good part, which shall not be taken away." What is that good part? It is the same of which our Lord and Saviour had spoken long before in His Divine psalm: "'The lot is fallen unto me in a fair ground, yea I have a goodly heritage." The good part is the lot and portion of Christ's Church: it is that which we, like Mary, choose for ourselves, as often as we enter these doors with a heart that tries to be lowly, penitent and obedient. The good part is being with Christ. Mary was with Christ, and therefore it was well with her. Therefore she did not cumber herself about much serving: when she had done her part as well as she could, in the household work, she did not suffer the care of it, nor any earthly care, to dwell upon her mind, make her fretful, interrupt her prayers: but she sought out the Lord Jesus where she knew He vouchsafed to be, and stayed with Him as long as she could, quietly hearkening to His blessed word. Well, my brethren, we also know, it is a blessed yet an aweful thing to know, where our Lord vouchsafes to be, in our time, at this very time. We know that wherever else He is or is not, He is surely *here*, in such houses of prayer as this: for we have His promise to His people, "'In all places where I record My Name, I will come to thee and bless thee." It is good then for us to be here, it is the good part, let us choose it. Here is Christ, and here are His saints, all His saints: in spirit they are here with Him, for they are inseparable members of Him. This, if any, is the place on

<hr>

^f Ps. xvi. 6.   ^g Exod. xx. 24.

earth to be in comfortable communion with those blessed ones whom we have known and loved, and with all others who have finished their course with joy. If bereavement, separation, widowhood, be hard things and bitter to endure, here is the place to soothe and assuage those griefs: here we are nearer to our departed ones than any where else on earth, and in a way to be perfectly with them: in our Holy Communions here we and they are together before our God in such a way as at no other time: if then we have any love, any affection for them, this is another reason why it is good for us to be here, why we should choose it as our good portion.

There is indeed this great difference between Mary's portion and ours, that our Lord was visibly with her, with us He is but invisibly, but then we have the comfort of surely knowing that if we try in earnest to have such a mind as she had, a mind to love Him best of all, every hour we spend here will be an hour of real preparation for heaven. And in this respect we Christians are even more favoured than Mary was at that time, that she saw Him indeed face to face, but could not yet sacramentally partake of Him : we who do but see Him, as the Church says, under the form of Bread and Wine, are permitted verily and indeed to take and receive His Body and Blood. And this is that gate of heaven, the figure of which Jacob saw in his dream: which was to be in the true house of God on earth. And is not this a good portion indeed, the best of all portions, to be here, preparing ourselves by Sacramental communion for the open and perfect Communion promised here-after ?

But now, if this be a true account of what is going
on here: if Jesus Christ really and truly comes here
every day for you to sit at His Feet and hear His
word, and every Sunday to be your Meat and Drink
indeed: do you not plainly see what a loss it is to
us, if we-fail to come as often as we can, and to communicate, those who are of age, as often as we can
prepare ourselves? Would not holy Mary have
counted it a severe loss, had our Lord ever come to
Bethany, and she missed seeing Him? Would she
willingly have let Him go away without her sitting
at His Feet and hearing His word? Can you doubt
that she ordered all things, when she knew that He
was to be there, so as to give herself the best chance
she could of seeing Him and hearing all she might
of His gracious words? I seem to see her, how
sweetly and wisely she disposed of her ordinary business, not neglecting it, but putting it well out of
hand, in order that she might be ready when her
Lord came: and when we care for Him as she did,
we also shall say to ourselves, every week of our lives,
'Jesus Christ is coming here next Sunday: I must
order my affairs, inward and outward, so as not to
lose the blessing of His visit.' O, depend upon it,
the work which is going on here is not a mere im-
pressive form, not a mere course of edifying lessons,
which if you miss, you may make up for it elsewhere:
but as Jacob said, "[h] This is the gate of heaven," and
as our Lord promised, the eye of faith can see here
the heavens opened, and the Angels of God ascending
and descending on the Son of Man. Can you think
it right or safe, to come here only now and then,

[h] Gen. xxviii. 17.

now in a morning, then in an evening, quite irregularly, just as you have a fancy, and as that kind of way is sure to turn out, very seldom, once only in many weeks or months? If men really believed that Christ and His saints are here, so as they are nowhere else, could they so entirely forget and omit all attendance on saints' days, as (alas) they do in this parish? Believe me, there is some great mistake, some weakness of faith here. I will say nothing of the week-day prayers, nor of the early morning Litany: only this one thing: Let those who can, try how those services will help them, when they are in trials and afflictions. If they come humbly then, surely they will find our Lord: and in choosing Him, they will find in the end that they have chosen that good part which shall not be taken away from them.

It shall not be taken away from them, but they may cast it away themselves. We may and shall lose Christ, if we are not careful to carry with us the spirit of the place, the spirit of devotion, the mind of that blessed Mary, out of the Church doors, to our house and to our work. No good feelings, no regular attendance here, will save us, if our ordinary lives be in any respect unholy. What would Mary have been the better for sitting at Christ's Feet and hearing His word, if she had not been careful to obey it? Never forget this: pray to God to write it in your hearts: for on this eternity depends.

SERMON XXVI.

THE BLESSEDNESS OF GIVING
PERFECTED IN OUR EUCHARISTIC SERVICE.

ACTS xx. 35.

" Remember the words of the Lord Jesus, how He said, It is more blessed to give than to receive."

THERE are two things very obvious to remark on these words of S. Paul. First (and it is a very noticeable fact) they are, I believe, the only distinct saying of our Lord in the days of His flesh, related any where in the New Testament except in the four holy Gospels. So many things as Jesus said and did, the which if they had been written every one, the world could not have contained the books that should have been written: and so entirely as the Apostles and other disciples hung upon His sayings and doings while He was with them, and lived upon the same afterwards; one should have expected very frequent reference, very many passages supplemental to the direct Gospel history, very many more than we find in the Acts and Epistles. It is plain that such things were not kept back, from the clergy at least, even by the manner of S. Paul in introducing

this very saying. " I have shewed you," set you a
pattern of, " all things, how that so labouring," i.e.
working with your own hands, "ye ought to support
the weak" and indigent, and to " remember the words
of the Lord Jesus, how He said, ' It is more blessed
to give than to receive.'" Do you not see how familiar he supposes them to be with that particular saying of our Lord? and if with that saying, no doubt
with innumerable others, which from time to time
he had taught them, in order to ground them in
their duties, whether as Christians, or as priests or
Bishops of the Church. For S. Paul was "*not a
whit behind the very chiefest Apostles;" and one of
the high prerogatives of the Apostles was, we know,
the being taught by the Holy Ghost, and having all
things brought to their remembrance, whatsoever
Christ had said unto them. It could not be then
for want of knowledge, that S. Paul did not say a
great deal more in his Epistles, in the way of what
would now be called ' personal anecdote' concerning
our Lord. One is led to think whether it might not
be so ordered by the Holy Spirit, reserving to the
four Gospels exclusively the privilege of informing
Christ's members of the sayings and doings of their
Head. But whatever the reason might be, such is
the fact, that of all the sayings uttered by our Lord
in the days of His flesh, this one only has been reported to us in Scripture, elsewhere than in the Gospels: for I reckon the first chapter of the Acts a
part of the Gospel of S. Luke. This is one circumstance calculated to draw attention to the words, and
to fix them in a Christian's memory.

* 2 Cor. xi. 5.

Another striking particular regarding them is this; that they are the *last* words of S. Paul to the Ephesian elders: his farewell words. He had just said "I know that ye all, among whom I have gone preaching the kingdom of God, shall see my face no more." The prophetic Spirit had taught him, that even if he should come to Ephesus again (of his ever doing which there is not much proof), he would find the present elders or Bishops of that province no more. It was to be their last meeting on earth. What then is the thought which he by the Holy Ghost would fain leave impressed upon their hearts? "I have coveted no man's silver, or gold, or apparel. Yea, ye yourselves know, that these hands have ministered unto my necessities, and to them that were with me. I have shewed you all things, how that so labouring ye ought to support the weak, and to remember the words of the Lord Jesus, how He said, It is more blessed to give than to receive." "[b] Be ye followers of me as I am of Christ," rather giving up what you might fairly take, than doing anything whereby a weak brother may be offended. The sentiment, if I mistake not, is parallel to that with which the beloved disciple S. John concludes his first Epistle, "[c] Little children, keep yourselves from idols," not of course from material idols alone, but from all covetousness and from all selfishness. Only S. Paul's words have that incommunicable ground of reverence, that they are also the words of the Lord Jesus Himself.

But what have the words to do with our service to-day? A great deal, my brethren; if we consider

[b] 1 Cor. xi. 1.　　　[c] 1 S. John v. 21.

them patiently. Our service to-day is a service of especial joy, a great thanksgiving, a very solemn Eucharist. And what is the immediate blessing for which we give thanks? No other than this, that He has graciously accepted the gift and offering and sacrifice of certain of His servants, into whose heart He had put it to repair and renew this His ancient sanctuary and render it, if it might be, less unworthy of its work. We acknowledge to-day, not so much any one of God's outward gifts to us, as His inward and spiritual gift, freely given to some of our brethren, a heart to give largely to Him. For such a day no words could be more apt, than His Who made us what we are, telling us that to give is in itself a more blessed thing than to receive. And I suppose that many an one here, thoughtfully listening to the lesson, may have felt how specially appropriate that portion of it was: the rather, as the words occur incidentally in the course of the daily lessons, and were not in any sense chosen out for the day: a kind of thing most satisfactory when it does happen, and occurring, I believe, quite often enough to reconcile us in good measure to the comparative scantiness of our service-book in respect of proper lessons for special occasions.

Perhaps a little further consideration may shew that, as the words have undoubtedly a far deeper meaning, so they are even more appropriate than we might imagine at first sight.

"It is more blessed to give than to receive." Even in our first and lowest way of taking it, this proverb, we know, expresses a great truth. To give belongs to superiors, to those who have enough and to spare, and all men naturally prefer the more favoured place. This is very plain: but so far there is nothing amiable, nothing that we can understand our Blessed Lord to be recommending. It will be more to the purpose if we observe that all men, even the worst, have in them a sort of natural kindliness, a delight in pleasing and helping others, for the sake of so doing. Who has not observed the ways of little children, how willingly they hold out their hands, when they have received any gift, to impart it to any one who happens to come in their way? And in spite of the corrupting and hardening world, and after all that may be too truly said of the growing selfishness of elder years, is it not true that a niggardly and miserly heart is the exception, not the rule among men; and that even those who appear most greedy of gain find a deeper and truer pleasure in those instances, many or few, wherein they have had courage to part with it for the good of others, than ever they found in the mere act of accumulation?

So far, the Divine words express an ordinary and natural feeling. And do they not also put before us a wonderful and mysterious law of our being, arising out of our peculiar relation to the great Lord and Governor of all things? We are made and renewed after His Image, and our happiness must be in some sort after the pattern of His happiness, and we know that as God it belongs to Him to give all and receive nothing. To give, is the more Godlike, and therefore the more blessed of the two. And therefore divines use to say that we need not stand amazed at the distinction of Persons in the Deity, for when the fact is made known to us, it seems quite according to reasonable expectation, that the Almighty Father should have had with Him to all eternity His Son and His Spirit communicating with Him perfectly in all things. See, my brethren, what a great thought is here. When we willingly and cheerfully impart of any good thing to another, we are in our poor way, yet really, in the sight of God and of good spirits, shewing ourselves His special offspring, both made and new-made in His Image, after His likeness. As Moses was made a god unto Pharaoh, because he had to impart unto him the knowledge of God's will: and as the Jews, the special children of God, kings and princes under Him, His royal priesthood, His peculiar people, are called gods, because the word of God came to them and was to be transmitted by them to others: so is each Christian, not only a king and a prince, but in some sort a god to his brethren, by reason of the great unspeakable gifts which he has continually to impart to them. We are gods to each other, could we but realize it, since we have constantly to give as well as to receive one of another.

Yet I should not wonder if the saying, "It is more blessed to give than to receive," may appear to some hard and perplexing as to the generality of mankind. For the more part by far of the children of men would appear to be by this rule cut off almost or altogether from one great source of happiness. If the blessedness lie in giving, how can they be blessed whose lot in life is never to give, always to receive? And may not the poor, so far, with reason feel a kind of spiritual envy towards those, whose

x

condition puts it in their power to be bountiful?
This is a sophistry which will scarce bear to be put
in words, and yet I should not wonder if it had
exercised a very evil influence on many a heart.
People have said to themselves like that discontented
prophet, 'I do well to be angry, even unto death; at
my froward and perverse lot in life, that I have a
heart desirous to do good to others, but none or
very scanty means of doing it.'

No Christian indeed need be deceived by this:
seeing that we all know perfectly (the history of the
widow's two mites has told us too plainly to be
mistaken) that it is not the amount of what we offer,
which God cares for, but the mind and temper and
devotion with which we offer it. He does much, it
has been said, who loves much. And since the poorest may love, and abound in love's little gentle services, as earnestly and as abundantly as the wealthi-
est, there is really no stint nor measure to limit the
degree of his blessedness, even in that province of
giving, from which he would seem, at first sight, entirely cut off. All men of course understand, that
a gift does not here mean, only or chiefly money or
money's worth. It includes every kind of service:
a word in season, a kind look, a draught of cold
water: an encouraging or warning tone of voice. In
all this men may just as much abound, whether they
have much or little in the way of possessions. Although of course, where a man *is* rich, it is idle talking of bounty, if he do not give largely: which is so
plain that one would be ashamed to mention it,
were there not some, (more than we might at first
imagine,) who quiet themselves in their scanty obla-

tions, by some vague recollection of what Scripture has said concerning the willing mind, a pleasure surely intended for the comfort of a very different class of persons.

Once more, It may occur to some, that if it be really and generally more blessed to give than to receive, then, *as* really and generally, our happiness must be greater in loving and serving men, than in loving and serving God. For to men, it might seem, we are able to impart something; but in our dealings with the Most High God we are debtors every way. We have nothing which we have not received from Him: how then can we really give Him anything? And in this way I can imagine men palliating to themselves, a very deep degree of indevotion, not to say profaneness. We had better, so they seem to say, spend our time and our thoughts upon our brethren, to whom we can really give, than upon our God Who is All-sufficient unto Himself. And so they become, if He permit, active helpers, kind moral men, but men of prayer, devout religious men, they cannot become: they are even content to go down to the grave without it. Now (not to speak of the danger to their own souls) what a loss, what a perverse waste is here, of the merciful provision made by our heavenly Father for His own glory and His creatures' good! He by His special favour hath given you a kind, willing, bountiful spirit, disposed to be full of mercy and good fruits towards men; and it was His purpose to train you by such exercise to the higher work of love and devotion to Himself; and you frowardly make that very bounty of His an occasion of drawing back from Him: you

say, 'I am friendly and forgiving to my brethren,
What lack I yet?' This is indeed very sad: but let
us observe well what it is owing to, and in what way
alone it can be cured. It is owing (as almost all
that is amiss in Christendom is owing) to men's poor
low unreal apprehension of the high and saving
truth of the Incarnation of our Lord Jesus Christ.
For see His miraculous condescension. He made
Himself Man, with this intent among others, that we
truly and really, and not in figure only, giving to
Him, might obtain the full blessing promised to
those who give rather than receive. It is not only
that He allows us to make, as it were, a virtue of
necessity, and by surrendering His gifts, when He
recalls them, with a willing, resigned, thankful spirit,
to obtain a place in the list of those who make
free-will offerings at His Altar. It is not only that
He counts as given what is lovingly yielded for His
sake, when we have no choice about keeping it. I
have known a bereaved mother, whose resort in
overwhelming moments, was to this one text more
especially: "'God loveth a cheerful giver." With
those words she stayed herself and quieted from time
to time the rush of sorrow, which otherwise might
have been almost felt as a sacred duty. But she
could not have done this; the words could not have
so come home to her, except she had a strong faith,
that all our bereavements, duly borne, are accounted
as free-will offerings, true gifts to our God and
Saviour. Though we have no choice, as our father
and pattern Abraham had, about actively offering
up those whom we love best, we have a choice whe-

¹ 2 Cor. ix. 7.

ther or no we will school our minds by His grace to
perfect resignation, and go on with our duties cheerfully: and if we make that good choice, we shall be
in His sight as cheerful givers: a portion in Abraham's blessing will be ours.

But, as I said, the point on which I am now speaking is somewhat even beyond this. Since the Incarnation of our Lord Jesus Christ, we are not only
accounted as givers, but He has made it possible for
us really and literally to give to Him. We do so,
every time we relieve one of our distressed fellow
creatures, for they are His brethren, He bears a true
blood-relation to them, and what we do to them, He
tells us is done to Him. And again as they were
true and literal *gifts*, wherewith His creatures and
servants, living in the days of His Flesh, waited on
Him from time to time, and that, not only in the
way of relieving the bodily wants and infirmities,
which He vouchsafed then to feel, but which have
now passed away, but also in doing Him honour and
shewing Him reverence: as the gifts of the Wise-
men and Mary of Bethany were real gifts given to the
Most High God, no less than the draughts of water
and morsels of meat which He asked of such as the
woman of Samaria or Zaccheus: so, now that He is
gone out of sight, we are not to doubt but earnestly
to believe that in both kinds He is well pleased with
the offerings which He puts in our heart to make,
I mean both with what Christian men bestow upon
the poor and needy, His brethren, and with what
they bestow on Himself immediately, whether here
in His holy Church and worship, or elsewhere in the
whole tenor and conduct of our lives. Our life, all

of it, may now be spent in literally giving to God, Who has made Himself one of us, that He might be literally capable of receiving from us. As by grievous sin we mysteriously crucify Him afresh, so by true sacrifice of whatever kind we refresh Him, thirsting for our good. "[g] He seeth of the travail of His soul and is satisfied:" "[h] He rejoiceth in the presence of the angels over every sinner that repenteth" with an earnest self-denying repentance.

Thus in our duty to God, as well as in our duty to our neighbour, we are wonderfully made partakers of that peculiar blessing, which belongs to those who give rather than receive.

And of all this the Holy Eucharist, with the services appertaining to it, is the great unspeakable pledge, token and exemplar. Consider it, as the providence of God hath bestowed it on us of the Church of England, in our own Liturgical offices from beginning to end. Is it not throughout a kind of descant, as musicians might say, on a theme given by David, by him whom Scripture sets before us as a pattern for cheerful givers? "[i] Who am I, said David, and what is my people, that we should be able to offer so willingly after this sort? For all things come of Thee, and of Thine own have we given Thee." "Of Thine own have we given Thee," surely they are prophetic words, surely they are fulfilled in our holy Eucharistical sacrifice in a sense probably far beyond what David himself then knew of. Let us take them, as I said, for a text to our own Communion service. That service

[g] Isa. liii. 11.   [h] S. Luke xv. 10.
[i] 1 Chron. xxix. 14.

begins, as you know, with the Lord's Prayer: God Incarnate hath given us His own Prayer, and we offer it back to Him: He hath given us thoughts in our hearts, and we try to offer them back to Him, purified by love: He hath given us His holy commandments, and we offer them to Him, by obedience or by penitence: He hath given us the Creed of His holy Catholic Church, and we offer it to Him by the confession of a true faith: He hath given us this world's good, and we offer it to Him in the offertory, properly so called: He hath given us food and gladness, and we offer to Him Bread and Wine: He hath given us an interest in all His whole Church, and we offer all to Him by intercession and commemoration: our very sins (the only thing we have which is not His gift) we are permitted to offer to Him in sincere confession and hearty prayer for amendment: He is our Lord God, our All in all, and we offer to Him, as is meet and right, the very best of our thanksgiving: greatest of all He hath given us His Son, our Saviour, and we offer Him to the Father in the way which He Himself ordained. And last of all, seeing that, in His Son, He hath given us a renewed being, we offer ourselves back again to Him, as a whole-burnt-offering, a reasonable, holy, and lively sacrifice, not only throughout the short remainder of our lives here, but throughout the long eternity which He is preparing us for.

It is but one instance more of the same spirit of devotion, if we try to offer Him the best we can in the way of outward service, reverential and beautiful. It cannot displease Him in itself that His children take such ways as they can, according to the

skill and sense of beauty which He has given, of
shewing their love for the habitation of His house,
and for the place where His honour dwelleth.   True,
it is nothing without the rest; the signs of love are
nothing, worse than nothing, without love itself: and
love cannot be without careful keeping of the commandments.   These outward gifts are nothing without the rest; but with the rest surely they are a
great deal.   For it was on occasion of outward gifts
such as these, that the comfortable word was spoken,
"kShe hath done what she could."   And who would
desire more than that? to hear those words must
have been a very heaven on earth.   Only let us who
in any way draw near to such offerings, either as
presenting or approving them, let us take it all upon
our heart and conscience as one pledge more given
to our Saviour that we will not, by His grace, be
wanting in any known duty: let it be to us a renewal
of our whole baptismal vow: let us not forget such
days as this, but try as we best may, to recall the
fragrance of them, and see if so improved they bring
not a great blessing.

k S. Mark xiv. 8.

SERMON XXVII.

CHRISTIAN BURIAL.

S. Matt. xv. 12.

" And His disciples came and took up the body and buried it; and went and told Jesus."

THREE persons there are, and three only, in the New Testament whose burial is especially spoken of as well as their death. Two of them are great saints, among the greatest: and in one way of looking at them, they are the very nearest to our Lord. One of those saints is S. Stephen, the first martyr: the other is he whom at this time of year especially the whole Church remembers, S. John the Baptist. You, my brethren, of this place, have cause just now to think of that blessed saint even more than the generality of Christian congregations have, because those who by God's good providence founded your Church here in the wilderness eleven hundred and fifty years ago, were led to fix on him, as the saint who should be borne in mind and honoured, and his example followed, by their children and children's children to all generations. This Church of Frome, as you all know better than I, bears the name of S. John Baptist, and he, I say, is one of two saints who being nearest in one sense to our Lord, have not only their deaths, but their burials also, especially recorded in His New Testament.

In what sense, some may ask, are S. Stephen and S. John Baptist nearer to Christ than any others? In the time of their martyrdom, my brethren, they wait upon our Lord, (so to speak) one on each side of His Cross: S. John being the last who suffered for Him before He suffered for all; S. Stephen the first, after He had come to be glorified above all: S. John the last martyr of the law, S. Stephen the first of the Gospel. I call S. John a martyr: the Church has always called him so; a martyr, and one of Christ's martyrs; although he did not shed his blood directly, and expressly, as S. Stephen did, in witnessing an article of the faith of Christ. The unbelievers rushed on S. Stephen, because they could not bear to hear him say, "ᵃ I see the heavens opened, and the Son of Man standing on the Right Hand of God," i. e. in other words, "I believe in our Lord Jesus Christ, the Only Begotten Son of God, Who ascended into heaven, and is at the Right Hand of the Father." Not so in the case of the Baptist: Herod and Herodias and Herodias' shameless daughter had no thought of faith or religion one way or the other, when they took counsel to take away his life: they could not endure him because he had disturbed them in their sins; because he had put the king in mind of God's law against a man taking his brother's wife. But John was a martyr just the same, for that law was a portion of the great seventh commandment, a part of the truth of God and of Christ,

ᵃ Acts vii. 56.

just as much as any article of the Creed is: therefore
S. John, dying for it, died for Christ's truth, and
was a true martyr; and let this be an encouragement to us all, in standing up for God's holy commands, as well as for His saving Faith: if it brings
persecution and trouble, so much the better: there is
something like a martyr's crown laid up for them in
heaven. But as I said, the point in S. John's history
to which I would draw your attention to day, is this,
that he and S. Stephen, with one besides, are the
only persons in the New Testament whose burials
are especially recorded. Of S. Stephen, you know
we read, "[b] Devout men carried him to his burial,
and made great lamentation over him." Of the Baptist, you heard just now; when his disciples came to
know of his being beheaded in the prison, they "came
and took up" his corpse; what seemed to them but
his poor headless "body, and laid it in a tomb, and
went and told Jesus." They only saw it as it was
then, in the deformity and indignity of that cruel
death but in the sight of God and His holy Angels
it was of great price, far more precious than rubies;
for *they* saw it as it will be hereafter, shining with
his Master's glory; changed after the likeness of
the glorious Body of our Lord Jesus Christ, and
wearing the crown which it will wear in the kingdom prepared for it. Therefore God put it in the
heart of John's faithful disciples, not only to bury
his body out of their sight, but to lay it carefully
in a tomb or monument: just as in the case of
S. Stephen, the good Christians did not only take
care that he should be buried, but came together

[b] Acts viii. 2.

to wait on him to his grave; made a point of being there, and joining in the solemn lamentation that was made over him. And when they departed from beside his grave to their ordinary duties in the world and in the Church, and when S. John's disciples, as in the text, after burying him, went and told Jesus, no doubt those holy tombs were not left unguarded, nor the bodies of the saints left alone sleeping in them: we need not doubt that the blessed Angels watched and still watch over them, as part of their Lord's treasure, even as in life they had charge over them to keep them in all their ways. Were there no more in the Gospel than this, my brethren, on the subject of Christian burial, and reverence for the dead, it were reason enough for Christians to think a good deal of it: but there is more than this, infinitely more. As I said at first, there are *three* persons mentioned in the Gospel as having been carefully and religiously buried: two of them great saints and martyrs: but I need not tell you Who is the third: you know it is our Saviour, the Lord Jesus Christ Himself, Saint of saints; and King of martyrs. You have not forgotten the last moments of that aweful Friday evening, the taking down from the Cross and laying Him in the grave; how gently and reverently every thing was done, so soothing to read or hear of, after the great tempest and power of darkness in which His Soul had passed away: you remember the fine linen and the spices, and the anointing, the new tomb prepared in the garden, freshly hewn out of the rock, and dutifully offered by the rich man Joseph, for Him Who being rich, had made Himself poor for us all. You remem-

ber Nicodemus and S. John, S. Mary Magdalene, and
the holy women, one of them at least very near akin
to our Saviour, who by Divine providence were permitted to be around Him at that time, and to fulfil
their loving duties towards Him as they best might,
undisturbed by those, so many and so near at hand,
who no doubt would have delighted in offering
Him the worst indignities: how two of the women
especially were protected in watching His Tomb to
the very last moment that their sabbath duties allowed. All these things, my brethren, all of you
I trust know and remember; for they are part of
the history of that most holy week, in which every
heart that has but a spark of faith and love feels especially drawn to our Lord. And the Church our
mother will not allow us to forget them: since she
has taught us, whenever we repeat our Creed, to
confess Christ not only crucified and dead, but also
buried: and she would have us keep Easter Eve, as
well as Good Friday and Easter Day.

We may well believe that His main purpose herein was to shew us and cause us to feel, how entirely
Christ is all in all to us: how having become Flesh
He sanctified as it were by His touch our flesh and
all its great changes, going through all His own
Self. For infants He became an infant, for boys a
boy, for men a full-grown and most perfect Man.
In like manner, because we die, He died; because
we go into an unseen world He descended into hell;
and because we are buried He was buried. The Head
was to be one with the members in all that is not
sin; and the members were to know, that neither
death nor burial, nor anything but their own wilful

apostacy, could ever separate them from the Head.
They were to be made sure that He would be with
them in the grave and in the unseen world: with
their bodies as well as with their souls, as an immortal seed, to keep them for the day of Resurrection.
Christ's sepulchre on Mount Calvary, as it is the
place to which in ages past devout men resorted in
outward and visible pilgrimage, so it is the place to
which, in all ages, they have resorted in heart and
mind, for comfort against the day of their death, and
the time between death and judgement.

That is the mystical or sacramental meaning of
our Lord's Burial, and of all that the Gospel teaches
us concerning it. But those places have a moral
meaning also. They teach us a certain great duty,
and encourage us in performing it. What is that
duty? Our own hearts tell us at once: it is reverence for the dead. As we sit in spirit by the grave
of our God and Saviour, we seem to hear a voice from
it, a voice which we cannot but attend to, telling us
that even the mortal remains of departed friends are
not to be forgotten, but to be thought of with loving
respect, for His sake, Who vouchsafed to lie a while
in that grave, and to have dear friends weeping by
it. That tomb on Calvary seems to say to us, ' Look
round the world, and you will see everywhere tokens
of a strong instinct abiding in every one's heart from
the beginning, strong among the heathens who know
not God, and even among many of those worse than
heathens, who when they knew God in Christ, have
chosen to cast Him and their own souls away.'

As to the heathens, there is hardly any where a
race or tribe so cruel and degraded, as not to have

some thought of respect and reverence for the bodies of some at least of the departed. To their enemies perhaps they are cannibals, absolutely devouring their flesh; but for those of their own tribe, kindred or household, for those whom for any cause they love and honour, they have their funerals and solemn mournings, and places for the safe keeping of their remains: it is a matter very near their hearts; their fathers' burial places are the spot of earth to which their wild spirits cling with a feeling of subdued love, grief, and reverence, more like true devotion than any thing else about them. And it is not the mere instinct of the animal man, such as even dumb creatures have frequently shewn towards the places where their human protectors are laid. It is no piece of barbaric childishness: it does not pass away as civilization comes on. Assyria, Egypt, Greece, Rome, Arabia, India, South America, the Empires which from time to time have embodied the greatness of this fallen world, did not, as they grew in arts and philosophy, cast away this care for the dead, but exemplified it in their several ways, by works which to this day constitute one of the main links, which bind them to after generations, and to us among the rest.

And what in some respects is still more remarkable, this feeling towards the departed often lingers in the hearts and minds of wicked and fallen Christians, in the very extremities of their ignorance and sin. Those, of whom one would judge by their ordinary living and talk, that holy and profane are to them all one, or rather that profane things are more welcome to them than holy, even *they* many times cannot bear the thought of being buried elsewhere than in holy ground. Though they have kept away all their lives long from everything belonging to God, it is intolerable to them to think of their insensible bodies lying in any other place than that which is under the shadow of the Church's wing: under the immediate shelter and protection of God. And if any one belonging to them dies, though for years they may have been doing their best, or rather their worst, to keep that person away from God's House, and to shew him the way to the places of riot and lewdness, that is to say, the houses of the devil: yet they are affronted beyond measure, if the Church wishing for her old godly discipline, make any difficulty about allowing that person to be brought like an ordinary Christian into God's House, and buried with the same holy psalms and lessons and prayers which would be said over the greatest saint among us. Whatever else may be thought of this, at any rate it is human nature; it is the old heathen instinct, shewing itself in those who might be thought to have less religion than the heathen. And if such, by God's special grace, could be brought to think really on what they themselves say and do at such times, how they are then without intending it, bearing witness to the truth of the Gospel, which at other times they scorn; it might be a good help towards bringing them to a better mind.

As to God's own ancient people, whether the patriarchs and their families before the Law, or the whole race of Israel after it, I need only just remind you how much of their history is taken up with burials, from the time when Abraham bought the cave in Hebron to be a burying place for Sarah, (which cave, by providential order is among the few holy places known with absolute certainty unto this day), to the hour when the good and dutiful Nehemiah pleaded it for a reason why he longed to return and rebuild Jerusalem, That it was "the place of his Fathers' sepulchres." You remember the patriarchs, how one after another they gave commandment, as Joseph did, concerning their bones, where they should be buried; and all in the Holy land: and how punctually Holy Scripture has recorded the fulfilment of each of those injunctions; and how the good and wicked kings of Israel and Judah, have their burials mentioned, as well as their death, often with some circumstance which is to be received as a token of God's favour or anger. And so from beginning to end, both before and outside of the Gospel, the Creator has made and acknowledged it to be a natural instinct among His creatures of mankind, that the living should honour the dead, that when one departs, the survivors should not be satisfied without due tokens of love and respect to his memory and his mortal remains.

This natural tendency and instinct, like others, the Gospel when it came took up, and turned it to Christ's own high and holy purposes, telling the true signification of it, and adopting it into the service of the kingdom of heaven. Christians, whether Jewish or Gentile, were used from the beginning, were taught of God to remember the departed and cherish what remained of them, with no less intensity and constancy than the most ardent among natural men, but with a deep tenderness and reverence, which nothing but

the most Holy Spirit could infuse. Their 'moanings,'
to use an expression of the Psalmist, were 'dovelike.'
To them it was more joy than grief, to think of those
gone before, so vivid was their faith in the good
things to come, and so unselfish their love to their
brethren. And so they spoke and wrote cheerfully
to each other, and did not usually put on mourning.
When heathens, they had been used to burn their
dead and bury their ashes. But as Christians, they
followed as nearly as circumstances allowed, the
example set in our Lord's own burial; they committed the body to the dust, with myrrh and sweet
spices, to signify that they were still His members,
kept by Him against that day. And they were very
careful to make their memorials, their tombs, tablets,
inscriptions, and whatever else they used as a token
to remind them of the dead, and honour their memories. All this they were careful to make as distinctly Christian as they could. They did in a manner put our Lord's mark, the sign of the Cross, upon
every thing connected with their funerals. Because,
as they knew and felt from the very bottom of their
hearts, that they could not do without Christ themselves, neither in this world, nor yet in the world to
come; so neither could they have borne to trust their
dead to any but Him; and this they signified by
their monumental and memorial crosses, and other
tokens of the same kind: it was as if for their dead
friends and themselves, they kept on saying day and
night to God and His holy Angels, to the spirits of
just men made perfect, and to all other: 'Christ died,
was buried, rose again the third day from the dead:
we desire to have no hope but in Him, neither for

ourselves, nor for these our dear friends departed. In Him believing, we believe in the Communion of saints, and the resurrection of the body, and the life everlasting.'

And there was another thing, my brethren, which the old fathers constantly taught, and the old Christians bore witness to, by these their Christian funerals, and graves, and memorials; viz: that even before the great Day, the reward of good Christians begins: that they are by no means in sleep, and forgetfulness, though they are in perfect rest. They have departed and are with Christ, which is far better than the very best of this world.

And one thing more: these special remembrances of each one who died in Christ, taken separately and apart from the rest, helped to keep up in their minds, that most Christian, comfortable, and true belief, that in that world (D.V.) we shall assuredly know each other: that the tender love of parents and children, wives and husbands, brothers and sisters, friends who are each to the other as his own soul, these affections in which we have been trained and educated, by His good providence, while we are here, will not leave us in the world to come. There will of course be nothing carnal, nothing earthly in that joy, which we are taught to call the Joy of the Lord; it will not in that respect be like marrying, or giving in marriage, here in this short life. There will be all the love, and more; yes, infinitely more: but it will be as much purer and more perfect than the best love we can feel here, as the spiritual body in which we hope to be raised will be more glorious than this, our frail, weak, perishable body. Of this

Faith especially, the holy Cross upon a Christian's grave is a token and pledge; it is a strong link, to bind us unto our friend that is gone: it is one link more, to bind us to Christ.

I have no need to explain to you, my brethren, why on this day of joyful anniversary, I have thought good to draw your attention especially to the duties we owe to the invisible portion of our congregations. For all Christian congregations are partly invisible: they have some belonging to them who are now out of sight, viz: all those who have ever belonged to them, and are deceased in the true faith and fear of God. They lie, my brethren, by hundreds, we trust around you. For nearly twelve hundred years, since first that good Bishop from Sherborne planted the Cross in this spot, the seeds of the all glorious harvest have been sowing here: graves have multiplied, and for every grave, we know, there is an immortal, a baptized soul, somewhere in God's keeping. Graves have multiplied, and generations as they passed, have taken more or less care of them: but until of late years, in various ways, the care has been less successful, I fear I must add, less earnest; but now the people of God here, and the friends of this good work afar off, are invited to offer of their substance for completely doing away with this reproach. You will do so, and that cheerfully, my brethren, I am certain; were it only for reverence towards one holy grave, one blessed memory in particular, for whose venerable sake this your Churchyard is thought of far and wide all over Christendom; at any rate by those in communion with the English Church. Were it only for Bishops Ken's sake, you

will be ready with your free-will offerings to make
and keep these graves secure, these monuments
Christian, this whole place such as may help Christ's
little ones to penitent, thankful, courageous, heavenly thoughts.

And when you have done your duty in this respect, and still more afterwards, as often as the loving but severe hand shall be upon you, as you know
it is continually upon one or another, to lead you
into this or some other Churchyard, to commit the
body of some brother or sister, perhaps your dearest
on earth, to the ground, O still try to bear in mind
as well as you can, the mystery of Christ's Burial.
Then doubt not but earnestly believe that it is far
better for them to be with Christ in the grave and in
Paradise, than to go on longer in this anxious world :
far better even for you to be without their bodily
presence for a while, if so be you may be drawn
the nearer to Christ. Do not grudge their bodies to
Him Who ever makes much of the bodies of His
saints. Try to go home with somewhat of the same
mind as those first Christians returning from the
grave or tomb in which they had laid some blessed
Martyr : with the Baptist's disciples, "go and tell
Jesus ;" with the devout bearers of Stephen "make
great lamentation" (you are not forbidden to do that:
your Saviour once wept by a grave): but do also as
they did afterwards : do not go away and forget the
departed, as the poor shallow unnatural world makes
so much haste to do : neither yet, as some have done,
idolize him to the neglect of God and your neighbour, giving yourself up to unprofitable repining,
like a sort of sentimental heathen : but make a sa-

crifice to Christ of your tears as well as of your delights: and as for the departed one himself, just keep the unfailing rule, do as you would be done by. Do what your own heart tells you that he whom you mourn would wish you to do, if he could now appear and tell you his mind. Believe that he is still very near to you; for if he died in Christ is he not still a member of Christ, and are not all Christ's members infinitely nearer to one another than heart can tell? Cherish his memory with a loving quietness, to help you in well-doing and patience. It will not hinder duty, nor make life dismal. How should it hinder duty to know that we are doing what our best beloved would have done? How should it make life dull, to have good hope that every moment we are a step nearer to seeing our best beloved again? It is all a part of the life of faith: it will by God's mercy help not hinder you, as you are helped not hindered by devout faith in Him to Whom your friend is gone. And do not fear to remember the departed if your heart tells you to do so, in your prayers. You may do that without believing in Purgatory: the early Christians made a rule of doing it. You cannot be wrong in commending their souls to Him, and asking Him to bless them as He knows best. And if you fear and tremble how it may be with any, let this urge you to live so on your own part, as to cheer those whom you must soon leave behind, that they may have good hope for you.

One parting word more, my brethren. I pray you, in Christ's Name, one and all, to think of the dead as still living, and of the living as of those who will very soon be dead. And when you stand by an open grave, think with yourself, 'That grave will be opened again, and I shall be there; he and I shall meet again. God grant for Jesus Christ's sake, that for both it may be with joy and not with grief.'

SERMON XXVIII.

THE ABOUNDING OF INIQUITY.

S. MATT. xxiv. 12, 13.

"Because iniquity shall abound, the love of many shall wax cold. But he that shall endure unto the end, the same shall be saved."

WE have here a most alarming prophecy indeed, from the mouth of Jesus Christ Himself, concerning what might be expected after the setting up of His kingdom. We might all of us naturally look for peace and joy, and a kind of heaven on earth: but the actual result, He tells us, owing to the perverseness of men, would be in a great measure quite contrary to this. There were to be false christs and false prophets, wars and rumours of wars, many to be offended, and to betray one another, and to hate one another: and to sum up all in a word, towards the end of Christ's earthly kingdom, and His second Coming to judge the world, so complete was to be the decay and falling off, that love and charity, the very note and mark by which His disciples should be known, were almost to vanish out of the Church.

Because iniquity, i. e. wilful sin, disobedience to God's plain commands, should abound, the love of the greater part should wax cold. I say, of the greater part; there being no doubt whatever that this is here the meaning of the word *many:* it describes the ordinary state of things, the effect which would be generally produced by the iniquity of the latter times. So great will be the falling off among Christians, sin and wickedness will be so exceedingly multiplied, that not one or two only, nor only a great number among them, but absolutely the greater number, will have waxed cold. Their love towards God and man will be almost or altogether extinct, like a fire burned out, or only just alive: so very general will the failure be, that hardly any will be as earnest in Christ's service, as if he had lived in earlier and better times.

This is the great disappointment of all: this is the disheartening sight which every where meets the eyes of God's people; nay, concerning which God Himself vouchsafes to speak as one wondering at the failure of His own work. " [a] What could have been done more in My vineyard, that I have not done in it? wherefore, when I looked that it should bring forth grapes, brought it forth wild grapes?" And again, " [b] When the Son of Man cometh, shall He find faith on the earth?"

Now if the great deliverance of all, the deliverance of all mankind from the power of darkness by the Death and Resurrection of Jesus Christ, and the setting up of the kingdom of heaven, if even this appear in a certain sense to have failed and been made void

[a] Isa. v. 4.   [b] S. Luke xviii. 8.

by the unworthiness of those for whom it is wrought:
much more might we expect the same in respect of all
lesser, all partial deliverances, such, for example, as
that for which we acknowledge God's mercy to-day:
the recovery of this Church and kingdom from the
captivity into which they had fallen for a time under
the enemies of both. This, like all God's temporal
gifts and deliverances, was in its measure a shadow
of the great gift, the Spirit of Christ sealing us to
be His; and the great liberty and deliverance from
the bondage of sin and death, which He gave us when
He made us Christians. Indeed, one might say more
than this: one might say that the Restoration of our
Church and king after the confusion of the great Rebellion was the actual setting up of the kingdom of
God afresh in a country which was in great danger
of losing it altogether: it made the difference to
hundreds of thousands, whether they should be
Christians at all or no. For if the kingdom of God be
in truth that one holy Society which began at Pentecost by the coming of the Holy Spirit; which was
founded on the Apostles and prophets, Jesus Christ
Himself being the head Corner-Stone: it must needs
be confessed that this nation, as a nation, had thrown
off the kingdom of God entirely, in that it had separated itself from the control of the Bishops, the
Apostles' only successors, and that as many as were
separated, in themselves personally, from the communion of the Apostolic Church, had so far ceased to
be Christians, and either by their fault or misfortune,
had lost their place in the kingdom of God. It was
not then, as I said, a small blessing, which Providence
restored to us by this day's deliverance, but it was

to the whole country and to very many of us seve-
rally, the blessing of being within God's Church and
kingdom, instead of being, by His just judgement
on our many sins, excluded from it. And the manner
in which God gave the blessing was such as to lead
all men's thoughts to Him as the only author of it.
When all hope from those in power, either abroad
or at home, seemed gone, the hearts of men were
turned as it were suddenly, were bowed as the heart
of one man, and the king was invited to return with
such unanimity that he said himself, he thought it
must be his own fault that he had not come back
sooner, every one seemed so glad to receive him. It
was evidently the finger of God, turning men's hearts
almost suddenly from confusion to order, from separation to unity, from rebellion to obedience, from
Satan's kingdom to God's. Who but would expect
that so great mercies should be met by a great love
and obedience, a new and fresh growth, if one may
say so, of holiness and virtue, all through the realm
which had been so highly favoured? But alas! all
history tells us how sadly such expectations were
disappointed. Those who had been so wonderfully
spared and restored too commonly forgot God, as if
He had done nothing for them, and made light of
His holy Name. The Court first, and too commonly afterwards the country, was overspread with
a dissolute profaneness: which has far more generally
than could be wished remained as a stain on the
character of our nation ever since. We see it to this
day with our own eyes, that iniquity, disobedience to
the great law of God, does abound, and has abounded
among us to a fearful degree. I mean especially the

law of purity, "[c]Blessed are the pure in heart, for they shall see God." "Fornication, and all uncleanness, or covetousness, let it not be once named among you, as becometh saints : neither filthiness, nor foolish talking, nor jesting, which are not convenient." How has it been among us in times past, how is it even now among us, in respect of this prime law, which if it be not duly observed, there is an end of Christian holiness: no chance of seeing the Lord. Alas, the evidences of the shame of our country and neighbourhood are too open and too many to be overlooked.　There is no doubt that in this great virtue of purity we Englishmen, favoured and instructed as we are, must own ourselves as a nation inferior to others which are generally supposed far blinder and more degraded.　It is most painful even to speak on the subject, far more to speak in public: but indeed the histories told in most villages by the registers we keep of marriages and baptisms are sad histories and very shameful, and such as to call for deep humiliation and penance if ever God's wrath is to be pacified.　Indeed our condition in this respect is too like that of the chosen people when the prophet cried out concerning them, "[d]Shall I not visit for these things, saith the Lord: and shall not My soul be avenged on such a nation as this?"

And along with impurity of heart and conduct has gone, as might be expected, extreme irreverence towards holy things.　How could it be otherwise? How could it be supposed that such as see God nowhere else, because wherever they go their eyes and their hearts are after their own ungodly lusts, that they

[c] S. Matt. v. 8.　　　　　　　[d] Jer. v. 9.

should be able to discern His Presence in His holy
Church, in her prayers and Sacraments ? It cannot
be : if men permit themselves without scruple to be
unclean elsewhere, their very coming to Church
(except in humble penitence) is an act of profaneness :
they cannot possibly come in due fear though they
may be occasionally moved for a time : and therefore
(a thing almost too frightful to think) their very
prayers do but serve in one sense to deaden their
hearts, make them more irreverent, and take them
further from God. No wonder then that the generations, in which impurity has so abounded, as it has
in our country ever since the Restoration, should be
remarkable for profaneness also. No wonder that so
many think of the Lord's holy day as a day of mere
rest and diversion, and spend it without scruple any
where rather than in His house : that of those who
do come, so few behave with entire reverence, and a
true sense of His Presence : that they seem to make
so little difference between a Church and another
place : that they talk so freely and in all companies
of the holy Scriptures, of God Himself, of His will
and of what is to come in eternity. These and a
thousand more instances might be given, of the cold
indifferent disrespectful way, in which, too commonly, the people of our country have for many
generations conducted themselves toward holy and
sacred things. We have too many of us got into a
way of priding ourselves on our common sense; we
say in our hearts, ' What use, what profit is there in
being so very scrupulous and serious, in making so
much difference among things that are outwardly
alike ?' and thus we give ourselves and one another,

for the most part, full license to behave as may suit
our fancy at the time.

Another sort of irreverence there is, most plainly
and undeniably too common among us: commoner
than it used to be even within the memory of man.
So almost all seem to confess: I mean, disrespect for
those whom God has set over us, to be, in any manner or measure, in His stead. Parents, e. g. how
seldom do we now hear them speaking as with absolute right to command their children, if grown to
any age; and when they do command, how coolly are
they often disobeyed! Towards kings, how greatly
has our reverence been diminished by the modern notions of liberty! how little do we fear to speak evil
of dignities, whether in Church or state! how easily
do most of us believe what we hear amiss of them!
how freely do we answer and argue, instead of obeying! how little conscience do too many make of
slighting or thwarting their known wills, when out
of sight! On the whole I know not how to deny or
doubt that these two sorts of iniquity, uncleanness,
and irreverence, have in a sad degree overspread our
land; and spoiled the fair fruits of thankful obedience
which we owed to the Almighty as Englishmen, were
it only for His great mercy to us as upon this day.
Two kinds then of iniquity, impurity and irreverence,
it must be confessed with shame, have abounded:
and the consequence too plainly has been what our
Saviour foretold: the love of the greater part has
waxed cold, it is no longer, with them, the most important thing to serve and please Him. Even among
good and decent sort of people, the old martyr spirit,
the spirit of zeal and self-denial, has to a sad extent

vanished away. We confess this miserable truth against ourselves, in that it has become a proverb, 'As cold as charity.' Charity has indeed waxed cold, in our ways both of serving God, and denying ourselves, and making sacrifices for the good of our brethren. How grudgingly do very many apply themselves to devotion! in how complaining a tone do they reckon up the minutes they spend in Church, and the money they spend (if any) in helping to provide for God's being duly honoured there! how coldly and scornfully do they think of those parts of the Prayer-book, which direct daily service, the keeping of Saints' days, more frequent Communions, and a worship in any respect more troublesome than we have been accustomed to! Again, as to denying ourselves: our Lord takes it for granted that all Christians will fast as regularly as they pray; He gives directions for one as well as for the other; but how many years of our life have many of us spent with little or no regard to that great and blessed duty! Neither can it be questioned, that the New Testament, both our Lord's own words and the writings of S. Paul, give great encouragement to those Christians who stand stedfast in their heart, and abstain even from lawful marriage that they may be free to serve God the better. Our Lord and S. Paul give them great encouragement, but what sort of encouragement do they find in the common talk and judgement of even good sort of persons? I fear that on the whole our tendency in this land is to speak of such things with scorn and dislike: though we really might with just as much reason scorn and dislike prayer itself, because many pray hypocritically.

Lastly, as to making sacrifices for others : no doubt there is a great deal of good and charitable almsgiving among us : and we know that even a cup of cold water, really given in the name of Christ, shall in no wise lose its reward : but so much the more may we mourn and lament, that those who do so much have not the heart to do still more : that few or none should be found to long and labour for such a blessing as our Lord offered to the rich young man, when He bade him give up *all* that he had, and take up the Cross and follow Him. Great numbers we know in the early days of the Church followed this gracious invitation : but now, I know not how, it almost seems out of the question ; for no other reason that can be given, but that the spirit of sacrifice and self devotion, the spirit of holy love, has in some degree departed from the Church. Charity has waxed cold, because iniquity abounds : we see so many plunged deep in gross sin, that we account it a great thing if we do but keep ourselves in tolerable order, and go on decently in the world : going on unto perfection is with us quite out of the question. Not to mention the many mournful ways, in which the evil spirits themselves of uncleanness and irreverence work their way into our hearts almost before we are aware, and set us positively against holy self-denial : there is also the evil habit of making comparisons ; our measures become of course evil and untrue, when we look away from God and towards our brethren, making their conduct our rule. And what is most fatal of all, the Spirit of love is withdrawn : He departs from those hearts which He sees wilfully persisting in uncleanness and irreverence : He diminishes the measures of the help and light which He bestows, when He sees that neglected which He had bestowed before. From him that hath not to any good purpose, He takes away even that which he hath.

Such, it cannot well be denied, is our condition. Whether or no ours are the times of which our Blessed Lord was speaking, in this one very sad token they certainly agree: iniquity does really abound in them, notwithstanding all the great things which have been done for us to make us good: wickedness, especially impurity and irreverence, does really abound among us, and the love of the greater part, their love both to God and man, has really waxed cold in consequence; if their lamp is not quite spent, at least it burns far more dimly than it otherwise would. This is our present condition. What are our prospects for the future? For each one in particular, all depends on perseverance. " * He that shall endure unto the end, the same shall be saved." The worst of times need not be our ruin, if we hold fast that which was given us at our Baptism: our crown cannot be taken against our will. To this one point, my Christian brethren, we must look before all: that no wilful sin, especially no impurity nor profane irreverence, lurk in our hearts, and spoil all our prayers and our works; we must submit our thoughts, words, and actions, morning by morning, and evening by evening, to the searching and trial of His Spirit, Who is to us also a consuming fire: so may we go on, with purified and trusting hearts, to consider the aweful things which

* S. Matt. xxiv. 13.

z

are further foretold concerning the Church and the world in general. After saying that times may be expected, in which because of the great abounding of iniquity, the charity of the greater part will die down and be extinguished: the Saviour and Judge of all prophesies: " 'This Gospel of the kingdom shall be preached in all the world for a witness to all nations, and then shall the end come." Most wonderful, yet most certain! when the Church is at her worst and coldest, even then her message is to be published, and do its work as a witness to the whole world. And God's word will not return unto Him void: though the whole world seem to be against Him, His own will know His Voice, and will be gathered together to Him. The powers on both sides, the world and the Church, will go on (as it seems) increasing in might and eagerness, as their time waxes short: some mighty evil, called by Christ the abomination of desolation, will seem for a time to prevail, and the faith of the saints, we have reason to think, will be tried by a more fearful persecution than the world has ever yet seen: and then shall the end come: " like a snare shall it come on all them that dwell on the face of the whole earth."

How near the beginning of these last trials may be, it is not for man to say: but it is safe to keep them very continually in thought, and to let ourselves be reminded of them by all great dangers and deliverances; all serious events, whether public, such as that for which we thank God to-day; or private, such as from time to time befal ourselves and our families. The prophecies of our Lord and the work-

<hr>

[1] Ib. xxiv. 14.

ings of His providence, are no doubt intended, not to fill us with a restless and curious fear of what perhaps may happen, but to keep us soberly prepared for that which *must* soon happen : the return of the Great King, to take unto Him His power, and judge the whole earth. May we be found in that day on His side and not on the side of Anti-christ.

SERMON XXIX.

OUR BLESSED LORD THE FOUNT OF ALL BLESSING.

Rev vii. 17.

*" The Lamb which is in the midst of the throne shall
feed them, and shall lead them unto living fountains of waters: and God shall wipe away all
tears from their eyes."*

THERE is reason to think that in the precious promises like this which abound in the prophetic Scriptures, so far as they are to be accomplished in this
world, the Holy Spirit meant to turn our minds especially to the blessed fruits of Christian worship in
holy times and holy places. Something has been
said already on this subject, that is, reasons have
been given, why even according to what we can see
and understand, the Sacraments and ordinances of
Christ as dispensed by His Church should be sought
as the appointed cure for sick and weary souls. But
now let us go on to that, which on this subject as on
all others is the true stay and rest of the believing
heart: let us reflect that if the Church be indeed a
Church, that is, Christ's own Body and Christ's own
place, the comfort and support, as well as other
blessings, to be obtained by waiting on it, must be

more, very far more, than any reasoning, or words
of man can explain to us. As Abraham went after
God's voice, not knowing whither he went, nor in
what particular way God intended to reward him:
so Christ's faithful people having truly Abraham to
their father, will of course follow Him, the Lamb of
God, whithersoever He goeth, not expecting nor
waiting to be told exactly beforehand what particular grace He will give them on this or that occasion,
or how. As S. Peter speaking in the name of all
Christ's true disciples, when asked, "[a] Will ye also
go away ?" made answer and said, "Lord to whom
shall we go ? Thou hast the words of eternal life,"
not pretending to understand, how Christ should be
our life, but firmly believing it, and resolved to take
all consequences : so the true spiritual worshipper
and worthy receiver of the Holy Communion comes
to the Church and Altar of Christ, not because he
can understand and explain the great things which
are there said and done, but because Christ has promised to be there, and to whom else can he go but to
Christ ? Where else can he find the words of eternal
life ? Clear views, and a regular understanding of
things, in the sort of way wherein people understand
the several parts of worldly skill and knowledge—
this he does not at all depend on ; if the heavenly
Teacher appear to shew him any thing in that way,
he is very thankful for it, and very much afraid lest
he make a bad use of it, knowing that knowledge is
a most dangerous gift : but the knowledge which the
true believer seeks with all his heart, and which God
has promised to give him, is simply the knowledge

[a] S. John vi. 67.

of his duty, instruction and guidance at all times what he is to do next and how: this is what we want, and this is what we may depend on, if we set our hearts earnestly to do right when we know it: for this is the word of Him Who is Wisdom : " [b] If any man will do His will, he shall know of the doctrine." Yes you may quite depend on it, whoever comes to serve God in His Church with a true desire to please Him, and to be where He is, that person though he be ever so dull of understanding, unable to read, very deaf, scarce able to attend through infirmity of mind or body, yet if he come to Church to meet our Lord, trying at the same time, honestly trying, to keep His commandments out of Church, he will find himself fed and guided, he knows not how : to himself he may seem to carry nothing away, but bye and bye, in the other world, to his own wonder and amazement, he will know of his own spiritual growth ; and in the meantime what is his comfort ? The presence of his Saviour, His pledged and promised Presence. Wherever else He is or is not, we are quite sure He is there, where but two or three are gathered together in His Name, that is, as members of His Body, the Church, in the place which is called by His Name, and where He has promised to come with a blessing.

Christ, Who cannot lie, hath promised to be here : here therefore is the place of consolation and refreshment, here is where they must come, who desire to have all tears wiped away from their eyes.

What would you have done, had you lived in Judea in His time, and had been in any kind of

[b] S. John vii. 17.

trouble or affliction? Suppose, for example, any one of us had his home in Capernaum or Bethsaida, and news came that the Holy Jesus was at hand, and we perhaps in care and trouble about ourselves or some dear friend, What should we have done? Do you not think we should have come to Him as those in the Gospel did, crying out, "°Lord help me;" "ᵈJesus, Master, have mercy on us;" "°Sir, come down ere my child die:" or if we could not come, should we not have tried to find some one to help us, if possible to bring us before our Lord, though the roof were to be broken up and we let down in our beds to be near Him, but at any rate to cry out for us, and beseech Him, as that centurion, to heal us at a distance by His Almighty power. The one thought which would have possessed us in such a case would have been, how to come as near to Him, to put ourselves as much in the way of a blessing from Him, as we could.

Even in that time there might perhaps have been people near us who would have said, ' Why do you take all this trouble, why go out of your way to seek Him? If He be indeed so gracious and so powerful, if, as they say, He can read our hearts, may we not just as well expect Him to heal us, though neither we ourselves nor any one else for us, join the multitude of those who think it necessary to call on Him in person?' Thus people might have reasoned in that day, but if they did so, we have no reason to think they were healed by our Lord, either in body or soul: all the cases of miraculous mercy that the

° S. Matt. xv. 25.   ᵈ S. Luke xvii. 13.

• S. John iv. 49.

Gospels tell us, yes every one of them, were cases in which people more or less put themselves out of the way to wait upon our Lord, either for themselves or for some one in whom they were interested. Now His miraculous mercy was a type of His ordinary mercy: His outward and visible Presence then was a type of His inward and mysterious Presence now in His Church; and if mourners and sufferers in those days were required to seek Him to the best of their power, else there was little chance indeed of a cure; depend upon it, so it is now.

You may think perhaps, What signifies my offering so trifling a service as walking to the Lord's house and waiting on Him diligently there? a thing which any child almost can do; you may find it hard to believe that such a simple matter should be made the condition of so great a blessing: to believe and pray, you may think to yourself, surely that is the great thing: and that is what one can do just as well at home. Very many people, I believe, without being quite entirely irreligious, do allow themselves to think thus: but let them only consider what would have been the consequence of their thinking so had they been afflicted persons in our Lord's time. They might just as well have said then, So slight a matter as going out and putting one's self in His way cannot make so great a difference; I will just stay where I am: and yet you see it would have made the difference of their being healed or no. Let us make up our minds, by God's blessing to come where Christ is, lest we miss the touch of His healing hand. Let us be rather of the number of those who followed Him if so be they might touch but the hem of His garment, or of those who brought the sick on beds and couches, and laid them before the door where He was, not of those among whom it is said even He could work no miracle, because of their unbelief. He could do no miracle! what a word is that to be spoken of the Almighty Son of God! what a fearful notion does it give us of the sad effects of our unbelief and sin! that it seems in a manner to set bounds to the very power of the Almighty: He would gather men under His wings, but they would not: He would heal Babylon, but she would not be healed. So it was in those places where the Son of God came to heal, and where the people had not faith to come and be healed: and may we not fear the same or the like condemnation for those places where even now He is present by His holy Church, and they will not come near to be instructed, and comforted and healed by Him? "'woe unto thee Chorazin, woe unto thee Bethsaida, for if the mighty works, which were done in you, had been done in Tyre and Sidon, they would have repented long ago in sackcloth and ashes. But it shall be more tolerable for Tyre and Sidon at the Day of judgement, than for you." Who can say that this sentence or something like it may not be hanging over the heads of those hundreds of Christian towns and villages, where few in comparison of the inhabitants shew any true and thankful sense of Christ abiding among them by His Church: where afflicted persons seek any where for comfort, rather than to the holy prayers and psalms and Sacraments which have been the stay and consolation of the saints in all genera-

ᵗ S. Matt. xi. 21.

tions: where day by day, and week by week, the
doors of the Lord's house are thrown open, He is
there to hear their prayers, and to absolve them by
the voice of His priest, and they think not at all of
it, or if at all, only to slight and scorn it, or let it
pass idly out of their minds?

But rather let us think of the blessings they enjoy,
who come here regularly in faith and reverence, and
sincerely wish themselves here when they cannot
come.　They come here seeking for Christ, and surely
they fail not to meet Him.　Every thing here is a token of Him; just as when you enter the house of some
honoured and beloved friend, although he be himself
out of sight, you cannot turn your eyes any way but
they fall on something which brings him to your mind:
the books, the furniture, the way in which things are
ordered, the objects he delighted in, all remind you
of him, and make him in a manner present though he
is absent.　So within these walls everything to the
eye of faith is a token of Christ.　The book out of
which we read, the very printed letters as we see
them in it, especially the letters of the most holy
Names of the Three Divine Persons, are pledges to
the very outward sight of our having Them exceedingly near us: they tell us, "This is the house of
God," this is even more than the gate of heaven, for it
is a part of the kingdom of heaven, a room in the palace
of the great Lord of all.　We look upon the white
robes of the priests and other ministers of Christ, and
they seem to tell us of the fine linen, clean and white
which is the righteousness of Christ and His Saints,
the wedding garment proper for His sacred Feast:
where that holy garment is worn, there is He with

His holy ones to crown or to chastise us, according as we come worthily or unworthily. We look westward, towards the chief entrance of the Church, and we see the Font, the holy laver of regeneration, where the Holy Spirit is given continually to make young children what by nature they cannot be, members of Christ, and so children of God, and so again inheritors of the kingdom of heaven. And the fathers and mothers who bring their little ones in faith are as certain of His being there to receive them, as if they saw Him take them up in His arms, put His hands upon them and bless them. We see the aged and poor people, and the little children, constant attendants in this place, and we may well remember that where Christ's poor are, and where His little ones are, there is He, and more especially when they come to place themselves, in a manner, under the shadow of His wing. Lastly we look eastward towards the chiefest part of the Church, and what is it which we see there? We see that most holy Place, where the Lord, from time to time comes to His people, to be their meat indeed and their drink indeed. His table we may call it, for there He distributes to us that which nourishes to eternal life; and His Altar too we may surely call it, as S. Paul does in the epistle to the Hebrews, since there we make the Offering and Sacrifice, which He has ordained in memorial of His precious Death. We see that Altar table, and it is to us a sure pledge and sign of Christ's being with us in a nearer and more aweful way than He was with the Jews of old, when the cloud of glory hovered over the mercy-seat.

By all these signs, and by many more, we are

assured that we shall find our Lord here, if we seek
Him in true faith and repentance: and if we find
Christ we find consolation, patience in our sorrows,
refreshment in our anxieties, relief in our wants and
doubts. It was the way of the holy men of old:
when they were in trouble they called upon the
Lord, if they possibly might, in His house, and He
heard them. Wherever they were, of course they
prayed, but if they could, they went and prayed in
the temple; if not, at least they turned towards it
to pray. Hezekiah, for example, received a letter
which troubled him greatly, full of profane threat-
enings, from Sennacherib king of Assyria: and
what did he with it? Where did he go for comfort?
Did he shut himself in his chamber and pray over
it by himself? Did he call to him pious and religious friends and tell them his grief, and beseech
them to pray with him and for him? Either of
these would have been a good way, and would no
doubt have obtained a blessing from the God Who
heareth prayer. But we are not told that the good
king took either of these ways: what we do read of
him is, that he took the letter into the house of the
Lord, and " ᵇ spread it before the Lord ;" appealing,
as it were, in his great cause, from all human and
created power to the Judge of all the earth: and that
his call was answered immediately. God would not
keep so faithful a servant waiting, but sent a message
to him immediately, and through him to the king of
Assyria, to assure both that He Himself would defend Jerusalem and save it: and so it was that same
night, that God's Angel smote of the Assyrians a

ᵇ 2 Kings xix. 14.

hundred and eighty five thousand.   And we in like manner, when we hear any evil tidings, let us not sullenly or despondingly brood over it at home, but let us too go up to the house of the Lord and spread it before the Lord, i. e. let us first resolve to try and be even more diligent and attentive in Church than usual, and then let us remember this our trouble when saying the Church prayers.   Let us spread our letters of evil tidings before the Lord, and see if we cannot get them turned into good tidings. Let us hasten here when the world torments us, if it is only that we may see, in the regular order of things here, a sort of image of what shall be in the holy Jerusalem, when all change and chance shall be over.   If we cannot come to Church (as ninety nine times in a hundred we cannot) let us at least turn our faces towards Jerusalem; let us with holy Daniel kneel on our knees to pray and give thanks to Him, wishing ourselves in His Church, as feeling certain that He is there.   If men want any lameness, or blindness, or palsy, or leprosy, to be cured by the touch of Christ, let them bring their patient to the temple, at the hour of prayer; as S. Peter and S. John.   If we want forgiveness of sin, here the Publican sought and found it.   If we want guidance in our doings, here S. Paul looked for it; he was praying in the temple, and Christ appeared to him saying, "[1] Depart, for I will send thee far hence unto the Gentiles."   The public service, where it may be had, particularly the service for the Holy Communion with the priest's absolution going before it, is the regular and appointed service for a trou-

[1] Acts xxii. 21.

bled mind: as much so as coming to touch the hem of Christ's garment was in His time the regular appointed service for a distempered body. And be ye quite sure of this: that the more earnestly we try, in quiet and untroubled times, to love the Church services and enter into their meaning, the more readily shall we draw comfort and refreshment from them in the hard and trying times. When Christ was upon earth in sight, those who came punctually and earnestly to seek Him might seem indeed to be kept waiting, for the trial of their faith, but were sure to find Him at last, and finding Him, to find health and consolation. And so it is, even more surely, now that He is nearer to us than ever, though out of sight. His gracious invitation is, "[k] O tarry thou the Lord's leisure: be strong and He shall comfort thine heart; and put thou thy trust in the Lord." May our devout answer always be, "[l] We wait for Thy loving kindness, O God, in the midst of Thy temple."

[k] Ps. xxvii. 16.   [l] Ib. xlviii. 8.

SERMON XXX.

THE DANGER OF PRIDING OURSELVES ON OUR RELIGIOUS PRIVILEGES.

ZEPH. iii. 11.

"Thou shalt no more be haughty because of My holy mountain."

"HE came unto His own, and His own received Him not." And why? because they were too proud of being His own. A marvellous thing to happen and a marvellous reason for it. And accordingly the Holy Spirit of God vouchsafed to speak of it beforehand by the prophets, that it might not be too great a distress and scandal when it really came to pass.

For in this passage of the prophet Zephaniah as well as in many other places, we are doubtless intended to think not only of the sins of the people of Israel just before the Babylonian captivity, but also, perhaps much more, of their great and final downfall, when they rejected and crucified the Lord of glory. The prophets of Jerusalem in that day, it was foretold, would be light and treacherous persons: and such were the Scribes and Pharisees, declared by the Eternal Wisdom to be fools and blind. Her

priests would pollute the sanctuary, and do violence
to the law: and did not Caiaphas and the rest meet
in the temple to pay Judas for betraying the innocent Blood? Did they not, under colour of the law,
condemn and murder and hold accursed Him Who
alone of all men ever entirely kept the law? "The
just Lord," saith the prophet, "is in the midst of that
city, every morning He doth bring His judgement
to light: He faileth not." What is this but the
Evangelist or rather Christ Himself telling us in
other words; "ᵃI sat daily with you teaching in the
temple," and "ᵇwhich of you convinceth Me of sin?"
"but the unjust knoweth no shame," they could not
answer Him, therefore took they up stones to cast at
Him. In His providence He had cut off the nations,
one after another, Assyria, Babylon, Tyre, Egypt,
Persia, Greece, but Jerusalem would not be warned:
their hearts were still set upon being great in the
earth after the manner of earthly kingdoms. Thus
and then came their ruin: they would none of their
Saviour, because He was not such a Saviour as they
desired, not a great one of this world. The Lord
poured out all His fierce anger upon them. A remnant only might be saved, and observe what is the
mark, the especial token whereby that remnant should
be known, "I will take away out of thee them that
rejoice in thy pride, and thou shalt no more be
haughty because of My holy mountain."

There it is, my brethren, you see clearly the rea-
son of the judgement. The Almighty Teacher lays
His finger as it were especially on the pride of the
Jews as the cause of their rejection: and it is their

ᵃ S. Matt. xxvi. 55.   ᵇ S. John viii. 55.

spiritual pride, for it related not to any outward or worldly advantages which they had or thought they had; but what made them proud, what they valued themselves on, was their spiritual privileges, their singular nearness to God. "They were haughty because of My holy mountain." Does the prophet only say this? or saith not the Gospel the very same? "ᶜThou art called a Jew, and restest in the law, and makest thy boast of God." They said, "ᵈWe be Abraham's seed, and were never in bondage to any man: how sayest Thou, ye shall be made free?" "ᵉHow can ye believe," said our Lord to them, "who receive honour one of another, and seek not the honour that cometh from God only." The Pharisee in our Lord's parable was a type and sample of the greater part of the nation. They were regularly in the temple or in some appointed place, praying: or rather seeming to pray, for all the while they were praising themselves in their hearts, and saying, "ᶠGod I thank Thee, that I am not as other men are." And as he knew no better than to scorn the publican even in his private addresses to God, so we remember how these haughty men, (haughty because of the holy mountain in which they fancied they had a high place), we remember, I say, they scorned their brethren of the common people, who were beginning to think reverently of our Lord. "ᵍHave any of the rulers of the Pharisees believed on Him? But this people who knoweth not the law are cursed."

You might think that this abominable pride would only damage a few persons, those who were in the

---

ᶜ Rom. ii. 17. ᵈ S. John viii. 33. ᵉ Ib. v. 44.
ᶠ S. Luke xviii. 11. ᵍ S. John vii. 48, 49.

highest places; but it was not so, my brethren, it had
its effect on the common people also, for they also
knew themselves to be Abraham's seed, as well as
the Pharisees, and they also were glad to be shewn
the way to a light and easy religion, a religion which
would save them the trouble of true repentance and
amendment. And they too very generally and very
quickly learned to say, "We have Abraham to our
father;" and in that they trusted: God would not
cast them off, they thought, whatever they might do,
because they were Abraham's seed. The promises,
they fancied, were made to them positively and absolutely, and could not be forfeited, be their sins
what they might. They had the same kind of confidence in God as those whom we call spoiled children have in their parents who deny them nothing.

And this proud selfish scornful temper mixing
itself with their very religion, was no new thing
among the Israelites. It was the very same which
had been complained of so many hundred years before, when it had shewn itself among the foulest
idolaters, as it did in our Lord's time among the op-
pressors and murderers. Hear Isaiah, speaking in
the Name of the Lord, "[b] I have spread out My
hands all the day unto a rebellious people, which
walketh in a way that *was* not good, after their own
thoughts; a people that provoketh Me to anger continually to My face; that sacrificeth in gardens, and
burneth incense upon altars of brick; which remain
among the· graves, and lodge in the monuments,
which eat swine's flesh, and broth of abominable
things is in their vessels; which say, Stand by thy-

[b] Isa. lxv. 2—5.

self, come not near to me, for I am holier than thou. These are a smoke in My nose, a fire that burneth all day." Only think, brethren, how wonderful, how horrible! that persons thus provoking the Lord should yet be bold and shameless enough to keep others at a distance, as not holy, not good enough to come near them! Again, hear another prophet, "'They build up Zion with blood, and Jerusalem with iniquity. The heads thereof judge for reward, and the priests thereof divine for money: yet will they lean upon the Lord, and say, Is not the Lord among us? none evil can come upon us." And once more, listen to Jeremiah crying out and warning them yet more passionately, as he saw the cloud gathering, and ready to burst upon them; "ᵏTrust ye not in lying words, saying, the temple of the Lord, the temple of the Lord, the temple of the Lord, are these. Behold, ye trust in lying words, that cannot profit. Will ye steal, murder, and commit adultery, and swear falsely, and burn incense unto Baal, and walk after other gods whom ye know not; and come, and stand before Me in this house, which is called by My Name, and say, We are delivered to do all these abominations? Is this house, which is called by My Name become a den of robbers in your eyes? Behold, even I have seen *it*, saith the Lord."

In all these instances, brethren, as in our Lord's own sayings, it is the same thing which seems to be wondered at: it seems to astonish as it were, and shock even Him Who is the Wisdom of God, not so much that they should prove so wicked but that

ˡ Mic. iii. 10, 11.   ᵏ Jer. vii. 4, 8—11.

being wicked they should pride themselves in their holiness: not in mere hypocrisy, pretend to trust in it, but really trust in it and think themselves good enough.

As this was the case in the Old Testament with Judah, more than with Israel, so in the New with the Pharisees, more than the common people. With Judah more than with Israel, because they had the true temple and priesthood, and were under the house of David; they had not so openly and entirely given themselves up to the ways of the heathen. With the Pharisees more than the common people, more than the other sects, such as the Sadducees, because they came nearer the right faith and the true meaning of the Scriptures. But for this very reason, even as we read in the prophet Jeremiah, that "the backsliding Israel had justified herself more than the treacherous Judah:" so we read in the Gospels that the Scribes and Pharisees received from our Lord and Judge, the severest condemnation of any persons. "Woe unto you hypocrites" (it is eight times repeated) "[1] ye serpents, ye generation of vipers, how can ye escape the damnation of hell?" And "[m] the publicans and the harlots go into the kingdom of God before you."

And now, dear brethren, I come to the most serious and aweful part of what I have to say: serious and aweful, because it directly concerns the very soul, the immortal life, of every one of us. For you are not to imagine that this most dangerous temper, being haughty because of God's holy mountain, is gone by and passed out of the world, that it

[1] S. Matt. xxiii. 33.   [m] Ib. xxi. 31.

cannot be found among your temptations and mine,
because we are Christians, and those who were
warned of it are Jews. Far from it: we are in
some respects even more exposed to it than they.
For what is God's holy mountain but the Christian
Church? Sion—that hill in the city of Jerusalem on
which David's palace stood, and also that blessed
upper-room, in which our Lord was hed His disciples'
feet, ate the last Passover, instituted the Holy Communion, promised the Holy Ghost to His disciples,
interceded so solemnly for us and for His whole
Church, to which room also finally the Holy Ghost
came down—Sion, I say, where these holiest things
were done, came indeed to be God's holy mountain, far holier, more gracious, more aweful than
Sinai, where the Lord had spoken to the people from
the top of the mountain out of the midst of the fire.
But neither Sion itself, nor any other place, is
really intended by the holy mountain. No single
place, for our Lord had said, "[n] The hour cometh
when ye shall neither in this mountain nor yet at
Jerusalem, worship the Father;" i. e. not so as that it
should be better to serve Him there, than in other
places. But our Sion is the Christian Church in all
the world, the city of the living God, the heavenly
Jerusalem to which as Christians we are come, and
in which by God's grace we hope to abide for ever,
and be saved among the remnant of the true Israelites. That is our Sion, and who can ever speak or
think worthily of the inestimable benefits of having
a portion therein? for it is indeed all one with being
a member of Christ, a partaker of the Divine Nature.

[n] S. John iv. 21.

We cannot think too much of it, but we may think wrongly of it, as of every thing else, and of every person, however great and good and holy. And you do think wrongly of our holy mountain the Church, if you allow yourself on account of it or of any thing belonging to it, to be proud and *haughty* and self-satisfied or to look disdainfully on any others. Perhaps it may be hard for some to imagine what I can mean by this. Because all persons now here call themselves Christians, and so to any one of us it is no distinction to be called a Christian: you never dreamed of being proud or lifted up by *that*: in that respect you know you are but as the rest of your neighbours. Very well; but although you are all Christians alike, no two of you all are exactly in the same circumstances as Christians, no two of you enjoy exactly the same privileges. Only look round you, my brethren, round the Church, round the parish, round the neighbourhood, round the country, round the world. To take one of the most ordinary distinctions, neither in this, I suppose, nor in any other mixed congregation, can we suppose every one able to read, every one having a Bible, much less every one equally able to study and comprehend that Bible. And it is the same with other privileges: a Church near at hand, room in the Church, pastoral ministrations sufficient and suited to your needs, both in the Church and out of it: or again, the family in which a man lives; whether holy and good ways, the ways of the Church, are kept up in it or no, and the neighbourhood, whether its tone and temper in such things is faithless or believing, religious or scornful; whether the air which

a man breathes, in-doors and out of doors feel like
air of Christendom, or no; all these things, and
many more, make an immense difference between
one man's condition and another's, and it is but too
possible for a person who feels himself to be well off,
better off than many others, in such things as these,
to look down on those others, to presume on his own
good estate, to watch himself the less strictly and
humbly; to allow in himself somewhat of the sad
temper of that Pharisee: and what is this but being
haughty because of My holy mountain? the very
temper which the Lord has said should no more be
in those who give themselves to Christ. Yes, brethren, it is but too plain, if you think on it for a
moment; from the highest to the lowest in the
Church of Christ, from the least little child sitting
by another child on a form in a Sunday school, to
any the most dignified among Bishops and pastors,
there is a temptation and a trial in respect of humility: we are one and all tempted to be self-satisfied and proud, instead of simply thankful for the
portion and standing which God has given us in this
His Church, His holy mountain: much as when
choral music is going on, and a whole company or
congregation are singing or playing every one his
own part, there is a temptation (especially to the
skilful ones) to be thinking of one's self, how well
one is performing, instead of throwing oneself heart
and soul and voice into the work, how sacred
soever.

And this disposition to praise one's self in one's
heart is always accompanied with a tendency to despise others. This is brought out among ourselves

far more plainly, alas! than could be wished by the sad and unhappy divisions now for so many ages existing in the Christian world. Whatever line of separation we look at, whether to Catholic Christians as compared with those who deny more or less of the Creed: or to Churchmen compared with dissenters: or to "good Churchmen" (so-called) compared with such as seem to think less of the Church: can we deny that in proportion to people's earnestness and zeal, Satan is sure to whisper to their secret souls more or less of vain imaginations, how good it is of them to keep so exactly to the right, and to teach them a kind of scornful pity for those whom they see to be in the wrong? And this on both sides alike of the line: for I am now supposing both to be equally serious and well-intentioned.

Again, to put a case somewhat different, who cannot see that among Churchmen some are far more diligent and thoughtful, and avail themselves more freely of Church privileges than others; that some communicate as often as they can, some so rarely, that they seem as if they would be glad to stay away altogether if they dared? And that each of these has his temptation to be haughty, in respect of those who seem not so high in the mountain as himself; the constant towards the occasional communicant, the rare one towards him who never comes at all!

This whole subject on which I have been speaking, I feel to be a delicate and rather a distressing one, as indeed every thing is that brings up the thought of 'our unhappy divisions:' and it may seem so far unsuitable to the joyfulness of this good day. But perhaps it is not altogether out of season, to warn one's self and others of this particular danger, in places and at times which stand out as it were, in any respect from among others; as, for example, where special endeavours have been made, as in this Church, from the hour of its first opening, to serve God in the beauty of holiness, and to do all things decently and in order. I wish to say to you and to myself, that while we are truly thankful for these things, which are real duties and privileges both, we ought to beware of so setting our hearts upon them, as to indulge any scornful feeling towards such as do not see the need of them, in the Church, or out of the Church: and God forbid that any one of us should give way to the thought, which is sure to be suggested to him, that his being regular in these services, and taking ever so much delight in them, will in the least lessen his guilt and his punishment, if he go on, openly or in secret, breaking any one of God's plain commandments.

Alas it is far otherwise. The higher any one is, by God's favour, in the holy mountain, whether in knowledge or in Sacramental privileges, the worse and more shameful is every known sin. O beware, for what a pity it would be, fenced as we are in this sacred ground, to let the great Owner when He comes, find it ravaged and devoured by evil spirits, as by wild boars and beasts of the field, all through our grievous fault. Remember, he that "° knew his Lord's will and prepared not *himself*, neither did according to his will, shall be beaten with many *stripes.*" Use yourself to look on each attendance

° S. Luke xii.˙47.

here, each participation of the means of grace, not as a debt paid, a duty done, but as a privilege mercifully granted, and lovingly to be accounted for. Think often, what you may be sure is most true, how much better use others would have made of your privileges than you have done. Thus you will apply to the disease its appointed cure: you will subdue the gay proud thought, how well you seem to be going on in comparison with others, taking part with the publican; praying and striving always to be of "[p] God's afflicted and poor people," whom He has left in the midst of His fallen Church trusting in the Name of the Lord.

[p] Zeph. iii. 12.

SERMON XXXI.

THE USE OF SUNDAY.

Ps. xlvi. 10.

" Be still then, and know that I am God."

ALL who have any religion at all think more or less of Sunday. This is so much a matter of course, that it is, we know, a kind of proverb, when one is describing an utter heathen and unbeliever, to say, 'all days are alike to him, he makes no difference between Sundays and working-days,' and the saying, like all common sayings, is not without a great and deep reason. It is quite true, that although, of course, a man may keep Sunday outwardly, and still be in heart and life a thorough heathen and unbeliever; yet no one who profanes the Sunday, can by any possibility be a truly religious person.

Now what is the great and deep reason of this? Not simply, because God has given through His Church a plain and positive command that Sunday should be kept; though that ought to be reason enough for any one who fears God; but in this instance He has been pleased to let us see the reason and principle of this His plain command. Hear what He says to His first people Israel: you have already heard it again and again from the prophet Ezekiel in the first lesson this morning. There He points it out to them as one of the chiefest things which He did for them on bringing them out of Egypt, "ᵃ I gave them My sabbaths, to be a sign between Me and them, that they might know that I am the Lord that sanctify them." He reckons up the sins of that generation in the wilderness, and twice He repeats, "ᵇThey polluted My sabbaths; My sabbaths they greatly polluted." And as their sins were repeated, so was His fatherly warning: "ᶜI said unto their children in the wilderness, Hallow My sabbaths, and they shall be a sign between Me and you, that ye may know that I am the Lord your God." And in the long course of sin which led to their sad captivity, this again is especially set down, over and over, "They polluted My sabbaths." The sabbath, therefore, was one main part of God's dealings with His ancient people for their good, and we are not to doubt that the Sunday is a main point of His dealings with us Christians. Polluting the sabbath was one of the worst provocations, in the wilderness and in the land of Canaan : so doubtless profanation of the Sunday will be a sore part of the burthen of deadly sin which will weigh down Christians in the day of account. And the Lord has added one at least of the reasons, why the sabbath was of so great consequence. It was to be "a sign" He says, " between Me and you, that ye may know that I am the Lord your God." Not to other people only, but to themselves; the right keeping of the day of rest, was to be a sign between God and His people;

ᵃ Ezek. xx. 12.   ᵇ ib. 16, 13.   ᶜ ib. 18, 20.

Ezekiel repeats it after Moses, for the Lord had spoken unto Moses from the beginning, "[d] Speak thou also unto the children of Israel, saying, Verily My sabbaths ye shall keep, for it is a sign between Me and you throughout your generations, that ye may know that I am the Lord which do sanctify you." There could be no real knowing that He was the Lord, without real keeping of His sabbaths. How and why is this? We must consider what sabbaths are, what the word sabbath means. It means as you all know, rest. Rest from what? Of course from labour and toil, from the ordinary work by which men carry on the course of this world: even as God is said to have rested after the creation when He had finished making new things and putting the world in that course in which it was afterwards to go on. He left off creating, as a token that we should leave off working: and He would have us leave off working in order that we may come to know Him; as it is written in the text which I read to you out of one of the psalms, "Be still then, and know that I am God." A man must be still, he must give himself time to think, he must pause in his earthly cares and labours and in his wild impatient fretful hurrying on after earthly things, else he will know nothing of God: he may say good words, he may remember prayers and psalms which he has learned, he may now and then have good thoughts hurrying across his mind, as bright spots of clear sky come out for short intervals in a wild windy day among the clouds. I say, a man who is always in this world's work may now and then have thoughts of God, but he cannot

[d] Exod. xxxi. 31.

really come to know Him without being sometimes
"still:" without having sabbaths, i. e. times of rest,
and hallowing them, i. e. giving them to God.   Observe, I am speaking here, not of the seventh day only,
which was ordained to be the Jews' sabbath, nor of the
first day only, which is ordained to be our Lord's day :
but of all the appointed times, whether they be days,
or hours, or minutes only, which God Almighty gives
us, wherein to draw near to Him that we may know
Him.   E. g. His providence allows us, every evening
and morning of our lives, some time, more or less,
wherein to say our prayers to Him : and I hope we
all make a rule of doing so, however sorely some may
be tempted, by hurry or other circumstances, too
often to break that rule.   Now with what mind, my
brethren, in what temper would you wish to be, when
you kneel down to pray to God ?   Surely you would
wish to be serious and composed, not full of worldly
profits or pleasures, not carried away by any passion
or fancy ; you would not choose to be in a rage with
any one, nor out of breath with searching after something which you vehemently desired, just at the very
moment that you were kneeling down to speak to the
Most High.   If a voice came at that moment from
heaven and said, " Be still now, and know that I am
God," you would acknowledge that it came season-
ably ; because your own heart would tell you, that
in order to have that sense of God's Presence which
is most desirable in all devotion, you must try to
subdue all outward and sensible excitement, you
have need to be as calm, as serious, as attentive as
ever you can possibly.

In like manner, when our Almighty Father is

speaking to any of us, by some turn of His providence; our own sickness, suppose, or approaching death, or the sickness, death, or danger of any one near and dear to us: or if it be a matter of great joy; life preserved, health restored, a happy marriage or birth, or whatever other gift of God it may be, that would go nearest to a good man's heart: whether it be for rejoicing or for mourning, we all feel that it becometh us well to be as "still," i. e. as serious and composed as we can, when we are receiving it at God's hand, otherwise we shall not in our hearts really know that it is His doing, and we shall not be any the nearer to Him for it.

Now for the very same reason that would make one wish to be thoughtful and serious when one is about to say one's prayers; or when the Almighty is shewing Himself especially near, in the way either of chastisement or mercy: for that very same reason all Christians know in their hearts how they ought to keep Sunday, not as a holiday, a *mere* day of leisure, but as a holy day, a day of *religious* leisure. The Lord says, 'Be still on this day, in order that ye may know that I am God:' "Hallow My sabbaths, that they may be a sign between Me and you, that ye may know that I am the Lord."

It is a plain command which no man can break without sin, and it is also a distinct promise of a very great blessing. Keep the sabbath, the Lord's rest holy; keep it *as* the Lord's rest, and ye shall know that I am the Lord which doth sanctify you. How many are there who go about saying in their hearts, "* Shew me some token for good:" some in a

* Ps. lxxxvi. 17.

restless kind of devotion, like Zacharias when he
said, "'Whereby shall I know this?" some in a discontented fretful unbelieving way, like the Jews
seeking a sign. Now to each one of these our Lord
comes every Sunday morning, and says, ' Here is
My sign, a sign from heaven, the very sign of the
prophet Jonas ;' for as that which happened to Jonas,
his deliverance from the whale's belly, was a figure
of our Lord's Resurrection yet to come, so the Sundays kept by the Church throughout the world are a
token and memorial of it, now that it has come.
Whoever then shall duly keep Sunday, the feast of
Christ's Resurrection, he shall know that Christ is
the Lord, and more ; he shall know that Christ is the
Lord sanctifying him : for Sunday is also the day on
which Christ began to sanctify His Church : the
Holy Spirit came down this day on the Apostles.
Therefore, as I said, as soon as we wake on Sunday
morning, would we but believe it, the Lord speaks
to us from heaven, to each one according to the several mind he is in ; and His word is, ' Behold, I am
come to bless you, if only you will be still, really
trying to rest from other things, you shall know Me,
know that I am God ; and My sure word is, "* This
is Life eternal, to know Thee, the only true God,
and Jesus Christ whom Thou hast sent."' This is
our Lord's offer made to you, every Sunday morning of your life. Suppose you are inclined to discontent and fretfulness, on account of something that
goes wrong: your schemes perhaps are disappointed,
your substance seems diminishing, your friends fail
you, you meet with ill usage and ingratitude, all the

<hr>

*S. Luke i. 18.   * S. John xvii. 3.

week perhaps you have felt low and desponding, as if nothing prospered with you: well, but now the Lord's day is opening, and the Lord Himself is here to greet you; do you open your heart to Him: trust Him with all your anxieties, pour out all your cares, all your fears, into His Bosom; He will not turn away from you, He will not say He has no leisure to attend to you. His Holy Spirit came down to-day to be the Comforter of His Church: He will not deny His comfort to any, the least, the unworthiest of His members.

Perhaps your cares and fears are not earthly, but spiritual: you have not that perfect assurance in your heart which you would wish to have of our Lord's forgiveness and favour: you wonder whether you are really in His Church or no: you are ashamed and afraid, because you cannot pray as you ought; the remembrance of your old sins comes fearfully over you, and you are in sad doubt whether your repentance has been, or will be, sufficient. Alas! Who can wonder or blame you, if you are in sorrow of heart? But yet, if you will but believe it, there is consolation and relief for you every Sunday of your lives: every Sunday of your lives He invites you, "[h] Come unto Me, and I will give you rest." All that happens in the ordinary course of that day; the very sun rising in the morning, the bells going for Church, the quietness of the fields, streets and roads, from the usual works not going on; the cattle resting according to the commandment; almost all whom we meet wearing their best; and much more, the circumstances of our holy worship itself; all this, I

[h] S. Matt. xi. 28.

B b

say, we are to take as so many signs from heaven,
that God is among us of a truth, that He is our God,
that His will is to save, forgive, sanctify and bless
us for ever, if we prevent Him not, by refusing
to improve the helps and opportunities He giveth.
Be still then, and know that He is God, all ye that
are doubtful and discontented. A large portion, of
the younger ones especially, are but too happy and
contented with their present condition; they seem to
be prospering and enjoying themselves thoroughly:
what has the Sunday to say to these? Why, it comes
to them as a grave and kind friend might come to a
thoughtless schoolboy, and say, 'Take care how you
go out in the morning, or lie down at night, without first saying your prayers.' It is as if the heavenly voice should speak again, and address them
in this way: 'Your care is to enjoy yourselves; yet
surely at the bottom of your hearts you would wish
for God's blessing on your enjoyment: and you who
are thriving in the world, hard-working industrious
people, you know, one and all, that you cannot go
on thriving unless it shall please God to bless your
work; make up your mind then, by God's blessing,
to the little sacrifice of time and trouble which the
holy day requires of you; do not think it too much
to consider in the morning, not how you may enjoy
yourself most on this your welcome holiday, but
how you may best advance in the knowledge of God
on this His own day; how you may best shew yourself thankful, and help others to be so.' Depend
upon it, there will be no loss of cheerfulness by your
setting yourself such a rule as that; your holiday
will not be the less delightful for being in earnest

kept as a holy day.   If you are a young boy or girl,
do not start with contriving how you may manage
to have as little of Church, as little of school, as ever
you can : but rather think this with yourself : Christ
is in the Church, I know : and Christ is in the Bible
which I learn at school: I must not scorn either
school or Church, lest I should be scorning our Lord
Christ, and then where shall I find a Saviour? If
you be a grown-up young man or woman, O beware
of making the Lord's day a day for merely seeking
your own pleasure.   Remember this is the very account which the Holy Scripture, by the prophet
Isaiah, gives of a holy time well spent : "[i]Thou shalt
call the sabbath a delight, the holy of the Lord,
honourable, and shalt honour Him, not doing thine
own ways, nor finding thine own pleasure, nor speaking thine own words:" and this is the promise with
which he follows it up, "Then shalt thou delight
thyself in the Lord."   It is God's own word most
plainly spoken : a boy or a girl, a young man or
woman, who will truly and really make it his endeavour to make the best use he can of his Sunday, will
soon begin to find it more delightful by far, than
if he had just made it a day for the most pleasure
and diversion he could get.   Only try ; only make
proof of it : see whether going to Church twice, and
keeping up your Sunday thoughts out of Church will
not make the whole day pass in a far more cheerful
and refreshing way than that other too common custom of just giving the least that you can to worship,
none at all to good thoughts, and your whole heart
and spirit to amusement.   Which of the two ways

---

[i] Isa. lviii. 13, 14.

is pleasantest to think of, when you lie down at night?
Which will seem more comfortable to look back upon,
when you are at your work the following week?
And think not that you may, when you please, make
up for these wasted Sundays, and then it will be the
same thing in the end.   Surely you know that time
lost can never be recovered ; it is gone for ever : and
if you will think on it for a moment, you will perceive that Sundays thrown away are far worse than
time merely lost.   Alas ! it is too true that they are
so many steps to utter unbelief and ruin.   For as
hallowing God's sabbaths, being religiously still, is
the way to know Him as God, so profaning and polluting His sabbaths, refusing to enter into His rest,
is the way to lose what little knowledge, what little
faith one has.   Make sure of it : if you will not in
earnest give your Sundays to your Saviour, you will
find, at last, that you have unawares given them to
the devil.'   For as the devil is always at hand to
spoil our greatest blessings if we will let him, to
turn our Communions into damnation, our marriages
into self-will and self-indulgence, our prayers into
taking God's name in vain : so if we will let him,
he can but too easily find out a use of his own for
our Sundays.   And as times go, I much fear that
that good day is, to very many, by far the worst day
in the week.   And what alas ! will be the end of it
all ?

I beseech you, my brethren, do not reject this warning.   The time of year is now come again, in which
many of you have more leisure on the week days to
think on the Sundays.   Your Lord invites you to be
still, in order to know that He is *God :* to rest from

your own works, that you may practise yourselves a little in the perfect rest, for which you hope. Do not despise, do not turn away from Him. And if you will listen to Him, these are the kind of rules you must keep. On week-days look back to the last Sunday, and on Sundays make yourselves good rules for the week following. In your meat, drink, and diversions, on that good day, be very cheerful and thankful, but never forget Who is watching you. Think of others as well as yourself, how sad it would be to help them on in the knowledge of the devil, on the day when *Christ* invites them to be still that they may know Him. Try to regard every Sunday as a step toward heaven, and by His grace He will make it so. These few hours well-spent will happily leaven your whole life, and insure you a joyful and eternal sabbath after a very short time.

SERMON XXXII.

CONVERSION.

Jer. xiii. 23.

" Can the Ethiopian change his skin, or the leopard his
spots ? then may ye also do good, that are accus-
tomed to do evil."

Two things there are especially, my brethren, which
hinder backsliding Christians from earnestly turning
themselves towards Him, from Whom they have
deeply revolted, two "*sore evils under the sun,"
which we are all apt to make too light of. One of
these is the evil and bitterness of sin, that men will
not believe, till they have tried; the other, that they
think far too little of the labour, and hardship, and
difficulty, of true, entire conversion and amendment.
As to the first, I spoke to you last Sunday, and tried
to point out to you some few of the innumerable evils
and bitternesses, in which men lose themselves when
they forsake the Lord. At present I will say no
more of that, than only just to beg of you, as you
love your own souls and care for your Saviour, that
you would make much of every thing, that would
cause you to be serious in your judgement of your

* Eccles. v. 13.

own sins, and would shrink from every thing that would encourage you in making light of them. As we go about the world, there is nothing we ought to be more afraid of, than 'a false peace and a silent conscience.' It is easy to damage other men's souls and our own by admitting vain excuses and clokes for sin, and making the heart easy, when it ought to be broken with religious fear and godly sorrow : but it is very very hard to repair the damage, to undo the mischief, to recover the lost ground. Therefore, I say it over and over again, be very jealous, my brethren, of any conversation, any reading, any thoughts, coming into your mind, which would make you easy in any known transgression of any of God's plain commandments, as if such transgression were a small matter, a thing tolerable. Do not use yourselves to smile, nor be amused at such doings : never allow yourself nor any one else to speak of them, except as of evil things and bitter. It is sometimes a hard rule to keep, but it is always a safe one.

And for the like reason, my brethren, be very much afraid of making out repentance to be easy. This is another of Satan's deep devices, by which he would keep us fast-bound in the chains of our sins. If he can, he will keep it from galling us, that we may be content to go on bearing it : and if we are disposed to get rid of it, he is sure to suggest, 'There is no hurry ; the work is easy enough, and bye and bye will do as well as now : the knot is one which you can undo at any time.' He whispers, 'You may repent whenever you please ; and repentance is never too late.'

My brethren, listen not to him : it *is* not at all true
that repentance is an easy work, or that bye and
bye will do as well as now. It is natural enough,
certainly, that we should think it easy : since we
think so little, most of us, of the mischief of sin,
which it was intended to cure. Persons who have
used themselves to make light of their bodily com-
plaints commonly imagine, when any thing is the
matter, that very simple treatment will heal it : and
there are many of confident and sanguine tempers,
who will not be put out of their way, even when
they know the attack is serious : they rely upon the
strength of their constitution, and will not be directed. Such have often found themselves deceived.
Much more must sinners expect to pay dear for the
grievous error and presumption of deferring their
conversion, as if they could set about it at any time,
or as if, whenever it took place, it would be their
own work, not God's ; or as if there were no law of
His just and severe providence, to make it harder
and more unlikely for every moment that it is volun-
tarily delayed. Yet so it is, not seldom. People
who know and are willing to confess that they are
in sin and that they know their sin to be mortal, will
coolly put off their repentance, saying, they mean to
turn to God some day or other, they are aware that
they must do so or be ruined, but it shall not be now.
And if you expostulate with them, they make it plain
by their talk, that they imagine holiness to be a
thing so much in their own power, that they may
take to it, and leave off their sin, whenever they
please, and in ever so short a time : and that whenever they begin to do so, He, for Christ's sake, will

forgive them at once and entirely. And so He will, if they truly and thoroughly repent, but true thorough, consistent repentance is a much greater work than they dream of, a work which cannot be begun, much less accomplished, without very special grace from Almighty God: and you, alas, what are you doing, but trifling with the hope of that grace, and provoking Him to withdraw it from us once and for ever? And then, better were it for you that you had never been baptized, never been born.

Do you not see, do you not feel, (if you will be but ever so little in earnest in attending to what passes between you and your God) how very much mischief you are led into by indulging the notion that the cure of your sins will be easy, and need not take a long time? The consequence is, first of all, that you lightly put away warnings: you say to yourselves, perhaps to others, ' We have heard all this before, and no doubt shall hear it often: to be sure it is all true, but it is a great weariness : no need to think of it at present: bye and bye our time will come to look after such things: till then we will enjoy ourselves: and we shall do well enough at last.' My brethren, is not this too true an account of the way, in which very many of us have been behaving to the Holy and Good Spirit these many years? And He hath spared us so long, and hath not ceased warning us: but will He bear it, do you think, for ever? He hath sent unto us all His servants the prophets, all their sayings in His holy Bible, and the teaching of His holy Church, heavenly messages without number, and we (must we not confess it?) have hearkened not: because we thought we could hearken and repent when we pleased.

And not hearkening to God's warning, of course, when temptation comes strong, men repeat the sin: and every time it is repeated, it blunts the edge of their conscience, and they vex themselves less and less about it. They come nearer and nearer to the prophet's miserable account of the Jews filling up the measure of their iniquities. "[b] Were they a-shamed when they had committed abominations? nay, they were not at all ashamed, neither could they blush." We are shocked when we see men and women in certain shameful ways, who have become so hardened as this: but alas, it is but the natural fruit of our own presumptuous doings, in deferring our repentance under the notion that we may repent when we will.

It is part of the same profane daring, when men put themselves in the way of temptation, when they seek out rather than avoid the sights and sounds and companions which they know are most apt to seduce them: when they go as near to deadly outward sin as they dare, thinking they can say to themselves at any moment, 'Thus far will I go and no further:' whereas after such wilful indulgence they have no more power (without special grace) to stay their own evil passions, than they have to stand on the sea-shore, and cause the tide to stop from rising at any point they please. Thus, one way or another, while the backslider is deceiving himself with a sort of good intention, the custom or habit of doing evil is formed: such a custom, as, according to the proverb, is even

[b] Jer. vi. 15.

a second nature : they can no more break it by their own power, than an Ethiopian, or African negro, can change his skin, or a leopard his spots. He that hath made us, you see, assures us that it is so. " Can the Ethiopian " (saith He) " change his skin, or the leopard his spots ?" Can a person who is naturally black make himself white by any effort or contrivance whatever? Or if a leopard wanted for any reason to be otherwise marked than he is, hath he any power at all to make the alteration ? No more may ye do good, that are accustomed to do evil. Not, of course, that our very nature is bad, as it came to us by our Creator's will : " God saw all things that He had made, and behold they were very good : " but ever since man's unhappy fall, he hath become weak through the flesh and unable to command himself. We were in sin when we came from our mother's womb, in original sin, the sin we inherited from Adam, and that alone was sufficient to hinder us from so working as to please God ; but our own ill-practice and ill-behaviour has made our condition much worse : too many of us, at one time or other of our lives, have become " accustomed to do evil." And when it once comes to that, the chances of effectual entire amendment are very much lessened indeed. The bad habit has a double power to make the sinner's condition more incurable : a power of its own, and a power from God's just judgement.

Wonderful in itself is the dominion which custom or practice gains over man's heart as well as body : I need hardly give instances of it : you know without being told, how that even in the most indifferent

* Gen. i. 31.

matter, the most ordinary postures, movements, and actions, when once people have got into a way of practising them, it seems next to impossible to leave them off. We come to do things without being a-ware that we do them: and when our attention is drawn to them, we feel as if we could not leave them off. Such is the power of habit or custom, put into our minds and bodies by Almighty God, that we might be tried, whether we will make a good or bad use of it. How fearful to think what a turn it too often takes ! how exceedingly horrible to be aware of shameful, corrupting, deadly sins, in a man's own self or his neighbour, having come to be so habitual as to be committed without the sinner being aware of it: or, if he is aware, with the feeling that he cannot at all help it. How shocking, how loathsome to the holy Angels, to behold Christian people, members of their and our Lord, so given over to the worst habits, that they even seem to be part of themselves, and the question may be asked of them too, 'Can the thief leave off his stealing, the drunkard his strong drink, the unclean his wicked pleasures, the liar his deceivings, the common swearer his oaths, the fretful and envious man his unkind ways?' 'Can these do good, now they are accustomed to evil ?' Can profane swearers ever be cured, seeing that it so often goes on all day long without the speaker being himself aware what he is saying, so entirely are the oaths become natural to his tongue ? Can stealing be cured, when the thief's hand has so used itself to take and conceal his neigh-bour's goods, that it does so without questioning, as a matter of course, whenever things come in its way ? or lying, when it has come to the tongue quite na-

turally perhaps ever since one learned to speak, as
often as truth seemed inconvenient? or drunkenness,
or other shameful pleasures, when they have taken
such hold upon a man that he feels as if he could
not live without them? or rage, or fretfulness, or
envy, after years and years in which the heart has
permitted itself to be kindled with those fires? Can
they be all cured, their evil lesson unlearned, and
the graces most contrary to them received to abide
in the life and heart? Yes, dear brethren, to all
these questions the Word of our gracious God saith,
Yes: it may be so, these evils may be uprooted, and
the good take root and grow in their stead: it may
be done, but not by us: it is too hard for us, but
nothing is too hard for the Lord, the Holy Spirit,
Who implanted Himself within us at our Baptism, to
be as it were the seed and germ of all these graces.
He is Almighty as ever, and near us as ever, and
full as ever of unutterable love for us sinners (for
He is the very Love of the Father and the Son), He
therefore, if we will let Him, both can and will revive the faint sparks which remain and are ready to
die. He is All-merciful and Almighty: He could
change the skin of the Ethiopian and the spots of
the leopard, if such were His holy will. Doubt ye
not therefore but earnestly believe that He is with
you to help you to do good, how inordinately soever
you have been accustomed to evil: but there is no
promise that He will do it in a moment or without
your earnestly working under Him: He was six days
in making heaven and earth: and to renew a lost
spirit and prepare it for eternal salvation, we may
boldly say, is a greater work than creating the visible

earth and heaven : therefore, my brethren and fellow-sinners, we had better make up our minds to be a long time under His Hand, patient scholars learning our lesson by degrees, " [d] precept upon precept ; line upon line, line upon line, here a little, and there a little," or as sick men submitting ourselves to the rules of a wise physician, who warns us at the beginning that the cure will be tedious, because the disease is very inveterate, and has been allowed to come to a head very dangerously. Why, my brethren, only think what a difficulty men experience in taking up as it were the thread of duty again, of the plainest and simplest duties I mean, when they have been long neglected : think, for instance, how hard people find it to go to Church after they are quite convinced and own that they ought to go : they feel as if they *could* not move a limb that way : and yet it is, bodily, as easy that way as any other : the difficulty is in the habit of mind ; it seems as if there were a spell on them, rendering it impossible for them to attend God's public worship any more. And it is much the same with other religious services, diligent prayer, confession of sins, holy reading, Holy Communion, Christian care of those committed to our charge : nothing so easy as to get into a habit of neglecting these blessed duties : one Sunday ill-spent will often suffice for that : few things harder than to break that evil habit, and force one's self again into Christ's aweful and comfortable presence.

These surely are great and sore evils, as great almost as any which the enemy of souls can put in our way to separate between us and our God.   And we

[d] Isa. xxviii. 10.

cannot cure them for ourselves: we cannot by our own strength break the chain of evil custom. Must we then go on in bondage? No, God be thanked, no, surely: for as it is in bodily sickness, so in this sickness of the soul. A man is unable to cure himself, but he does not therefore give himself up: he goes to the physician, he prays to God, he observes rules, he takes medicines: and so by God's mercy he very often recovers. And thou, O sinner, though without Christ thou canst do nothing, mayest yet assure thyself out of God's holy Word, that through Christ thou mayest do all things. He can and will save thee to the uttermost, if thou wilt come to Him, and hold by Him in earnest. The chains will fall off from thy hands, as from S. Peter's hands when the Angel came to him in prison, and power will be given thee, step by step, to follow Him Who cometh to deliver thee. He will train thee, not only to break off thy sins, but to form the contrary habit of all holy obedience. Much distress and agony will there be, many disappointments, many backslidings: but let us go on trying to trust and follow Him, renouncing ourselves: He will bring us out into a large place, a state of perfect freedom: a state in which it will be as impossible for us to do evil as it was at first to do right. Only lean entirely on His grace, and be always seeking it. In His strength, not in your own, make good resolutions, and be watchful in keeping them: and see if in the end He do not, make you like unto the Angels whom He keepeth in perfect peace, their minds being stayed on Him, because they trust in Him.

SERMON XXXIII.

THE BITTERNESS AND MISERY OF BACKSLIDING.

JER. ii. 19.

*" Know therefore and see, that it is an evil thing
and bitter, that thou hast forsaken the Lord thy
God, and that My fear is not in thee, saith the
Lord God of Hosts."*

I need not say that it is an evil thing, one of the
worst of evils, never to have known the Lord, to have
gone on from youth as mere heathen and unbelievers,
having no hope, and without God in the world.
Which of us all would deny or doubt this? But
there is a condition worse than this, the condition of
those who have forsaken the Lord, after they have
known Him: who have had hold of Him Who is the
only hope of our souls, and have wilfully let Him go;
like froward children pushing away from them the
nursing, upholding, guiding Hand, to cast themselves down on the ground, to wander along their
own ways, to follow they know not whom, they
know not where.

Ignorance is evil, but apostacy, wilful backsliding
is not only evil, but bitter. The sense of it comes

over the heart with a peculiar loathsomeness: as
when some pleasant meat that a man had specially
delighted in, has become utterly corrupt, it is more
shocking to the taste than the ordinary sort of unpleasant things.   So in respect of the common evils
of life; men think it bad and hard to be born in
extreme poverty: not to have known from their
youth up, what fulness of bread is: but every one
feels that it is still worse to be reduced to starvation
after having seen better days.   To be born among
rude barbarians, far from the decencies and comforts
of what we call civilized life, never to have known
anything of them, would seem to most of us a very
pitiable circumstance: but it would be much more
pitiable, surely, for one who, having been bred up in
the enjoyment of those advantages, was banished
from them for the rest of his time, to abide with
savages in some wild and desolate island.   And it is
commonly observed that those who from their youth
up have never known, what pain and ill health are,
find it much harder to bear when it comes, than their
less favoured brethren do, who have been more or
less sickly all their lives long.

By the same rule, evil as it is, never to have known
the Lord, it is far more evil and bitter to have forsaken Him after you have known Him: I say, to
have forsaken Him: I do not say, to be forsaken by
Him; because in truth He never forsakes any who
have not first forsaken Him: and as in the case of
poverty, banishment, or sickness, it is a most intolerable weight added to the burden, when conscience
tells us, that the misery was our own fault, so it must
always be in this worst of miseries, the misery which

c c

comes, sooner or later, upon those who have known God, and refused to obey Him: the bitterest drop in their cup is the feeling, day and night, that they chose, it should be so; they brought it all upon themselves. And no wonder: for in very deed to have forsaken the Lord for ever, and to be forsaken of Him, and that by one's own wicked choice, and to be continually aware that it is so, this is no other than hell itself. For hell is more than the everlasting fire and other torments which shall take hold of the poor lost bodies; hell, to the inward soul and spirit, is eternal separation from God; separation and alienation from Him Who only is comfort, and pardon, and love, with the full consciousness that it was the person's own doing. No wonder the beginnings and foretastes should be bitter, when the end is so inconceivably horrible.

That backslidings do in a certain way bring their own punishment and misery with them, that to forsake the Lord is bitter as well as evil, the word of God expressly affirms, and each man's own experience, fairly consulted, will soon show. "*Thine own wickedness," saith the prophet, "shall correct thee, and thy backslidings shall reprove thee," i. e. in the very course of thy sins there will be always something to make thee ashamed and afraid of the consequences of them. For think of the adulterer, the thief, the murderer, at the very moment when they seem to be carrying out their wicked designs most prosperously and with the highest hand. Look carefully upon them: attend to their low whispers, watch their uneasy countenances, their restless actions. They can-

* Jer. ii. 19.

not be at ease, for they are afraid of discovery. Hear
how the prophet writes of them, taught by Him,
Whose eye is never off them. "ᵇThe murderer, rising
with the light, killeth the poor and needy, and in
the night is as a thief. The eye also of the adulterer
waiteth for the twilight, saying, no eye shall see me:
and disguiseth his face. In the dark they dig through
houses which they had marked for themselves in the
day time: they know not the light. For the morning is to them even as the shadow of death; if one
know them, they are in the terrors of the shadow of
death." So full of fear and anguish are the ways of
bad men, who would fain be out of sight, and know
that they cannot be so. Again, those who refuse the
true light, how greatly do they suffer from a sense
of blindness and darkness; they have a feeling that
they are all wrong, but they have not the heart to
follow after the way of deliverance, and this is their
condition, the Spirit of God bearing witness to it.
"ᶜWe wait for the light," say they, "but behold
obscurity: for brightness, but we walk in darkness:
we grope for the wall like the blind, and we grope,
as if we had no eyes: we stumble at noon day as in
the night: we are in desolate places as dead men."
Well might the apostle cry out to those who had recovered from this forlorn condition, "ᵈWhat fruit had
ye then in those things, whereof ye are now ashamed?" What fruit indeed? What is there in the pleasures of sin to make up for fear and darkness, such
as this? and then, overshadowing all, is the dreadful certainty coming nearer and nearer, as this short

ᵇ Job xxiv. 14—16.   ᶜ Isa. lix. 9, 10.
ᵈ Rom. vi. 21.
c c 2

life wears away, the end of those things is death, everlasting death.

O ye who have forsaken your God and Saviour to walk in the paths of sin and unbelief; He calls on you now to look back, and consider what warnings He has been giving you all along, even you yourselves, each one of you: how, when you turned from Him, He still met you and confronted you in your downward path : how He left you not without witness, when you were hiding your eyes from Him. Remember (many may be able to do so) when you first fell away into deadly sin, when you permitted yourself to listen to the tempting spirit, and to plunge into the known sin, the thought of which perchance had been haunting you for months and years, but hitherto God's grace and good providence had kept you from quite losing yourself in it. Remember the misery and disquiet it was, after the first intoxication had passed, and you waked up with the thought, 'I was innocent, I was pure, but all that is now passed away: can it ever be again with me as it was in times past? How shall I ever bear myself? How will God or man bear with me?' And then would come the miserable thought, as it came to our first parents after the fall, the thought and wish of hiding one's self from all that one had loved and trusted before, from our best friends, from those whom we most looked up to, yea even from Him, the Fountain of all love and trust, the Father and God of our whole life. Yes, the fallen Christian, in the first pangs of his remorse, would fain, like Adam, hide himself from God, but there are no trees in the garden thick enough to veil you from His Presence; you knew it

well, and in your despair you were tempted to sin
again worse than before, that you might drive away
the thought of God, since you could not drive away
God Himself. And it may be, you were for a time,
able to do so. The Evil one was at hand, and by
his help you were able to go on some way in a kind of
wild dream of false enjoyments, undisturbed by conscience, undisturbed by the fear of God, undisturbed
by the thought, 'What will be the end of all this?' It
might be so for a time, but it could not continue so
always. Bye and bye some trouble came on; or your
wicked pleasures ceased to satisfy; your very soul
began to ache and be weary, and you knew not which
way to turn for help: you had driven the Creator
to a distance from you; you would not let Him be
your Friend and Saviour, and now the creatures, the
world in which you had trusted, seemed as it were to
take part against you. When you sought to enjoy
yourself, there was gall and wormwood in the draught.
Your blessings were cursed; the good fruit, like the
apples we read of near the Dead sea, turned to dust
and ashes in your mouth. When a little comfort
did come, it was all dim and uncertain, you could
not depend upon it: it was chased away the next
moment by some sudden recollection of death, and
what will come after death, or at least by an indis-
tinct sense of being very miserable at heart, like
what men feel in a horrible dream. When people
were kind and good to you, there was the sharp
pang of feeling, 'How entirely all this is contrary to
what I deserve! how different would it all be, did
they know what I know of myself!' All this and
very much more must those expect to feel,—thousands

have felt it, and are feeling it daily,—who have given ear to the deceiver and have turned away from their God; fallen Christians, yet in their impenitence. They must be miserable, for they are forcing Him to look on them in anger, by Whose forgiving love only they can stand any chance of salvation. Who shall make atonement for them? Who shall speak a good word for them? For they are treading under foot the Son of God, they are counting His Blood an unholy thing, they are bringing on themselves the wrath of the Lamb. And again, who shall turn their hearts, since they are driving away the Comforter, they are doing despite unto the Spirit?

O backsliding Christian, miserable thou art, and miserable thou must and wilt ever be, until thou begin to repent in earnest, to repent and turn thyself from all thy transgressions, to turn to that Saviour from Whom thou hast deeply revolted, to turn to Him, not in word only and in feeling, but in heart and in life.

Perhaps all these sayings about thine own sad condition do not at all come home to thee: perhaps thou hast no notion at all, that thou art wretched and miserable; perhaps, as yet, it is not, to thee in the least bitter, to have forsaken the Lord. This is too likely: the prophet in the text signifies that such may be the case: for he exclaims to fallen Israel, "Know now, and see, that it is an evil thing and bitter, that thou hast forsaken the Lord." Why, how could they choose but know and see it, seeing His commandments were so plain, their sins so notorious, His judgements so fearfully surrounding them on every side? But it seems that those gross

idolaters from among the Jews were not aware of the
situation they had brought themselves into. And
in like manner we find it every day, and it is well
nigh enough to break a thoughtful person's heart,
that men and women, made in infancy children of
God by holy Baptism, often when they have been
carefully taught the aweful issue of what they do,
lose themselves in deadly sin, abide in it for months
and years, and are hardly aware that it is deadly;
they have no horror, it does not come over them
with any thing like a thrill of alarm, when they consider how they stand towards God. What must
become of them, if there be any truth in Scripture,
were they to die at this moment! They could not
endure it, if they found themselves suddenly poised
over a dreadful gulph, on the steep edge of a rock
or point of a steeple; or sleeping, as the wise man
says, on the top of a mast: but it is no concern at
all to them that they lie down night after night in
the full guilt of fornication, or other grievous sin,
concerning which God is pledged, and they know
it, that no man doing such things shall inherit His
kingdom. O miserable quiet, false peace, fatal and
shameful security! It is even as people do not feel
dirt and loathsomeness, because they have become
thoroughly used to it: or as a leper might have
ceased to feel his leprosy. Who would choose such
consolation as that? Nay rather, my brethren, let
our prayer be to know and feel the worst of our
condition, that in proportion to its evil, so we may
feel its bitterness. Fear nothing so much as "* feed-

* S. Jude 12.

ing thyself without fear." Shrink from nothing so
much as from the poisonous sweetness of the flesh,
the bold voice of the world, and the subtle whispers
of the Evil one encouraging thee to follow the pleasures of sin. Force thyself every now and then to
meditate seriously on what is to come. Make thyself leisure for such thoughts : thou wilt find it, bye
and bye, quite worth the while. Try to draw in
thine heart a picture of the days which will soon
come upon thee, if God spare thy life in this world,
and thou continue impenitent; the powers of thy
mind and body decaying, and at last dying away,
under the wretched influences of sin: no care, no
anxiety to be serving God in good works: no hearty
desire to pray; no faithful and dutiful approach to
our Lord in Sacraments. Think of thyself thus
drearily making thy way towards thy grave, weary
of the world, yet afraid to leave it : leaning on all
manner of bruised reeds, though thou be sure they
will go into thy hand and pierce thee: ever turning
away from the Judge, before Whom thou knowest
thou must presently stand. And think too what
the effect will be on others, how day by day more
and more souls will be the worse everlastingly for
knowing thee and living within thy reach, and day
by day the hour will be drawing on, when thou and
they shall have to stand together before the throne
of Him Who died for them, and will require their
blood at thy hands.

Whoever thou art, that art tempted to go on in thy
sins, especially foul and corrupting sins, it will be
well for thee to be very often looking on to those

days of darkness, when the evil and bitterness of
forsaking the Lord will begin to appear such as it
really is: and sometimes again it will be well for
thee to strive and pray, as thou mayest, to draw in
thine heart the contrary picture: of one entering
into his rest, in peace, because he hath walked in
uprightness. Imagine the true and loyal soldier of
Christ, after a brave adherence to duty, after vows
kept, temptations overcome, good works wrought in
the Name of Christ and to His glory, by the help
of His good Spirit, humble and constant repentance
for his many sins and infirmities, imagine such an
one as he will lie on his death-bed, cheered and
strengthened, morning by morning, by his Lord's
gracious messages of pardon and peace, the Holy
Comforter bringing home to him the Church's absolution; think of his sure and blessed hope, brightening in the light of Christ's Sacraments more and
more unto the perfect day; the Angels waiting
around him to receive his spirit in peace when his
time shall come, as surely as if men saw them with
their eyes, and the moment of his departure blessed
by those treasures of Divine consolation, which He
is sure to reserve for His own, whether man discern
them or no: "'for precious in the sight of the Lord
is the death of His saints."

O Christian, backsliding Christian, whoever thou
art, think deeply on these things, look well upon
these two pictures; for one of the two must be thine
own, and this day thou art called upon to choose
which it shall be. Shall thy death be the death of

'Ps. cxvi. 15.

them that die in the Lord, or shall it be the evil and bitter death of those who have forsaken their God, and have made light of their Saviour's Blood ? Thou must choose, and thine heart can have no doubt which of the two is the right choice. May the good Spirit give thee courage and dutifulness to make it, and having made, to *abide by it !*

SERMON XXXIV.

WEARINESS INDULGED, THE BEGINNING OF UNBELIEF.

HEB. x. 37.

" Yet a little while, and He that shall come will come, and will not tarry."

ARE you tired sometimes, my brethren, with coming here so often, hearing many times the same lessons out of Holy Scripture, the same prayers out of the Prayer-book, the same kind of instruction in sermons, perhaps, in some cases, receiving the same Holy Communion over and over again, so many times in the year? and are you tempted to say in your hearts, 'After all, what good comes of all this? how am I the better for it? surely there is no need to keep so very strictly to my rules: surely it will do me as much good, if I come only now and then, when I feel in my heart that it will be good for me.'

I am speaking, as you may perceive, to those among you more especially, who have set themselves a rule, and try in earnest, to come to Church as constantly as they can. I have no doubt that many if not all of them are, or have been, or some day will be, tried and tempted with thoughts such as I have been speaking of, tempted to say, "[a] It is vain to serve God in His Church and what profit is it that we have kept His ordinances?"

One has but to look round a Church, and see with one's eyes that so it is very commonly. For why else is it that so many, who were used to come for a time, who perhaps for some considerable portion of their lives made a rule to wait upon their Saviour here in His own house and at the Altar where He gives us Himself, how is it that so many of those have either left off coming at all, or when they do come, drop in so irregularly : as if serving God and keeping His ordinances were a matter of fancy, in which a man might please himself, without being called to any account? I do not, I will not, I cannot believe that this slackness in all or the greater number of cases is caused by persons giving themselves up deliberately to some known sin which makes them hate being in God's Presence : as Adam and Eve, when they hid themselves from the voice of the Lord among the trees of the garden. I am not now speaking of such, whether they be many or few, but of well-meaning persons, who have unhappily allowed themselves to grow weary of waiting on Christ in His Church, or have listened to the sayings of others, scornful or discouraging. Too well may we all of us understand what passes in their minds. If not in respect of going to Church, yet in respect of private prayer, or of reading Holy Scripture; of one religious duty or another, we have all at times more or less felt, 'What a weariness is it! may we not as

[a] Mal. iii. 14.

well give it up?' It is the trial of us all, my brethren. But still the truth must be told concerning
it: it is neither more nor less than the beginning of
unbelief: I say again, it is want of faith which
occasions that weariness and unwillingness of spirit,
which makes almost all of us slow to attend holy
services, languid while there, and glad when they
are over, unless so far as it may be owing to some
bodily infirmity. It is want of faith and nothing
else, which makes men say to themselves and others,
'What is the use of so many prayers and Sacraments?'

Look, my brethren, at the first lesson this morning,
and see what God teaches us there. The prophet
Habakkuk, who lived in very bad times, just before
the captivity of the Jews in Babylon, describes himself there deeply meditating: " [b] I will stand upon
my watch, and set me upon the tower, and will
watch to see what He will say unto me, and what I
shall answer when I am reproved." Here is a
thoughtful Christian person, hearkening after God's
instruction: considering what he had best say, what
will be the fittest answer for him to make, if he
should be reproved, called to account, for his faith in
Christ and dutiful obedience to the Church. And the
Lord's answer is, in the first place, " [c] Write the
vision, and make it plain upon tables, that he may
run that readeth it." As if He should say, 'The holy
and heavenly Gospel which you must all learn, and
all teach, is by God's mercy made so clear in the
sight of all men, that he that hath least leisure, he
that might seem to be most hurried with worldly

[b] Hab. ii. 1.   [c] Ib. 2.

cares, may nevertheless read, hear, understand, and
practise it." It is indeed written and made plain
upon tables, as the ten Commandments were from
the beginning, which commandments with the Creed
and the Lord's Prayer, are indeed the chief parts of
this Gospel law. That is the first portion of the
answer which the Holy Ghost instructs us to make,
when our faith is in danger of being disturbed by
evil thoughts within or by foolish talking around us.
Say, This is what I have learned from the beginning,
even the Creed, the Lord's prayer and the ten Commandments. God has so far made His truth plain
to me, and by His mercy I will cleave to it. And
then, when the bad thought or the scornful tempter
goes on and suggests to you, that it is but a poor
dull wearisome thing to go on, all one's life long,
learning and practising such ordinary things as these,
when he asks, 'What good do you get by it, in return
for the manifold pleasures and profits of this world
which you are obliged to give up?' then do you take
up the second part of the answer provided by the
Holy Ghost, and say, "[d] The vision is yet for an appointed time, but at the end it shall speak, and not
lie: though it tarry, and be long in coming, yet by
God's grace I will wait for it: because it will surely
come, it will not tarry." Or as S. Paul teaches us
to understand the words, "Yet a little while, and He
that shall come will come, and will not tarry." This,
brethren, must be our reply to our own feelings and
to the sayings of others, when they would tempt us
to be unfaithful and impatient, first impatient and
then unfaithful. We must say to our tempters and

[d] Hab. ii. 3.

to ourselves, Our Lord has had our duty and our belief written out for us so plainly, that he may run
that readeth it: therefore we believe, and by His
grace we will always believe. And again we must
say, 'Our Lord has taught us that we must not expect
to see and feel at present, how happy we are: we are
not to long to have our good things here: He hath
warned us before, that we shall have to wait for Him:
and by His gracious help we will wait, and not permit our faith to be disturbed: for though to flesh
and blood it seem long, we know for certain that it
will not be long in earnest: a very little while, and
He that is coming will have come: our future will
have become present, our seed will have borne good
fruit, our hope will be turned into everlasting joy.'
This is our answer, when we are reproved as to our
faith and religious duty: we know by God's teaching in the Scriptures and the Church that we are
right, and for the proof that we are so, we are content to wait patiently until He that is coming shall
have come.

For instance: serious persons know well how busy
the tempter often is in checking and disturbing their
prayers: as if one should whisper to them, 'Here
you have been, I know not how many years, beseeching the Almighty God night and morning not
to lead you into temptation: yet the old temptations
continue, and you often feel as if you could have no
peace. Surely you may just as well leave off your
prayers, they are but a trouble; and seemingly, do
you no good.' One is almost ashamed to put such
a blasphemous thought into words: it is however a
thought, which more or less distinctly troubles many

when they pray : how may we best put it down, or
hinder it from hurting us ? Why, by using ourselves
steadily to consider, that although our Lord hath promised us all good things in answer to prayer, He hath
not promised us, *when* we shall have them.   Thus,
we have no right, because we are still tempted, to
say that the prayer, ' Lead us not into temptation' is
not heard and answered according to God's promise.
He hath ways for our escape, which we cannot yet
understand : bye and bye, if we persevere, we *shall*
understand them, and acknowledge with adoring
gratitude that when He most seemed to tarry, He
was very near us, preparing the way to come to our
entire deliverance.   Again, both in Church and at
home we and all Christians pray continually for the
Church.   We pray, 'Give peace in our time, O Lord :'
'Rule and govern Thy holy Church universal in the
right way :' and in the Lord's prayer, 'Thy kingdom come :' and yet from year to year and from generation to generation it almost seems as if there were
more and more strifes and divisions ; more grievous
errors, the children of men less and less willing to
submit themselves to His kingdom, the Church.
Are we then to conclude that we may as well leave
them off ? God forbid : He Himself hath graciously
instructed us far otherwise.   "*He spake a parable to
this very end, that men ought always to pray for the
Church and not to faint," not to tire, nor cease from
their prayer because for the time it seems fruitless.
The unjust judge, though he cared not for God or
man, did yet in the end do what was right by the
poor widow, because she was so earnest and constant

* S. Luke xviii. 1.

in asking: much more will our Righteous Judge
avenge the cause of His own elect, His own adopted
children, for whom He shed His Blood: though He
bear long with them. But then, they must cry unto
Him day and night: our intercessions, whilst we
are on our warfare on earth, must keep time, as best
they may, with the cries of our martyred brethren
resting beneath the Altar in paradise: He will have
us to be crying out with them, "Lord, how long?"
O wait for Him: continue asking Him: because He
will surely come: He will not tarry.

Again; the devil will tempt you, if he can, to leave
off Holy Communion, even after that by God's mercy
you have made a good beginning. Alas, that we
should have so much reason to say it! But so it is,
that in this parish, and I suppose in many more, we
can count by scores, almost by hundreds, the persons
who have fallen away from Christ's Sacrament and
Sacrifice, i.e. (for I must tell you the truth) they
have indeed fallen away from Christ: since His own
word is, '*If any man draw back, My soul shall
have no pleasure in him.' If any such be here, I
would say to them, Hearken, dear brethren, to your
Saviour Who calls you in a manner this very day,
and says, 'Why, having begun to come to Me that ye
might have life, do ye thus trifle with the life that ye
had received? Why will ye die again, after ye had
been made partakers of My Death and Resurrection,
so as that ye need never have tasted the death of sin
any more? Why starve yourselves, when ye had
actually fed on the Manna and were invited to feed
on it continually?'

* Heb. x. 38.

D d

Surely it was one of two great evils, either you have fallen into deadly sin, and are still abiding impenitent; or you are giving way to slothful unbelief, as concerning the virtue of our Lord's Sacrament and Sacrifice. You found it no such entire comfort, such full delight and joy in the Lord, as you expected: but you should have remembered that for such open vision of the Blessed God the time is not yet come: it tarries, and you were bidden to wait for it: but you have gone away, and would not wait. What if, when He comes, you find that you have cast away your part in Him? Or perhaps it was not so much your own misgivings and the whisperings of the devil, as the open ridicule and censure of the wicked world, which turned your feet from this only way of peace: perhaps people said, or you fancied them saying, 'How good such an one is become, here he is, taking the holy Sacrament, and setting himself up to be better than others:' and you did not meet the temptation in a manly and Christian way: you turned your back on your Saviour for fear of being counted particular. But how will it be when He shall come openly, in His own Form, not under the veil of the Sacrament? Then, in that aweful shipwreck of the whole world, when you are lost with the greater part of the crew, will it be any comfort to you to reflect, that at any rate you had saved yourself for a little while from being thought foolish and over-scrupulous by those who must now be partakers of your misery? The Gospel gives us reason to believe, that a few only will be saved. And when our Lord invited you to your first Communion and gave you grace, if so be, to receive it worthily, you for the time were one of those few. O shame and misery, should you have to confess bye and bye, that because they were *but* a few, you made haste to withdraw yourself from among them : because your Lord and Saviour had few in comparison who loved Him well enough to keep His last command, therefore you would not continue to be one of the few !

More instances might be given : but these, if I have made them plain, will be sufficient to make you understand that wilfully allowing yourselves to grow weary of your regular devotions is indeed the beginning of unbelief. And when a Christian is in any manner asked, 'Will you or will you not keep up your rules for prayer in public and in private and for Holy Communion ?' it is in fact as if he were asked, 'Will you or will you not begin to take your part with the unbelievers and enemies of Christ ?' In S. Paul's time it was at peril of their lives, when Christians held their solemn meetings for common prayer and receiving the Eucharist : yet he says most earnestly, or rather the Holy Ghost says by him, " ' Let us not forsake the assembling of ourselves together, as the manner of some is." It might be death for them to assemble ; yet they were commanded to do so, and it was unbelief if they drew back. How much more inexcusable, my brethren, is our unbelief, if we calmly consider it ! when we give up going to Church, or Holy Communion, or regular prayers, or reading of our Bibles, for such slight reasons as are very commonly alleged ! or rather for no reasons at all, but for the mere dislike of trouble, and fancy what some foolish people may say of us ! Is it not

' Heb. x. 25.

something like selling our birthright for less than a mess of pottage? Not that I mean to say, it is always easy to keep to our good rules, and wait on our Saviour as we ought. Our Lord Himself in peculiarly aweful words, signifies that it would prove a hard and rare thing. For after He had said so much to encourage us always to pray and not to faint, after He had pledged Himself and His Father to answer the prayer of faith speedily, He ends with that saddest of prophecies, " ⁵ Nevertheless, when the Son of Man cometh, shall He find faith on the earth?"

It is hard and rare then, no doubt; harder and rarer perhaps in our days, than in the very days of persecution, to pray and not to faint, to communicate and not draw back; to wait patiently for the vision, though it tarry: to keep it before our mind's eye that He Who is coming will soon have come: and then we shall find that He has not tarried: then the time will seem, as it is, very short. It *is* hard: but it is far from impossible: for He is with us by His Spirit, to Whom all things are possible. Only persevere a little while, and He will be with you in the body also: you shall see what you now believe, and feel what you now imagine faintly, as in a dream. Only be not cowardly: pray, strive, persevere: *He* never draws back: why should you?

⁵ S. Luke xviii. 8.

SERMON XXXV.

THE INTIMATE CONVERSE OF CHRIST OUR LORD WITH EVERY CHRISTIAN SOUL.

Ezek. xx. 35.

" I will bring you into the wilderness of the people,
and there will I plead with you face to face."

SINCE every word of the Old Testament is written
for our learning, for the admonition of us Christians
upon whom the ends of the world are come, so also
doubtless is this verse, and the whole wonderful
chapter from which it is taken, as you heard it just
now in the first lesson. It is spoken to *us*, brethren,
to all of us members of the holy Catholic Church, to
each one of us having a soul of his own, a soul redeemed by the precious Blood of Christ, and to be
saved, or lost hereafter, as it shall be found to have
welcomed, or neglected so great salvation. And it is
spoken to us for a special message, even on this very
day, to be thought over, and laid to heart before we
lie down to sleep. You know it must be so, brethren,
because you know that the providence of God reaches
to the smallest things, to the fall of a sparrow, to the
number of the hairs of a man's head: much more

will He take notice of the way in which we receive
His own words, read to us in His own house by the
special order of His Church.

Read to *us*, I say, and spoken to *us :* let there be
no mistake in that. The elders of Israel were sitting
before the prophet, and he was speaking directly, and
in the first place to them, but through them the Lord,
by his mouth, was speaking to the whole house of
Israel, and to us who are His spiritual Israel, that
is, to all Christian people. For Ezekiel is as truly an
evangelical prophet as Isaiah. Isaiah is known by
that title, because the Holy Spirit guided him to describe so exactly the Life, and Death of our Lord, and
the glory of His Church : and no less evangelical is
the word spoken by Ezekiel, declaring the trials, the
sin and chastisement, and the final triumph of the
same Church. Isaiah preaches the Gospel of Christ
Himself in His natural Body on earth : Ezekiel, the
Gospel of Christ's mystical Body, Christ still on earth
but mystically by His Spirit.

And what is the special message which He brings
us to-day ? "I will bring you into the wilderness
of the people, and there will I plead with you face
to face." What is "the wilderness of the people ?"
or rather of " the peoples," for such is the meaning of
the word. It means the condition of the Christian
Church in this world : you may wonder how this
blessed condition, this state of salvation should be
called "a wilderness." I will try, please God, to
explain it to you. God's ancient and chosen people,
the children of Israel, chosen for no goodness or
merit of their own, but because the Lord loved them,
and because He would fulfil the promises made to

their fathers, were not at once brought to their full rest and inheritance, when they were delivered from Egypt and Pharaoh. They found themselves in the desert, not in Canaan; in the land of trial, not in the land of promise. The Lord their God led them a long way round about; for forty years He shewed them their way in the wilderness, to humble them, and to prove them, to know what was in their heart, whether they would keep His commandments or no. The prophet, putting them in mind of this and of all God's gracious dealings with them, says that the same kind of thing should take place, when after their long captivities, among the Assyrians, or among the Babylonians, or wheresoever else they were scattered, He should bring them in, and make them His own people again. " I will bring you out from the people, and will gather you out of the countries wherein ye are scattered. . . . . And I will bring you into the wilderness of the people, and there will I plead with you face to face. Like as I pleaded with your fathers in the wilderness of the land of Egypt, so will I plead with you, saith the Lord God."

This then is the state of a converted Israelite, when he is made a member of Christ, which the Church plainly tells us he *is* made by the Holy Ghost in Baptism: he is free to love and serve God; the devil need not prevail against him; his past sin, and the sin of his forefathers Adam and Eve, is freely forgiven him, and the Good Spirit is offered him for the future, to prepare him for Heaven; but he has not yet past his trial. He is brought, not as his fathers were, into the wilderness of Egypt, but into the wilderness of the peoples: into the place whither God's children

are gathered, not from Egypt only, but from all people, nations, and languages; and where they are put
on their trial, in a new and marvellous way.

This is the condition of a penitent and converted
Israelite. But as God has but one way of redemption, by the precious Blood of His dear Son: so He
has but one way of penitence, conversion, and salvation. Christ is the same, and the Church is the
same; there is the same Holy Spirit, the same Bible,
and the same Sacraments for us sinners of the Gentiles as for the children of Abraham after the flesh.
We, as they, are brought into the wilderness of the
nations; the region, where Christ's servants are on
their trial in their way to heaven. We are not safe,
but we are on our road to safety. Christ has put
us in the road, but He does not force us to move
onward. We never could have saved ourselves, but
He leaves us free to destroy ourselves, if we will, to
cast away the salvation which He so dearly purchased
for us. Even S. Paul says, "[b]I count not myself to
have apprehended: but this one thing I do, forgetting those things which are behind, and reaching
forth unto those things which are before, I press toward the mark for the prize of the high calling of
God in Christ Jesus;" and, "[c]I keep under my body
and bring it into subjection, lest that by any means,
when I have preached to others, I myself should be
a castaway." And he says, "[d]All our fathers were
under the cloud, and all passed through the sea: and
were all baptized unto Moses in the cloud and in the
sea: and did all eat the same spiritual meat; and did
all drink the same spiritual drink: for they drank of

[b] Phil. iii. 12—14.   [c] 1 Cor. ix. 27.   [d] Ib. x. 1—6.

that spiritual Rock that followed them, and that Rock was Christ. But with many of them, (even the greater part) God was not well pleased; for they were overthrown in the wilderness. Now these things were our examples," both their mercies, and their trials, and both are written for our admonition: as the Church also reminds us, every morning of our lives, teaching to us sing; "* He is the Lord our God: and we are the people of His pasture, and the sheep of His hand," (therefore) "To-day if ye will hear His voice, harden not your hearts: as in the provocation, and as in the day of temptation in the wilderess; when your fathers tempted Me, proved Me, and saw My works."

Ye see your calling then, brethren, how great and blessed, yet how alarming, and aweful! so that every one, the least and the lowest, yea even the least of God's people may take up the words of our father Jacob at the foot of the mysterious ladder, and exclaim, "'How dreadful is this place, this is none other but the house of God, and this is the gate of heaven." How is it that we who believe these things can help saying to ourselves when we wake in the morning, ' God is giving me one day more in this life, this wilderness of trial: here I am again with all my sins, and infirmities, my weak frail unbelieving heart, my senses so apt to wander, the chains of mine evil habits yet hanging about me: and here all around me is the world as it was yesterday—with its bad company, its vain shows and pomps, its scorn, and laughter, so hard to bear when one is trying to do a little better, its tempting pleasures, its calls of busi-

* Ps. xcv. 7—9.   ' Gen. xxviii. 17.

ness that leave no time for prayer; here also, as yesterday, though I see him not, yet I know, I almost feel, that the Evil spirit is at hand, resolved, if he may, to do his worst against me, remembering well alas! how much encouragement I have hitherto given him and hoping to-day to complete my ruin. Here I am still at the gate of heaven: the ladder is still let down, and the door open, and the Lord standing above, and calling me by name, but alas! there are all these chances against me: what, if after all, I should be lost and miscarry for ever!'

Yes, indeed, my brother; thy burden is indeed sore, and far far too heavy for thee to bear alone: the burden, I mean, which is laid upon thee of answering to thy Lord's call, improving His gifts and mercies, working out thine own salvation. No wonder thine heart should die within thee, when thou thinkest of thyself only, and of thy condition, such as thou seest and feelest it here in the wilderness of the people; now, in the day of temptation in the wilderness. Responsibility in all kinds is a burden, and men generally do what they can to escape from it; but especially that greatest responsibility, the having to answer for their own souls. But be not deceived: thou canst not escape from it. Is it not written "⁶ Every man shall bear his own burden?" Think not of putting it off from thee: that was the mistake of the wicked and slothful servant. That was what came into the mind of the degenerate Israelite. The cumbrance, the burden, the strife must be borne as long as thou art on thy trial: but, let this be thy comfort, that thou art not called to

⁶ Gal. vi. 5.

bear it thyself alone. He Who laid it on thee did both proportion it to thy needs, and hath promised to be with thee along every step of thy way, to help thee in bearing it: even as He was with our father Jacob, not only by shewing Himself at a distance, on the landing place of the stairs that led to heaven, but also by accompanying, and keeping him along the way in which he was to go, every step of it, from the beginning to the end. This is the other part of the promise by Ezekiel, God's promise renewed to each one of us to day. He says not only, 'I will bring you into the wilderness of the peoples, I will set you on the way to heaven, putting you at the same time, on your trial, whether you will be a good Christian or no.' If that were all, though it were far more than we deserved, yet well might we fear, and tremble, and almost wish to be as the heathen: but now that other promise is added, and surely to a loving believing heart it makes all the difference, "There will I plead with you face to face."

Consider what this means. When the Lord had delivered Israel out of the land of Egypt, and brought them through the Red sea, He by no means left them to find their way by themselves: His Holy Spirit was among them as a pillar of a cloud by day, and a pillar of fire by night, to shew them what course they should take: He spake to them from mount Sinai, He shewed them from time to time the skirts of His glory. He sent messages by Moses: He fed, refreshed, guided, chastened them by miracle: when they went wrong, as they were constantly inclined to do, He warned them beforehand, and reproved them afterwards; He would never let them alone. This

the Scripture calls "pleading with them," condescending to reason and argue with them, to try this
way and that, as a loving father with froward and
unwise children : ordering matters so, that if they did
go wrong, and came to a bad end at last, all might
know that it was entirely their own fault. He, their
King and Father, would be justified in His saying,
and clear when He was judged. And certainly every
one who reads the history of God's people in the
wilderness must see most clearly that He was all the
while doing whatever could be done to His vineyard :
that the blame was theirs, not His, when only wild
grapes were brought forth.

Well then, here the Holy Ghost tells us that the
same and more would be true of the spiritual Israel ;
that is, among us Christians. "Like as I pleaded
with your fathers in the wilderness of the land of
Egypt, so will I plead with you, saith the Lord God."
But with this difference : God pleaded indeed with
all His people Israel, but He did not plead with all
of them face to face. That was a privilege reserved
for Moses only, as it is written, "With him will I
speak mouth to mouth," and after his death, "[h] There
arose not a prophet like unto Moses, whom the Lord
knew face to face." In the new Israel, on the contrary, that is, in the Church and people of Christ,
this astonishing promise is made to every believing
soul, man woman, and child : according to our
Lord's own declaration, " He that is least in the kingdom of heaven is greater," that is, is a greater prophet, has more knowledge and higher privileges,
"than John the Baptist," who was himself as great as

[h] Deut. xxxiv. 10.

Moses or any other prophet. Moses saw so much of the glory of God, that when he came among his brethren again, his own face was too bright for them to endure: but that was only just for once: it was no constant privilege: but concerning the privileges of us Christians it is written, "[1] We *all*, with open face, beholding as in a glass the glory of the Lord, are changed into the same image from glory to glory, even as by the Spirit of the Lord."

Here, brethren, is our relief, and is it not enough and more than enough to help us to bear our burden? What if a man's waking thought, as I said just now, be of the greatness of his task, of the great eternity which is fast coming on, and how little he is prepared for it? What if his heart within him feel desolate, when it comes over him, how much he has to do before he can be ready for his account, how little he did yesterday, and the day before, and the day before that; how the sad words, 'too late,' seem to haunt him wherever he goes: how his life, as he looks back on it, seems all made up of lost opportunities, grace trifled with, love unrequited, duties deferred, time, health, and talents wasted: and what small chance there is of his doing better for the little time that remains? Where can a man go, or what can he do, in such a case, unless he has a true and living faith in Him Who has promised to be with His people all along their way in the wilderness, pleading with them face to face, as He is in heaven pleading with His Father for them. To that very end, as well as to be our Sacrifice, He became one of us at His Incarnation, and His delight ever since has

[1] 2 Cor. iii. 18.

been to abide with the sons of men. As He was the
true sufficient Comforter of His disciples when He
was with them after the flesh, so and much more has
He been our Comforter since He went out of our
sight, dwelling with us by His Spirit. Thus He
vouchsafes to plead with us continually, Face to face,
Soul to soul, Thought to thought, assuring us of pardon through the Blood of His Cross for all the past
that is heavy on our heart, and assuring us also, for
the time to come, of the help of His Almighty Spirit
to amend our ways.

Face to face He pleads with us again in His holy
Gospels, as often as we hear, or read them, with an
earnest mind, and in the spirit of prayer. In every
page He comes to us as the Word of God, living, and
powerful, " [k] sharper than any two-edged sword,
piercing, even to the dividing asunder of soul and
spirit, and of the joints and marrow, and a discerner
of the thoughts and intents of the heart."

But above all He pleads with us Face to face, when
He comes to us in the Sacrament of Holy Communion.
To the soul that takes Him at His word, to the conscience that is awed by His Presence, it is even as
seeing Him, to see that of which He affirms that it
is His own Body and Blood. And what is the self-
examination and confession, by which He offers to
make you ready, but His Spirit both asking you questions, and helping you to answer them. Thus He
pleads and strives with you continually, in a way
most mysteriously near to you, which Scripture calls
"face to face," outwardly by His Bible, His Church
and His Sacraments, and inwardly by His Good Spi-

[k] Heb. iv. 12.

rit. He never leaves you, nor forsakes you, until you force Him to do so, by incurable impenitence.

O, my brethren, if this be indeed our condition, if Jesus Christ did not only, once for all, redeem us by His Death, but vouchsafes also continually to abide with us in this near and peculiar way, as our constant Watcher and Guide, by day and by night; how can you bear, any of you, to have Him and His blessed Presence any while out of your thoughts? How dangerous to your souls! How unloving, how unthankful to Him! For observe, it is not merely that He is always *present*, but more, He is continually *speaking* to your souls. If you will listen reverently, there is no hour of your life, but you may hear His word behind you, saying, "[1]This is the way, walk ye in it, when ye turn to the right hand, and when ye turn to the left." It is unkind and affronting not to hearken after His words: much more, when they *do* come to your hearing, to turn from them with scorn and impatience. It may have seemed to you a light thing, a pardonable frailty, to go on occasionally indulging your eyes, your thoughts, or your tongues, when the inward voice said, ' Forbear;' or again to turn away from good advice and holy example, under the notion that you need not be so very particular. O pray do so no longer! Consider Whom you are resisting, with Whom you are trifling.

Once more; when afflictions or when comforts have befallen you, you have most likely owned God's providence in them in a general way; but have you looked at them in this particular light, that it was the Son of God our Saviour, His own Self, pleading with

[1] Isa. xxx. 21.

you, to correct such and such faults, to encourage you
in such and such good ways, to win you more entirely
to Himself? Once use yourself to do this, to see God,
God your Saviour, in all that happens to you, sad
or joyful; and you know not what a blessing it will
prove, what a glory it will pour over your path: observe Him in little things as well as in great, for in
both, in all, His way is to strive and plead with sinners;—When accidents happen, to hinder dangerous
purposes;—When opportunities come suddenly for
performing some holy work;—When words pierce
you, like arrows shot at a venture;—When you wish
to pray, and cannot, and contrariwise when He helps
you to be fervent;—When He gives you means of
grace, and when He takes them away;—In the seasons of the year, and of life, and especially of the
Church's year; It is still the same gracious Master,
Friend, Father, Comforter, 'changing His Voice.'

He has one end in all His dealings with you to
guide you with His Counsel, that He may after that
receive you into glory. Do you try to have one end
in all your dealings with Him, to love and pray for
the glory, and to follow the guidance,

SERMON XXXVI.

GOD THE HOLY GHOST ALONE TEACHES US OUR LORD'S GOOD DEALINGS TO US, OR OUR ILL-DEALINGS TO HIM.

S. John xii. 16,

" These things understood not His disciples at the
first : but when Jesus was glorified, then remem-
bered they that these things were written of Him,
and that they had done these things unto Him."

The beloved disciple here marks a circumstance
which had clearly made a great impression upon him,
and to which he adverts in other places : the Holy
Ghost by which he was moved guiding him so to do
for our learning.   It is this : how little our Lord's
chosen disciples understood at the time that which
they were witnesses of, the sayings and doings of
their Blessed Master and ours, and how they gradu-
ally came to understand them, not by any diligence
and clever reasoning of their own, but by the help
of God's Word and Spirit : when He was glorified,
and the Holy Ghost had fallen on them, not before,
they remembered and understood aright both what
the Scripture had said of Him, and how it had come
to pass, unawares to themselves.

E C

Thus when in course of manifesting Himself at the first Passover after His Baptism He had spoken of raising up the Temple of His Body, His meaning was a secret both to friends and enemies, until He was risen from the dead, then says S. John, "[a] His disciples remembered that He had said this unto them : and they believed the Scripture, and the word which Jesus had said." We all know from all the four Gospels that so it was in regard of His Death and Passion : how plainly soever He may now seem to us to have spoken, His hearers constantly misunderstood Him. "[b] They understood none of these things ; and this saying was hid from them, neither knew they the things which were spoken." And S. John has set down for us some of Christ's parting words, which shew that this was not altogether their simplicity and slowness of heart, but that it was a rule or principle of His dispensation, a part of His fatherly dealings with them. "[c] These things have I spoken unto you, being yet present with you. But the Comforter which is the Holy Ghost, Whom the Father will send in My name, He shall teach you all things, and bring all things to your remembrance whatsoever I have said unto you." And most especially in His words to S. Peter, when he objected to his Lord's demeaning Himself, "[d] Lord, dost *Thou wash* my *feet?*" The answer is very emphatic and plainly refers to a great deal more than that one particular action, "What *I* do *thou* knowest not now ; but thou shalt know hereafter."

Indeed when a man considers really, and puts his

[a] S. John ii. 22.   [b] S. Luke xviii. 34.
[c] S. John xiv. 25, 26.   [d] S. John xiii. 6, 7.

mind to it, that this Jesus of Nazareth was truly and literally the Most High God walking on earth and conversing with men, it stands to reason that all, even His most ordinary actions, and what most appear matters of course, would have in them a depth of power and meaning incomprehensible without God's special inspiration; as the wisest of men writes, "°I know that whatsoever God doeth, it shall be for ever."

But I wish to consider now more particularly what we are to learn from the ignorance of the disciples concerning that of which S. John was speaking, the solemn act of this day, our Lord's entry into Jerusalem, riding on an ass, the multitude and His disciples rejoicing around Him. They had taken part in it indeed by His direction, had dutifully brought the ass and colt, and set Him thereon, had lovingly and joyfully united their voices to the salutations of the multitude "'Hosanna: Blessed is the King of Israel that cometh in the name of the Lord," but they knew not what it all meant; it did not occur to them that it was literal fulfilment of a prophecy in Zechariah: their Lord's order, and His way of entering the place appeared, I suppose, simply strange to them: and in their own and the people's doings they saw no more than the expression of what was natural at the time. We know that our Lord by entering Jerusalem on that day, the tenth of the first month, was in fact setting Himself apart as the Very Paschal Lamb to be slain on the following Friday for the sins of the world; that the disciples by bringing the ass and colt were a sign of their own work when they should

° Eccles. iii. 14.　　'S. John xii. 13.

go forth two and two and begin to bring in both Jew
and Gentile to the obedience of Christ, that the multitude which went before and followed were as the
law and the prophets on the one hand, and the
Church on the other, before and after our Lord.
The Holy Spirit when He came instructed Christians
so to interpret the doings of that first Palm Sunday,
but the persons who took part in them "understood
not these things at first."

From all this we may make out three rules (so to
call them) commonly observed by our Lord and
Saviour in training up those whom He trusted to be
His Apostles: three sorts of things in which as yet
they were not fully informed, but must wait until
He was gone, and the other Comforter was come in
His stead. They could not as yet understand either
(1) the meaning of the Old Testament concerning
Him, or (2) what He was doing in their sight from
time to time: or (3) what they themselves or others
were doing to Him. There was a depth of hidden
meaning and power in their dealings with Him, and
much more in His with them, far beyond what man's
heart could imagine. On none of those things could
they speak worthily in words which man's wisdom
taught them, they were to wait for the words which
the Holy Ghost should teach them. "*When He is
come," said our Lord, "He will teach you all things,
and bring all things to your remembrance, whatsoever I have said unto you."

This holy season, as it passes over, will bring before
us daily instances of such ignorance in those nearest
our Lord. They still missed the meaning of the

* S. John xiv. 26.

Bible in a way which would have seemed to us almost incredible. When our Lord put them in mind that He was to be numbered with the transgressors, S. Peter took it as a call to be ready with his sword to fight with those who should use his Master so ill. Even S. Peter and S. John went away from the Sepulchre, not knowing the Scriptures, "[h] that He must rise again from the dead." Even the two on their road to Emmaus, after that they had heard of the Angels' report continued "[i] slow of heart to believe all that the prophets have spoken."

Again as to His own doings they could not of themselves read the lesson of humility which He taught by washing their feet. He had to explain it to them, "[k] Know ye what I have done unto you? ye call Me Master and Lord: and ye say well; for so I am. If I then, your Lord and Master, have washed your feet; ye also ought to wash one another's feet. For I have given you an example, that ye should do as I have done to you." And at the last moment just before His Ascension, when He was on the point of leading them out to Bethany, they could not get rid of the idea that He was about to restore the kingdom to Israel.

Lastly, for their own doings towards Him, how little did S. Peter, after at least three warnings, given to him in the course of that very night, realize what he was doing, when he disowned and denied Jesus of Nazareth; at first, it may be, to get admittance where He was, afterwards in fear of what might happen to himself. How far were the chosen three from imagin-

[h] S. John xx. 9.   [i] S. Luke xxiv. 25.
[k] S. John xiii. 12—15.

ing what a thing it was for them, that night, to sleep, when He earnestly bade them Watch! and the whole number of them, how their behaviour must have appeared to the holy Angels looking on, when, one and all, they forsook Him and fled, having but a few minutes before pledged themselves, 'Though we should die with Thee, we will not deny Thee in any wise[1].'

Do you sometimes wonder, my brethren, at this unthoughtfulness in our Lord's holy Apostles? Does it seem to you almost childish? Do you feel as if it could not be your own case? Nay, let us consider how matters stand with ourselves. God's providence has just now brought us to the last week of another Lent, and we are so much nearer the last week of our lives. If we have been at all using the precious holy season as we ought, we can judge in some degree of our own way in times past, whether we too have not been guilty of strange unthoughtfulness towards our Lord and Saviour, Whom we knew to be always by us, always at hand to do us good. For you know that the season of Lent is appointed especially for such self-examination as shall reach back during a person's whole life, as far as he can remember, and lead him to pour out *all* his heart before God. If we have tried, and are trying, so to exercise ourselves in earnest, I am sure we must be learning from day to day the same three things concerning ourselves which we hear S. John confessing of himself and his fellow disciples. First, we have hitherto fallen very very far short of the meaning of Holy Scripture : we have not applied it to ourselves as we might and ought to have

[1] S. Mark xiv. 31.

done, to help us in loving and serving God: no, not
even those portions of it which His providence has
made familiar to us. E. g. is it not too possible to
go on day after day and perhaps many times a day,
saying to our Saviour in His own words, ' Forgive
us as we forgive,' and yet to indulge an unforgiving
heart towards some at least of His and our brethren?
or to beg of Him, on your knees, ' Lead us not into
temptation,' and when you arise, go the way in
which you know you will be most tempted? But if
your conscience tells you such things of yourself, and
so humbles you in the dust, does it not also tell you
something to encourage and raise you up with hope
of pardon and restoration? Have there never been
moments, in which by God's great mercy some saying of our Lord or S. Paul, some verse in a psalm or
prophecy, familiar perhaps to you all your life long,
but hitherto passed over lightly, as nothing in which
you are particularly concerned, has flashed upon
you, you know not how or why, in a new light, and
seemed different from what it ever was before; a
ray from the All-seeing Eye, an arrow aimed by the
unerring Arm, lighting exactly where you needed
warning or correction, as "[m]a certain man drew a
bow at a venture and smote the wicked king of Israel
between the joints of his harness?" Then you were
like the disciples who understood not at first the
meaning of Moses and the prophets, until the Holy
Spirit came down at the intercession of Jesus glorified, and taught them. O beware, as you love your
soul, how you behave at such moments! God is then
dealing directly with *your* heart and conscience in

[m] 1 Kings xxii. 34.

particular. It concerns you beyond measure that He deal not with you in vain.

Now, when the meaning of the Bible is thus brought home to a man, one token of his better mind will be his confessing with shame before God his own grievous sin in not having long ago laid to heart the holy words which now for the first time he seems to feel: and when he looks carefully after the cause of the mischief, he will most likely find that he missed the meaning of God's Word because he would not attend to God's providence: as the disciples fell short of the sense of the prophecies concerning their Lord for want of understanding what He was doing with them and before their eyes. They, for the most part, could not help it, and it was no fault in them. But how, too generally, has it been with us Christians? Have we attended, as we might, to the ways of His grace and providence with us, with each one of ourselves especially? Have we seen His hand in all things? We knew from the beginning it was there: have we watched for it, committing all our cares to Him beforehand: not merely saying as of course, 'It must be as God pleases,' but embracing that great truth in our hearts, and glad to have it so? Have we particularly marked and treasured up the order of His dealings towards ourselves and those dear to us, in regard of our temporal good? When He has over-ruled matters so, that things seemingly most against us have fallen out, as in Joseph's history, to our great good, have we thankfully and humbly owned His hand? Have we accepted our disappointments and troubles as also from Him, sure that if we will they shall prove the best things that ever happened to us? Then have we been so far happier than those who knew Christ after the flesh, that we have felt and known what He was doing for us and with us all along: yet never will there be any, no not of the best among His servants, to whom as long as he lives here the word will not seem to be spoken, " ª What I do thou knowest not now, but thou shalt know hereafter."

Lastly, the disciples looking back after a time remembered that they had done such and such things to their Lord, and comparing their doings with Holy Scripture saw the drift and purpose of them to be far more serious and important than they had at all imagined at the time. Do you, Christian penitent, look back on what is written in your memory and conscience, and say—say to God on your knees—how many things you find there registered, which seemed to you at the time mere trifles, matters of course, but now you are sadly convinced, you cannot hide it from yourself, that God had a will in those things, and in the bottom of your heart you knew His will and ought to have chosen it. Observe, I speak especially of man's behaviour *to our Lord.* This indeed reaches to all our doings, since all is done in His Presence, in love and duty towards Him, or the contrary. But I am thinking just now of what is plainly *personal* to Him. Sit down calmly, now before Lent is over, sit down, if you have not yet done so, and consider how you have treated your Saviour at times when you knew and owned Him to be present: in prayer, in Church services, in solitary thought, when your conscience has been struggling, and the thought,

ª S. John xiii. 7

'He is here,' or some word of His, came across your mind, and might have helped to keep you from sin, or urge you on in goodness.

Alas, for the inadequacy of most of our examinations and confessions, in time past, when we try them by this measure! and what if we should have gone on, many of us, for some good part of our lives, without any real examination or confession at all ? In any case, the saying will hold, Not without Jesus glorified, not without the light of that Spirit Who vouchsafes to come to us though His glorification and intercession, can we see the true greatness either of our own transgressions or of His mercies; and the true meaning of His holy and saving Word. But this light may be ours, every one of us, if we will. It may be had for asking, if you ask but sincerely and constantly. The disciples did so: amid many wanderings and infirmities, nay and some serious backslidings, they continued on the whole loving and faithful to their Master while yet with them, and when He was gone, they continued in prayer and supplication, until the Comforter came upon them. And when He came, He taught them the two great lessons which the saints have always prayed to be taught, to know themselves, and to know God. If you will wait and pray, pray and wait as they did, the same knowledge will be granted to you.

One sure effect and token of the blessing will be, the happier and better use of Holy Scripture. I cannot but apprehend that much of the unbelief as well as immorality of this time may be due to men's not using themselves to think thus seriously of God's universal providence, and of the deep, everlasting consequences of their own behaviour towards Him. They stumble, e. g. at the history of the Israelites in the Wilderness, because they have never realized their own supernatural condition; God's miraculous mercy to themselves. Just as on the other hand, too many of us never indeed think of doubting the history, but neither do we ever think of saying to ourselves " we are the people" etc.

God grant us better minds both for this Holy week and for the rest of the year and for all the coming weeks and years of our life ! And for our encouragement let us remember, (1) how when people turn to Him in earnest, presently their small beginnings, their widow's mites and cups of cold water, and poor weak prayers become great by His loving acceptance; how (2) a new light shines on their Bibles, and treasures undreamed of occur to them for their special use ; how, lastly, His ordinary providences are turned into means of grace and edification to the watchful, lowly, penitent and obedient heart. Every way the saying is fulfilled, "° If any man be in Christ, to him it is a new creation, a new heaven and a new earth : the old things are passed away ; behold all things are become new."

° 2 Cor. v. 17.

SERMON XXXVII.

JUSTIFYING FAITH.

Hab. ii. 4.

" Behold, his soul which is lifted up is not upright in him : but the just shall live by his faith."

THIS is one of the solemn passages, which are not uncommon in the old prophets, where their minds are in deep thought on the difference between the world and the Church, and the fierce warfare which is to come on between them in the last days before the Judgement. 'Mind not,' he tells us in the Name of God, 'though the time seem long, and the trial of your faith harder and harder. God's work is still going on; you must not measure it by your own sense or imagination; you must not at all hurry, or be impatient. God's time is set, and He will keep it; our not knowing it makes no difference. "The vision is yet for an appointed time, but at the end it shall speak and not lie: though it tarry, wait for it: because it will surely come, it will not tarry."'

And then it goes on; "Behold, his soul which is lifted up is not upright in him: but the just shall live by his faith." As if he had said, 'Depend upon it, when this world has done its best and its worst, it will plainly appear that the great question between

it and the Church is, whether it is better to trust
in one's self, one's own wisdom, and fame, and riches,
and high spirit, or to go altogether out of one's self,
and to live entirely by faith upon the heavenly
righteousness which God gives to His own people.
The world rests upon itself, the Church lives by
faith. The last day will shew to all God's creation,
as every man's hour of death will shew to him and
convince him for ever, which is the right of these
two, and which is the wrong.'

It is the great concern of us all to make up our
minds to this in good time; to make it the very
rule of our life; that when the shadows of this
world pass away, we may not depart helpless and
unprepared into that other world, where are no shadows at all, but dying with Christ's mark on us, and
with our hearts full of Him, may both be acknowledged by Him, Whom we shall there meet face to
face, and may ourselves know Him even as we are
known. This should be our great care; all our life
we should be looking on to this; all our life we
should be turning towards Him, Who hath brought
us already so very near Him: by this faith, this
heavenly and spiritual mind, God promises that we
shall live; He will meet our dutiful and obedient
longings with His unfailing gift of grace: such faith
He will make the continuance of heavenly life to us.

I say *the continuance;* because by His distinguishing mercy we who have been baptized in infancy
were then made partakers of that life; we then had
our new birth unto righteousness; we began to live
by that life which the members of Christ have from
Him, as the branches of a tree live by the sap which

they secretly draw from the roots. If we had not been called to that blessing until we were grown up, the Church would have required of us actually. and really to have this faith in our minds: according to what we learn in the Catechism, that in persons to be baptized the Church requires faith, whereby they stedfastly believe God's promises. As it is, the unspeakable Gift was made ours before we could know any thing of it; it was breathed into us, like the breath of life, by the free and bountiful grace of the regenerating Spirit; yet still we live by faith. Faith is that by which we abide in Christ, and keep our portion in the good and Holy Spirit. By faith, as the Apostle says, " we stand:" that is, the spiritual life within us depends in some special manner on this grace. We are justified, made holy, made members of Christ, once for all, as infants in Holy Baptism. But just as our bodily life would decay and die away, if we took no care to preserve it, so will our spiritual life, if, when we grow old enough, we do not constantly turn towards Him, Who was the beginning of that life in us, and graciously offers Himself to be the support and end of it also, if we do not prevent Him.

Such turning towards Christ is faith. It is, as I have said, looking out of ourselves, and entirely depending on Him for every good thing, and for deliverance from all evil. It is not, as I suppose, turning to Him as our Saviour only, but as to our Judge also, and our Teacher and our King: it is seeking His favour before all the good things of this world, and willingly parting with them to please Him; it is remembering His Presence when we are most alone, and keeping our very thoughts in order, that we may not displease Him Who is for ever reading our hearts.

This is some account of that faith, by which the just live, and by which Christians are graciously enabled to keep that heavenly righteousness, which God gave them when He made them His own: which faith if we lose, we draw back unto perdition, but if we continue so to believe, it is the very saving of our souls.

Thus we may understand how impossible it is, that those men should have true faith, who allow themselves in what is commonly called self-righteousness, that is, I suppose, any sort of notion, that they are good enough, and need not much fear the sentence of the last day. The Pharisees of old seem to have gone far in this temper, trusting to their being children of Abraham, to their knowledge of the law, and to their very exact observance of some particular portions of it: as also to their punctual and regular performance of such outward duties as fasting and public prayer. They did not so much try to deceive others, but were themselves greatly deceived about their own condition, by their carefulness in these things. They were deceived, and thought themselves good enough, because they looked to themselves and their fellow men, instead of looking out of themselves into the perfect law of God, and the deep sayings of Holy Scripture, requiring truth in the inward parts, and declaring that "the very heavens are not pure in His sight: how much less man that is a worm!"

We are in continual danger of erring as they did,

and losing both faith and the rewards of faith, in this way particularly: that we take up with what we find in ourselves, or with what others seem to find in us, as if it were good enough to please God, instead of lifting up the eyes of our heart to the Cross of Christ, and to Him Who hangs upon it, and seeking from Him more and more of the heavenly righteousness.

Some of us are inclined to trust in our readings and prayers, and in our regular attendance at Church: perhaps also in our being punctual at the Holy Communion. Let such consider, whether they are not the very persons to whom our Lord gave that solemn warning, "*Many will say to Me in that day,.We have eaten and drunk in Thy Presence, and Thou hast taught in our streets: and then will I profess unto them, I never knew you: depart from Me, ye that work iniquity."

Others imagine all is well enough with them, if they have their neighbours' good word, as honest, kind, friendly people. They do not consider that He, with Whom they have to deal, requires also purity of heart.

And so in many other ways: there is perhaps no part of goodness, which has not one or other of us depending upon it, in such sort, as that we willingly forget what God requires of us in other respects. It is sad and humbling to think, how ready we are to content ourselves, in this way, with what we may have already done, our poor weak beginnings in goodness, and take no pains to go on daily to something better. Whereas our Lord has

<hr>

ᵃ S. Luke xiii. 26, 27.

distinctly warned us, though we had done all that
is required, not at all to trust in it, but to feel that
it is no more than our duty, that after all we are
but unprofitable servants, and that if He is so gracious as to give us a reward at last, He will but
be rewarding His own work in us.

But some perhaps may say, they consider this
to be most true, they account it very dangerous and
unchristian to trust in works, their whole reliance
is on faith: and in this they think the New Testament bears them out, because it says so distinctly,
that we are justified by faith. I would say to all
such persons, Take care that you are not deceiving
yourselves, and falling into the very error which you
think yourselves most free from. What difference
can it make in point of pride and presumption, whether a man trusts in his own faith, or in his own
works? In either case he trusts in something of his
own, and not in the only sure trust, his crucified Saviour: in either case he goes about to establish his
own righteousness, instead of submitting himself to
the righteousness of God. To be sure, it is the extreme of rashness and folly, for any man to think
that his poor blemished works are good enough to
claim eternal life at his Maker's hands: but is it
not as foolish to imagine one's faith, taken in itself,
so perfect and precious in God's sight, as that it shall
make up for wilful disobedience, and cause God to
accept us though we live carelessly? Nay, it is
neither our faith nor our deeds, but the merit of our
Lord and Saviour Jesus Christ, such as true faith apprehends it, alone and all-sufficient: this it is whereby we are justified: for His sake God is moved

F f

both to forgive us our past sins, and to pour His sanctifying Spirit into our hearts, to make us truly righteous before Him.

Such faith as this, the faith which keeps hold of our Lord, not only as bearing our sins in His own Body on the tree, but also as uniting us to Himself and making us members of Him, strong in the strength of His Spirit to keep all we have vowed to Him: such faith as this leads immediately to the obeying all His commandments : not one or two which may happen to come easiest to us, but all. For since He was so good and merciful as to forget our natural sinfulness, and take us into His favour, before we could love and serve Him : much more, being made His, will He bless our true love and service, weak though it be, with more and more of His grace. According to the Apostle's reasoning, " *If, when we were enemies, we were reconciled to God by the death of His Son, much more, being reconciled, we shall be saved by His life."

Again, if our faith really tell us that we are in very deed brought so near to God in Christ, as the New Testament every where implies: if He be indeed the Vine, we the branches ; He the Body, we the members ; bone of His bone, and flesh of His flesh ; so that the life we now live, is not so much ours as that of Christ living in us, and we may cry out with S. Paul, " ᵇI can do all things through Christ which strengtheneth me :" if these things are so indeed, how heavy must their account be, who wilfully break any of their Saviour's laws, who scorn and slight Him, actually abiding in them ! How certain must we feel,

* Rom. v. 10.　　　ᵇ Phil. iv. 13.

as we think on these things, on the one hand, that none of our labour can be vain in the Lord, that He counts and treasures up every one of our good thoughts, and actions, and self-denials : and on the other, that every wilful sin must tell for the worse upon our spiritual condition ; it may be truly repented of, confessed, forsaken ; but there is reason to fear that it never may nor can so vanish, as if it had never been. It will make some difference to us, for ought we know, to all eternity. Surely, if a man really believes in eternity, nothing at all that he does here can possibly seem altogether trifling to him. He will feel sure that he shall hear of all again, and that it will be the better or the worse with him for ever.

On the other hand, faith in Christ Jesus, faith in Him as our present Saviour, just in the same proportion as it makes our actions important, will make our fortunes in this world of small consequence : because this thought will be ever in our minds : God has put us on our way to heaven : Christ is abiding in us by His Spirit to help us thither : what real difference can it make how we fare, and how we are employed, in the worldly matters through which we must pass here ? How we behave, how we think and feel, what our hearts are set upon ; *that* makes the difference : not, how well we are provided for in this world. Therefore a thoughtful Christian will never like to be at all forward in choosing his own condition.

But if he must at any time choose, and if he will take the Bible at its word, he cannot doubt that the way of the Cross, the way of suffering and self-denial for Christ's sake, is to be chosen before all others. "'Blessed are the poor, Blessed are they that mourn, Blessed are they which are persecuted for righteousness' sake." It is our Lord Himself Who speaks thus earnestly: and if we will obey His teaching, we must really believe that there is some special virtue and blessing in these things, so bitter to flesh and blood; in poverty, mourning, desolation, persecution. As they make us outwardly more like our Master, so He has endowed them with an inward and spiritual power, to bring Him really nearer, and do ourselves more good, if we will try and strive to take them rightly.

But then they must not merely be endured patiently; they must even be welcomed with a sort of devout joy, for the hope's sake that they really will bring us nearer to Jesus Christ. We must have learned, for God's sake, to subdue our earthly natures so far, as to be even comforted and refreshed in our mind, by every vexation and grief that comes upon us; considering with ourselves, that this is the way by which Christian people are to be made like unto Christ.

Devotional exercises, prayer and the like, are another great trial of the faith, by which the just are to live. As one of the best signs of bodily life, not mere living, but healthful life, is our having a relish for our proper food and exercise; so is the life of faith known by our loving to pour out our hearts before God, to call upon Him in all temptations, to commit ourselves to Him in all dangers; and above all, by our earnestly hungering and thirsting after

c S Matt. v. 3, 4, 10.

Him Who is our Righteousness: hungering and
thirsting after that Bread and Cup which are the
very Communion of His Body and Blood.   This is
why the holy ordinances of the Church, why prayer,
especially in public, and the Holy Communion, are
so very great a part of the Divine life.   It is not that
every such devout exercise is a good work done, and
so an end; but by those things, in a certain sense,
we spiritually live: to delight in them, not now and
then, but constantly, is the very token of the Holy
Spirit working within us: they are as the act of
breathing, by which we continually inhale, so to say,
more and more of that good Spirit, the quickening
breath of the Almighty.   If we can live without
breathing, then may we hope to live spiritually without constant prayer and partaking of Church ordinances.   And if we can live without food, then we
may live the life of faith without receiving the holy
and blessed Supper of the Lord.

I speak in this place more particularly of public
Church prayers: because, blessed as all good prayers
are, the Church prayers more especially are those to
which the great promises are made; our devotion,
then, is not simply our own, but that of all the members of Christ, all our brethren everywhere; and so
our communion with Him is more perfect: as the
limbs of the body derive strength and nourishment
from the head in greater perfection when all are exercised together, than when any one is in action, the
rest remaining still.

It is a bad sign, therefore, of the Divine life, when
a man is contented to remain at home, and say his
prayers, and read the Scriptures there, under the

notion that place signifies little, if a man is employed
in reading or hearing that which is good. It proves
that such a person has little or no faith in Christ
present in His mystical Body, but is rather apt to
put his trust in his own private thoughts and devotions; which kind of thought is surely a sort of self-
righteousness.

And on the other hand, if a person be earnest and
anxious about public prayer *only*, he has reason to
suspect himself, lest his own fancy, or the praise of
some fellow-creature, or some other poor low motive
be really what brings him to Church, instead of the
true faith and fear of God.

Thus the two, public and private prayer, will mu-
tually encourage and bless one another. The prayers
we make at home, when nobody sees us, will prepare
us for those in Church, and will be a test of our
sincerity in them: and the prayers of Christ's body,
in which we join, will draw down blessings on the
whole course of our lives; and among the rest, on our
private prayers.

And the more earnest and constant we are in thus
addressing ourselves to Almighty God, either in
Church or at home, the less leisure and occasion shall
we have to talk and discourse about Divine things, except where duty requires it. It is to be apprehended
that much talk of holy subjects is often rather a
token of lightness and irreverence, than of the true
love and fear of God Most High, dwelling in the deep
of a man's heart. If we read on to the end of the prophetic warning from which the text is taken, we shall
see that he who speaks so earnestly of justifying faith,
was also instructed to teach men a holy silence, few

and grave words, and hearts full of awe and soberness, when they are in the Presence of God, in His
solemn worship, or in such discourse as seems especially to bring us near to Him. " ⁴ The Lord," he
says, " is in His holy Temple : let all the earth keep
silence before Him."

It will be another part of the same dutiful temper
—the proper temper of him whom Christ has justified—to be very patient and humble in all perplex-
ities and discomforts : in no wise expecting always
to see his way clearly, but content even to seem to
" walk in darkness and have no light," so he may but
be permitted and helped to " ᵉ trust in the name of
the Lord, and to stay himself upon his God."

Finally, and above all, such an one will cherish in
himself a very deep and earnest fear of relapsing, by
any wilful habitual sin, into that miserable state from
which Christ has delivered us, or a worse. He will
pray to be even haunted and possessed, with the
thought and dread of such a dangerous downfall :
knowing that as the just is to live by faith, so he will
most surely die by such unbelief as must go along
with all wilful sin : it wastes and destroys, more or
less quickly, the powers of his regenerate soul, the
spiritual and heavenly life, which he has from Christ
dwelling within him by His Spirit. Full of this great
fear, he will pray to God to make the remembrance
of his sins more grievous to him than it is, and so to
withhold him from ever wilfully repeating them.
And he will see to it, that what faith he has be never
suffered to lie idle, but rather that it be continually
exercised in little every day matters, so that like the

ᵈ Hab. ii. 20.   ᵉ Is. l. 10.

love of a dutiful child, living in the house with its parent, it may grow and thrive from day to day, and spread itself quietly, like a holy leaven, through all his thoughts, words, and actions.

These are the things by which we should try our faith : by little obediences and self-denials, occurring every moment, rather than by our feelings and imaginations, when particularly moved. He that despiseth these small things shall surely fall by little and little. But he that in these things watches himself and serves Christ, the Holy Spirit will prepare him for the great trials, whenever they come ; and of him there is the best hope, that he will not be one " of them that fall back unto perdition," but of them whose faith shall last " to the saving of their souls."

SERMON XXXVIII.

GOD TRIES US BY LOVING US.

Ps. cxxx. 4.

"There is mercy with Thee: therefore shalt Thou be feared."

"God is Love." What a word is that, my brethren! "God is Love," and wherever God is, there is Love: and surely God is everywhere with us, therefore Love is everywhere with us; whether we perceive it or not, it encircles, it compasses us on every side; it pervades our whole being. For if God did not love us we should not be: never would He have made us had He hated us. So reasons a holy writer of old, and so the inspired Word plainly teaches, declaring that His mercy is over all His works, and that He willeth all men to be saved, and that the miserable ones who will finally go wrong, will not be lost for want of love on His part, but for abusing His gift of free-will by rejecting His love.

"God is Love;" we all, all Christians, know and acknowledge it; but even as we know and acknowledge in words, and in reason we cannot deny, that God is everywhere, Immense, Incomprehensible, Omnipresent, that He is "about our path, and about

our bed, and spieth out all our ways: " and yet we
live, and move, and think, we lie down and rise up,
we go out and come in, too often, alas! inattentive
to His aweful Presence: so it is in respect of His
love; it is on all sides of us, it is in the very air we
breathe, and yet how many live and die without
really and truly feeling it in their hearts!

And, O my brethren, what a difference does it
make in a poor sinful soul, what a change in every
view and feeling, what a light cast on all around,
what a life animating all within, when love ever
present love, begins really, however imperfectly, to
be perceived, apprehended, realized, by one who has
unhappily been hitherto a stranger to it! Think
what it would be in a battle, in a fire, in a shipwreck,
for any one of the poor sufferers to catch the eye of
some one who he could not doubt was able to save
him; to perceive that eye fixed lovingly and compassionately upon him! what a thrill of hope, and
consolation, and thankfulness, would presently take
place of the feeling, ' there is no hope, none! '

Think of that saying in the Gospel, " * Jesus, beholding him, loved him." Imagine the eye of Him
Who is Love fixed upon you in love, and you suddenly becoming aware of it, after that for a long time,
perhaps for your whole life hitherto, you had walked
in desolation, " having no hope, and without God in
the world." It is no dream nor fancy, my brethren:
in all countries, all generations, in every town, in
every village, in every rank, degree, occupation of
life, this, by God's mercy, is the history of thousands
of souls. After many years they have come to ap-

* S. Mark x. 21.

prehend their Saviour's love towards them, to discern somewhat of His gracious countenance, which had been watching them all the while, and they knew it not.

Perhaps they had been wanderers in such a city as this, uncared for, unguided, unprotected; their hearts hardening from year to year by reason of the hardness and selfishness of those among whom they lived; hardly hearing of faith, or of a Saviour, except in the way of scorn and blasphemy: like the poor prodigal in the Gospel, their life has been a dreary famine, and their only resource has been to sell or hire themselves to one after another of the evil spirits, who lay in wait for them, for such miserable husks as they might afford them. But He Who died for them, and had never ceased to love them, He in His own good time had pity on them, and caused them to have a sense of His love, dimly perhaps and doubtfully at first, and with many intermissions, like a star appearing and disappearing; and they have not turned away, they have not been altogether disobedient to the heavenly vision, and the touching, winning, attracting power, was His deep love wherewith He loved them.

It matters not how this happened in each instance: in the inexhaustible riches of His providence and grace, it is probable that no two among the millions who have been converted since Pentecost have come to Him exactly in the same way: but it was always Divine Love, in one shape or another.

'Jesus, beholding thee, loved thee,' when at first thou wast brought to the font, else why did He move thy parents to bring thee? Why did He take thee up in His arms, lay His hands upon thee, and bless thee ?

Again, Jesus, beholding, loved thee, when He caused thee haply to fall in the way of some kind and good adviser, whom He moved to speak a word to thee in season, just when it was wanted to check thee in thy dangerous ways; or when He opened and set before thine eyes just the very page in His holy Word which He had prepared beforehand for thee, and by His secret inspiration guided thine eyes and thy mind to read, and mark, and think over these words in particular, until thy heart burned within thee, and thou saidst to thyself, 'Surely I have a friend; surely there is One Who careth for me, and knoweth what is in my heart, to walk with me in the way as I am sad, and to open to me the Scriptures.'

'Jesus beholding thee, loved thee,' as often as His severe but merciful hand hath touched thee in the way of affliction, or in the way of relief. Did He strike thee suddenly down in thy young days, by some violent fall or blow, by fire or water, by loss or damage of eyesight, or any other of thy precious senses ? or hath He chastened thee in any time of thy life by long-continued, wearying illness, and made all thy freshness to consume away like a moth? Hath He touched thee with want or bereavement, with destitution or loss of friends? Hast thou seemed to be alone in the world, none to pity, none to help, conscience whispering to thee that it was thy own fault? And then did He come to thee in thy darkness and dimness of anguish, either by thoughts of hope and penitence, darting into thy mind thou knewest

not how, or by some kind messenger, some inter-
preter, one among a thousand, leaning over thee as
the angel over Hagar in the wilderness, some friend
of soul or body, whose very presence was felt by thee
as a token that there was love and hope for thee,
when thou hadst ceased to think of either? Or was
it the affliction, the sickness, the departure, the death,
the alienation, or, worse than all these, the treachery
and sinful misbehaviour, of some fellow creature on
whom thou hadst been used to depend, father,
mother, brother, sister, wife, or husband, child or
friend, which was as thine own soul,—was it losing
any of these, or the being near to lose them, which
caused thee to feel for the first time what a nothing
we are without God?

Whichever of all these methods, or what means besides them, He took to open their eyes, thou knowest,
Christian brother, that it was Jesus beholding and
loving thee; it was just as much a miracle of His
spiritual grace, as the mighty works in the Gospel
were miracles of His power over earthly things, and
of His compassionate care for earthly sufferers. For
I need not tell you that those works, each and all of
them, were as types and shadows of what He is continually doing for lost souls. His beholding, and His
loving, His Word, and His Touch, are daily and
hourly healing spiritual lepers, raising the dead in
sin to the life of righteousness, opening the eyes of
the blinded understanding, setting free the palsied
and perverse will, causing such as are wilfully deaf
to hear the words of the Holy Book, unloosing the
tongue of the dumb to speak the language of His
people, and shew forth His praise.

Now, my brethren, you plainly see that this special love of our Redeemer, manifested to each of those sufferers according to their special and several needs, laid each one in his turn under special and particular obligations. They could not be as they had been before, having once become aware that Jesus, beholding, had so loved them. That leper who had approached our Lord in such deep and trembling loneliness, the first, seemingly, who had ever ventured to come near Him to seek relief of that loathsome disease, bowing down and kneeling, and falling down on his face, and crying, "[b] Lord, if Thou wilt, Thou canst make me clean," think you that he could ever forget the touch of the great physician's hand, and His Voice saying, "I will; be thou clean?" The man out of whom the legion of unclean spirits had gone, was not content to remain for a short while, "at the feet of Jesus, sitting, and clothed, and in his right mind," but prayed Him that he might be with Him. The blind men, that were healed near Jericho, made use of their eyesight to mark which way Jesus went, and to follow Him. That other blind man, whose eyes were opened upon washing in the pool of Siloam, lost no time in confessing Christ before men, and had a confessor's reward, that he was persecuted by Christ's enemies.

That persons so favoured should so acknowledge the favours which they have received may appear to some of us as we read almost a matter of course. You may say to yourselves, 'How could they do otherwise? they would have been the most ungrateful of men had they at such a time turned away from

[b] S. Luke v. 12.

the loving eye of Him Who had just relieved them.'
Most true, my brethren, none may deny it; but do
you not see, do you not feel, what follows concerning
yourselves, concerning each one who has ever felt
the Lord's Eye of love fixed upon him, whether in
providence or (much more) in grace? Surely all
the dutifulness and humble love we can in any way
practise towards Him ought to be a matter of course
with us, after any such special mercy as may at all
answer to the gracious doings of our Lord in the
flesh, when He went about healing men's bodies, for
a token of what He would do for their souls. Surely
all His special providences and calls, inward or outward, secret or open, all the thrilling glimpses and
flashes of His fatherly care, wherewith from time to
time we have ever been any of us visited, will come
back one day as consuming fires to devour us, if we
have not made much of them, and suffered them to
kindle in us also some faint sparks at least of true
heavenly love.

O, depend upon it, my brethren, Love, the Love
of the Most High God towards us miserable sinners,
as it is the most blessed, so is it the most trying of
all things. It puts all who are the objects of it
under a probation keener and more searching than
any other that we can imagine. Think once again of
the miracles recorded in the Gospel; the greatness
of the mercy shewn in them did not take away but
enhance their effect as modes of trial and probation
from beginning to end. Before they were wrought,
they were trials of faith; as He said, "° According
to your faith be it unto you;" and again, " If thou

° S. Matt. ix. 29.

canst believe, all things are possible to him that
believeth." And afterwards (as we have seen) they
were trials of love and gratitude, of dutifulness and
constancy ; as He said again, " [d] Sin no more, lest a
worse thing come unto thee." " [e] Tell no man, but
offer for thy cleansing that which Moses commanded."
" [f] Go home to thy friends, and tell them what things
God hath done unto thee." " [g] Labour not for the
meat that perisheth, but for that meat which endureth unto everlasting life." " [h] Dost thou believe on
the Son of God ? Thou hast both seen Him, and it is
He that talketh with thee."

As the favour shewn by the Redeemer to the children of Israel in making them a peculiar treasure to
Himself above all people, a kingdom of priests, and
a holy nation, did not exempt them from severe and
perilous trial, but on the contrary, caused the inqui-
sition made on them to be stricter and more rigid
than on any other people (as saith the prophet,
"You only have I known of all the families of the
earth, therefore will I visit you for all your iniquities "); so you may be sure that each one of those
on whom our Lord wrought His gracious miracles,
and to whom He addressed Himself in a marked
and peculiar way, had more to answer for in despis-
ing and rejecting Him than the ordinary multitude,
who were about Him in this place or in that.

And can ye at all doubt, are ye not equally sure,
that in whatsoever manner or degree the gracious
Saviour hath at any time touched you with a sense
of His love, His converting, restraining, chastening,

[d] S. John v. 14.   [e] S. Mark i. 44.   [f] Ib. v. 19.
[g] S. John vi. 27.   [h] Ib. ix. 35, 37.

consoling love, He hath made you so much the more responsible, hath put you so much the more on your trial, hath entrusted you with so much the more of His choice treasures? If He calls, will He not expect an answer? if He is trying, will He not judge? if He have put a trust in your hands, will He not exact an account of you?

Therefore, dear brother or sister in Christ Jesus, whosoever thou art whom Jesus beholding, hath loved, drawing thee to Him out of the midst of this great Babylon, this type of the dreary world, wherein, as we wander up and down it is hard not to think of the psalmist's sayings, "[i] I have spied unrighteousness and strife in the city: Day and night they go about within the walls thereof; mischief also and sorrow are in the midst of it:" thou, I say, who here or elsewhere hast found, or art finding, a shelter in the arms of thy Lord, and of His Church; do not think it hard to be told, that although thy condition is very blessed, thy deliverance wonderful, nay miraculous, and such as thou canst never thank Him enough for, yet thou art not taken out of trial: rather (as I said) thy trial is more searching, and in one sense more hazardous than ever; by how much the shame and the loss must be the greater, when a soul falls from a more favoured place.

Perhaps the services of this very Lent may have been, as it were, messages from God to thee; perhaps words and thoughts have been caused to enter into the depths of thy soul, which before flitted only over its surface; perhaps thou art ready to say to God, "[k] I had heard of Thee by the hearing of the

[i] Ps. lv. 9, 10.   [k] Job xlii. 5.

ear, but now mine eye seeth Thee." If so, it is well, thank God for it; praise Him with humble joy, for so graciously drawing nigh to thee; but observe what has ever been the mind of His true and dutiful servants, whenever He hath made them aware of any nearer or more especial Presence of His; they have feared always, as they entered into the cloud; their cry has been like that of S. Paul newly converted, "[1] Lord, what wilt Thou have me to do?" or of the child Samuel, long before, "[m] Speak, Lord, for Thy servant heareth;" or of her, the most blessed of all the daughters of Eve, "[n] Behold the handmaid of the Lord; be it unto me according to Thy word." The saints did not allow themselves to be carried away by the sense of Divine favour, of relief, or deliverance; they presently composed themselves in the attitude of servants, or rather of Angels, waiting humbly round the Throne; watching to learn what next He would have them do or suffer for His Name's sake. And now, in this good and solemn season, if God has in any respect shewn Himself nearer to thy heart and conscience, answering thy prayer, forgiving thy sins, dispelling thy temptations, breathing into thee good desires, God forbid that thou shouldst throw away the intended fruit of such mercies by simply brooding over them as marks of favour, by indulging the temper, too natural to us all, which would lead thee to say, "[o] God, I thank Thee that I am not as other men are."

Listen to the great and holy penitent, how he, taught by the Holy Ghost, behaves himself under the

---

[1] Acts ix. 6.   [m] 1 Sam. iii. 9.
[n] S. Luke i. 38.   [o] Ib. xviii. 11.

mighty hand of God, stretched out to deliver him.
He cries out of the deep, even as any poor lost soul
among ourselves may have cried out of the deep of
its sin and misery, "P Lord, hear my voice: O let
Thine ears consider well the voice of my complaint."
He is struggling in the deep mire, where no ground
is; the waves and storms are gone over him; he
finds no footing of his own; all his hope is that a
saving hand may be reached out to him, not for any
good desert, any innocency of his, for he is sadly
convinced that, "If Thou, Lord, shouldest mark iniquities," none could stand. But 'There is mercy,
pardon, propitiation with Thee; Thou hast an infinite treasure, an inexhaustible store of indulgence;
an atonement which can never wear out, nor lose its
virtue.' 'That, that alone, is my hope; there is
mercy with Thee, therefore,' now mark what follows,
" *therefore shalt Thou be feared.*" He does not say,
' Therefore shalt Thou be loved, therefore shalt Thou
be trusted in, therefore shall the people give thanks
unto Thee;' and yet who can doubt that love, trust,
thanksgiving, are very meet, right, and the bounden
duty of those to whom God hath shewn especial
mercy? The Psalmist, however, mentions none of
these, but what he does say is, " There is mercy with
Thee, therefore shalt Thou be *feared.*"

How is that? how cometh it to pass that God's
mercy and compassion through Jesus Christ should
cause Him to be more *feared* by sinners? Why,
surely any one of a thoughtful mind may understand that grace and pardon poured out in such
abundant measure, heaped together, and running

P Ps. cxxx. 2.

o g 2

over, will add to our burden and debt of dutiful
gratitude; that as our condition is infinitely more
blessed, so it is also infinitely more aweful, than it
would have been if the work of redeeming Love had
never been wrought for us, or we had never been
told of it. The wrath of the Lamb—final condemnation from Him Who did love us so dearly that He
gave Himself to take our nature upon Him, and to
die for us—such wrath as will cause even Him at
last to say, "'Depart from Me, ye cursed;"—this
would seem from Holy Writ to be reserved especially
for the children of the kingdom; not for those who
have lived without grace, but for those who have
received grace, and thrown it away.

"Wherefore, holy brethren, partakers of the heavenly calling"—for so I may venture to speak unto
you all, since the very fact of your being here in
God's house is a token of your having at some time
or other known and believed that Jesus beholding,
loved you;—let me beseech you not to give ear to
the seducing spirits who would rob you of the fruits
of that Love, by suggesting, in their several ways,
that it takes away or lessens the need of holy fear
and exact watchfulness. Beware of imagining that
because God is Love, therefore it is impossible that
wrath should come upon any to the uttermost. The
same Scripture that tells us, He will have all men
to be saved, tells also of some who will be punished
with everlasting destruction from His Presence. The
one saying is as plain as the other; and He Who is
Truth and Love Himself has plainly signified His
will that we should think much of these His severer

' S. Matt. xxv. 41.

declarations, by uttering so many of them with His own Divine Lips. It is Jesus Christ, not one of the prophets or apostles, Who tells us most expressly of "[r] the worm that dieth not," and of "the fire that is not quenched;" of "[s] a great gulph fixed," and one beyond it, whose portion is "to lift up his eyes, being in torments;" of its being possible for a man's latter end to be such, that "[t] good were it for that man if he had never been born."

O, my brethren, believe your Saviour; take Him at His own word; listen not to those (in our days, alas! too many) who either in scorn or in mistaken charity, would persuade you that "the wicked shall *not* be turned into Hell." Verily, it is one of Satan's snares when a poor fallen sinner has come to know in good earnest the winning power of our Master's Love, and to feel that it is indeed inexhaustible,—I say, it is one of Satan's devices to whisper in such a person's ear, and say, "Love is almighty, irresistible: as it hath come to you, so it will come to all : ye shall not surely die for ever, any of you, whatever the Bible seems to say." And so he contrives, if he can, to separate our love, and the love which would teach others, from that holy reverential fear which belongs to plain simple faith in the Bible.

Sometimes he takes another way, and would fain persuade the newly converted, that there are indeed everlasting torments, and 'very many,' he says 'will fall into them; but you are safe. God does nothing in vain; He hath sealed you with His own seal, and His seal cannot be broken; trust Him therefore, and

[r] S. Mark ix. 44.   [s] S. Luke xvi. 26.
[t] S. Mark xiv. 21.

be very thankful; but why should you account yourself still bound to such exact watching and prayer
and self-denial, as if you had no assurance from Him?
You are called unto liberty, why enslave yourself
again to the law?' Thousands there are whom the
great enemy deludes by fancies of this sort, and
tempts them by little and little to " forsake their own
mercy :" but let us pray God to keep it in our hearts,
and in the hearts of all His people, that His loving-
kindnesses are for our trial, as well as His severe
judgements; let us beseech Him beforehand, that
when the sense of deliverance comes, it may come so
chastened and tempered with warning, that we may
be kept humble and watchful; that according to His
promise to His Church, when our light is come, and
the Glory of the Lord risen upon us, and we see His
boundless Love, and flow eagerly towards it as a river
towards the ocean, then our hearts may " fear, and
be enlarged"—may *fear*, and not be lifted up—may
be *enlarged*, and not straitened—enlarged to receive
more and more of heavenly inspirations of His good
Spirit; enlarged to offer Him more and more unre-
servedly the spiritual sacrifice of holy desires, good
counsels, and just works.

In what particular respects Our Lord, by commending His Love towards us, lays us under special
probation, it is not hard to understand. Recollect
once more the deep and blessed saying, " " Jesus, beholding him, loved him." What might angels, looking on, expect of that young man, when the Gracious
Eye had so rested upon him ?

First, that this converting look should abide in his

" S. Mark x. 21.

heart and memory as a special ground of thankfulness, to keep him cheerful and contented in all earthly anguish, sorrow, bereavement; even as the blessed S. Paul never forgot the glory and the Voice which came to him in the moment of his conversion, and was accustomed, in memory of it, to call himself, "[1] he that had obtained mercy."

Next, it will be expected that our Lord's loving aspect, seen, it may be, but on that one occasion, should be treasured up in the believing heart as an earnest and token of that vision of transforming power which shall be hereafter, when the faithful penitent shall see his Lord as He is: not as then, after the flesh: not as now, through a glass, darkly: but face to face, as He is; beholding Him, and beheld by Him, in that Presence which is the fulness of joy. God's special, spiritual vouchsafements here, are so many glimpses and tokens of Heaven, meant to abide with us, and help us to think much of Heaven; and after them we are on our trial, whether we will so use them or no.

Again, was it possible, think you, for one to discern our Master's eye fixed on himself in Love, and not to catch one faint spark at least of loving thought towards his brethren? All fire is spreading, and surely he to whom it has been given to kindle himself at that Divine Fire will not rest until he hath kindled others also. Not for pride, but for love and dutifulness, he will walk so as that his light cannot but shine before men; he will be on the watch for quiet and effectual means to help those around him, and shew them the good way, knowing that the

[1] 1 Cor. vii. 25.

promise, "' Inasmuch as ye did it to one of the least
of these, ye did it unto Me," stands true as concerning heavenly and spiritual even more than concerning bodily and earthly relief. Indeed there is nothing
so converting as the sight of a true penitent. For
his sorrow shews us what true sin is; his gentleness
and charity reflect the love of God, and proclaim Him
waiting to be gracious; his evident acceptance is an
invitation to all to come, wash, and be clean; his
calmness and peace convince us that there is rest to
be had even by such world-troubled and sin-troubled
transgressors as we, and smooth the rugged road of
penitence to those who shrink from the pilgrimage.

Who dreads weeping whilst he watches Mary
Magdalen's tears? Who thinks penitence grievous
when he sees her departing with the "' Go in peace"
expressed in eye, feature, and step, the "Go in
peace" which is manifestly no going away, but a
continual abiding in and with Jesus?

In short, my brethren, when our Saviour hath once
let us know that He loveth us, from that day forth
we have a deeper and more serious account to give
of all our conduct towards God and man than ever
we had before. It is, in a certain sense, as He taught,
a new yoke and a fresh burthen laid upon us; yet
not a grievous yoke, nor an oppressive burthen, for
the sense of His unspeakable Love will constrain
us in our turn to love Him, and love, willing, thankful, adoring love, will make the yoke easy, and the
burthen light. Love bears a burden, saith the saint,
without burthen. Yea, like the Cross itself, such a
duty of love carries rather than is carried, as the

' S. Matt. xxv. 40.   ² S. Luke vii. 50.

wood lifted up the axe from the depths of the river, in token and prophecy of the delivering and upholding power of that which it foreshewed. Be fearless, then, beloved. Take up this responsibility, bear it about, and so bearing rejoice in the sense of God's past mercy, and in the hope of His future, resting on His first free gift and your own thankful improvement of it.

So be it, O Lord, for Jesus Christ's sake, Who loved us, and gave Himself for us, to Whom, &c.

SERMON XXXIX.

GOD TRIES US BY ENABLING US TO LOVE HIM

Song of Solomon iii. 4.

" I found Him whom my soul loveth: I held Him and would not let Him go."

" [*] WE love Him, because He first loved us :" that is, not only is it reasonable and right, not only does it follow as by a kind of moral necessity, that out of mere gratitude we should love Him, in acknowledgment and return of His unspeakable love : as if one should say, ' We have known and believed the love which God hath to us, how then can we choose but love Him ?' Not only so, but in another sense also, " we love Him because He first loved us." That is, if we have the heart to love Him at all, this also comes of His great love towards us; it is one gift more, the precious and crowning gift, in whatever measure we are able to love Him; it will not come of itself, immediately upon our knowing and believing, but it is a distinct and fresh gift from Him, Who is all good gifts in one, the Holy and Almighty Spirit of God, in whose Unity Christ Jesus our Saviour liveth and reigneth with the Eternal Father, that Spirit

[*] 1 S. John iv. 19.

whom the Church teaches us to acknowledge as the eternal and essential Love of the Father and of the Son.

"[b] The love of God is shed abroad in our hearts by the Holy Ghost which is given unto us." That is the most excellent gift, the gift which seals and secures all the rest. Tribulation, patience, experience, hope, may fail at the last, may disappoint and make one ashamed, but so long as the Holy Spirit poureth His love into our hearts, we are safe from so sad an end. Therefore it stands first among the blessed fruits of the Spirit, love, joy, peace and the rest: which whoso beareth, it is written concerning him, "[c] against such there is no law:" his sins are forgiven, and his pardon sealed in heaven, if only he persevere.

'If only!' But what an *If* is that, my brethren! and how seriously does it bring before us this great and aweful truth, that as every instance of Christ's love towards us adds something to His yoke and burden laid on us, an easy yoke and a light burthen, because it is Christ's, but still a yoke and a burthen, somewhat added to our responsibilities; so are all especially answerable for the right use and improvement of the love of God, shed abroad in their hearts. Do not suppose that this rule applies only to those confirmed in holiness, to those who are by comparison undefiled in the way. It is a rule for all; it is simply this, that the love of God, be it much or little, it is a talent, and must be improved. Love may be in all degrees, from the first faint intermittent spark, which seems every moment on the point of going

[b] Rom. v. 5.   [c] Gal. v. 25.

out, to the steady, fervent, spreading, brightening glow, which seems by God's mercy sure to go on, shining and warming more and more unto the perfect day. But in every portion and stage of it, it is the free gift of God, "[d] more to be desired than gold, yea, than much fine gold : " and if we are accountable (as who dare deny ?) to the Maker and Giver of all for the use we make of our money and other such outward endowments, how much more for these inward and spiritual treasures !

All this is so plain and obvious, that it might seem hardly needful to put you in mind of it. But there is a reason for doing so, my brethren, a reason well known to those who have had occasion to watch at all carefully their own and other men's consciences. When God in His mercy visits a sinner with a touch of earnest, thankful love, causing him to feel His tender care, and drawing up his heart to Himself in a way which the sinner had seldom or never experienced before; at such times there is a joy, a sweetness, a comfort, in all that we do or suffer for our Saviour's sake, which seems to carry the soul on for the time, without consideration of any duty, or calculation of any reward : it is all for love; no further question is asked. As a mother waits upon her infant as a matter of course, and seeks no further recompense or encouragement for doing so, the mother's love which she bears in her heart is its own reward : so, many times, it comes to pass in those whom the Lord hath begun to convert unto Himself : they seem for a while to be borne along upon the wings of love, and of love only; and when the

[d] Ps. xix. 10.

charm of this feeling begins to fail and die away
(as sooner or later, by His providence, it is sure to
do) presently there arises a temptation to faint and
be weary in trying to please God, and something
whispers in their hearts, 'it is too cold, too dull a
thing, to go on praying and keeping the commandments, for duty's sake, for fear's sake, or for anything but mere love's sake;' and so people are
tempted to give up, one after another, their holy and
good observances, and the works which were under-
taken to please Christ. I have known this feeling
allowed to prevail so far as to cause a Christian
person to leave off private prayer entirely, under the
notion that it was no use to pray, unless we could
pray with sweetness and comfort. This single instance, my brethren, if you consider it, is sufficient
to show that we are responsible in a very peculiar
way for the use we make of the flashes and gleams
of Divine love which it may please the Holy and
Good Spirit from time to time to awaken in our
hearts.

I say 'flashes and gleams' of heavenly charity, because I fear that in the lives of ordinary Christians
it is rare indeed to find that which goes much beyond these. If the very truth must be told, if you
will try and go deep down into the dark places of
your conscience, and endeavour to see what God sees
there; how often, think you, shall you find that
you have said a thoroughly good prayer, thinking of
God all along, and really meaning what you said to
Him? How many times, since you were a communicant, have you drawn near to receive those
most Holy Things with so true a heart, with so full

assurance of faith, as to have kept up your sense
of Christ's Presence and of His wonderful and mysterious coming from beginning to end of the service? How many confessions have you made to Him,
either alone or through His Priest, which you can
now look back on as an exercise of real and earnest contrition?

However, we may hope and believe that there
have been glimpses, please God, to some, to many,
or to all of us, of true adoring love, for which we
cannot be thankful enough. We may remember
brief seasons at least in our past lives, in which it
was given us to know in some small measure, what
it is to love God. In early youth, mere change of
place, and withdrawal for a time from objects which
had come to be too tempting, have been blessed to
some in a remarkable way, leaving the heart and
mind again open for pure and innocent thoughts and
associations to flow in, and for the child-like love of
Him Who is purity and goodness to revive. Were
they not times of trial as well as of comfort? Is it
not a humbling thought to remember how little profit we reaped from them; and a comforting thought
again, to be assured, that even now, if we will offer
up the memory of them with mingled regret and
thankfulness to Him Who gave them, He will accept them for His Son's sake, and by His Holy Spirit
make them helps to effectual penitence?

And then, my brethren, what an ordinary thing
it is to be lifted up or brought low by what we hear
in sermons, or read in spiritual books, God's providence so adapting the words spoken or the speaker's
manner to our mood of mind and spiritual necessities

at the time, that we feel it not as the word of man, but as in such case it is in truth, a word from God, His good instrument to make us for a short time forget and lose ourselves in the love of Him! And were we not answerable to Him, when through carelessness or worldly desire we permitted such good impressions to die away?

To speak of a Gift yet more sacred; none of us surely needs to be told, how greatly it concerned him to make much of his Saviour, newly received in the Holy Eucharist, and of any heavenly aspirations and holy desires which at such a time may have been granted to him. The evening of a Communion day is always in this respect a very trying time.

So are times of bereavement and affliction, and still more, to some tempers, times of narrow escape and unlooked for relief. At such times the Almighty Teacher "° openeth the ears of men and sealeth their instruction;" the truth, the warning, the lesson of love, comes to them as the commandments did on Mount Sinai, not only spoken, but written and engraved, written and engraved in our hearts, and we are apt to feel, for the time, as if nothing could ever erase it. "'He sendeth out His word and melteth them:" hardened spirits, frozen hearts, that have continued impenetrable perhaps through a long life, give way at once when that Word commands, "ᵍWho calleth for the waters of the sea and poureth them out upon the face of the earth." "He bloweth with His wind," the rushing mighty wind that came down upon the Apostles, "and the waters flow;" and the heart that was like a flint stone becometh a well of

° Job xxxiii. 16.　　ᶠ Ps. cxlvii. 18.　　ᵍ Amos v. 8.

living water. So it was, above all other days, on the great day of Pentecost: "[h] the windows of heaven," the outlets of Divine grace, were opened as they never before had been, and "the fountains of the great deep," the hearts of sinners were broken up. There was "[i] poured upon the house of David and upon the inhabitants of Jerusalem the spirit of grace and supplication ;" and they began to "look on Him whom they had pierced," and to "mourn for Him as one mourneth for his only son."

Thus it was on the birthday of our Mother the Church, and thus it has been ever since: to each one of us, would we but watch for them, there have been days of grace, acceptable times, special out-pourings of the Blessed Spirit, when God vouchsafed unto us, in a peculiar degree, some earnest and fore-taste of the blessedness of loving Him; and Holy Scripture is full of notices how much we lose if we fail to mark those times, and to improve them to our soul's good.

Moreover the Bible very carefully teaches, that however *we* may neglect our Blessed Master's lessons of love, there are those who will make much of them for their own several purposes. First, there is one watchful enemy who is never (probably) far off, when and where God is dispensing His grace : when the sons of God "[k] come to present themselves before the Lord, Satan," we are warned, may be expected to "come also among them:" and can you doubt with what mind he comes, or how he is employed on such occasions? He watches to see how he may rob God's children of the blessing newly received:

[h] Gen. vii. 11.   [i] Zech. xii. 10.   [k] Job ii. 1.

he takes advantage of men's natural weariness and
infirmity to entice them a little way off their guard,
to draw away their eyes for a moment from looking
at their Lord: and then he tries his deadly sugges-
tions of pride, lust, vanity, selfishness, sloth: he tries
his worst against thee more keenly in proportion
as God hath shewn thee favour, and is giving thee
grace to acknowledge it: for whom will the Evil one
most envy? Those, to be sure, whom he apprehends
to be best beloved of God, and to love Him best.
He never made such an assault on any as on our
Head and Master, just after the Voice from heaven
had declared Him the beloved Son.   Therefore men
are not to be dismayed, but calmly to consider that
it is no more than they had cause to expect, if they
find their comparatively happy intervals, when they
have seemed able to love God more steadily than
usual, followed by times of unusual distress from the
crafts and assaults of the devil.   It has always been
so, and they must not be dismayed, but they cannot
be too serious, watchful and humble.

Think, my brethren, of the sad downfalls recorded
in Holy Scripture, when persons originally visited
with God's favours neglected to hold fast what had
been given them.   Remember God's chosen people
at the foot of Mount Sinai: they had just been admitted into covenant: God had avouched them to
be His peculiar treasure above all the nations of the
earth, and they, with obedient and willing hearts for
the time, had avouched the Lord to be their God,
and had promised to do all that He commanded.
They had learned the lesson of devout fear, and their
need of a Mediator, according to His purpose in

causing them to hear His Voice out of the midst of the fire: and He had sent them that gracious message, "They have well said all that they have spoken." What is the next thing we hear of them? They have made them a golden calf, and are offering sacrifice to the works of their own hands.

Remember Balaam, the man who not only heard the words of God, knew the knowledge of the Most High, and saw the vision of the Almighty, but also spake those noble words (and who can tell but that for the time he was in earnest, or at least seemed to himself to be so?) "[1] Let me die the death of the righteous, and let my last end be like his." And yet we know what happened to Balaam; for earthly treasure and preferment he sold himself to do the devil's work. No doubt the wicked one was close at hand to spoil the good words as they came out of his mouth, to quench whatever devout feeling might for the moment go along with them, perhaps by inviting him to praise himself for them in his heart. O, be very watchful, when you seem drawn towards your Saviour; suffer not your thoughts to dwell with complacency on any good thing in yourself, but go out of yourself, go on to something better, humble yourself before Him more and more, put yourself more entirely in His hands, for so only will you be safe from the enemy.

Remember David, and remember Solomon: the sad falls which Holy Scripture relates of them followed in both instances upon their undertaking a great and holy work for the love of God: David had devoted himself to the planning and providing for

[1] Num. xxiii. 10.

the temple, Solomon had carried out his father's plans,
had builded and consecrated the holy place according
to all that was in his father's heart: and to each of
them the Lord had vouchsafed His gracious acceptance of their work, and of the love which caused
them to offer it: and now, what is the next thing
we read of them? David's miserable doings in the
matter of Uriah, and the perversion of Solomon, seduced into idolatry by his many wives. And when
Solomon's sin had borne its fruit as was foretold,
and the people at last had returned from captivity
cured of their fondness for worshipping other gods,
how passionately does Ezra, that holy and humble
reformer, deprecate in them the tendency which was
shewing itself, then, as in all great revivals, to presume on God's favour, and begin taking liberties
again. "*After all that is come upon us for our evil
deeds, and for our great trespasses, seeing that Thou
our God hast punished us less than our iniquities
deserve, and hast given us such deliverance as this;
should we again break Thy commandments and join
in affinity with the people of these abominations?"

Would you have a sadder instance still, my brethren? Remember the multitudes who cried 'Hosanna' when our Lord entered Jerusalem, they were
the same with those who cried 'Crucify Him' when
Pilate gave them their choice between Him and
Barabbas. The Evil one who seduced Judas had
been busy no doubt among them: he had great
wrath, seeing the world in appearance going after
Christ, and he was restless and active, as he would
be now in any place or parish where the number of

<hr />

* Ezra ix. 13, 14.

H h 2

penitents and communicants seemed increasing, and souls were being one after another converted to God.

I know not whether it would be right to put down Simon the unhappy sorcerer as another instance of advantage taken by the devil of a transient gleam of good feeling towards God: certainly we read that he believed, and continued with Philip, and wondered, and the last thing we are told of him in Scripture is, that he asked the Apostles to pray for him: grievous indeed it were to think, but it seems not unlikely, that those relentings (if they were such) were perverted by the enemy as encouragements to Simon in his sin.

By instances such as these Holy Scripture warns us, that times when we seem to love much are apt to be times of especial temptation, and as such are eagerly seized on by the haters of our souls. But there are other and more cheering examples: the glorious saints and faithful servants of Christ have ever been no less anxious on their part to yield unto Satan no such advantage. Their hours of spiritual strength and gladness, of conscious drawing nigh unto God, put them as they well knew on their trial in two ways especially: first in respect of perseverance, and again in respect of submission and humbleness of mind. In both, by God's mercy, the saints have been enabled to prevail. Did the feeling of human weariness come on, that bitter ingredient in the cup of God's wrath against sinners, which makes simple continuance in well-doing, *as* continuance, so hard and painful? The saints, in His strength Who never slumbers nor sleeps, have refused to give way to this weariness: they have prayed without ceasing, they have continued instant in prayer, they have served God with fastings and prayers night and day: having received some grace, they did not draw back from seeking more; they were not like that wicked and slothful servant, who hid his talent, for fear, as he said, of losing it, but in reality because he hated the trouble of improving it, and wished, if he could, to have less to give an account of; he was indolent and he feared responsibility; such are they, who, when Christ blesses them by suggesting good thoughts to their hearts, shrink from the toil and the risk of carrying out and improving these good thoughts: whereby the saying of a wise man is seen to come fearfully true, 'Hell is paved with good intentions.'

Not so the holy men either of the Old or of the New Testament: they have ever been such as Jacob wrestling with the Angel, violent with a holy violence, taking the kingdom of heaven by force, still urging their way onward from strength to strength, from one step to another of the ladder that reacheth unto heaven. Jacob's wrestling, his importunate earnest prayer, had lasted all night until the breaking of the day, and still he went on; and when the Mysterious and Holy One, making Himself weak in compassion to His creature, said, "ᵃLet me go for the day breaketh," Jacob, the head and pattern of God's chosen Israel, was taught of the Spirit to reply, "I will not let Thee go, except Thou bless me:" and He did bless him; giving us all to understand, that the way to please God in the use of His grace, is to ask for more grace: He loves to be so detained. He

ᵃ Gen. xxxii. 26.

indeed for our trial makes as though He would go further, but His wise and true disciples, like those two at Emmaus, constrain Him, saying " °Abide with us." And He condescends to their devout importunity : He goes in to tarry with them : He makes Himself known to them in breaking of bread. That is, the Blessed Sacrament of the Eucharist, as it furnishes very special occasion for trying the perseverance of beginners in the school of God's love, so by His gracious bounty does it often bring the reward of such perseverance, He whom we love revealing Himself therein to be loved more and more.

In all such instances, the Divine Lord and Lover of souls (if we may speak it with reverence) would seem to be carrying out a certain law which He hath set Himself, for the perfecting of His Spouse the Church, and of each one of her faithful members. He withdraws Himself for a while, that He may be sought more earnestly, and found with an increase of blessing.

"ᴾ By night on my bed I sought Him Whom my soul loveth, I sought Him, but I found Him not. I said, I will rise now, and go about the city, in the streets, and in the broad ways : I sought Him, but I found Him not." The devout soul seeketh her Lord, sometimes in silent, lonely meditation, sometimes in the assembly of the faithful, and the public offices of Christ's household, in the streets, as it were, and broad places of the city : she is broken-hearted at not finding Him : she asks the watchmen, the guides and guardians of souls, stationed by her Lord to find and to help her, Saw ye Him Whom my soul loveth ?

° S. Luke xxiv. 29.   ᴾ Cant. iii. 1.

That is her one thought; she perseveres in loving and in seeking: and she shall not wait long for her reward: for His rule is, "⁹ Seek and ye shall find."

"It was but a little that I passed from them, but I found Him Whom my soul loveth:" and then mark what follows, my brethren; "I held Him and would not let Him go."

Such is divine love, unwearied, unabashed, undaunted, unremitting, yet full of deepest reverence and adoring submission: for she knows that by such importunity she is simply doing the will of the Beloved.

What indeed is the history of the blessed S. Mary Magdalene, as it will shortly come before us in the Easter lessons, but this same parable of the Spouse enacted in a real instance before men's eyes? Early in the morning, while it is yet dark, she seeks Him Whom her soul loveth: she finds Him not: she asks those whom Christ had set to watch, even two of His chiefest Apostles: and still she finds Him not: but no thought comes into her mind that she should therefore leave off asking: she enquires of the next person she sees, and behold it is her Lord Himself: she hath found Him Whom her soul loveth, and she calls Him most earnestly, but it is with a word of reverence, "Rabboni, that is to say, Master:" she seeks to hold Him, but it is by the Feet, that she may worship Him. When she is bidden not yet to touch Him, but to wait until He hath ascended to His Father, she repines not; when she is sent away out of His sight on a message, she lingers not, but departs quickly with fear and great joy, and runs to

⁹ S. Luke xi. 9.

bring the disciples word; and while she (with the other holy women) is so employed, behold Jesus meeteth her again, and she is permitted this time to hold Him by the Feet and worship Him.

Surely never was such encouragement to make much of any loving, adoring thoughts, which our gracious Saviour may at any time put into our hearts! Except indeed in that one case, to which from the nature of it no other *can* be compared, the case of that other Mary, the Blessed Virgin, Mother of our Lord and our God, Jesus Christ. As none was ever favoured like her, so we cannot imagine any other making so perfect a return of love as she in her constant maternal offices towards Him: and yet we know that He said, "'Whosoever shall do the will of My Father, the same is My brother and sister and mother:" and she in her divine hymn is the Church's abiding pattern, yea, and the pattern of each Christian, how mean soever, in the blessed duty of making the most of the love of God shed abroad in our hearts. "*My soul doth magnify the Lord, and my spirit hath rejoiced in God my Saviour. For He hath regarded the low estate of his hand-maiden: for behold, from henceforth, all generations shall call me blessed." One might expect, perhaps, that a soul favoured as she was, would be able to do nothing but spread her wings, as it were, and glide upwards, rejoicing in the clear light: but behold, she addresses herself to the same ordinary and simple duties which are the portion of any one of us, whom God hath revealed His love unto, and enabled in some measure to love Him. Whatsoever things are

<hr />

* S. Matt. xii. 50.   * S. Luke i. 46—48.

thankful, whatsoever things are humble, on those she thinks, those on occasion she will do: the verses of her holy song alternate between thankfulness and humility: but the very first thing she does is to arise in haste, and pay that seasonable visit of charity and sympathy to her cousin Elisabeth.

But you will say—some at least will say to themselves—All this supposes that we have some love at least in our hearts, to meet His great love for us: and I cannot feel as if I ever had any love: my endeavours, such as they are, are common, cold, dull and dry: there is no comfort in all this for me. Nay, but there is the greatest comfort if thou wilt but go on with thy duties, desiring to love: in such cases, the desire of loving *is* love in His sight: the irksome dullness and dryness is the thorn in thy flesh, the messenger of Satan to buffet thee. But fear not: His grace is sufficient for thee, His strength will be made perfect in thy weakness. Only set yourself in earnest to obey His voice: say to Him night and day, "'Behold the servant of the Lord, be it unto me according to Thy word." And then, if you have not always the comfortable consciousness of loving Him, make sure that it is good for you to be kept low; trust yourself with Him, as it were, in the dark: if you have that comfort, pray Him to temper it always with holy fear: remember that there are some who fell from heaven.

Use thyself to discern our Lord's presence in the ordinary and repulsive ways of common life: not only in His sick and poor, in Lazarus lying at the gate full of sores, but in the very worst of thy bre-

ᵗ S. Luke i. 38.

thren, provoking, unbelieving, selfish as they may be, like that unpitying rich man, or worse; yet if they are Christians, do thou use thyself to acknowledge Christ's presence in them, and try to love and serve them for His sake. It is one of the likeliest ways to obtain the sense of His more convincing and endearing presence in thy heart.

Finally, since both lessons are of course infinitely too hard for thee, both that of submitting for a while to the seeming absence of Him Whom thy soul loveth, and that of holding Him fast, when He hath allowed thee to find Him: go thou to the only school where those lessons are to be learned: to the school of thy dying Lord, now especially about to be opened for thee: sit down with His Mother and His penitent servants, those two holy Maries, under the shadow of His Cross: and thou shalt be taught all His will, and what is more, thou shalt be enabled to do it: whether it be that thou shouldest work for a time in darkness, or at once come out, and rejoice in the clear light.

SERMON XL.

CHRIST AND HIS CHURCH IN A BAD WORLD.

S. John viii. 59; ix. 1.

" Then took they up stones to cast at Him; but Jesus hid Himself, and went out of the temple, and so passed by. And as Jesus passed by, He saw a man which was blind from his birth."

This escape of our Lord was no doubt a great miracle. As a very old divine remarks on it, 'Christ here hides Himself, not by shrinking behind partition walls, nor by interposing any thing else between them and His own Body, but by the power of His Godhead making Himself invisible to those who sought Him.'

Once before, as it seems, He had wrought the same wonder, but not in the same place, nor among the same people. Very early in His ministry, when He first preached at His own city Nazareth, the people of that place, being offended at His reproving them for their especial want of faith, "* rose up, and thrust Him unto the brow of the hill whereon their city was built, that they might cast Him down headlong. But He, passing through the midst of them,

* S. Luke iv. 29, 30.

went His way." "Passing through the midst of
them;" they are the very words which S. John uses
in the text. Thus, as another old writer observes,
you may understand that our Lord's Passion was
endured not of constraint, but willingly: that He
was not so much taken by the Jews, as offered by
Himself. For when He will, He is taken; when He
will, He escapes: when He will, He is hanged on a
tree; when He will, they can lay no hold on Him.
So here He is on the brow of the hill, whither He
had gone up to be cast down; and behold, through
the midst of them, changing or astounding their
minds in the midst of their rage, He passes safely
down: for the hour of His Passion had not yet come.'
S. John says, He hid Himself, S. Luke does not say
so: therefore it may be, that in the one case His
enemies could not see Him, any more than Balaam
could the angel; in the other case, that though they
saw Him, the hand of God was on them in some
remarkable way, to keep them from laying hands
on Him.

Another circumstance much to be observed, in our
Lord's manner, in both these two several miracles,
is His passing immediately from His danger and the
midst of His enemies, to the performance of works
of mercy among worthier and more thankful people.
When He became visible again, it was to heal those
who had need of healing. Thus from that hill at
Nazareth He went straight down to Capernaum, and
healed in their synagogue a man who had a spirit of
an unclean devil. And as He passed out of the
temple, where the Jews had been seeking to stone
Him, He saw the man blind from his birth, on whom

He wrought that wonderful miracle, putting clay on his eyes, and causing him to wash and receive sight.

Thus did our Lord very wonderfully both manifest and hide Himself at the same time, according as men were willing to receive Him or no. Thus did He prepare His disciples' minds for His Passion, and shew, that when He did suffer, it was not through weakness, but of His own most merciful will. But the particular way in which at present I wish to consider this great miracle is the following: how it throws light on the true condition of Christ and His servants here in this evil world. It shews us what the true Church of Christ and what true Christians must expect: and it shews us also how they may behave themselves, in such trials, worthy of Him Whom they serve.

The plain doctrine of Scripture is, that as affliction is the lot of all men, for man is born to trouble as surely as the sparks fly upward, so persecution is the lot of Christians. They declare themselves in Baptism bound to be always at war with the world and the devil: and the world and the devil for their part will never leave them alone. On this point our Lord and His Apostles are quite plain and express. Our Lord in that prayer, wherein, departing, He recommended His Church to His Father, particularly mentions its condition as one of continual war with this evil world, where it remains now for its trial. "[b] I have given My disciples Thy Word," He says, and "the world hath hated them, because they are not of the world, even as I am not of the world.

[b] S. John xvii. 14, 15.

I pray not that Thou shouldest take them out of the world, but that Thou shouldest keep them from the evil one." You see, our Lord's own intercession is not that His people should be free from persecution and hatred, but that they should so behave themselves in it, as to give the bad spirit no advantage against them.

To the same effect, He told them that they must take up the cross, and pronounced it as one of the regular blessings of a Christian to be persecuted for righteousness' sake: as much so as to be poor in spirit, pure in heart, merciful, or a peace-maker. And when His kingdom was set up, it was a regular part of His Apostles' instructions, that " ᶜ we must through much tribulation enter into it." And S. Paul tells Timothy in so many words, " ᵈ All that will live godly in Christ Jesus must suffer persecution." And S. Peter comforts them, not with a promise of ease and quiet, but with the thought, ' Who is he that can harm you, if ye be followers of that which is good?' And S. John, writing to his fellow Christians, describes himself to be their " ᵉ companion in tribulation, and in the Kingdom and Patience of Jesus Christ." As much as to say that tribulation is the condition of Christ's kingdom, and patience the virtue which properly belongs to it.

If we then have no persecution, no tribulation to endure; if all men speak well of us; if we are such that the world cannot hate us: is there not some reason to fear that we are not such as He would approve? The cross is distinctly declared to be Christ's mark: if we have it not clearly upon us, we have

ᶜ Acts xiv. 22.   ᵈ 2 Tim. iii. 12.   ᵉ Rev. i. 9.

the more reason to stand on our guard, and tremble, lest after all we should prove not to have been His true soldiers and servants. If we are among the unbelieving Jews, and they take up no stones to cast at us, I do not say that it is at once a sign that we are altogether not on Christ's side, altogether in a bad way: but surely it is a reason why we should be very humble; why we should fear and suspect ourselves, and look narrowly into our own doings, and punish and deny ourselves in secret.

I will try to explain what I mean, by an example, ordinary and mean enough in comparison. Any young person among his companions, entering into their sports and amusements, and generally praised by every one of them, called universally kind, and frank, and goodnatured, and high-spirited: such an one will do well to take himself to task, lest he be encouraging sin in others: rioting, or lewdness, or profane mirth, or idle useless ways; even if he be not exactly guilty of such sin himself. Any one who goes much into company, and is not noted as at all stricter than the rest, let him watch his own ways diligently: he may be far gone, before he is aware of it, in loose ungodly ways of talking and thinking: he goes a great way with the friends of the world: let him see to it, that he is not the enemy of God.

But further: the attack on our Lord on this occasion seems to shew what way of thinking it is, and what particular part of the Church's doctrine, which is most apt to draw on itself the censure and enmity of the world. Why did the Jews try to stone our Lord? Because He represented Himself as having

been before Abraham. So a while after, when He
plainly said to them, "'I and My Father are one,"
they presently took up stones to stone Him. And
His final condemnation to death by the high priest
went on no other ground. Caiaphas asked Him in
the council, putting Him in a manner on His oath,
whether He was the Christ, the chosen of God?
And when He said "I am," and told them for a
token of it that they should see Him one day coming
in the clouds of heaven, they at once condemned
Him to be guilty of death.

Thus it has ever been between Christ and the
wicked world. They would bear Him to teach many
things, to speak in praise and love of charity, or to
utter His great unspeakable promises. But when it
comes to this, You are members of Christ, walk worthy then of the vocation wherewith ye are called :
Christ, Who accounts you part of Himself, is the Most
High God ; you, as united to Him, are partakers of
the Divine nature ; therefore you must really keep
the commandments, you must be inwardly and really
holy as He is Holy : when this kind of doctrine is put
forth, and urged home to the hearts of men, they
grow uneasy, and start objections, and make difficulties, and say it is requiring too much ; they never
can come up to so high a standard : and they take
people to have become their enemies, who talk to
them in such a tone.

They can bear to think of Holy Baptism as a religious dedication of their infants to Almighty God :
but they do not love to hear it called Regeneration.
The Holy Communion they consider a true memorial

¹ S. John x. 30.

of the Body and Blood of Christ, but they do not like to say that in it they really and spiritually partake of His Body and Blood. And so in other things; the spirit of the world mixes insensibly with our views and thoughts, and tries to hinder us from considering our communion with Christ so very near as the Church constantly teaches. And if we indulge this unbelief and dislike, we shall come in time to hate the high doctrine and its maintainers. Like a certain persecuting emperor of old, it will make us angry to hear persons confess that they bear about within them Him Who was crucified.

This too we may often see, in a small way, in men's conversation. They like to see people good to a certain degree, but that high and angelic goodness, that perfect separation from the things of earth, which becomes men who know that their life is hid with Christ in God, this is not to their liking, they hardly believe it sincere when they see it, and they generally have some word of contempt to describe it by. All such cases are but so many tokens, that the true spirit of those Jews, who then took up stones to cast at our Saviour, lives, and is active and mighty among us now.

This of course makes our duty, in respect of God's truth and worship, harder to perform; but it does not in the least make it obscure or doubtful. Whether men will hear, or whether they will forbear, it is their pastor's business to urge on them the truth, and their duties; it is their brethren's business by practising the duties, to shew that they believe the truth. We must not neglect or forget high and mysterious doctrines or severe rules, because those

I i

with whom we are concerned are impatient at being put in mind of them: yet again, we must so teach them as they may be able to bear; tempting them as little as possible to irreverent hearing or careless forgetting.

Thus our Lord, though He punished the hardened obstinacy of those Jews, by openly declaring His Godhead, which He knew they could not endure, yet in His mercy withdrew Himself from their sight: He would not yet suffer them to crown their unbelief with murder. 'The Word,' says a great Bishop and saint of old time, S. Athanasius: 'The Word Himself, having been made Man for our sake, condescended, when sought for, to hide Himself: and again, when persecuted, to fly and avoid the snare laid for Him. For it became Him, not only by hunger and thirst and affliction, but also by concealment and flight, to shew Himself clothed with flesh, and made Man. Thus at the beginning, just after He had been made Man, in His childhood, Himself by the Angel commanded Joseph, "Arise, take the young Child and His Mother by night, and flee into Egypt, for Herod will seek the life of the young Child." Afterwards, when He was shewing Himself as God, and had healed the withered hand, the Pharisees went out and took counsel against Him to destroy Him. But Jesus knew it, and departed thence. So, too, when He raised Lazarus from the dead, from that day, we read, they took counsel to kill Him: "[h] Jesus therefore walked no more openly among the Jews, but went away into a place near the wilderness."'

[h] S. John xi. 54.

In all these instances, Jesus Christ, His hour being not yet come, retired out of the way of His enemies, and gave them time to consider and repent. So, it becomes us, when we bear witness to the truth,, to be full of that great charity, which will make us put ourselves in the gainsayers' place, and always, consider what is most likely to do them good, and bring them to a better mind. As for example: if a bad or profane word is spoken in our hearing, it can, never of course be right to seem amused with it, or in any way to become partaker of the sin: but it may often be best not openly to rebuke it at the time, but rather to turn the discourse for the present, and, await some opportunity, when we can speak with the offender alone, and he is otherwise more disposed to listen to us. This is withdrawing the name of our Lord out of the way of reproach, as He did His person from the stones that were cast at Him.

Only we must be very careful, that we do not so, retire through cowardice or sloth, or out of care what men may say of us: and the proof of this will be, if we seek anxiously afterwards for opportunities of doing the good, which we thought we could not do at that time; and if we deny ourselves something for the sake of doing it.

Moreover, when we hear persons speak disrespectfully, I will not say of our Lord and Saviour Himself, since that kind of blasphemy is not yet so common among us, but of His great manifestation of Himself in His Church, her ordinances and doctrines; I say, when words of reproach are spoken against the Church, the clergy or the sacraments; our great and chief care ought to be, 'What if I, by some sin of mine, have helped to give occasion to this great evil?'   We should consider how far our own behaviour has been from the pure and mild, the exact and self-denying precepts of the holy universal Church; how we have tempted men to slight it, by our careless or self-willed ways.   We should call to mind any private sins, to which we may have unhappily given way, more or less wilfully: we should consider in our hearts, 'How could God hear the prayers of such as I have been, so inclining to wickedness in my heart?   No wonder if, when I have prayed in Church that God would make all Christians agree in the truth of His word, and live in unity and godly love, my unworthiness should have hindered in some measure the petition from being granted: no wonder if, where I am concerned, evil spirits have great power, and the work of God seems to go backward instead of forward.   God grant that I may do better in what time yet remains, and never again put a stumbling-block in the way of Christ's little ones.'

Such seem to be some of the thoughts which would come most naturally into the mind of a considerate Christian, especially if trusted with others, when he meets with the contradiction of sinners: when being a parent, for example, he finds his children disobedient and unthankful; when he is a master, and his servants prove unruly; when being called on by his office to warn and guide others, his advice is set at nought, and his labours seem without fruit. Instead of spending his thoughts on their sinfulness, he will do well to consider his own ways,

beseech God to shew him where he has been wrong;
in what respects, secret or open, he has either given
scandal to his brethren, or stained his own conscience, and forfeited the blessing of Christ.

And lastly, whatever trouble has come upon any
man, either by his own fault or those of others, in
the way of doing his duty: we learn by this example
of our blessed Lord, that it should not make us cold
or lukewarm in doing our duty afterwards. He
having withdrawn Himself from the wicked malice
of the Jews, did not the less go on with the great
work which He had to do. He saw the man born
blind, begging at the gates of the temple, and without any delay He healed him, giving as His reason,
"¹I must work the works of Him that sent Me while
it is day: the night cometh, when no man can work."

The danger which He had just been in from the
malice of the Jews, was to be a warning to His disciples, of what both He and they might expect from
the same enemies bye and bye. His hour was not
yet full come, but it would come before long, and in
the mean time His care was, to finish the work
which His Father had given Him to do.

Let us, all in our several stations, take the hint
which our Master and only Saviour thus graciously
vouchsafes to give us. When untoward and perplexing things happen, let us go on the more earnestly with what we are sure is good and right, the
fear of God and the keeping of His commandments.
When we are hindered from doing good in one way,
let us go on straight, if God permit, to do some other

¹ S. John ix. 4.

good, or the same in some other way. Or if our
hands seem entirely tied, at least let us do ourselves
that great good of humbling ourselves before God,
searching and confessing our past offences, and beseeching Him that the cross, which He has laid on
us, may be in His own mysterious way united to
the Cross of His Son, and made profitable to our
salvation.

SERMON XLI.

CHRISTIAN ENERGY.

1 Cor. xvi. 13.

" Watch ye, stand fast in the faith, quit you like men, be strong."

THESE words are addressed to Christians, as the soldiers of Jesus Christ. They are such as one might imagine a wise commander speaking to his men on the night before a battle, that they might rise up in the morning full of considerate courage, and steadily resolved to do all their duty, cost what it might. "Watch ye, stand fast in the faith, quit you like men, be strong."

Every one must feel, on merely reading or hearing this, how truly great and noble the character is which S. Paul here recommends us to imitate; how a person, who should diligently practise this rule, would, as it were, walk on high, and though he lived in the world, would be above the reach of its storms and temptations.

And we shall feel this yet more strongly, when we recollect, besides, what sort of a person it was who wrote these words, and how completely all his life was spent, after he became a Christian, in prac-

tising the lesson they teach. It was the Apostle
S. Paul; of whom it might be said, more truly perhaps than of any other saint either in the Old or New
Testament, that his whole life, after God had once
called him, was a life of continual watchfulness.
He never seems to have forgotten, for a moment,
that he was a Christian. Whatever he did and suffered, was done and suffered quite in a different way,
and with a different mind, from what it would have
been if he had not been a disciple of Jesus Christ.
When anything happened to him, whether pleasant
or unpleasant, the first question in his mind seems
always to have been, not 'how can I make this turn
to my own profit, or my own enjoyment?' but
'how must I act, to make the most of it for the
glory of my Master and Saviour, and the good of the
souls committed to my charge?' You cannot doubt
upon a little consideration, that such a man had
found out the true secret of happiness, as far as it is
to be had in this life.

Now then, if there be any truth in the Bible, it is
in the power of every one of us, to be this great and
noble character; to be like S. Paul, if we will. His
example is not set before us merely like a beautiful
picture, for us to look at and admire, and wish we
were like it. But it is the very pattern which our
Blessed Lord has set before us, to help us in copying
His own Divine example. We are to be followers
of him, as he was of Christ.

This is not the less true, because the generality
of Christian people seem to think so little of it.
The world, they seem to take it for granted, is so
altered since S. Paul's time, that the rules by which

he conducted himself will no more do for us. We praise and admire him, but excuse ourselves, though we follow examples and indulge desires most completely opposite to his.

He tells us, for example, that it made little difference to him whether he was rich or poor. "* I know both how to be abased and I know how to abound. I have learned, in whatsoever state I am, therewith to be content." How many of us have heard and read these words over and over again, and have admired S. Paul, and praised him, for the temper of mind he shews in them, without a single thought of practising the same; without once considering, that if S. Paul was thus careless about money, it little becomes them to be so anxious about it, as they allow themselves to be every day, and all day long!

It is indeed a shameful and painful recollection, how continually we live in the midst of noble and good examples, yet how little we profit by them. Our only comfort should be, that it is not yet, by God's mercy, too late to amend. We may this very day, if we will, begin accustoming ourselves, from time to time, to remember in our daily doings the high thoughts and rules of conduct which we read of in the Bible.

We have all of us, I suppose, at times, had pious thoughts and good resolutions in our minds. We have wished to serve God as faithfully as S. Paul: to be as contented and cheerful as he was, and to care as little for the world. Perhaps we have even tried for a time, to live in earnest by his rule: to make the most of ourselves, and all that we had, for

* Phil. iv. 11, 12.

the honour and service of our God. Although we
are too soon tired of such steady and devout purposes,
yet if we have ever fairly tried, I am sure we must
feel and own, that we were never so happy as in
those hours.   We may have been more gay and
mirthful, but we were never so happy ; for we never
were, we never could be, so sure that God approved
of our enjoyments, and that they would not leave a
sting behind them when they were gone.

What hinders us from recalling those happy
hours? from lengthening them to days and weeks
and months and years? from keeping them by us
all our lives long, to store us with pleasant recollections for ever and ever?   It is only making up our
minds to live steadily by faith in things not seen;
to deny our wandering thoughts resolutely and manfully ; and our happiness is in our power.   We may,
by God's grace and mercy, begin it any hour, any
minute, we choose.

Any hour, any minute, we may begin 'watching
ourselves,' considering our own words, purposes,
and actions, like men who are awake and alive to
what is passing around them; who know they cannot stay where they are, and are desirous to make
sure of going the right way.

I do not say that this will be altogether pleasant,
or, for a long time, easy.   Most men have lived, hitherto, so much at random, that it must cost them
some trouble to rouse themselves, and reflect in earnest on what they are doing, and where their journey will end.   They are like persons only half
awake, who can hardly, for a while, be brought to
attend even to their most necessary cares and em-

ployments. But to go on thus in spite of warning, is indeed both childish and unchristian. It is childish carelessness of what ought to be dearest to them, the happy place which God offers them in heaven, and which they are throwing away for want of firmness in keeping their attention that way. It is most unchristian ingratitude for the great mercies which Almighty God has bestowed on them, not so much as to cast an eye towards the crown of glory which He holds out, promising Himself to be "*b*our shield, and our exceeding great reward."

But, it will be fancied, 'This rule is too hard and strict for every-day life. It will take away all the pleasant freedom of thought, and happy carelessness, which made our childish days so delightful. Surely, if we mean no *harm*, we may enjoy ourselves without the trouble of considering whether we actually mean *well* or no.'

So it may seem beforehand. But if you would give God's command a fair trial, you would find it very far otherwise. The watchfulness and wakefulness which He enjoins, does not mean that you should be always in a state of painful alarm. At first, of course, it must be an effort, but the longer and more regularly you go on with it, the easier and more natural will you find it. He will help you to the habit of watching yourself, and restraining your inclinations, more and more entirely: as a good rider restrains an unruly horse that he is used to.

One reason why watching and controlling one's self seems to most men a hard and painful task is,

b Gen. xv. 1.

the irregular and unsteady way in which it is too commonly practised. Those who have long done it most effectually, are least seen to do it: their goodness sits easy upon them. But those who do it only now and then, and then suffer themselves to fall into their former carelessness, are of course discontented and uncomfortable in themselves, and can afford but little temptation to others to follow their example. The way for them to mend themselves, and to do good to their neighbours, is to follow the second part of this apostolical advice, and not only to watch themselves continually, to be always awake to their duty, but also "to stand fast in the faith, to quit them like men, and be strong." In other words, not only to *think* of their duty, but to *do* it without delay as soon as ever it is made known to them what God would have them to do.

"[c] I made haste," says the Psalmist, "and prolonged not the time, to keep Thy commandments." This is the only secret for being watchful and comfortable at once. Once make up your mind never to stand waiting and hesitating when your conscience tells you what you ought to do, and you have got the key to every blessing that a sinner can reasonably hope for. Then you may, by God's blessing, experience even in this world how true those promises are, which are scattered up and down the Scriptures, of the happy effects of Christian obedience; such, for instance, as the following verses of the Proverbs of Solomon: "[d] My son, let not them depart from thine eyes: keep sound wisdom and discretion: so shall they be life unto thy soul, and

[c] Ps. cxix. 60.   [d] Prov. iii. 21—26.

grace to thy neck. Then shalt thou walk in thy way safely, and thy feet shall not stumble. When thou liest down, thou shalt not be afraid : yea, thou shalt lie down, and thy sleep shall be sweet. Be not afraid of sudden fear, nor of the desolation of the wicked, when it cometh. For the Lord shall be thy confidence, and shall keep thy foot from being taken."

This delightful sense of God's Presence and guardian care, which in the common course of things accompanies our sincere and steady endeavours to please Him, is surely enough, being remembered, to overpower that common objection to Christian obedience, that it brings with it a constant strain and weariness, turning our thoughts at all times exactly the same way; so that it is supposed impossible, but that one should get more and more tired of it. It cannot be altogether denied, that we must expect to meet with something of weariness and painfulness, even in the course of Christian love and duty. It is the condition of human life; a part of the cross appointed for us to bear in imitation of Jesus Christ. It is vain to think of escaping it, and happy he who bears it best. But then it is equally plain, that when once the fresh spirits of early youth are past, there is the same weariness and painfulness to be looked for in every other service, as well as in God's. All men have their dull and irksome hours to endure: only he who stands fast in the faith, finds them pass more lightly over him than others, so far as he is more deeply impressed with the remembrance of the Presence of his Maker, and the hope of eternal life.

Neither can a man have any idea, before he has

tried, of the constant variety which may be found, even in the soberest exercise of our duty to God and man, in the quietest walks of life. Suppose, for instance, a man only bound himself to recollect, in all his dealings with others, that plain and easy rule, which every child is acquainted with: "*Whatsoever ye would that men should do unto you, do ye even so to them." No two persons that we meet with being exactly like one another, it is evident our conduct to each would be different; and here would be one continual exercise of our Christian wisdom, to consider how we might best suit the reasonable wishes of each out of so many various persons, some more and some less near to us. Still further; scarce any person could be found, whose condition and circumstances are exactly the same for two days together; so that here, too, will be continual employment for our discretion and Christian charity, in changing the manner of our kindness according to the change of their wishes and necessities. It is easy then to see, that we need not be afraid of want of variety, in the happy art of keeping God's commandments. Once set your heart upon that task, and you will not long complain of its being dull and wearisome, or of its keeping you too much under restraint, and checking the natural spring and freedom of our affections.

Christian watchfulness, then, and standing fast in the faith, would effectually overcome those inward feelings, which stand most in the way of our perfection and happiness. Join to them Christian courage, which is the virtue next recommended by

* S. Matt. vii. 12.

S. Paul, "Quit you like men, be strong," and you will be equally armed against the worst of those outward difficulties, which are sure, from time to time, to embarrass and distress you. You will not be moved by foolish objections, or apprehensions merely relating to this world, from doing your very best for yourself and others. 'What will people say or think of me? how will they bear to have such and such things said and done, so different from what they are accustomed to say and do?' These are questions very proper to be asked and considered, when we are considering how we may employ what God has given us to the best purposes. But they are not considerations which ought to frighten or stop us, when we are once convinced that saying or doing so and so is on higher accounts our duty. We may safely follow S. Peter's example, and make appeal, on such points as these, to the common sense of the world itself. "'Whether it be right in the sight of God to hearken unto you more than unto God, judge ye." If we shew ourselves steady and resolute in the sober discharge of our duty, we shall find ourselves not only more comfortable within, but more quiet also from without; less disturbed by other people, than if we were unsteady in our good meanings, and only went half way in religion. 'Let men alone, and they will let you alone,' was a wise and kind warning; to all those, especially (and they are not a few), who are apt to look anxiously around, and watch what their neighbours are thinking of them.

It may sometimes happen, that though a man is

' Acts iv. 19.

certain by God's word what it is his duty to do, he
shall find himself puzzled and embarrassed by the
difficulties and objections of other men, not because
he fears they may be true, but because he cannot
find proper words, or distinct thoughts, to answer
and silence them with. Something of this sort
appears to have befallen the prophet Jeremiah, when
"ᵍthe word of the Lord was made unto him a reproach and a derision daily." He said to himself,
"ʰI will not make mention of Him, nor speak any
more in His Name." There was the temptation ; but
the sense of duty, duty which had become natural
to him by long practice, very soon prevailed against
it. "ⁱHis word," says he, "was in mine heart as a
burning fire shut up in my bones, and I was weary
with forbearing, and I could not stay." A resolute,
practical sense of duty is the one thing needful in
such a case. It is not possible, perhaps, to help
being annoyed, if you find men disliking or mocking
you, either for doing your duty, or for some indifferent trifle in the manner of your doing it. But
it is very possible, and the only safe and comfortable
way, to apply yourself to the same duty the more
diligently for all their scorn and dislike: and to
many people it is surely rather an advantage than
not, to have little power of *talking* well on serious
subjects. If they had that power, it is but too likely
they would content themselves with merely talking.
This ought to satisfy them and make them thankful
in their want of it; only taking care to glorify God
the more constantly by their lives, the less they are
able to glorify Him with their lips.

ᵍ Jer. xx. 8.　　　　ʰ Ib. 9.　　　　ⁱ Ib.

It seems, then, there is no danger, either from within or from without, which we may not overcome, if we will, by Christian watchfulness, perseverance, and courage. For if ridicule and mockery can be so overcome, we may be sure every thing else may. And all the excuses which we daily hear in the mouths of others, and perhaps still oftener make to ourselves, of the world being too hard for us, though we wish to keep the commandments, come in the end to no better than this: That we should be very well content to serve God, if it cost us little or nothing. If you would not die in such a temper as this towards your Father and your Saviour, there is but one thing for you to do. Though that which makes you sin be your right eye, the thing you are most used to and love best in this world, you must pluck it out and cast it from you: "[k]For it is better for thee that one of thy members should perish, and not that thy whole body should be cast into hell."

[k] S. Matt. v. 29.

к k

SERMON XLII.

OUR LORD'S GREAT DESIRE.

S. Luke xxii. 15.

" With desire I have desired to eat this passover
with you before I suffer."

WE all know how our thoughts are apt to be employed when some beloved friend or kinsman is
removed out of our sight, though it be but for a
short time, on a journey or visit. We pursue him
as it were along the road or voyage : we say to ourselves, 'Now he is passing such and such a place,
now he is looking on such and such an object, now
he is very likely conversing with this, or that friend,
now he is at his journey's end, and refreshing himself
in this or that well known place, and so and so are
enjoying his society.' Or we look back on the time
past, and call up in our minds how he and we were
employed together yesterday, on this day week, or
the like. Our memories are busy in retracing the
time he spent with us, hour by hour, and his way
of employing it. Much more if he have set out on
the great journey of all: if the separation is that of
death. The loving heart never tires of the tearful

pleasure, as we picture him to ourselves going out
and coming in, on the several hours of the day and
days of the week, in times of business or times of
refreshment, his customary sayings and the tones of
his voice. Now and then our thoughts so bring
him back, that we almost seem to have him among
us again: those more especially who were with him
in the last days and hours of his life. Who does
not know of such recollections, and feel what a treasure they are, laid up in his heart for the rest of his
life?

So it is, brethren, at this time with the holy Church,
the Spouse of Christ. The days are come round
again in which the Bridegroom was taken from her:
the joy of His visible Presence removed for a time;
and as by His appointment she fasts in those days,
so of her own natural piety, because she loves Him
and cannot help it, she keeps account of His doings
and sufferings for every day, almost for every hour,
of five days in this the last week of His life: His holy
week, and our Great week: the week of the great
crime wherein all our sins are summed up, and of
the great Sacrifice which made atonement for all.

The Bride in the Canticles kept musing and imagining where her Beloved was from time to time:
"[a] Tell me, O Thou Whom my soul loveth, where
Thou feedest, where Thou makest Thy flock to rest at
noon." "[b] My Beloved is gone down into His garden, to the beds of spices." Thus she inquires, and
thus she answers herself. So the Church in loving
meditation traces her Lord through this season of
love and sorrow; on Sunday, from Bethany by the

[a] Cant. i. 7. [b] Ib. vi. 2.

mount of Olives to Jerusalem and the Temple, where He presented Himself as ready for the Friday Sacrifice, the true Paschal Lamb set apart on the tenth of the month. On Monday and Tuesday we accompany Him in His solemn farewell to the temple, and in His prophecy on the mount of Olives which is a sort of leave-taking to this wicked world. But from Tuesday evening to Thursday evening there is silence nearly total. We are told how our Lord's enemies were employed, but not what He was Himself doing. They were plotting against Him, and Judas making his bargain: but of Him we are only told that He gave His disciples warning of the intended mischief: "ᶜ After two days is the feast of the passover, and the Son of Man is betrayed to be crucified." In that stillness may be the Scripture was fulfilled, "ᵈ He sitteth alone and keepeth silence, because He (the Father) hath borne it upon Him." The burden is of His Father's laying on: He willingly accepts it, and answers not a word.

Once in the course of that time, probably early on the Thursday morning, He breaks the silence, and for what? To give directions about the passover. His disciples come to Him, taking for granted, by reason of His former custom, that He would keep the feast, and ask Him where they should get it ready for Him. He gives them a token by which they may find out the place, and no word or doing of His (after that,) is recorded, until they were actually set down at the feast together. And then His word is, "With desire I have desired to eat this passover with you before I suffer: For I say

ᶜ S. Matt. xxvii. 2.   ᵈ Lam. iii. 28.

unto you, I will not any more eat thereof, until it be fulfilled in the kingdom of God."

May we not from this feel certain that the eating of that passover with them was a matter near His heart? that it was at least one of the subjects on which He had been meditating in silence now for nearly two days? that He had looked forward to it, with a sort of yearning, as He had all along to His Passion and to His work? He Who had said a while before, "*I am come to send fire (the blessed life-enkindling fire of My Holy Spirit), and what will I (i.e. what want I more on earth), if it be already kindled?" and again, "'I have a Baptism to be baptized with" (i.e. a deep sea of pain and anguish to plunge into) "and how am I straitened till it be accomplished." He, the same Saviour longed in His human heart to eat this passover with His disciples. He longed to go, but also before He went He longed to partake of that feast with them. And so we may think of Him as having been partly taken up on that Thursday morning, to-day, and more than half to-morrow, perhaps at this very hour, with Divine thoughts and purposes concerning that Paschal Feast.

It was no new thing to the Holy Jesus to come up to Jerusalem to keep the passover. He had done so while He was under His mother's roof: He had done so, as we may plainly gather from the Gospel history, regularly during the years of His public ministry. Why should He have had that peculiarly earnest longing for it on this occasion rather than on any before?

* S. Luke xii. 49.   ᶠ ib.

If we may reverently muse on the springs of that sacred desire, it may occur, first of all, that that feast was to be (speaking after the manner of men) our Lord's solemn farewell to His twelve Apostles, who had been to Him for three years like companions in a warfare, or a voyage: whom He loved with all His human heart, not merely as His faithful servants, but as His children, and friends, and in a certain sense, His comrades. It has been truly remarked that such partings, both in Scripture and in daily life, are often solemnized by social meals: as when Elisha being summoned by Elijah to quit his home and his parents and devote himself to be prophet in his room, asked leave to wait till he had partaken with them in one more meal: and Levi the son of Alphæus, on giving up all for Christ, made a great feast in his own house by way of farewell to his friends, many of whom being publicans and sinners came and "sat down with Him and His disciples," and hearing His blessed doctrine might have been partakers of their friend's grace. Nay, and the marriage feast of Cana itself has been thought to have been connected with our Lord's quitting His Mother in order to give Himself up to His public ministry. Our Lord's desire thus interpreted, would be one instance more of His most gracious sympathy, whereby He vouchsafes to share our human feelings of affectionate regret on parting with those whom we love, and to sanctify our natural and harmless way of expressing it.

But as in all things which He said and did, especially as the end drew nigh, so in this, we may be sure there was a mystery and a great one. His last

Passover would repeat and finally seal the lesson which His Circumcision began to teach, that the law of Moses, ceremonies and all, was His law: altogether holy and just and good. He gave His sanction to it even in the moment of superseding it by something better. When we look at Him thus partaking of the sacrificed lamb, and afterwards sitting down to the Supper, we see what must have been a joy and consolation to all loyal Israelites, and an example given to the Church and to us all, of gentle and charitable dealing with those whom we are called on to help in the knowledge and practice of Divine things. We see Him by this significant action declaring anew the decree which He had promulgated in the beginning of His ministry, " *Think not that I am come to destroy the law, or the prophets: I am not come to destroy but to fulfil." 'This will be My last passover. And something else will immediately come in the place of it: but that which is coming will be the fulfilment, not the contradiction, of that which is departing. The one will follow close on the other, not as doing it away altogether, but as crowning, and completing it.'

This we are sure is His meaning, for what are His words? "With desire I have desired to eat this passover with you before I suffer! For I say unto you, I will not any more eat thereof, until it be fulfilled in the kingdom of God." He signifies how welcome that last Paschal Feast would be to Him on account of its fulfilment, on account of that of which it was a type, and on account of that which was the answer to it in the kingdom of God which He was

* S. Matt. v. 17.

about to set up. Now we know what that is, my
brethren. The very Paschal Lamb is the Lord's
Body, offered once for all upon the Cross, and presented continually by our High Priest to the Father
in heaven: and the very Paschal Feast is our taking
part in that Offering, and partaking of that blessed
Body in the Sacrament of Holy Communion. And
our Saviour added words which fix our minds again
upon that Sacrament, by mentioning the other part
of it also. For "[h] He took the cup and gave thanks,
and said, Take this, and divide it among yourselves:
for I say unto you, I will no more drink of the fruit
of the vine, until the kingdom of God shall come."
Plain therefore it is, that whatever high prophetic
meaning there might be besides in our Lord's words,
not perhaps to be perfectly brought to pass, until
even the Sacraments give way to heavenly partaking
of Christ, still the Sacrament of the Lord's Supper
which was presently to be substituted for the passover must have been in His mind, must have been
part, and a great part of what He "desired with" so
much "desire."

Why did He desire it, my brethren? Because of
His deep love; because of His unutterable, incon-
ceivable, marvellous sympathy with us sinners! He
knew how vast the benefit would be to us, worthily
eating His Body and drinking His Blood: and He
felt the time long while we were kept waiting for
the blessing: His tender love made Him feel as if
He were to be the receiver, not the Giver. As once
He said, "[i] My meat is to do the will of Him that
sent Me." So here He intimates that it should be

---

[h] S. Luke xxii. 17. 18.   [i] S. John iv. 34.

meat and drink to Him for His people to be forgiven
and saved by being made partakers of Him. In
this sense it was and is His will to drink with His
disciples and with us the fruit of the Vine, new and
consecrated to be His Blood, in the kingdom of God
His Father.

In short, we have every reason to believe that our
dear Lord in the silence of these two days was preparing in ways known to Himself for the great work
of this evening, the Institution of the Holy Sacrifice,
and Sacrament of the Eucharist. With desire He
desired it for our sakes: from the beginning from
the very fall of Adam, and before, He had been preparing for it, as the types of the Old Testament
commencing with the Tree of life, abundantly shew :
and at some time in the earlier part of this day, perhaps about this very hour, He, knowing that which
His disciples knew not, the great miracle which He
meant to work that evening (and to repeat as often
as that Sacrament should be offered and received in
the Church), gave them directions where and how to
prepare for it. A man bearing water to be their
guide, as the Church which we know by her baptiz-
ing us is our guide to the Altar : a large Upper-room
to be the place, i. e. the Church Catholic which has
room for all and lifts men high above worldly things :
and the room is to be furnished and prepared, kept
clean or renewed by faith repentance and obedience.

All this providential care did He Who is the Wisdom of God spend upon the institution of the Holy
Eucharist : besides what we ought never surely to
forget, His setting His heart upon it so very earnestly. How then can they be said to have the mind

of Christ, to enter into His feelings, in whose mind this Blessed Sacrament takes up but little room? Who regard the reception of it as a right thing, perhaps, nay even as a positive duty, but still it is to them an outward thing, well enough to those who feel inclined to it, yet such as an earnest person may also do well enough without. Oh, if ever you are tempted to this way of thinking, do look back, I beseech you, for a moment to this Thursday morning, look and see how He was chiefly employed this day, the day before His death. His sacred Heart filled with longing anticipation of the moment when He should give Himself to His people, to be their spiritual Food and sustenance in that Holy Sacrament, as well as of that other moment, so soon to come after, when He should give Himself for them on the Cross. Here are you wavering and hesitating, and trifling with His gracious invitation, aware of your duty but shrinking from it, putting off and putting off, and glad in your secret heart to find an excuse for delay. Perhaps you come very seldom, once, twice, thrice, or four times in a twelvemonth : and you say you are afraid of coming oftener ; the service, if familiar, would become a form to you. Depend upon it, this is not all devout fear: there is something in it of spiritual sloth, if not worse. Those to whom our Lord first gave the Sacrament surely knew His will best concerning it: and their way, as you may see in the Acts of the Apostles, was to offer and receive it daily.

But perhaps you rather incline to come when our Lord calls: for one reason or another you are a communicant, possibly a frequent one, but you have

allowed yourself to grow careless in preparation: you
pass over your faults too lightly: you do not allow
time sufficient, nor begin soon enough, nor seek out
the best helps you can; above all, you do not pray
earnestly enough for help, in examining your consciences, and trying and proving your repentance.
This again is spiritual sloth in another form: and
against this also our Lord's preparation at this time
may well serve for a rebuke and warning. He being so to offer and give Himself, had stedfastly set
His face from the beginning towards that great work.
It was a main part of that Will of God, to do
which He had come into the world, and so His eyes,
and His heart had been perpetually towards it: and
He might on this sacred morning be compared to a
loving father, who knowing himself to be at the
point to die, and having in his mind to bequeath a
rich and unexpected legacy to his children, and to
tell them of it that very evening, muses much on it,
settles how he will speak to them of it, and rejoices
to think of the joy and help that it will be to them.
How disappointed would that father be, if he found
that his children having in some way come to know
of his intention, had thought little of it beforehand,
and shewed themselves cold and indifferent when he
told them of it.

For one sign by which we may try ourselves whether we have been careful enough in our preparation
for Holy Communion, it may be well to consider
what our tone of mind has been on the evening of
Communion days, and on the morrow, and the next
day: whether we have detained the Divine Guest,
and made much of Him; for He is more than an

Angel, and He did not come unawares: so that we are without excuse, if we quickly forget Him, if we easily suffer Him to depart. Would it not be a good rule, my brethren, if in fear of using our best Friend so ill, we made it our practice at each Communion to settle it with ourselves when we are to communicate next, and to present such our purpose to Him then and there on our knees in His Church, as part of the reasonable, holy, and lively sacrifice of our souls and bodies which we then offer in union with that of His Body and Blood? If we do so in earnest, adding hearty prayer to be helped in our preparation, doubtless He that heareth prayer (if we do not hinder Him by wilful sin), will be with us as He was with His disciples, both beforehand, shewing us how to make ready, and in the mystery, coming Himself to dwell in us as in all who approach Him with clean and prepared hearts. Then by His grace we shall offer to Him the like promise again, and He again will aid us to keep it: and so on, Communion after Communion proving to us as steps of that ladder which through the Incarnation of God the Son hath been let down from heaven to earth, and which through the power of His Cross we sinners are enabled to ascend, until upon our last Communion we reach the highest step, the landing-place of our eternal home, and find Him waiting there to receive us: as it is written, " [k] The Lord stood above it and said, I am the Lord God of thy fathers... And behold I am with thee and will keep thee: I will not leave thee until I have done that which I have spoken to thee of," "[l] Thanks be unto God for His unspeakable Gift."

[k] Gen. xxviii. 13.　　　　[l] 2 Cor. ix. 15.

SERMON XLIII.

THE VANITY OF ALL ATTEMPTS TO HINDER THE PURPOSES OF ALMIGHTY GOD.

S. Matt. xxvii. 66.

" So they went and made the sepulchre sure, sealing the stone, and setting a watch."

"THEY made the sepulchre sure :" the words almost sound like an expression of Divine and Holy scorn : they have a turn which in common talk we should call "ironical;" of which kind of speech examples are by no means wanting in the word of God. E. g. when the tower of Babel, the first great public work that we read of as contrived to assert man's independence of his Maker, when that was in building, "ᵃ The Lord came down to see the city, and the tower which the children of men builded ;" and He said, "This they begin to do, and now nothing will be restrained from them which they have imagined to do." As if He could not confound them as He presently did, with the breath of His nostrils, or with one rough word. So again in some of His aweful reproofs, "ᵇ Go and cry to the gods whom ye have chosen : let them deliver you in the time of your tri-

ᵃ Gen. xi. 5, 6.   ᵇ Judges x. 14.

bulations;" "ᶜ let them rise up and help you, and be your protection." And Michaiah to Ahab: "ᵈGo and prosper, for the Lord shall deliver the place into the hand of the king." And the prophet Amos: "ᵉCome to Bethel and transgress; at Gilgal multiply transgression; for this liketh you, O ye children of Israel:" and Ezekiel: "ᶠAs for you O house of Israel, thus saith the Lord God: Go ye, serve ye every one his idols, and hereafter also, if ye will not hearken unto Me: but pollute ye My holy Name no more with your gifts, and with your idols."

Such sayings all understand to be a very grave and terrible form of reproof, which the Most High God condescends to adopt, if haply He may make the faces of the wicked ashamed, that they may seek His Name; and perhaps it may be a like form of speech, when the Holy Ghost vouchsafes to take up Pilate's word, in which he hardly seemed himself to be quite in earnest, "Go your way, make it as sure as you know how," "So they went, and made the sepulchre sure, sealing the stone and setting a watch." Made it sure, by adding to the stone (which was very great and not easily rolled away), their own seals, and perhaps that of Pilate also: in token that whosoever should open that grave would be doing affront and violence both to Cæsar's authority and to the High Priest. Made it sure by obtaining besides, a party of Roman soldiers to guard the place. Very probably they were the same four, who had mocked and crucified our Lord, and had kept guard over Him as He hung on the Cross.

ᶜ Deut. xxxii. 38.   ᵈ 1 Kings xxii. 12.
ᵉ Am. iv. 4, 5.   ᶠ Ezek. xx. 39.

They have "made the sepulchre sure, sealing the stone, and setting a watch," and now, during the remainder of the sabbath, they think perhaps they may take their ease. Now they have succeeded in the plan, on which they have been setting their hearts for so many months or years; now He Whom they hated is taken out of the way. So they may go on flattering themselves for a few hours: but what is the first tidings they are to hear in the morning? 'It was all of no use, the stone is rolled away, the seals, both yours and Pilate's, are broken; He Who there lay dead, lies there no longer: He is risen, He is not here. There was a great earthquake; and one whose countenance is like lightning, and his raiment white as snow, came from heaven, and declared it, rolling at the same time the stone away; and "for fear of him," so these hard bold heathen soldiers are forced to confess, we shook "and became as dead" persons.' Thus they reported to their employers, the priests and scribes: who, if they came to the spot, would see nothing but an empty grave. So ended their notion of making the sepulchre sure.

Once more in the New Testament the like endeavour on the part of Christ's enemies comes to exactly the same issue. Paul and Silas are at Philippi; they work a miracle, dispossessing an evil spirit: they are seized, and a command is given, "keep them safely;" it is the same word as before, and their feet are made "safe" in the stocks; but again there is a sudden great earthquake, shaking the foundations of the prison, so that the doors of all the cells are thrown open, and the chains of all loosed.

See how Christ's enemies conspiring against Him,

and His friends, do but in their greatest success
bear more entire witness in favour of Christ. In fact,
what took place at the Grave of our Lord on that
first Easter morning, besides its other mysterious
bearings, was just a true sign and token of the final
triumph of right over wrong, good over evil, which
is to conclude the history of this world. Sign of
signs, token of tokens; such is the Resurrection of
Jesus Christ: and in witness of this, its deep moral
meaning, it was of old a custom in the Church, in the
midnight service by which they passed from Passion-
tide to Easter, to follow up the burst of praise, "ᵍThe
Lord is risen, Alleluia," not with any of those Psalms
which would more directly remind you of the Resurrection, but with the first of all the Psalms, "Blessed
is the man that walketh not in the council of the ungodly nor standeth in the way of sinners, nor sitteth
in the seat of the scornful. But his delight is in the
law of the Lord: and in his law doth he meditate
day and night. And he shall be like a tree planted
by the rivers of water, that bringeth forth his fruit
in his season: his leaf also shall not wither: and
whatsoever he doeth it shall prosper. The ungodly
are not so: but are like the chaff which the wind
driveth away. Therefore the ungodly shall not stand
in the judgement, nor sinners in the congregation of
the righteous. For the Lord knoweth the way of
the righteous: but the way of the ungodly shall
perish." Yes the Resurrection of Jesus Christ is to
men, perhaps to Angels, the great eternal token that
good shall prevail against evil, and light against
darkness, for that "ʰGod is Light, and in Him is no

ᵍ S. Luke xxiv. 34.   ʰ 1 S. John i. 5.

darkness at all." And the vain efforts of His enemies to prevent the Resurrection, are as the endeavours of the powers of evil from the beginning, to
stifle and overpower what is right and good. They
are turned backward, and their knowledge made
foolishness: whatever they do falls out or will fall out
in the end rather to the furtherance of God's good
and perfect will. See what a witness the unbelieving Jews were providing against themselves, by
taking such care that the grave should be closed and
watched, and then bribing the soldiers to give the
account which they had invented for them. By
their seals put on the stone they were unconsciously
attesting His truth. See what true words they spake
without knowing it "The last error shall be worse
than the first." Unbelief, now the Lord is risen,
will be worse than it was before He died. Just so it
has always been. Joseph's brethren said, Cast him
into the pit, "ᶦand we shall see what will become
of his dreams," and the very next step they took led
to the fulfilment of those dreams. Pharaoh drove
Moses away, saying, "ʲSee my face no more ;" and
when he would have overtaken the departing Israelites, the cloud and the sea came between him and
them, and Moses taking up his saying promised
them, "ᵏThe Egyptians whom ye have seen to-day,
ye shall see them again no more for ever," and it
was so. His hardness in driving away Moses, was,
humanly speaking, the cause of his death. So Ne-
buchadnezzar, "ˡWho is that God that shall deliver
you out of my hands?" And the Lord, so to speak, ac-

ᶦ Gen. xxxvii. 20.   ʲ Ex. x. 28.   ᵏ Ib. xiv. 13.
ˡ Dan. iii. 15.

L l

cepted the challenge, and compelled the tyrant to confess that " there is no other God that can deliver after
this sort." So Daniel's enemies in the time of Darius,
who even in the minute details of what they did, set
a kind of pattern for these chief priests and elders.
They could find nothing against Daniel, except they
found it against him concerning the law of his God :
so the Jewish council knew not anything for which
they could condemn Christ, except His declaring
Himself to be the Son of God; that was His preaching the law whereof the Lord had said unto Him,
"ᵐThou art My Son; this day have I begotten Thee."
"ⁿAnd they brought their stone, and laid it upon the
mouth of the den ; and the king sealed it with his own
signet, and with the signet of his lords." Daniel's resurrection, with no manner of hurt found on him, is a
type, no doubt, of Christ's rising with His glorious
Body : his call to the penitent Darius, "°O king live
for ever," is it not like the mercy sealed by the
Resurrection, to the very murderers of our Lord, if
they would truly repent :. the destruction of his ac-
cusers on the other hand, a sure token of what will
befall his wilful and persevering enemies ? So Judas
and the Jews, "ᵖWhat will ye give me, and I will betray Him unto you?" and when the time came, "Take
Him and lead Him away safely." Observe the word
" safely :" it is the very same as in the text, " let the
sepulchre be made *sure*," and see what the safety and
sure keeping of the wicked and of our Lord's enemies will most certainly come to at last. But all
these were but lesser instances and samples of the

ᵐ Ps. ii. 7.   ⁿ Dan. vi. 17.   ° Ib. iii. 9.
ᵖ S. Matt. xxvi. 15.

eternal confusion and disappointment of him who is the head and king of those wicked ones, in his great plan for undoing the Creator's work. The prince of this world thought he had made sure the ruin of our first parents; but the Unspeakable Wisdom and Mercy made it the occasion of the Great deliverance. And now that the promised Seed had come, and was about to give up His heel, His lower nature, to be bruised and crushed according to His promise: though Satan had come once and found nothing in Him that he could lay hold of, he failed to learn the whole truth by his disappointment. He had departed from Christ only for a season; now, Judas especially giving him the opportunity, he returns, and by him and his other agents carries on the conspiracy, and brings about the great crime, little thinking that he was thereby giving his own head to be bruised and crushed for ever. For, wise and knowing as Satan is in his way, two great things were hidden from him: the two mysteries which were united for us yesterday in one holy commemoration and thanksgiving. 'The prince 'of this world,' says S. John's disciple Ignatius, 'knew not the virginity of Mary:' i.e. he knew not that He Whom he was tempting was the Very and Eternal Son of God. And on yet higher authority we are assured that he knew not the virtue of our Lord's Sacrifice; for thus speaks the Holy Ghost by S. Paul, "ᵃ We speak wisdom among them that are perfect: yet not the wisdom of this world nor of the princes of this world, that come to nought; but we speak the wisdom of God in a mystery, even the hidden wisdom, which God ordained before the world

ᵃ 1 Cor. ii. 6—8.

L l 2

unto our glory: which none of the princes of this world knew: for had they known it, they would not have crucified the Lord of glory."

Thus the way in which God's providence over-ruled the precautions of the chief priests and Phari-sees to the more complete manifestation of our Risen Lord, was, as I said, but a sample of His dealings with Satan altogether, causing good in unknown and untold ways, to spring even from that evil which remains incurable because it refuses to be cured.

But as we wait here in spirit, now in these sab-bath hours, round the still closed Grave of our Lord and Redeemer, with the holy women, and the fa-voured disciples who were allowed to assist at His Funeral, and while we are looking forward to His glorious Resurrection to-morrow morning, there come naturally into the mind, thoughts of another triumph of the Son of God, another disappointment and discomfiture of God's enemy, not in this world, but in the world out of sight. The Church in her services, and lessons for the day—nay more—in the Creed which she taught us at our Baptism, and en-joins us to use daily, takes care to remind us not only of our Lord's Crucifixion and Death, but also of His Burial and of His Descent into hell; two points of deep humiliation, taking place after death, and needful to be remembered, if we are to thank Him at all worthily for His infinite condescension, for taking upon Him the form of a servant in all things. He was buried, and He descended into the unseen world: these two make up between them the state of man between death and resurrection. All of us, ex-cept those, few by comparison, who shall be alive to

meet the Judge when He comes at the last, expect
assuredly to come to a time when those words shall
be true in regard of ourselves, 'His body is in the
grave, his soul in the other world.'   We know we
must come to it sooner or later; and O how forlorn
and dreary would that knowledge be of itself to our.
poor frail nature, if we had never heard of the Grave
by which we are invited to watch to-day, and of
Him Who was laid in it!   The Church therefore, in
her motherly care, the time itself prompting her,
does in her services and lessons for this holy Satur-
day, this Sabbath of sabbaths, draw our attention in
a particular manner to what our Lord was at this
time doing and enduring for us, to Jesus Christ
our Surety and representative in the hours between
His Death and Resurrection.   As His Burial is the
pledge of His care of our bodies, in death, and
through death, and after death, so is His Descent
into hell, the token of His vouchsafing to be with
our souls.

As for our bodies, men may speak as they will—I
have heard, or read of many before now speaking in
a forced kind of carelessness, as if it were nothing
to them what became of *their own* remains;—but
even the hardest and most unbelieving have commonly some one or other for whose decent burial
they are anxious; and surely, brethren, there must
be many of us who have felt as comfortable beyond
expression, the assurance that when the coffin which
hides some dearly beloved form is disappearing from
our eyes, we are not simply committing "earth to
earth, ashes to ashes, dust to dust," but are intrust-
ing a body which is a member of Christ to the care

of Christ Himself, Who has promised to keep it safe, and raise it again : and that if we are worthy, we shall see it again, the same in substance, though changed in form, according to His mighty mysterious working.

Christ's Burial is His pledge that He will be with our bodies to take care of them in the grave; His Descent into hell is a pledge of something far higher, and more precious ; that He will be with our souls in paradise, if at least paradise be the proper word for the rest which remaineth for the people of God after they are delivered from the burthen of the flesh, until the number of His elect be accomplished, and His kingdom fully come. For the souls of the departed are not to be regarded as continuing in a sort of slumber, alive indeed but unconscious. Our Lord's own parable of the rich man and Lazarus is surely distinct enough to contradict such a notion : it shews the disembodied spirits not only living and thinking and feeling ; but retaining in some measure their earthly interests and affections. And so, no less distinctly, does the well-known vision of the souls of the martyrs in the sixth chapter of the Revelations; with this remarkable circumstance besides, that they pray, and an answer is given to their prayers, "'They cried with a loud voice, saying : How long, O Lord, Holy and True, dost Thou not avenge our blood on them that dwell on the earth ? And white robes were given to every one of them; and it was said unto them, that they should rest yet, for a little season, until their fellow-servants also, and their brethren that should be killed as they were, should

ᵗ Rev. vi. 10, 11.

be fulfilled." Their state is a blessed one, yet imperfect, and so far what is said of them resembles the account of the holy men of the Old Testament in the eleventh of Hebrews the thirty-ninth and fortieth verses, "*And these all, having obtained a good report through faith, received not the promise: God having provided some better thing for us, that they without us should not be made perfect."

Now of those same holy men, Abraham, Isaac, and Jacob, and the rest, our Lord more than once speaks, as preceding all others in the heavenly banquet in His kingdom; "'Many shall come from the east and west, and shall sit down with Abraham, and Isaac, and Jacob in the kingdom of heaven, but the children of the kingdom shall be cast out into outer darkness, there shall be weeping and gnashing of teeth." Those who should afterwards come into the assembly of the saved ones, would be in a certain sense gathered into them, as Lazarus was carried by the Angels into Abraham's bosom, to a place near him at the feast, where he might lean on the patriarch's bosom as S. John did once on Jesus Christ's.

There is an old Church tradition again which suits well with these words of our Saviour, and which those who have been taught to think anything of it must needs remember on Easter Eve. I will express it to you in the words of a very learned and holy prelate of our Church, Bishop Jeremy Taylor. In a devout thanksgiving to our Lord, going through the main particulars of what He did, and suffered for us, this good Bishop says, ' The grave could not hold Thee long O holy and eternal Jesus: Thy Body

* Heb. xi. 39, 40.   ' S. Matt. viii. 11, 12.

could not see corruption, neither could Thy Soul be
left in hell: Thou wert free among the dead, and
Thou brakest the iron gates of death and the bars
and chains of the lower prisons. Thou broughtest
comfort to the souls of the patriarchs, who waited for
Thy coming, who longed for the redemption of man,
and the revelation of Thy day. Abraham, Isaac,
and Jacob saw Thy day and rejoiced.' And he adds,
from the hymn called Benedicite, "O ye spirits and
souls of the righteous, bless ye the Lord: praise
Him and magnify Him for ever." You will understand that the notion is—a generally received one in
the first ages of the Church—that Christ's Divine
Soul being parted from the Body, passed into the
unseen world, and proclaimed His work of redemption to the saints of the Old Testament, ending with
the Baptist: and either then, or immediately after
His Resurrection, freed them from the restraint
under which they had been kept imperfect: caused
them in fact, to be first in the kingdom of heaven.
And with them, and with all after them who shall
from time to time, be admitted to a home in that region of rest and safety, Christ our Lord has promised
to be. So much at least is plain from the words of
the inspired Apostle. "*I am in a strait betwixt
two, having a desire to depart, and to be with Christ,
which is far better: nevertheless to abide in the
flesh is more needful for you." Think, my brethren,
if those who have died in the Lord were not immediately to be with Christ in some way nearer and
better than the best they can obtain here, would
S. Paul have so expressed himself? But you will

* Phil. i. 23, 24.

say, 'S. Paul was a great saint; his wishes, and prayers are no measure or warrant for me.' Nay, but remember how in another place he silences beforehand the like scruple in regard of his and our final reward. "ᶻ Henceforth there is laid up for me a crown of righteousness, which the Lord, the righteous Judge shall give me at that day, and not to me only, but unto all them also that love His appearing." Remember too how the same S. Paul studiously reminds the Thessalonians that our Lord when He comes will bring all His saints with Him: not the great saints only but all who sleep in Jesus "will God bring with Him."

Much more might be said, but surely this is enough to remind us all, how thankfully we ought to meditate on this among our other great Christian privileges: bought yesterday and sealed to-morrow— on the blessed portion which our dear friends departed have in Christ and on our assured communion with them. For as we and they are members of Christ: and as they are with Him in a sense in which we are not yet, their communion is more perfect, not only with Christ, but through Christ with us who remain. And they doubtless pray for us, if not individually (which yet we need hardly doubt) yet as included in Christ's militant kingdom for which we know they cry unto the Lord continually. Observe that this departing and being with Christ does not imply an equality of privileges in all to whom it is promised. As in the final glory, "ᵞ one star differeth from another star in glory," so in the intermediate rest. And it is reasonable to suppose

ᶻ 2 Tim. iv. 8.   ᵞ 1 Cor. xv. 41.

that they grow in grace, and in the knowledge of our Lord Jesus Christ. But indeed little or nothing is clearly revealed on that point. Let it be our comfort, as surely it must be our duty, to trust and commend our brethren departing or departed, with all their seeming imperfections to Him Who knows what they are, and Who loved them so that He died for them: as we must commit to Him the souls of such as never by His providence had an opportunity of knowing Him.

And now let us try to lift up our hearts in true Easter thanksgiving to Him Who as at this time was for our sake destroying the works of the devil, not only by His Resurrection but by His Descent into hell, not only by overcoming Death, but by opening the gate of Paradise.

SERMON XLIV.

THE LESSONS OF THE EMPTY GRAVE.

S. Matt. xxviii. 6.

" Come, see the place where the Lord lay."

Who that is but a little child among Christians,
does not know a Christmas or an Easter picture when
he sees it? In this way many who cannot read
come in a manner to know by sight the Manger at
Bethlehem, with the Divine Infant, Mary, and Joseph,
and the shepherds: much more the aweful Cross,
and Him that hangeth thereon, His Mother and His
beloved disciple standing by. And now what shall
hinder, but that we may every one of us form in his
mind's eye an image more or less lively and distinct of what we should have seen had we been waiting by our Lord's grave on the morning of His
Resurrection, to help our devout meditations during
what remains of the great forty days. For the present, my brethren, let us fix our thoughts on the
particular moment when the words of the text were
spoken. It is early, just after sunrise on the Sunday
morning: the sepulchre is open, and two women

standing by it, Mary the wife of Cleopas, our Lord's
Mother's sister, and Salome the mother of S. James
and S. John. Only these two women are there now:
for Mary Magdalene who had been with them in the
early morning, is gone to tell S. Peter and S. John of
the stone being rolled away. But in the meantime
a wonderful vision is happening. An Angel of the
Lord had been commissioned to roll away the stone
in sight of the keepers, not that our Lord might rise,
(for that He had done already by His own power),
but that the world, and especially His own faithful
followers, might know that He had arisen. This
Angel had shewn himself to the Roman sentinels,
"his countenance like lightning, and his raiment
white as snow." But the holy women drawing nigh
saw him not, until after Mary Magdalene had left
them : then he shewed himself to the other two and
uttered in words the first Gospel of the Resurrection.
See, he is sitting on the great stone which he had a
little before rolled away from the entrance of the
cave : for the sepulchre, you know, was not like one
of our graves, but like a cave or grotto hewn on the
side of a hill : there he sits, as one quietly rejoicing
in a good work of which God had made him a minister; and near him, but shrinking back for fear, afraid,
and bowing down their faces to the earth, stand the
two women, elderly persons both of them, for the
one is our Lord's aunt after the flesh, own sister to
His blessed Mother ; the other is mother to S. James
and S. John. They had come prepared with spices
and ointments thoroughly to anoint His blessed Body,
thus performing the last office of love, as the manner of the Jews was to bury : but now they are lis-

tening to words, which make them forget all that.
The heavenly messenger, seeing their fear, soothes
them, and speaks kindly to them: ' Fear not *ye* : '
well might those heathen soldiers shake and become
as dead men : but ye need not, "for I know that ye
are seeking Jesus which was crucified. He is not
here, for He is risen as He said. Come, see the place
where the Lord lay." Upon this they enter in as
he bade them, and behold another Angel, a young
man sitting on the right hand, clothed in a white
robe, such as S. John afterwards in the Revelations
saw worn by the saints in heaven. Again they are
overpowered with amaze : but he too speaks gently,
much as his companion had done. "* Be not affright-
ed : Ye seek Jesus of Nazareth, which was crucified : He is risen ; He is not here : behold the place
where they laid Him." And then the two Angels
join in delivering Christ's message to the two holy
women : they were to go to His disciples, especially
to S. Peter, and tell them as from Christ Himself,
that He was going before them, as a shepherd before
his scattered flock, into Galilee, and there they would
see Him. This message would be a token to His disciples that there was no mistake, that He was really
risen : for the former mention of Galilee to them had
been in the conversation the night before His death,
when He was with them alone. With it "they departed quickly from the sepulchre with fear, and
great joy ; and did run to bring His disciples word."
" And as they went, Jesus met them saying, All hail.
And they came, and held Him by the feet, and worshipped Him." But before He appeared to them,

* S. Mark xvi. 6.

He had already shewn Himself to their companion
Mary Magdalene, who had returned to the sepulchre
in their absence, and could not be comforted until
she saw her Lord. Such is the picture drawn by
the finger of God of that which happened on the
first Easter morning to those who first came in dutiful love to wait upon their departed Lord. For their
love's sake He perfected that which was lacking in
their faith. For them the Angels were sent, the
stone rolled away, the grave clothes laid carefully
on one side, and " the napkin that was about His
Head, not lying with the linen clothes, but wrapped
together in a place by itself : " and the very place
where the Body had been lying marked out exactly
by the Angelic stations. For Mary Magdalene as
she was weeping by herself—the other women, and
S. Peter, and S. John having departed, " [b] stooped
down, and looked into the sepulchre. And seeth two
Angels in white sitting the one at the head and the
other at the feet, where the Body of Jesus had lain."

The blessed words "Come, and see," had before
invited many to Jesus : as the two disciples that followed Him at the Baptist's saying, "Behold the
Lamb of God!" When they asked Jesus where
He dwelt, He said "Come and see." Nathanael
doubted whether any good thing could come out of
Nazareth. Philip said "Come and see." The Samaritan woman would have her neighbours "Come and
see " a man who told her of all things whatsoever
she had done : and here the loving women who as yet
understood not the Scripture, nor had been able any
how to take in the thought which He had so often

[b] S. John xx. 11, 12.

and so plainly taught them, are invited to "come and see," not as yet Himself, but the sure tokens of His being again alive.

And this you will observe is but a sample or specimen of our loving Lord's fatherly care to satisfy those whom God had chosen before to be witnesses of His Resurrection; that miracle of miracles, on which our all depends for Eternity. "Come," is the Divine message: 'come see, not at once your risen Lord Himself, but the place where He lay. His will is to try and prove you, whether you will believe without seeing, that your blessing may be the greater when you are permitted to see. There have been those already who have seen as much as you if not more: a pure and bright angel rolling the stone away, and shewing the inside of the sepul-chre emptied of Him Who had lain there. So much they saw, and feared, but their hearts were not turned towards Him Who was dealing so wondrously with them: they were too much like those of whom it is written that they believe and tremble. They are gone to tell our Lord's enemies, and take large money to deny what they have seen: be it yours to depart quickly and tell His friends with fear and great joy, and to bear witness to Him henceforth not only with your lips but in your lives.'

"Come, see the place where the Lord lay." The words are spoken, doubt it not, to others beside those holy women; to all who in earnest seek Jesus which was crucified. Come near in spirit, read, hear, mark, consider thoroughly, and pray God to make present to your minds, what the holy women saw on that Easter morning: the crown, and glory of it

being, that as they ran to bring His disciples word,
"behold Jesus Himself met them, saying, All hail.
And they came, and held Him by the feet and worshipped Him." Thousands, nay hundreds of thousands there have been, so impressed with this history,
that they could not be happy without going themselves to view that holiest place on earth, and to
worship Him on the very spot where He died for
them, and rose again. We are not of course called
outwardly to do as they did, but we are called, every
one of us, we have professed as they did, to be pil-
grims in heart. We have come before Christ as His
people, on this and on former Easters, we have stood
in spirit, by His grave with the holy women, we
have heard the voices of the Angels : can we ever
again be as persons to whom no such privileges had
been granted? What should we have thought of
our Lord's disciples, or of the women from Galilee,
if after all that they had seen and heard they had
gone away and thought no more of it, wondering in
themselves at that which had come to pass, but leading just such lives as they might have done if they
had never heard of any such thing? God keep us
from such hardness of heart, such contempt of His
mighty works. God give us grace to come and
come again and again, and in spirit watch by the
place where Jesus lay, not in these days of Easter
only, but every day of our lives, even as often as we
profess in our Creed that we believe in Him Who
on the third day rose again from the dead.

It is very sad that Christians should use themselves to let such a confession as that pass their lips
day after day without really laying it to heart. We

do not know what treasures of grace, and edification we throw away by such careless and thankless habits. Only just consider the Angel's invitation, "Come, see the place where the Lord lay:" how deep meanings you may gather from it, if you will but attend, besides confirming yourselves, please God, in the faith of *His* Resurrection and the hope of *your* own.

"Come, see the *place* where the Lord lay:" look well upon this cave, here lying open before you: it is a grave, a tomb, a place for the dead, a resting place provided by a frail sinful man for his body to be laid in and to moulder away according to the sentence passed on all the children of Adam. Consider it well: outwardly and in itself it is no more than any other grave, a token of man's sin and of God's wrath, a home where decay and corruption and loathsomeness may shortly be expected to come: and then consider Who has been lying here, and why. It is the Lord, the great God of heaven and earth: this is the place which He hath chosen to Him to be His rest, after all His work, His severe work, begun continued and ended for us. See the place where thy Lord lay, where He laid Himself down of His own free will, and be ashamed of thy pride and high looks.

Again, the other Angel, inviting the women not only to behold but to enter into the sepulchre, said, "He is risen, He is not here: behold the place where *they laid Him*," not "where He lay," but "where they laid Him:" by which words we are put in mind not so much of our Lord's humbling Himself as of the spite and cruelty of His enemies, who laid Him low. And who, and what are they? Not the Jews

M m

and Pilate only, but we, my brethren, we Christians, we and our worldly unchristian ways. His Angel speaks to us from His Grave, and says, 'See how low thy sins have brought Him, and pray and strive to hate them, how tempting soever, for His love's sake.'

And there is yet another sermon, another Gospel, most necessary, and most comfortable, if we will so take it, to every one of us, which the Angel sitting where Jesus had lain preached and taught to His faithful servants seeking Him. " Come, see the place where the Lord lay;" may well sound to a thoughtful Christian's ears, as if our Father in heaven were saying to him, by His Angel, 'From henceforth I would have thee look even on this created work of Mine—on that which we call this present world,—quite differently from what thou wouldest have done, had the Son of God never been Incarnate. By vouchsafing to become one of us, and to take on Him so entirely our ordinary ways and wants, our cares and sufferings, He has sanctified for ever this whole state of things, by which His good providence is trying and training us for a better, whether we regard it or no.' The whole earth has been from that day forward the place where Jesus lay for a time, where He lived and breathed, was born and died, ate and drank, slept and waked, moved and talked, did and suffered; having made Himself in very deed one of us children of Adam, both in flesh and spirit; partaking of our nature, of our tastes, powers, and endowments; of our sorrows, travails, infirmities: in short of all man's being, sin only excepted. The heathen, possibly,—the Israelites for

certain, might know that it is *God's* world: we
Christians know yet more, that it is Christ's world,
the world of God made Man: the world of which
the Creator Himself condescended to form a part, to
become Himself, bodily one of His own creatures.
The Church in its Creeds, and the whole New Testament, seem to take up the Angel's invitation, and
say, 'Behold this course of nature; this wonderful
arrangement of things, animal, vegetable and mine-
ral, fire, air, earth, and water; the simplest elements
mysteriously uniting and separating, separating and
uniting again, to work out the Lord's marvellous
purposes: behold it all, study it, think much of it,
search it out, learn from it, as He may graciously
help you, more and more of His adorable Love and
Wisdom, Who orders and moves it all by hidden
springs which He hath set in His own power: and
then add to all these thoughts this one overpower-
ing thought more: that it is "the place where the
Lord lay." He Who made it, and saw all that He
had made, and behold it was very good, hath in these
last times vouchsafed to come down and see it in
another sense, to acquaint Himself with it, as it were,
by His own experience, increasing (so the Bible
says) in wisdom as in stature.' Oh what a thought
for the lovers and for the students of nature and
for such as work under them! For the astronomer,
the chemist, the miner, the mechanic, and also for
such as take pure delight in the natural grace and
beauty of these outward things, in poetry, in paint-
ing, in music, and the like: that our Lord's mark
is upon them all, in all we are sure of His sympathy,
if only we seek His glory, and our neighbour's good.

How little do they know their own loss, who follow their art, trade, or skill, whatever it may be, for their own profit only, or for the praise of men, or for the pleasure of praising themselves in their own hearts, when they might turn it all into heavenly blessings, and ways of communion with their Saviour. He, we know, was on earth a poor tradesman for near thirty years. Can you doubt that He has a feeling for those whose calling is hard work, or skilled work in any kind? He uttered words of something like wonder at the beauty of the flowers which His own hands had made. "c Even Solomon," He said, "in all his glory was not arrayed like one of these." May we not be sure then that He is with us, to approve and bless the innocent and thankful enjoyment so natural to almost all of us, when we are soothed or lifted up, or carried even out of ourselves, by the beauty and glory of His creatures in their several kinds? He humbled Himself, so as to have need of them, and to receive help and satisfaction from them in the days of His flesh: on that account they all have His seal and ought to bring Him to our remembrance; and besides that, He has declared it to be His will, that they all, even these lower beings, the creature itself (so S. Paul speaks), shall be delivered "d from the bondage of corruption into the glorious liberty of the children of God." The Angels at the last day will in effect say again to each happy and forgiven soul, " Come, see the place where the Lord lay :" 'see this world in which and for which He humbled Himself so exceedingly: see what it is now become, by His merits, and through His Incarna-

c S. Matt. vi. 29.   d Rom. viii. 21.

tion : a new heaven and a new earth, wherein righteousness, and nothing beside shall dwell for ever.'

Or we may apply the angelical words not so much
to the works of nature as to what is commonly called
the course of this world, the doings of fallen man in
it, and God's gracious providence over-ruling and
turning them to good. "Come, see the place where
the Lord lay," see these souls and bodies of men to
whom He has drawn so very near. Whatever may
be said of other things, to be sure no soul, or body
of man can ever be looked on or thought of by a
believing heart, as it might have been if God had
not vouchsafed to become Incarnate, and die for it.
Since that day, you and I and every one born into
the world of the seed of Adam is a real blood relation, at a very considerable distance no doubt, but
still we are all really related by blood to Jesus Christ
the Son of God. Ought not this to make exceeding
difference in our way of judging ourselves and one
another? Thou art tempted to debase and corrupt
thyself, thy soul or body, to commit mean or shameful sins, sins of lust or sins of dishonesty, to tell a
lie, or to sin against thine own body. The temptation is great, the Evil one is at hand to say, 'Thousands have done the like, or have done worse, and
no great harm has come of it :' thy poor weak soul
trembles and wavers. O, think once again, think
Whose thou art and Whom thou dost serve, consider
that thou art in very deed akin to God's own Son,
to the great King of heaven and earth, and what it
will be to provoke Him to jealousy by so dishonour-
ing the great Name, and defiling the holy Seed. Or
it is in thy power to do something towards helping

the soul or body of thy neighbour: and again selfish
sloth tempts thee and it comes into thy mind to say,
' What is that to me? Am I my brother's keeper?'
Nay, but this thy brother does by birth appertain to
the family of the Most High God, possessor of heaven and earth: he is the acknowledged kinsman of
Him Who is King of kings and Lord of lords. Christ
Who loved him so dearly that He died for him, will
surely demand an account of him: the blood of his
body, much more of his soul if he perish, will surely
be required at thy hands. If he be a Christian
man, or a Christian child, his soul and body has become in an especial sense, the place where the Lord
hath laid, where in Holy Baptism He vouchsafed to
come. Take heed how thou dealest with such an
one: how thou despisest one of these little ones.

Once more: the Angel may be understood to invite us to mark how our God, and King, abiding
among us, took part in human *societies:* how, becoming a Jew among Jews, a true lover of His nation
weeping more over the misery of Jerusalem than
over His own Sufferings, He hallowed all the na-
tional love which men feel for the land of their birth,
its laws and its ways: how being a member of a
certain tribe, village, family, He declares His gracious sympathy with the partiality each man feels for
his own race, his own abode, and most especially his
own home. And if good men are disquieted, as
well they may be, at their own sins and the sins of
their people, and wonder sometimes whether the
All-Righteous can indeed continue to dwell in such
a world, still the voices of the Angels come to comfort us, every Easter and every Sunday (for Sunday

you know is our weekly Easter), and over and over
they keep saying to us, not only " Come, see where
the Lord lay," but also, "Behold the place where
they laid Him."   Mark in what a fallen country,
among what a wicked people, in what a disturbed
and debased state of things the great God vouchsafed
to have his abode on earth, how He put up with " the
contradiction of sinners against Himself," and learn
for His sake to make the best of all things, to bear,
believe, hope, endure, as He commands, and as He
has done before you.   Behold where they have laid
Him: in a grave close to His Cross, and made with
the wicked, and seeming like a malefactor's grave.
It was their doing not His. He only permitted and
controlled it: and so it is in the ways of His providence. The evil, the moral evil which we see in
His world and in His Church is the tares sown not
by His hand but by the enemy: yet amongst it all
He is there, to help His people to turn it to good if
they will: when we see it, we are not to be disheartened: for this too is a token of His presence:
these are the very things which He declared should
be in His Church: the best days, by man's froward-
ness, would become in a certain sense the worst.
Behold where men have laid Him: what sort of a
world, and what sort of a Church they have caused
this to become, in which they know He has come to
dwell: behold, yet doubt not, but earnestly believe
that here He still is, ready to work His miracles
of grace if we will let Him: here He is, sympathi-
zing with all of us who against hope believe in hope,
that we are the people for whom so great things
have been done, and that according to those first

days of our fathers coming out of the land of Egypt, He will shew unto us marvellous things, the more wonderful for our unworthiness.

The Psalmist has put it all in one word, " • The secret of the Lord is among them that fear Him :" His great secret, and the secret of our happiness, that although in the Body He is not here, save in His wonderful Sacrament, but is risen, yet His having been once here is our token that He is always here in heart. The moment you turn to Him in earnest in any joy, or in any trouble of your own or of others, little, or great, but especially in your soul's joy and trouble, there He is, there you find Him, watching as it were to catch your eye, feeling for you, and with you, with a true heart's love. O how infinitely beyond anything you can find out of Him ! Do you believe this? Then act on your belief. Turn to Him always : let it be the rule of your life. So shall you have grace to keep a perpetual Easter ; to worship Him standing as the Angels do ; with a humble and lowly yet brave and hopeful heart. So, as we stand by His open Grave, may we all sing a true Alleluia, the Magdalene with the beloved disciple : the penitents with those who have not defiled their garments.

• Ps. xxv. 14.

Even so, Come, Lord Jesus.

CPSIA information can be obtained
at www.ICGtesting.com
Printed in the USA
BVHW090351010819
554780BV00003B/73/P

9 780469 185418